# Digital Systems Design with Programmable Logic

**ELECTRONIC SYSTEMS ENGINEERING SERIES**

*Consulting Editor* **E L Dagless**
University of Bristol

**OTHER TITLES IN THE SERIES**

Advanced Microprocessor Architectures *L Ciminiera and A Valenzano*

Optical Pattern Recognition Using Holographic Techniques *N Collings*

Modern Logic Design *D Green*

Data Communications, Computer Networks and OSI (2nd Edn) *F Halsall*

Multivariable Feedback Design *J M Maciejowski*

Microwave Components and Systems *K F Sander*

Tolerance Design of Electronic Circuits *R Spence and R Soin*

Computer Architecture and Design *A J van de Goor*

# Digital Systems Design with Programmable Logic

*Martin Bolton*
*University of Bristol*

**Addison-Wesley Publishing Company**

Wokingham, England • Reading, Massachusetts • Menlo Park, California
New York • Don Mills, Ontario • Amsterdam • Bonn • Sydney
Singapore • Tokyo • Madrid • San Juan

Cover designed by Hybert Design & Type,
and printed by The Riverside Printing Co. (Reading) Ltd.
Typeset by CRB Typesetting Services, Ely, Cambs.
Printed in Great Britain by T.J. Press (Padstow), Cornwall.

First printed 1990.

**British Library Cataloguing in Publication Data**
Bolton, Martin
Digital systems design with programmable logic.
1. Digital circuits. Logic design
I. Title
621.3815

ISBN 0–201–14545–6

**Library of Congress Cataloging in Publication Data**
Bolton, Martin,
Digital systems design with programmable logic/Martin Bolton.
p. cm.
Includes bibliographical references (p. ).
ISBN 0–201–14545–6
1. Programmable logic devices–Design and construction.
2. Programmable array logic. 3. Logic design. I. Title.
TK7872.L64B64 1990
621.39′5–dc20 90–7
CIP

To John Birkner and Shlomo Waser,
who introduced me to the world of
Silicon Valley

# Preface

## Aims and Approach

The aim of this book is to teach a modern, structured approach to digital design through the medium of programmable logic, the semicustom technology which every digital engineer will come into contact with. Programmable logic allows digital systems to be designed so that functions can first be isolated into high level blocks in a well-planned way ('top-down design') and then each one designed in detail and finally optimized. This is the approach which is now essential for all types of semicustom design. The modern digital systems designer must be familiar with the concepts of abstract high level design as well as with classical switching theory and its recent developments.

During the twenty-year reign of 'catalogue' logic components, the digital systems designer had little opportunity for optimizing a design at the component level – it was more a question of adapting predesigned blocks. This has changed with the increase in the use of semicustom digital circuits. Programmable logic is the most accessible and widely used semicustom technology, and is thus a good place to start learning modern digital system design. Nearly all of the techniques learnt in this book relate directly to designing with other semicustom technologies such as gate arrays and compiled cells. It also gives a good grounding for a study of VLSI design.

The approach taken to design throughout this book is top-down, with decisions on implementation delayed as long as possible. This obviously has analogies in high-level language software design, and is, indeed, the approach now adopted in the more advanced programmable logic computer-aided design systems. At the stage of conversion of abstract blocks into programmable logic device specifications, the concept of **device resources** is stressed. Every block specification has a certain set of resources demands, which must be satisfied by the chosen device.

## Audience

This book is aimed at readers who have attended a first course on logic design, and have a knowledge of simple Boolean design methods and gate circuits. This makes it suitable for advanced undergraduates, beginning postgraduates and practising electronic engineers wishing to learn to use programmable logic more effectively.

The book is intended to supplement and extend the excellent application material published by the semiconductor manufacturers, by presenting more rigorous and systematic design methods. (Manufacturers tend not to include such material in the belief that it will scare away potential users.) For this reason, designs are considered complete when a suitable PLD has been chosen and a method of specification outlined. Full implementation details and circuit diagrams, while an essential part of a completed design, are best studied by looking at the examples given in the readily available application books.

## Chapter summaries

The first chapter introduces digital systems as abstract entities independent of any particular circuit implementation. This approach is necessary in the first stages of any design, where the architecture is planned. No prescribed design methods can be given here, only an orientation towards the type of thinking needed.

The second chapter is a brief review of the logic design principles and notations which are built on in the remainder of the book. For the intended readership, this should largely be revision. The treatment, however, has an emphasis different from that normally found; the techniques important for programmable logic design have been given a fuller treatment.

Chapter 3 deals with the principles of array logic, the basis of almost all programmable logic components. The principal types of programmable logic device are developed from a general model. This is presented with a historical bias, firstly to show the origins of the ideas and secondly because this allows a logical and coherent development.

In Chapter 4, the discussion of detailed design techniques begins. Minimization of the combinational logic of programmable devices is becoming increasingly important, with most computer-aided design packages containing a minimizer of some sort. The principles of minimization are introduced by means of the classical hand methods adapted for the programmable logic application. The algorithms underlying some of the well-known minimizers are then outlined. While many minimization problems will be too large for hand methods, an understanding of the techniques is essential background knowledge.

Chapter 5 covers techniques of implementing combinational logic in programmable devices. These include choosing the correct component and the partitioning of logic between more than one device. The practical issues of delay and hazards are covered, and, finally, the question of how many logic gates a programmable component replaces is approached.

Chapter 6 is concerned with the design of synchronous sequential circuits, with the emphasis on state machine controllers and the application of programmable sequencers. Specification methods, logic design and performance calculations are covered in detail. This material is extended in Chapter 7 where more advanced sequencer design techniques are introduced.

In Chapter 8, the main topic covered is the application of programmable logic in data path design. In particular, the principles and applications of special programmable devices ideally suited to these applications are covered. This chapter ends with a discussion of the problems in linking control and data sections.

Asynchronous design, while full of pitfalls, will always have its role in digital systems design. Chapter 9 covers the basics of asynchronous design and shows how these can be applied to programmable devices. An especially easy-to-use method is described for the design of self-clocked asynchronous circuits. The chapter ends with a brief treatment of the phenomenon of metastability, important even in synchronous designs.

In Chapter 10, some of the ideas underlying the computer-aided design tools now so necessary are reviewed. The general requirements of a specification method are given first, and then an outline of the features of some representative and interesting tools follows. The final part of the chapter deals with design verification by simulation and the problems of testing and producing testable designs.

The bibliograpical notes at the end of each chapter give the sources of the material appearing in the chapter, and give suggestions for further reading. Some of these suggestions are selective, because of space limitations. Of the vast number of articles and papers in existence, only a sample can be referenced.

The most complete list ever published of programmable device architectures, organized into tables according to device category is given in the Appendix.

Many more specialized techniques cannot be covered in a book of this size without the coverage becoming too shallow to be worthwhile. Topics to be covered in depth in a future volume include: parallel state machine design, self-clocked design, microprogrammble devices, partitioned arrays and programmable gate arrays, and further material on the problems of testable design and test generation.

## Acknowledgements

I must thank the reviewers and those colleagues, David Milford and Lawrence Crutcher in particular, who read parts of the manuscript. Their suggestions and criticisms were digested and acted upon in most cases. Many of the ideas were refined in the course of teaching parts of this material to students at Bristol and to engineers on short courses. I must also thank the staff in the Product Planning and Applications Group of the now sadly defunct firm of Monolithic Memories in Santa Clara, who gave me the opportunity of direct contact with some of the pioneers of programmable logic. Finally, it goes without saying that this book represents a personal view, and, of course, there is room for more than one of these!

Martin Bolton
*Bristol*
*February 1990*

**Trademark notice**

# Contents

CHAPTER 1

# The Structure of Digital Systems

---

**OBJECTIVES**

When you have completed studying this chapter you should be able

- to understand what is meant by the behaviour of a digital system;
- to appreciate why an algorithm is a suitable method for specifying a complex digital system;
- to outline the steps required to transform an algorithm into a digital hardware design;
- to understand the role of the control and data parts of a digital system;
- to appreciate that many architectures are possible for realizing any given specification;
- to understand the limitations of programming languages for specifying digital systems;
- to enumerate the advantages of programmable logic;
- to start to think about digital systems as abstract entities.

---

## 1.1 Introduction

In this first chapter the first stage of the design of any digital system – the planning of the architecture – will be examined. For this task there is no single set of rules which can always be applied to guarantee a good design; if this were possible there would be no place for human creativity. The aim of this chapter is to outline the common characteristics of digital systems at the architectural level and to suggest a way of thinking about digital systems design. Finally, some guidelines for producing a well-organized and efficient design will be given. Time spent at the initial stages of design is always well rewarded – especially when planning for the most effective use of programmable logic components.

A second aim of this introductory chapter is to introduce some of the concepts and terminology of modern digital systems design. To some readers these notions will appear rather abstract at first reading. Nevertheless, after studying some of the more practical parts of the book, a second reading should allow them to make better sense.

Some very general questions will be answered first, such as 'what do digital systems do?' and 'what are they made of?'. This leads on to questions of what constitutes a good structure, and how a design can be specified more formally. Formal specification is part of the design process; a sound and usable formalism is indispensable for designing reliable complex systems. Further questions arise when the performance of the system has to be evaluated – when for example is a standard architecture appropriate and when must a new one be contemplated?

Finally, the effect of the implementation technology, that is, the type of digital components used in the system, on the design process will be discussed. In particular, some of the features of programmable logic which make it so suitable for producing well-structured designs will be explained.

## 1.2 Signals, behaviour and algorithms

What is a digital system? A formal answer is that it is a system which processes information which is represented by digital (or discrete) signals. What are digital signals? Again, this can be answered formally by stating that they are those signals which have only a finite set of values. For example, an integer number in the range $0 \ldots 15$, a member of the set of symbols $\{AND, OR, ADD, JUMP\}$, and a telephone number are all digital signals. On the other hand, values of continuous physical quantities, such as speeds or temperatures, are not inherently digital signals, although by a process of quantization they can be converted into digital signals. In digital systems design, the term 'signal' is used in an abstract sense; it may not be something which has a direct physical analogue. For example, a signal representing a memory address in a microcomputer system cannot be directly measured.

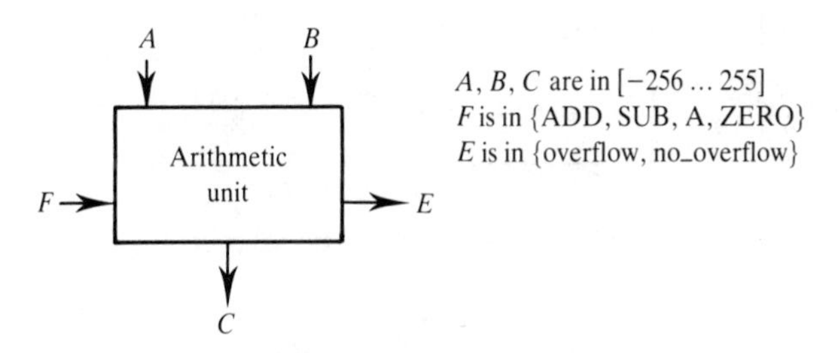


**Figure 1.1** A digital system.

We always start our thinking about a design by drawing a block diagram of our digital system. This single block, which is all that can be produced at this stage, has on one side digital input signals, and on the other digital output signals. The task of the system is to transform the former into the latter. This transformation is defined by the system's **behaviour** or **transfer function**. An example of this is given in Figure 1.1, which shows an arithmetic unit. The input signals are $A$, $B$, and $F$ and they have values in the ranges $[-256 \ldots 255]$, $[-256 \ldots 255]$, and the set $\{\mathrm{ADD, SUB, A, ZERO}\}$ respectively, and the outputs $C$ and $E$ have values in $[-256 \ldots 255]$ and {overflow, no_overflow} respectively. The operation of this simple system can be specified as follows:

**if** F = ADD **then** D = A + B;
**if** F = SUB **then** D = A − B;
**if** F = A **then** D = A;
**if** F = ZERO **then** B = 0;
**if** D < −256 **then** E = overflow, C = −256;
**if** D > 255 **then** E = overflow, C = 255;
**if** (D ⩾ −256 **and** D ⩽ 255) **then** E = no_overflow, C = D.

This set of conditional expressions is a specification of the behaviour of the system; it says nothing about how the system is to be built. Notice that an additional signal $D$ has been introduced to enable overflow detection.

This system is one which has no memory, since previous input values are never used; it is **combinational** (or 'combinatorial'). All except very limited digital systems need some memory to enable their behaviour to adapt to different sequences of input signals. For example, the security system of Figure 1.2 will only deliver an output $Z$ with value 'unlock' after the correct sequence of digits has occurred. Here the input $S$ has values in the range $[0 \ldots 9]$ and the output $Z$ has values in {lock, unlock}. Such a system is **sequential**.

There are various ways of describing the behaviour of a digital system. For a combinational system, behaviour may be described by expressions such as those given for the arithmetic unit, or explicitly by

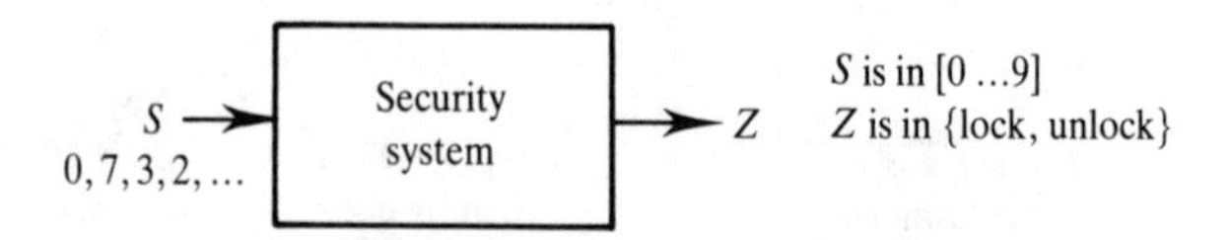


**Figure 1.2** A sequential digital system.

defining the output for every possible input in a **function table** (or **truth table**). The tabular method is only suitable for systems with a limited number of input values – the table would otherwise become too large to handle. Descriptions of sequential systems must take account of the values of the signals stored in the internal memory, and must also define how these values are changed in response to new inputs. This type of behaviour can also be described by types of function tables, but they can suffer from the same size problems as combinational tables. Details and applications of these descriptions will be reviewed in the next chapter.

More complex systems thus need a more manageable form of description, in the form of rules which can be applied to an input to generate the output without having to specify every possibility in a table. Such a set of rules can be thought of as an **algorithm**, and the operation of the system as a **computation**. This algorithm will have to be expressed in a formal language, just as it would be in a computer program. Unfortunately there is at present no universally accepted design language for digital systems; many exist, each with its own particular strengths and resulting design style. Such languages are examples of **hardware description languages** (not all hardware description languages are capable of describing algorithmic behaviour, however). Since conventional computer programming languages such as Pascal specify algorithms, are they not suitable for describing the behaviour of digital systems? The answer is, 'to a certain extent'. The problem with these programming languages is that they specify the behaviour of a certain kind of digital system – the von Neumann computer. Programs written in such a language assume the presence of elements such as program counters and stacks. However, algorithms specified in this way can be transformed into specifications of more freely structured systems which are not von Neumann computers, and in fact this is often a useful way of thinking about possible designs, as we shall see shortly.

Having defined the signals and behaviour of a digital system at this abstract level, it is now possible to study this behaviour by simulating it with a 'high level' simulator, a program which accepts the behavioural description as an input. Alternatively, if the system is described in a programming language, it can be simulated by executing the program. A simulation enables the responses of the system to a set of predefined inputs to be examined. Even better, if the system is described in a suitable formalism, it is possible to verify mathematically selected behavioural properties. The latter techniques are beyond the scope of this book. It is also sometimes possible at this pre-implementation, abstract stage to perform optimization of combinational and sequential systems to reduce the size of the circuit which will eventually be required. In simpler systems the design can now be converted into a form which is physically realizable as a logic circuit. A first step towards this is to **encode** all of the signals used, both internal and external.

Physical digital systems operate with signals which have a restricted number of values, two being by far the most common. These **binary-valued** signals take values in the set $\{0, 1\}$. **Multiple-valued** signals with values in $\{0 \ldots m-1\}$ are also possible but are at present not widely used. The problem of encoding is to represent abstract signals by a string of symbols, each of which can take on the values allowed by the physical system. For example, in Figure 1.1, $\{\text{AND}, \text{SUB}, \text{A}, \text{ZERO}\}$ could be encoded as $\{00, 01, 10, 11\}$ in a binary physical system. In a four-valued system, one symbol would suffice. In this book, only binary systems are considered.

Various methods are available for performing this encoding. The two principal options are **encoding by enumeration** and **encoding by rule**. In the former, all signal values are listed and next to each the encoding is given. Examples of encoding by enumeration are character set codes (such as ASCII) and processor instruction sets. The most well-known applications of encoding by rule are in the codes used for numbers. Here each binary symbol is given a weighting according to its position in the string (or word). The number represented is simply the sum of the weightings multiplied by the values of the symbols (1 or 0) at those positions. An encoding allows the computation of the digital system to be re-expressed in terms of binary signals, thus defining a lower level computation which can be performed by binary circuit elements. A third form of encoding is generated as a result of optimization; codes for inputs, outputs and internal signals can sometimes be selected to minimize the cost of the final digital circuit. In sequential systems the internal coding is the process of **state assignment**.

So far, a digital system has been viewed as a single block with no internal structure. Only the most uninteresting systems are like this. We must now look at how an internal structure, or an architecture, can be developed.

## 1.3 Architecture of digital systems

Having answered the question of *what* the digital system must do, we now have to decide *how* it must do it. In other words, a description of behaviour must be transformed into an architecture. By **architecture** is meant the configuration and interconnection of the major functional blocks of the

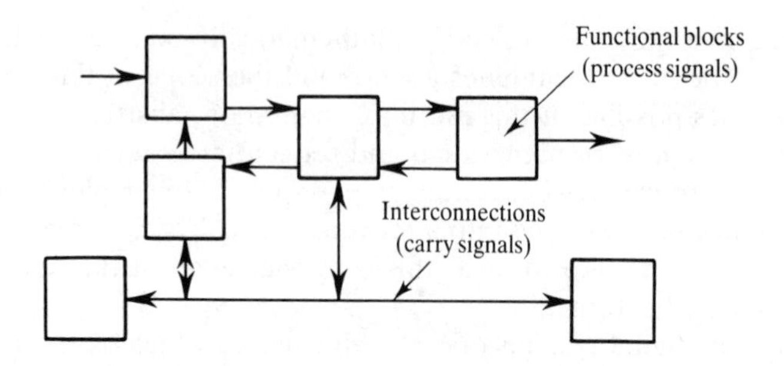


**Figure 1.3** An architecture.

system, like that of Figure 1.3. Functional blocks are just smaller digital systems which also process digital signals, while the interconnections carry these signals from block to block. This process can be continued by further refinement of the new blocks. Figure 1.4 shows how this process gives rise to a **hierarchy**. In Figure 1.5 an example is given of the types of blocks which may exist in a typical architectural hierarchy. Where the hierarchy ends will depend on the method of implementation, that is the circuit technology, chosen. Usually the lowest level of block corresponds to a component which can be bought 'off the shelf' or is the highest level of primitive component available in the library of a computer-aided design system, or which can be created automatically by a 'module generator'.

The architecture which is arrived at depends on

(1) the type of problem to be solved,
(2) the constraints given on performance and size, and
(3) the circuit technology to be used.

These points are now taken in turn. Firstly, the problem type can determine the architecture in those cases where experience exists in the solution

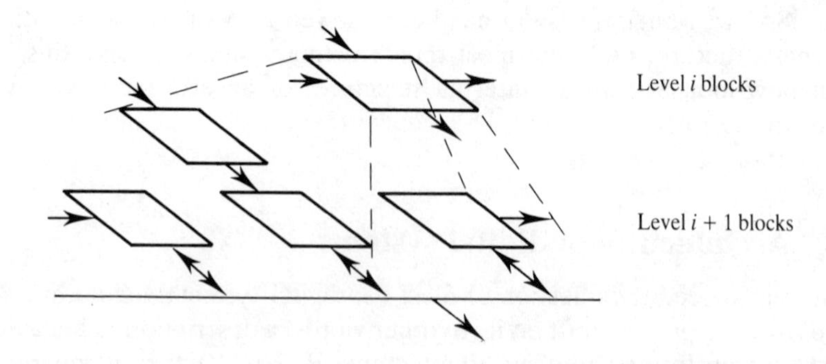


**Figure 1.4** Refinement of an architecture.

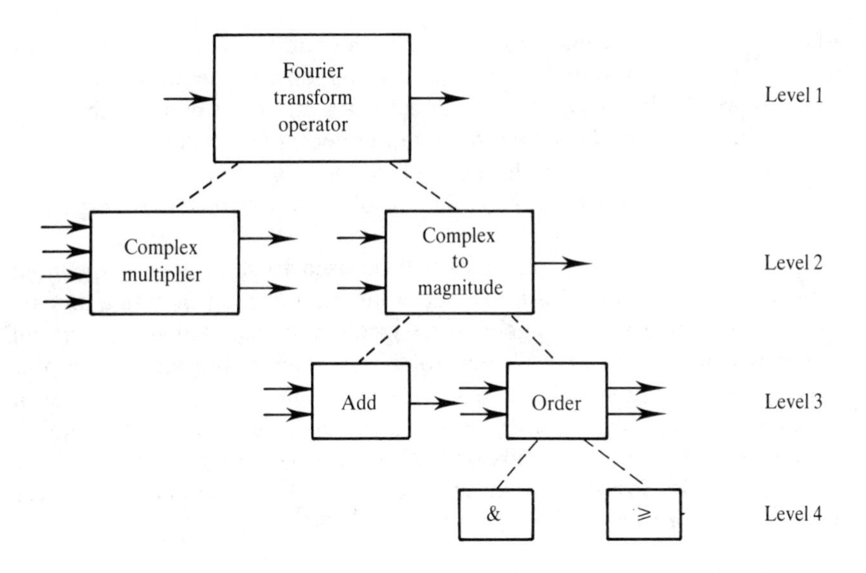


**Figure 1.5** Functional block hierarchy (from Denyer and Renshaw (1985)).

of that particular problem – indeed there would have to be a very good reason to change it. Secondly, performance and cost constraints always influence the architecture in practical design; very different constraints apply, for example, in the design of a home word processor and a computer system designed to track radar returns in real time. Finally, the components to be used can often constrain the architecture by reducing freedom to define arbitrary structures where a standard, if less 'elegant', structure would be more economical. The lower the level of the largest predefined block, the more freedom there is to define an architecture. It will be shown that the particular advantage of programmable logic is that there is great freedom in the choice of architecture without the need to decompose the design to the level of the most primitive possible digital component, the logic gate.

At this point it is worth saying a little about how hierarchical design is approached. Much has been written about this topic in the context of software engineering, where the concept of 'structured design' is now conventional. A structured design strategy consists of rules for partitioning a system into modules, for determining when a module partitioning is 'good', and for interconnecting modules. A **bottom-up** design will start with a set of available modules and connect these in a way which will achieve the behaviour and performance demanded by the specification. In **top-down** design the overall specification is decomposed into a set of specifications for simpler systems. These in turn may be decomposed further. At some point, these subsystems can be constructed from some collection of pre-existing modules or components. This last stage is thus bottom up. Real design is never purely top down – in fact, there are probably more digital systems designed in a bottom-up manner than top down. This does not, however, remove the necessity for devoting time to producing a well-structured design. Before looking into this more closely, it is necessary to understand the two kinds of block which all digital systems are made of.

A few very simple examples will be used to show how a specified behaviour can be converted into a set of interconnected functional blocks. The first system to be designed is a signal processor which delivers an output which is at all times equal to the average of the last two inputs received. The input signal is in and the output signal is out. The range of values of these signals can be ignored at this stage. This system must have a memory, as its output depends on a past input as well as on the present input. The following Pascal-like fragment describes the behaviour of the filter as an algorithm:

```
repeat
  out = (last_in + in) / 2;
  last_in := in
until false;
```

The internal signal (or variable) last_in has been defined as the content of the internal memory. The assignment := is used to indicate the act of storing a signal in a memory. The equality symbol = is used to indicate that the result on the left-hand side is not being sent to a memory, but that it is always equal to the right-hand side. The endless loop indicates that this filter continues its operation without end. A major assumption now has to be made about the operation in time of this system. The program has no way of denoting when things happen, only the sequence in which things happen (this is a major drawback of descriptions based on programming languages). For now let us assume that the loop will execute whenever a new input arrives. Figure 1.6 is a block diagram of the architecture of this system. The blocks required are two **data processing** units (or operators) – an adder and a divider – and a memory which can hold the value of one signal – a **register**. This system can be thought of as **passive**; it performs the same operation continuously regardless of the values of the input signals. Also notice that in constructing the block diagram **parallelism** which was not present in the program description has been introduced; the operations of storing the input and computing the output happen at the same time. The text and the block diagram are thus not identical descriptions. One has been transformed by the designer into the other.

A second example is a system which delivers an output which is equal to the largest input which has been received. The operation of this

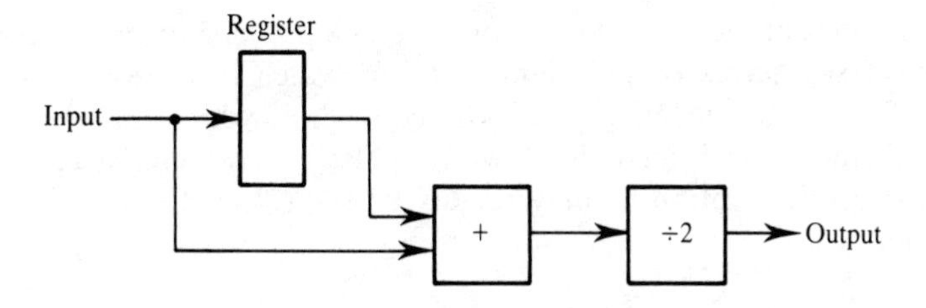


**Figure 1.6** Averager.

system can be described thus:

```
largest_in := 0;
repeat
  if inp > largest_in
    then largest_in := in;
  out = largest_in
until false;
```

As before, one register is required, here to store the signal largest_in. There is now a conditional action – the input is only stored if it is found to be larger than the value already stored. An architecture for this system is given in Figure 1.7. It is assumed that the initialization signal, 'reset',

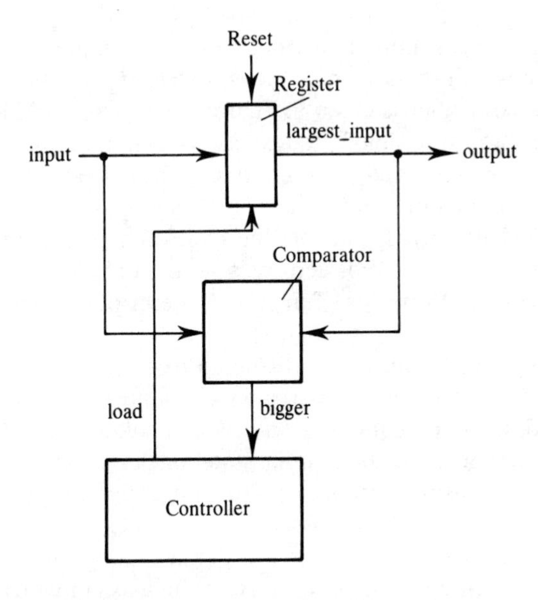


**Figure 1.7** Largest input detector.

is present once at the start of operation. A data processing block 'comparator' delivers a **status** output signal 'bigger' which has the values {true, false}. This signal is fed to the box 'controller' which has the task of producing the **control** signal 'load' which is also two valued. By referring to the program description, it may readily be seen that the function of the controller is

**if** bigger **then** load

In other words, the controller converts the status signal 'bigger' into the control signal (or **command**, **instruction**) 'load' which causes the register to store the current input. The controller is thus the **active** part of this digital system. This controller is particularly simple, as it is a combinational system; it does not need to remember previous actions.

The final example is a digital system which has an output which is updated to be equal to the input after every third input has been received. This can be specified as follows:

```
index := 0;
repeat
  index := index + 1;   {performed modulo 3}
  if index = 2
    then out := in
until false;
```

Figure 1.8(a) shows a simplified architecture of a digital system performing this function in which the action of the controller is not specified. A block diagram of the controller is given in Figure 1.8(b). Notice that storage has to be provided for the signal 'index' as well as a data operator '+1'. Therefore what was named as a controller has been decomposed into another simpler controller and a data processing part (the issue of timing has again been ignored). However, the controller of Figure 1.8(a) could also have been implemented directly as a sequential block, with no special internal structure, from its functional description without further decomposition.

Thus, digital systems are constructed from passive parts which process signals (data) and active parts which control and sequence these processing actions. (The combination of a controller and a data processor is sometimes known as an **algorithmic state machine**. Another term sometimes used is the **Glushkov model**.) There is usually more than one way of separating the control and data blocks in a complex digital system, and as will be seen in later chapters there are distinct design methods for these two classes of system building blocks. Next the ways in which these blocks are used in more complex architectures will be discussed.

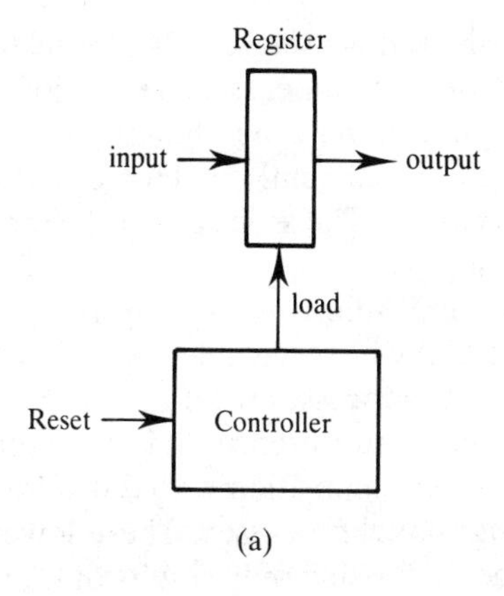


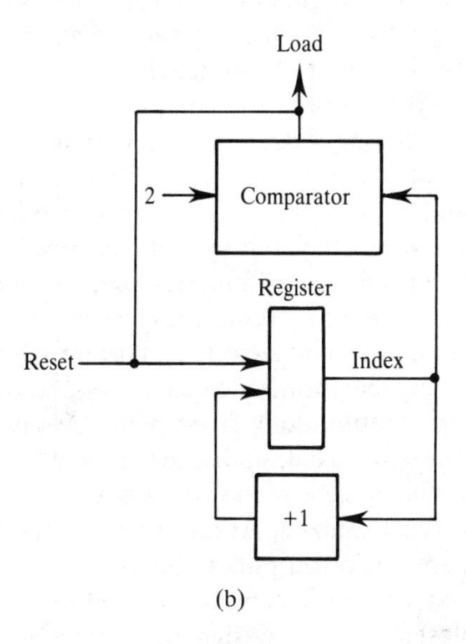


**Figure 1.8** Sampler: (a) first level architecture; (b) controller block diagram.

## 1.4 Structured design and architectures

A 'structured' system design is one which has a clear division into modules, each of which has a well-defined function and relationship with the others. Modules should be selected in such a way that interaction with others is minimized. In this way modules can be developed and tested independently, and in the case of a large system even by different people. When thinking about the operation of digital systems, the concept of a **process** or **task** is useful when a structure is being devised. At the simplest level, a process can be identified with the actions performed by a single controller and the data part to which it is attached. If a collection of controllers and data parts cooperate on the same task, this also can be regarded as a process. System design can now be thought of as a partitioning into processes which operate concurrently and a hierarchical decomposition of processes into subprocesses. These may be referred to as **horizontal** and **hierarchical** decompositions.

Horizontal decomposition is appropriate when, at any level, activities can be identified which are able, and are required, to operate in parallel. The division into processes would be such as to require minimum interaction both to reduce interference and to simplify the design of each module. A hierarchical decomposition would result in a higher level 'master' process controlling 'slave' processes. These lower level processes may operate at a higher speed, passing only results of their computations to the higher level. Another model of a hierarchically organized system is that of a **hierarchy of interpreters**, in which at each level the instructions of the next highest level are interpreted and acted on.

There is trade-off between the complexities of the control and data parts of a process. At one extreme a very simple data part could be defined, which would require complex control to allow a sequence of different operations to pass through it. This is what occurs in a von Neumann computer where the step-by-step sequencing of the program is the complex controller and the arithmetic–logic unit and registers are the simple data part. At the other extreme are systems with data paths containing multiple functional units connected in a pattern which relates closely to the computation being performed. Such a system requires little or no control as results are routed along fixed paths. Many high performance, special-purpose processors are designed in this way.

Decisions also have to be made about how the various processes will be coordinated and synchronized. At the top level there will be a supply of inputs and a requirement for outputs to be available at certain times. The inputs may arrive at regular intervals, at random times, or be sent on demand. The simplest systems to design are those where all operations can be synchronized to a **clock**. This is not always possible, however, as interfaces to other systems and signal transmission delays cause signals to arrive at unpredictable times. The handling of asynchronism will be covered at length in later chapters. In large digital system designs, the interaction of the various internal processes will have to be modelled, analysed and simulated at the architectural level in order to ensure correct operation and satisfactory performance. This topic is too large to be adequately treated in this book.

To conclude this general discussion of architectural design, some well-known architectures are examined to see how they can be placed into this context. It will also help to clarify exactly what level of architecture is being addressed in this chapter. The first to be examined is the so-called von Neumann computer, the most common digital system architecture of

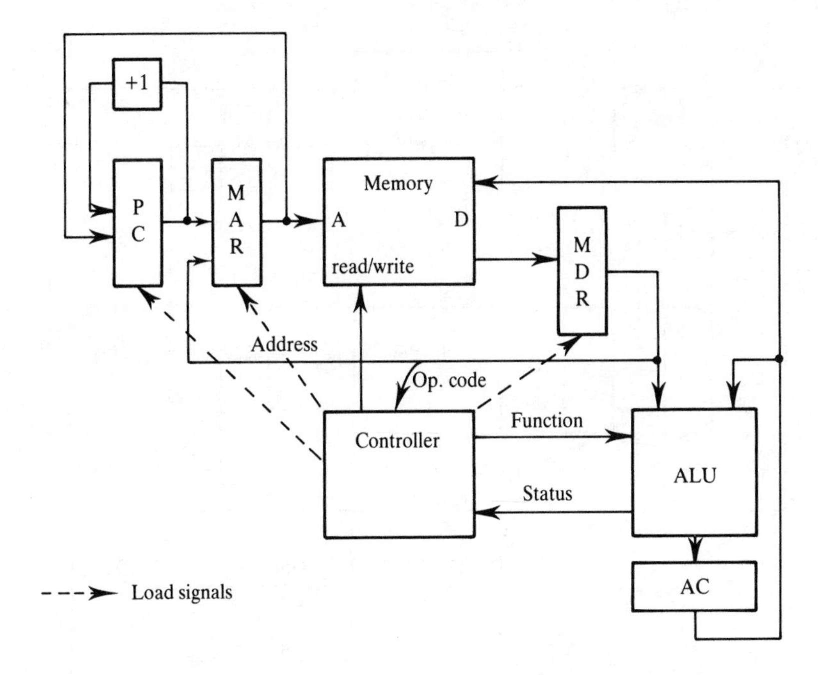


**Figure 1.9** The von Neumann architecture: PC, program counter; MAR, memory address register; MDR, memory data register; ALU, arithmetic/logic unit; AC, accumulator.

all, as it is the basis of the microcomputer (there is dispute as to whether von Neumann should be given all the credit, but his name is now irrevocably linked to the machine). Figure 1.9 shows the architecture of the simplest possible computer which could be built on this pattern. The four essential units are the memory, which holds both instructions and data, the controller (or sequencer), the program counter, and the arithmetic–logic unit (ALU) with its accumulator. Operation can be explained by examining the sequence of events occurring during execution of the different instruction types. Each instruction word is assumed to have an operation code (op code) part and an address part.

At the start of an instruction cycle, the memory address register (MAR) contains the address of the present instruction. This instruction is then available at the memory data output and stored in the memory data register (MDR). The op code part is an input to the controller, which then determines the next action. If the instruction is not a branch then the program counter (PC) is loaded with PC + 1. If the instruction references a data word in memory, the address part is loaded into the MAR. A data word is then either read from the memory into the MDR for use by the ALU or transferred from the accumulator (AC) to the memory. At the end

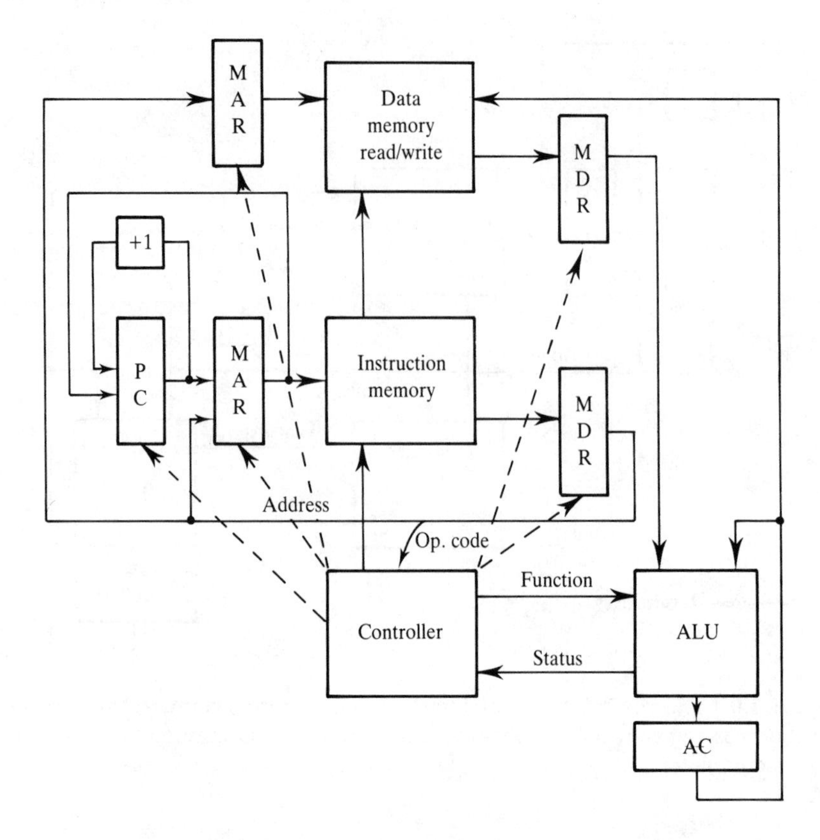


**Figure 1.10** Harvard architecture (for key see Figure 1.9).

of the cycle, the PC content is loaded into the MAR for the next instruction. If the instruction is a branch, the address part is loaded directly into the MAR for the next fetch. This address can then be loaded into the PC for subsequent incrementing.

This simple architecture illustrates well the problems of identifying the control and data sections of a digital system. Some blocks cause no difficulty – the controller is just that, and the ALU and AC are obviously data processing elements. The PC and its incrementer are concerned with control, but the MAR, memory and MDR hold both types of signal.

A drawback of this architecture is that instructions and data are fetched in alternate cycles, thus allowing only half of the memory bandwidth (measured in words per second) to be utilized for data processing. This scheme does allow instructions to be treated as data, however, which makes it possible to alter them. An architecture which keeps the ALU better fed is reminiscent of an earlier model, the 'Harvard' architecture. The Harvard mark I was a calculator-like machine which had separate control and data sections. Figure 1.10 corresponds to Figure 1.9 for this architecture. There are now two memories, one for instructions and one for data, which can be accessed in parallel. Data bandwidth is doubled, but instructions can no longer be altered, which is not considered a disadvantage nowadays. The Harvard architecture has recently become more widely known as a result of its use in high performance signal processing microcomputers.

These two standard architectures are known as **single-process** architectures because there is only a single controller and data path. Many types of multiple-process architectures can be defined; only a few general ideas can be mentioned here. A computation can be imagined as a network of processes passing data to each other. These data transfers can occur in a strictly predefined order given by a controller or in an order defined by the processes themselves. In the latter case, a process executes either when its input data is available or when there is a demand for its results. The two types of organization are known as **control flow** and **data flow**. In control flow, each process can be assumed to take a maximum time to execute, or the controller may use completion signals from the processes. There exist some highly developed control flow architecture design methodologies, especially for signal processing. The study of these topics belongs more with computer architecture than digital systems design.

## 1.5 Specification of digital systems

In an earlier section, behaviour was specified by expressing it as an algorithm in a programming language. As the examples chosen were very simple, a longer example will now be presented to show how the method works. The system is a video game controller which has the following two-valued input signals:

| | |
|---|---|
| from the machine | 2p_coin, 10p_coin, start |
| from the game electronics | 500_points, life_gone |

and the following two-valued output signals:

| | |
|---|---|
| to the indicator lamps | start_game, game_over |
| to the game electronics | clear_game, game_on |

The behaviour of the controller expressed in the style of Pascal is:

```
while true do
  begin
    clear_game := true; game_over := true;
    start_game := false; game_on := false;
    coin_count := 0;
```

```
    while coin_count < 10 do
      begin
        if 2p_coin then coin_count := coin_count + 1;
        if 10p_coin then coin_count := coin_count + 5
      end;
    clear_game := false; game_over := false;
    start_game := true;
    while not start do nothing;
    while start do nothing;  {wait for release}
    lives := 4; start_game := false;
    while lives > 0 do
      begin
        game_on := true;
        if 500_points then lives := lives + 1;
        if life_gone then lives := lives - 1
      end
  end
```

In addition to the input and output signals, two other internal signals (or variables) are used: coin_count and lives. Operations using these constitute the data part of the system, that is

```
coin_count < 10
coin_count := coin_count + 1 (or 5)
lives > 0
lives := lives +/- 1
```

From the other statements the behaviour of the controller can be extracted. This controller will have to generate additional signals to evoke the arithmetic operations in the data part and will need status inputs from it which indicate the result of the comparisons. It is thus possible to derive an architecture from a behavioural description. There are problems, however.

In order to perform this transformation, we had to interpret the program in a way different from the normal rules of Pascal. In particular, timing rules have to be invented, that is when things happen; it has to be decided which actions can happen in parallel, for example the output assignments in the example probably could. Rules about setting and resetting signals also have to be invented, for example does output := true imply that the signal stays true until output := false occurs? Despite these limitations, the method does aid the design process in that it is a way of expressing and experimenting with ideas on paper as a first step. (A program can be analysed for parallelism automatically by looking at dependencies among data operations and then transformed into a special-purpose digital system. These methods, however, are still at the research stage.)

As an example of a more suitable method of describing behaviour, the game controller is re-expressed in one of the many languages specifically designed for specifying the behaviour of digital systems, SML. The semantics of this language will not be given here as, in this simple example, most of it should be obvious.

```
program game_controller;

input 2p_coin, 10p_coin, start, 500_points, life_gone;
output start_game, game_over, clear_game, game_on;
integer coin_count[4], lives[4];

  loop
    parallel
      raise (clear_game) || raise (game_over) ||
      lower (start_game) || lower (game_on) ||
      while coin_count < 0 do loop
        switch
          case 2p_coin: coin_count := coin_count + 1;
          case 10p_coin: coin_count := coin_count + 5;
        endswitch
      endloop
    endparallel;
    parallel
      lower (clear_game) || lower (game_over) ||
      raise (start_game) ||
      loop if start then break endif endloop
    endparallel;
    while start do loop skip endloop;
    parallel
      lives := 4 || lower (start_game)
    endparallel;
    while lives > 0 do loop
      parallel
        raise (game_on) ||
        if 500_points then lives := lives + 1 ||
        if life_gone then lives := lives - 1
      endparallel
    endloop
  endloop
endprog
```

Parallel activities are now made explicit, so there is more than one way of describing the system, each with a different combination of parallel activities. A rule of SML is that time advances one step whenever a variable is changed; thus this aspect of behaviour is again built into the design. SML has only been introduced here to demonstrate that more unambiguous design languages can be defined. However, none are as widely used and known as programming languages, and many are still only a restricted or partial solution to the architectural design problem.

The **register transfer languages** (RTLs) belong in this class. These describe the operation of a digital system as a sequence of data transformations and transfers between registers. From this type of specification the function of the controller can be immediately derived but, before an RTL program can be written, a design for the data part of the system has to be drawn up. It can thus be thought of as the next lower level of behavioural description. RTL level notations will be used in later chapters.

## 1.6 Influence of circuit technology

The vast majority of digital systems are constructed as silicon integrated circuits (ICs). The complexity of the smallest IC unit can range from one containing a few transistors to one containing a few hundred thousand. The conventional names for the size ranges of these units, **SSI**, **MSI**, **LSI** and **VLSI** (denoting respectively small-, medium-, large- and very-large-scale integration) are loosely based on numbers of transistors, but today are generally used to identify the style of IC rather than a crude component count. ICs may also be categorized as standard, custom or semicustom. **Standard** ICs have their architecture and function defined by the manufacturer, while **custom** ICs are those which are fully defined by the user for a specific function. The **semicustom**, or application-specific, ICs (ASICs) have a standard circuit framework or set of cells which are wired in a pattern defined by the user to suit the application. Programmable logic fits into the latter category (the term ASIC, however, is mainly used for gate array and standard cell ICs).

The larger the number of transistors in a standard IC, the more constrained becomes the architecture of the digital system constructed with them; a number of design decisions are 'locked' into the IC. However, building a system with smaller devices, although giving the designer greater architectural freedom, is nowadays impractical for reasons of cost, size, weight and power consumption. This freedom is regained with custom design, which retains the advantages of a high level of integration while giving the designer the ability to design the system in a more efficient way than would be possible with standard devices. The design costs are very high and this method of design ('VLSI design') is still only possible for ICs destined for mass use or where unusual economics apply. This is an area, however, where developments in design automation are likely to have a large impact.

SSI and MSI components are generally thought of as fixed-function 'catalogue' parts, ranging in complexity from simple gates to arithmetic unit 'slices' and counters. Some of the more complex MSI parts are very suitable for building data paths, perhaps specified at the register transfer level. With LSI parts there is less freedom in system design. For example, LSI blocks such as 8-bit microprocessors and their peripheral controllers are intended to be used in stereotyped ways – the system function is defined by the software. Recent microcomputer ICs and memories are now considered to be in the VLSI category, but their mode of application is much as before – the recommended configurations are retained. Unfortunately, LSI and VLSI components do not remove the need for the less complex components. Linking complex standard components from different manufacturers or to user-defined interfaces often demands a certain amount of special-purpose processing performed by collections of small-scale circuits. This is the function of 'glue logic'. In fact, the circuit board area occupied by this can exceed that taken up by the major LSI or VLSI circuits themselves.

In most manufactured digital systems the cost of the ICs is a small fraction of the total cost – of the order of 10–20%. This figure may be verified by working out the IC cost as a fraction of purchase price of, say, a small computer or a test instrument. The additional costs are in power supplies, circuit boards, passive components, packaging, documentation, manufacture and testing. To a first approximation, all of these costs are proportional to the number of ICs in the system. The obvious conclusion is that a system must be designed to have the smallest number of ICs consistent with meeting the performance and other requirements. Custom ICs can achieve this, but at a high cost of design. If production economics do not allow their use, a good compromise can be to use semicustom components, or a combination of standard LSI or VLSI and semicustom components.

## 1.7 Why programmable logic?

Probably the most widely used type of semicustom component is programmable logic. **Programmable logic devices** (PLDs) are ICs whose ultimate function is determined by the designer; they leave the manufacturer in an unprogrammed state. Programming is performed either by loading internal storage registers or by inducing permanent or reversible physical changes in selected parts of the circuit. In the former case the device's program can be modified dynamically, whereas in the latter case this is not generally possible. By this definition, microcomputers are also programmable logic devices. However, the definition will be restricted here to include only *logic* components with programmable function and/or configuration.

Until recently, all PLDs were based on a single type of logic array. However, a number of new types of high density PLD now have been introduced and it is likely that more will arrive. Consideration of these devices, many based on well-known ASIC forms, is beyond the scope of this book. Attention here will be restricted to the conventional array forms.

These forms are described in Chapter 3. Such PLDs are now available in sizes which can allow systems of LSI complexity to be implemented in a single IC. Because of the wide size and speed range of available PLDs, there are many niches into which PLDs conveniently fit, from simple 'glue' to the implementation of entire systems. The particular attractions of programmable logic are as follows:

- System design does not have to be performed down to the logic gate level; functional descriptions of control and data paths can be compiled directly into PLD descriptions.
- Subsystems of complexities of up to 1000–2000 two-input gates can be implemented in a single package.
- With reprogrammable PLDs, errors can be corrected at the prototype stage without discarding a possibly expensive part.
- The demands on computer-aided design are small, except for the very largest PLDs.
- Modern PLDs have speed and power consumption comparable with those of high speed CMOS logic.
- Capital investment is low.
- Design time is much shorter than with other types of ASIC.
- The function of an existing piece of equipment can be modified by simply changing or reprogramming a PLD.
- Printed circuit board design can be simplified because of the freedom possible in signal allocation to pins.

## 1.8 An approach to design

The message of this chapter is that there is no single 'recipe' which can always be followed to obtain a good digital system design for all applications. However, the guidelines given in this section should be useful.

Before stating these, the design process is idealized by breaking it up into four steps, as shown in Figure 1.11. At level 1, the specification of the system's function exists; this should contain no details of the implementation. Level 2 is the system architecture; this is a description of the major functional blocks of the system and their interconnection. Control and data processing will be separated where this can be done conveniently. The architecture may be constrained by certain major components, such as microprocessors, on which it is based. At level 3, all the components have been selected and the first iteration of the detailed design exists. Finally, at level 4 the design has received its final stage of optimization, in which the

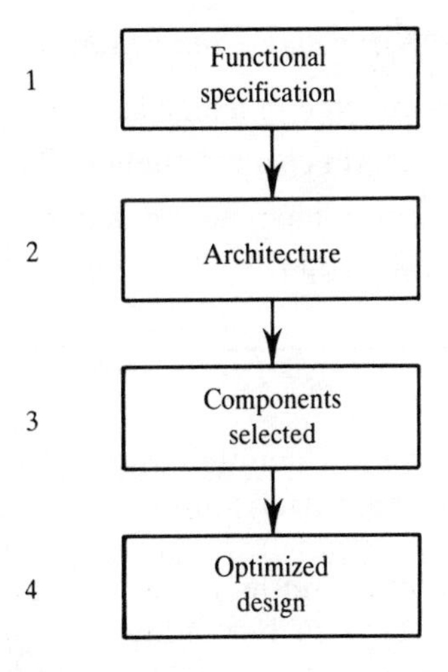


**Figure 1.11** Stages in design.

best circuit configurations are produced. The optimization criteria will depend on the intended use of the system.

With this model in mind, the design guidelines are expressed in the form of the following checklist:

*Level 1: functional specification*

- Can the specification be produced by modifying an existing specification?
- Can the specification be expressed mathematically?
- Can it be structured hierarchically, using more abstract signals?
- Are all links with other systems well understood and specified?
- Will it perform correctly for all input signal combinations?
- Are the performance requirements and constraints fully specified?

*Level 2: architecture*

- Does an architecture for this problem already exist?
- How much parallelism is necessary?
- Can standard LSI or VLSI blocks be used?
- Is a custom IC design permissible?
- Are some parts candidates for semicustom ICs?
- Can the function of each block be independently verified?

*Level 3: components selection and optimization*

- Is the design documented to a high standard?
- Will the design perform correctly under all physical conditions?
- Can a failure of each component be detected?
- Is any optimization possible?

---

## SUMMARY

A digital system is formally defined as a system which operates on digital signals, those which have only a finite set of values. The behaviour of a digital system, which could be combinational or sequential, may be specified by listing its inputs and outputs in a table, or by writing down an algorithm which computes the outputs from the inputs. An algorithm may be expressed in a programing language or, more unambiguously, in a suitable hardware description language. Algorithmic behaviour is converted into a block diagram by defining an architecture. Many architectures are possible for any given task, but all have control and data sections. Signals are stored and transformed in the data part, while the sequencing of operations is the function of the control part. Sometimes it is not easy to separate the two parts, as in the von Neumann computer. The architecture chosen is strongly dependent on the circuit technology selected and the complexity of ICs available. Programmable logic devices are available in a range of sizes and can be used at various levels in a design hierarchy, from the logic gate to the subsystem level. Their main advantage is that they can reduce the number of ICs in a system while requiring only moderate design effort and expenditure.

---

## BIBLIOGRAPHICAL NOTES

A more formal approach to digital systems at the level considered in this chapter, and one which has influenced the approach adopted here, is that of Davio *et al.* (1983). Ercegovac and Lang (1985) is an excellent practical textbook based on this approach. Bell *et al.* (1972) is a readable discussion of the design issues, although the examples are based on an obsolete technology. Newly developed techniques of optimization at the pre-encoding stage are introduced by De Micheli (1985). Prosser and Winkel (1987), Langdon (1982), and Comer (1984) all contain chapters on 'top-down' design and the process of defining control and data parts. Much of Section 1.4 has been drawn from Barton (1985). Hartenstein (1973) elaborates on the idea of a hierarchy of interpreters. A good sourcebook of standard architectures is Siewiorek *et al.* (1982). The Harvard mark I is described in Ceruzzi (1983). A highly developed type of control flow architecture specialized for signal processing using serial arithmetic is given in Denyer and Renshaw (1985). The game controller example is taken from Dagless (1983). Conversion of programs into digital systems is discussed by Davio (1984). SML is described by Browne and Clarke (1987). Register transfer languages are introduced in Friedman (1986). A book on digital design based entirely on a register transfer language is Hartenstein (1977). An example of a CAD system built around such a language is Gai *et al.* (1985). A recent language and design system for synthesizing multiple process architectures is described in Berstis (1989). Practical and economic aspects of digital systems are addressed by Blakeslee (1979) and Peatman (1980). Economic justifications of programmable logic are given in Vargas (1987) and Kamdar (1988). The trials of some of the programmable logic pioneers are entertainingly described in Kidder (1981).

## EXERCISES

**1.1** Which of the following are digital signals?

(a) the days of the week,
(b) the real numbers,
(c) the integer numbers,
(d) all the world's telephone numbers.

**1.2** Write the specification in two different ways for a digital system which accepts two inputs, one which has values in $\{0,1,2,3\}$, and the other which has values in $\{\text{PASS}, \text{MINUS}\}$. The output is equal to the first input if the second input has the value 'PASS'; otherwise, it is equal to the first input negated.

**1.3** A signal processing system is to be designed which accepts a continuous string of data signals and outputs the average of the last ten inputs at one-tenth of the rate. Write an algorithm which specifies the behaviour of this system and devise an architecture.

**1.4** A digital system is to be designed which sorts into ascending order 16 bytes stored in a read–write memory. Sorting commences on receipt of a command 'start' and the signal 'finished' is issued when sorting is complete.

(a) Design an algorithm for this task and express it using programming language statements. (One simple sorting method is to compare successive pairs of bytes and to reverse them if they are in the wrong order, doing 15, 14, 13, . . . , 1 comparisons.)
(b) From this algorithm derive an architecture for the sorter, showing any internal signals defined.

**1.5** A simple printer controller is to be designed. The controller accepts inputs in sequence which are codes for both printing and non-printing characters. The only non-printing characters are 'carriage return' and 'line feed'. The outputs are commands to the printing mechanism.

If the printer has reached the end of a line and a 'carriage return' has not been received by the controller, a bell must be sounded and the printer carriage returned.

Produce a block diagram for this controller. Identify data and control signals, and the functional blocks. Modify the design to allow inputs to be received in bursts at a faster rate than they can be printed.

---

CHAPTER 2

# Review of Basic Topics in Logic Design

---

**OBJECTIVES**

When you have reviewed the material in this chapter you should be able

- to construct simple binary encodings for digital signals;
- to specify binary functions as truth tables or lists of cubes;
- to use the theorems of Boolean algebra and to express Boolean functions in the sum-of-products and product-of-sums forms;
- to use K maps for minimizing functions of up to four variables;
- to specify Mealy and Moore finite state machines with state tables and diagrams;
- to construct an $n$-bit adder with and without carry lookahead;
- to use the direct polarity indication system for documentation.

---

## 2.1 Introduction

This chapter is concerned with the raw materials of digital systems: combinational and sequential logic circuits. The topics which will be reviewed are codes, Boolean algebra, canonical forms, minimization, finite state machines and arithmetic circuits. Finally, a system for the documentation of logic circuits is introduced, consistent with the latest international standards, which will be used in this book.

Most readers should be able to skip through this chapter very quickly, as the majority of the material is covered in a first course on logic design. This is not included merely for completeness, however – all of it has been selected as being essential for understanding the design methods in later chapters. It should also serve as a reference for more experienced designers who have lost touch with fundamentals. For a more complete coverage, the reader is referred to one of the textbooks mentioned at the end of the chapter.

## 2.2 From signals to Boolean algebra

### 2.2.1 Codes

In Chapter 1 it was stated that digital signals must be encoded into strings of symbols which can be processed by the circuit elements of the digital system. Throughout the book, these will always be the binary symbols '0' and '1'. In this section, some of the more commonly used encodings will be outlined.

An unsigned number, $N$, may be represented by a string of **bits**:

$$b_{n-1}b_{n-2}\ldots b_1b_0$$

where

$$N = b_{n-1} \times 2^{n-1} + b_{n-2} \times 2^{n-2} + \ldots + b_1 \times 2^1 + b_0 \times 2^0 \quad \textbf{(2.1)}$$

Numbers with a fractional part may be represented by defining a **binary point**. For example, the string 101.011 is interpreted as

$$1 \times 2^2 + 0 \times 2^1 + 1 \times 2^0 + 0 \times 2^{-1} + 1 \times 2^{-2} + 1 \times 2^{-3} = 5\tfrac{3}{8}$$

A code which is useful when numbers have to be converted to or from a human readable form is **binary-coded decimal** or BCD. Here each decimal digit of a number is encoded separately. For example, the number 805 is encoded as

1000 0000 0101

BCD codes are less efficient than the standard binary code as not all bit combinations are used.

The most widely used method of representing signed numbers is **two's complement**. The encoding rule is now changed to give the most significant bit a negative weighting, that is $-2^{n-1}$. Thus the string 101.011 is interpreted in two's complement as

$$-1 \times 2^2 + 0 \times 2^1 + 1 \times 2^0 + 0 \times 2^{-1} + 1 \times 2^{-2} + 1 \times 2^{-3} = -2\tfrac{5}{8}$$

The range of numbers that can be represented with the binary point in the position shown is $-4$ to $3\tfrac{7}{8}$. Two's complement encoding has the advantage that the same arithmetic circuits can handle both signed and unsigned binary numbers. Some details of two's complement arithmetic will be given in Section 2.4.

The **sign + magnitude** representation treats the sign as a separate bit. This form is most commonly used in floating point codes, in which the number is represented in two parts: a **fraction** and an **exponent**. Sign + magnitude representation of the fraction simplifies the normalization operation; this is a left shift to remove any leading zeros, thus preserving maximum precision.

Numerous standard codes also exist for non-numerical information, but even so it is likely that every digital system designed will have a new, custom, encoding defined for some of its signals. A binary string of $k$ bits has $2^k$ different combinations of 1s and 0s and can thus represent a maximum of $2^k$ signals. Put the other way, $l$ signals can be encoded by a string of length $\lceil \log_2 l \rceil$, where $\lceil X \rceil$ is the smallest integer $\geqslant X$.

For some applications it is important to construct codes with special properties. One such property is that, in a list of signals, the codes for adjacent signals differ in only one bit position, the first and the last signals in the list being considered as adjacent. The **Gray code** has this feature. The 2- and 3-bit Gray codes are shown in Tables 2.1 and 2.2.

By examining Table 2.2 it can be seen how it can be derived from Table 2.1. The first four rows are the same if the $x_1$ bit is ignored, while the second four are the first four in reverse order with $x_1 = 1$. This rule can be generalized for the construction of larger tables. Note that these tables are of length $2^k$ where $k$ is the number of bits in the code. Gray codes are useful for solving certain state assignment problems in sequential circuits, as will be seen in later chapters.

Another useful class of codes are those which have error detecting and correcting properties. Treatment of these is beyond the scope of this book. One simple error-detecting method which occurs frequently, however, is the **parity** bit. An extra bit is added to the code to make the number of ones or zeros in the augmented code odd or even. A single corrupted bit will therefore cause the parity to be incorrect when checked.

**Table 2.1**

| | $x_1$ | $x_2$ |
|---|---|---|
| 0 | 0 | 0 |
| 1 | 0 | 1 |
| 2 | 1 | 1 |
| 3 | 1 | 0 |

**Table 2.2**

| | $x_1$ | $x_2$ | $x_3$ |
|---|---|---|---|
| 0 | 0 | 0 | 0 |
| 1 | 0 | 0 | 1 |
| 2 | 0 | 1 | 1 |
| 3 | 0 | 1 | 0 |
| 4 | 1 | 1 | 0 |
| 5 | 1 | 1 | 1 |
| 6 | 1 | 0 | 1 |
| 7 | 1 | 0 | 0 |

### 2.2.2 Truth tables and cubes

The behaviour of a combinational logic block whose inputs and outputs have been encoded is most directly specified by a binary truth table. Truth tables have the form shown in Table 2.3. Here the input bits are $I_1$–$I_3$ and the output bits are $O_1$-$O_3$.

On the left-hand part of the table is a column for every binary input signal, and on the right is a column for every output. This table represents a **multiple output function**. The '*'s in the input side indicate that the value of the input is irrelevant in that row, in other words its value is **'don't care'**. The use of these '*'s in the input side has the effect of condensing the table, as a single '*' implies two rows, two '*'s four rows, etc. A '–' in the output side means that the output signal can be 0 or 1, whichever is the most convenient or economical in the implementation. This therefore also means 'don't care'. A function with 'don't care' values in the output part is described as being **incompletely specified**.

A shorter method of specifying functions is to use the decimal specification, in which rows are identified by the decimal equivalent of the input combinations read as binary numbers, and rows with identical outputs are collected together. For example, in Table 2.3 $O_1$ is 1 for inputs 101 and 111, that is 5 and 7. It is 0 for input 0, and is 'don't care' for inputs 1, 2, 3, 4 and 6. This can be expressed as

$$O_1 = \sum(5, 7)$$

or

$$O_1 = \Pi(0)$$

**Table 2.3**

| $I_1$ | $I_2$ | $I_3$ | $O_1$ | $O_2$ | $O_3$ |
|---|---|---|---|---|---|
| 0 | 0 | 0 | 0 | 1 | 0 |
| 0 | 0 | 1 | – | 1 | 1 |
| 0 | 1 | * | – | 0 | 0 |
| 1 | * | 0 | – | – | – |
| 1 | * | 1 | 1 | 1 | 1 |

with

$$d(1,2,3,4,6)$$

Alternatively, function $O_1$ can be said to have the **on set**, the **off set**, and the **don't care set**:

$$\begin{aligned} X^{\mathrm{ON}} &= \{101, 111\} \\ X^{\mathrm{OFF}} &= \{000\} \\ X^{\mathrm{DC}} &= \{001, 010, 011, 100, 110\} \end{aligned}$$

Another method used for expressing functions, widely used in the computer implementation of the more complex design algorithms, is the **cube notation**. The $n$ input variables of a function can be thought of as defining an $n$-dimensional space, each axis of which has coordinates 0 and 1. The $2^n$ combinations of the inputs define the **vertices (0-cubes)** of an $n$-dimensional cube, also known as an ***n*-cube**, or **hypercube**. Figure 2.1

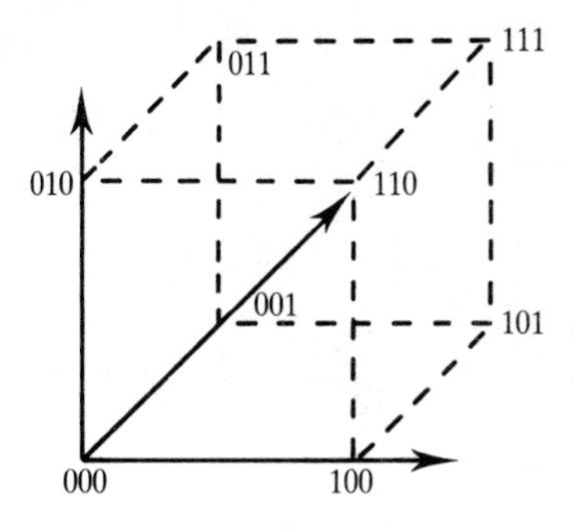


**Figure 2.1** A 3-cube.

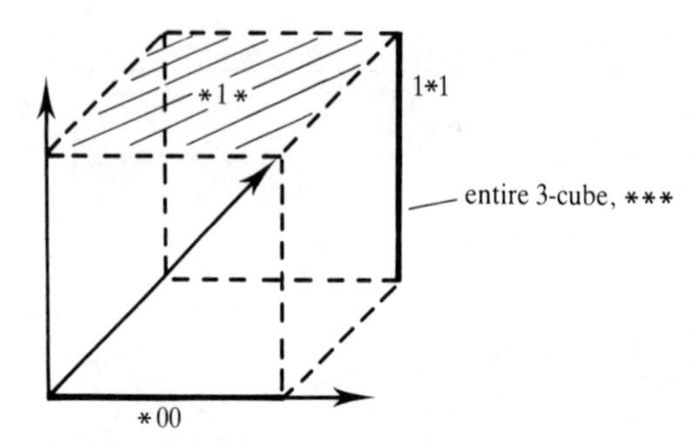


**Figure 2.2** Some subcubes.

illustrates this for $n = 3$. Notice that all adjacent vertices differ in only one variable. Thus for example the line joining 101 and 111 can be written 1*1 – this is a **1-cube**. In general, a cube with $k$ non-don't-cares defines an $n - k$ dimensional subspace, termed a **subcube** or **face**. Some subcubes are shown in Figure 2.2. Figure 2.3 shows the geometrical representation of function $O_2$ of the example. More will be said about this representation in Chapter 4.

### 2.2.3 Boolean algebra

The algebra of binary logic functions is Boolean algebra, whose most useful results will now be summarized. This algebra in its binary form is defined in terms of the set $\{0, 1\}$, (or $\{\text{false}, \text{true}\}$), the two operators $+$ (sum) and $\cdot$ (product), and a set of postulates. The following useful theorems can be derived using this algebra, some directly from the postulates. Every Boolean variable has a **complement**, as defined in theorem (4).

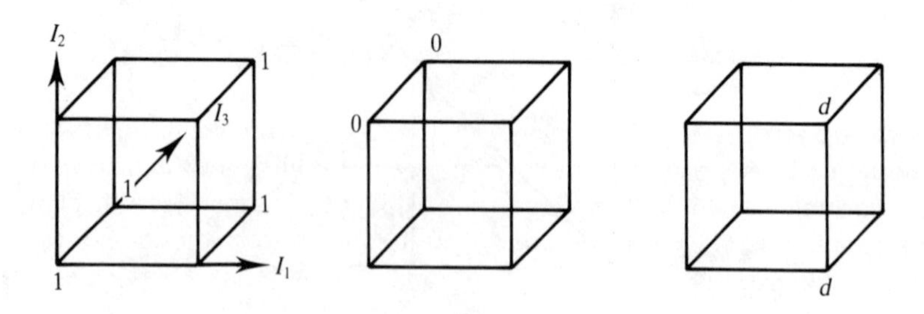


**Figure 2.3** Cube representation of $O_2$.

| | | |
|---|---|---|
| (1a) | $x + 0 = x$ | identity elements |
| (1b) | $x \cdot 1 = x$ | |
| (2a) | $x + y = y + x$ | commutativity |
| (2b) | $x \cdot y = y \cdot x$ | |
| (3a) | $x + (y \cdot z) = (x + y) \cdot (x + z)$ | distributivity |
| (3b) | $x \cdot (y + z) = x \cdot y + x \cdot z$ | |
| (4a) | $x + \overline{x} = 1$ | complementation |
| (4b) | $x \cdot \overline{x} = 0$ | |
| (5a) | $x \cdot x = x$ | idempotence |
| (5b) | $x + x = x$ | |
| (6a) | $x \cdot 0 = 0$ | |
| (6b) | $x + 1 = 1$ | |
| (7a) | $x \cdot (x + y) = x$ | absorption |
| (7b) | $x + (x \cdot y) = x$ | |
| (8a) | $x + (y + z) = (x + y) + z$ | associativity |
| (8b) | $x \cdot (y \cdot z) = (x \cdot y) \cdot z$ | |
| (9a) | $\overline{x + y} = \overline{x} \cdot \overline{y}$ | De Morgan's theorem |
| (9b) | $\overline{x \cdot y} = \overline{x} + \overline{y}$ | |
| (10) | $\overline{\overline{x}} = x$ | double complementation |
| (11a) | $x + \overline{x} \cdot y = x + y$ | from (3a) and (3b) |
| (11b) | $x \cdot (\overline{x} + y) = x \cdot y$ | from (3b) and (4b) |

Notice that, where the theorems are grouped in pairs, one can be derived from the other simply by interchanging '+'s and '·'s, and 0s and 1s. This is the principle of **duality**.

### 2.2.4 Boolean equations

It is now possible to apply this algebra to the analysis of the functions previously specified by truth table. Let us go back to output $O_1$ of the example in Section 2.2.2. We wish to obtain an expression for

$$O_1 = f(I_1, I_2, I_3)$$

This can be achieved in two ways. First, look at the conditions which make $O_1$ equal to 1. A **product term** is defined as a Boolean product of two or more variables or their complements (or **literals**). From theorem (1b), a product will have the value 1 if each of its literals has the value 1. So, in the example, the product

$$I_1 \cdot I_3 \quad \text{(or just } I_1 I_3\text{)}$$

is true whenever $I_1$ and $I_3$ are true, which is also when $O_1$ is true. Thus we can write

$$O_1 = I_1 I_3$$

It is also possible to include the 'don't care' cases by allowing them to assume the value 1. In the truth table there are three products which are equal to 1 when $O_1$ is '–'. These are

$$\bar{I}_1 \bar{I}_2 I_3 \quad \bar{I}_1 I_2 \quad I_1 \bar{I}_3$$

Now, by applying theorem (6b), another expression can be written for $O_1$:

$$O_1 = I_1 I_3 + \bar{I}_1 \bar{I}_2 I_3 + \bar{I}_1 I_2 + I_1 \bar{I}_3$$

This form is the **sum of products**. In this example the products correspond to 0-cubes and 1-cubes of the space spanned by the inputs. A sum-of-products form which contains only products with all input variables present (thus corresponding to 0-cubes or vertices) is the **canonical sum-of-products form**. The products in this case are known as **minterms**. Ignoring 'don't care' outputs, the canonical form for $O_1$ is

$$O_1 = I_1 \bar{I}_2 I_3 + I_1 I_2 I_3$$

A second method of producing an equation for an output is to look at those input combinations which cause the output to be 0. A **sum term** is defined as a Boolean sum of two or more variables or their complements. From theorem (1a), a sum term will have the value 0 if each of its literals has the value 0. So, for $O_1$, the sum

$$I_1 + I_2 + I_3$$

is false whenever $I_1$, $I_2$ and $I_3$ are false, which is also when $O_1$ is false. Thus we can write

$$O_1 = I_1 + I_2 + I_3$$

Now, by applying theorem (6a), and adding in the 'don't care' conditions, the **product-of-sums** form can be written down:

$$O_1 = (I_1 + I_2 + I_3)(I_1 + I_2 + \bar{I}_3)(I_1 + \bar{I}_2)(\bar{I}_1 + I_3)$$

Notice that this form was obtained by applying the dual argument to that which produced the sum of products. Sum terms which contain all variables are called **maxterms**, and an equation containing only maxterms is the **canonical product of sums**.

Minterms and maxterms may be identified with a decimal number, leading to the shorthand forms of specification used in Section 2.2.2.

A further sum-of-products equation may be obtained for the complement of the output, either directly by looking at the 0s in the truth table or by applying De Morgan's theorem (theorem (9a)) to the product of sums above. Similarly, a further product of sums may be obtained by applying (9b) to the sum of products or writing an expression directly for the output 1s.

## 2.3 Logic gates

To the Boolean operations of +, · and complement, there correspond the logic circuits OR, AND and NOT. All the theorems of Section 2.2.3 are valid if the operations are performed by logic gates. The truth tables of the AND and OR gates are identical to those for the · and + operators. These may be obtained by application of theorems (1b) and (6a), and (1a) and (6b), respectively and are given in Tables 2.4–2.6. Boolean algebra is thus also the algebra of logic networks.

Sum-of-products and product-of-sums expressions lead to **two-level** networks, as in Figure 2.4. In canonical form each of the input AND or OR gates has $n$ inputs for an $n$-input function. Figure 2.5 gives the canonical sum-of-products form for $O_1$. Notice that logical negations, or NOT gates, are also required.

The two-level form is the one in which all logical functions in this book will be expressed, for reasons to be explained in the next chapter. Designs will be conceived directly in this form except in those cases where a pre-existing design in **multiple-level** form has to be converted. This conversion is performed by applying the theorems of Boolean algebra to expand the expression into two levels. For example, the network of Figure 2.6 can be converted into two-level form. (Here NAND and NOR gates are used – these are just AND and OR gates with negated outputs.) First

**Table 2.4**

| AND (·) | | |
|---|---|---|
| $x$ | $y$ | $z$ |
| 0 | 0 | 0 |
| 0 | 1 | 0 |
| 1 | 0 | 0 |
| 1 | 1 | 1 |

**Table 2.5**

| OR (+) | | |
|---|---|---|
| $x$ | $y$ | $z$ |
| 0 | 0 | 0 |
| 0 | 1 | 1 |
| 1 | 0 | 1 |
| 1 | 1 | 1 |

**Table 2.6**

| NOT ($\bar{\ }$) | |
|---|---|
| $x$ | $y$ |
| 0 | 1 |
| 1 | 0 |

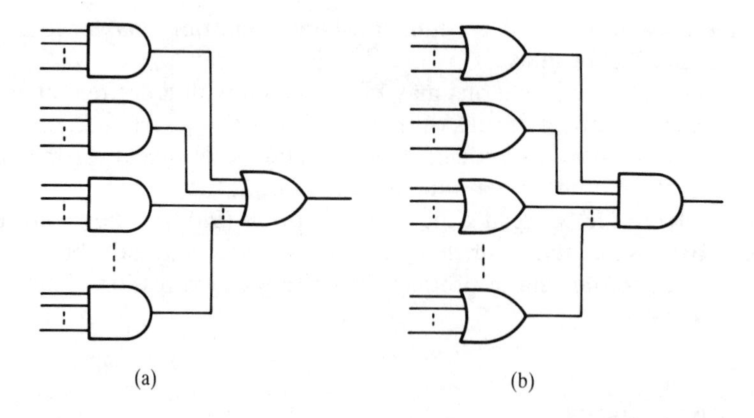


**Figure 2.4** Two-level networks: (a) sum of products; (b) product of sums.

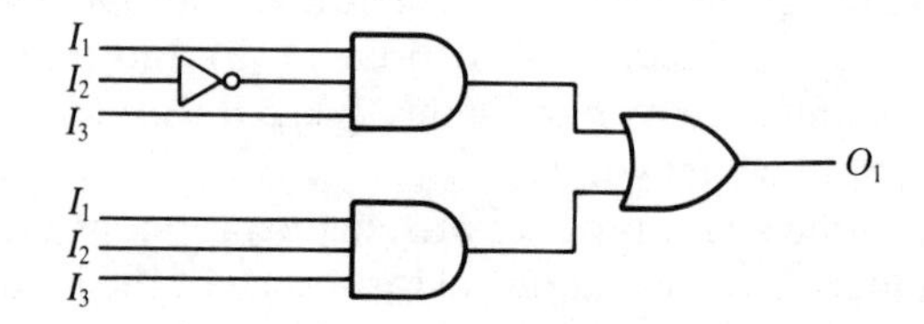


**Figure 2.5** Canonical sum of products for $O_1$.

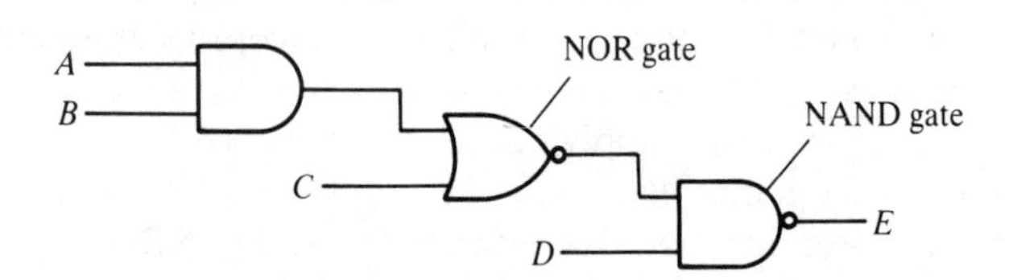


**Figure 2.6** Multiple-level network.

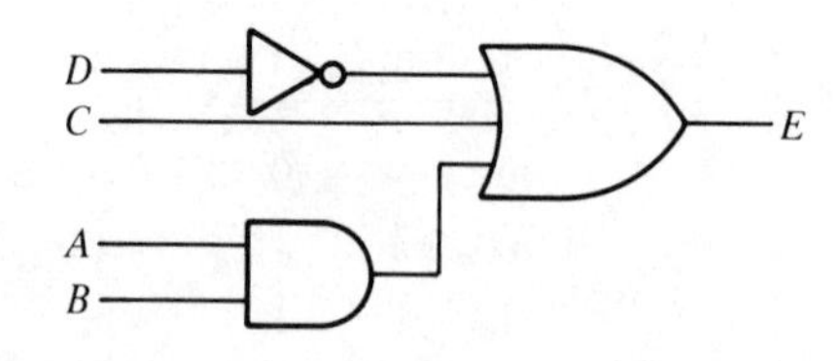


**Figure 2.7** Two-level form of Figure 2.6.

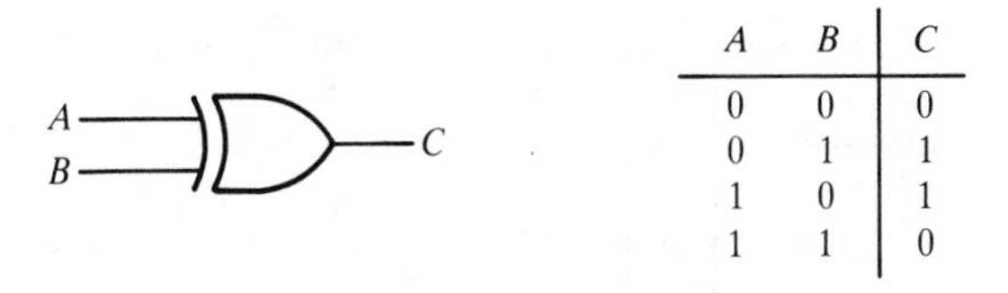


| A | B | C |
|---|---|---|
| 0 | 0 | 0 |
| 0 | 1 | 1 |
| 1 | 0 | 1 |
| 1 | 1 | 0 |

**Figure 2.8** The exclusive OR gate.

the equation for the output is written down; it is usually easiest to start from the output terminal. Note that the multiple levels of gating give rise to factorization in the equations. The equation for the output, $E$ is

$$E = \overline{D \cdot (\overline{C + A \cdot B})}$$

This can be expanded, by applying De Morgan's theorem once, into

$$E = \overline{D} + C + A \cdot B$$

which now is in the desired sum-of-products form. The new network is shown in Figure 2.7. This is not in canonical form, as the AND gates are not connected to all input variables.

One other type of gate which is used frequently in programmable logic is the exclusive OR. Its truth table and symbol are given in Figure 2.8; the output is true when the two inputs are different.

## 2.4 Minimization

The two-level forms produced so far have been designed without regard to optimality; the number of logic gates used has not been considered. That there are more and less economical designs is obvious from the truth table of Section 2.2.2. The '*'s in the input side represent a compaction of two minterms into one product with fewer inputs. Minimization algorithms are systematic procedures for finding the **minimum cover**, that is the most compact table of this form – the one with fewest rows, and thus product terms. Other minimization criteria can be added, such as minimum number of gate inputs, but, for the programmable logic devices to be studied in this book, reducing the number of products is the sole aim. We shall only be concerned with sum-of-products implementations, but dual procedures apply for products of sums. In this section, the minimization problem will be discussed generally, and some simple manual procedures for minimization will be reviewed. Chapter 4 will discuss minimization algorithms in more detail.

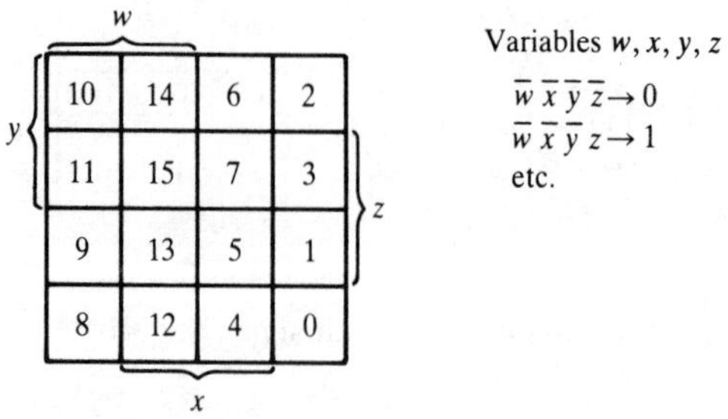
w
10 14 6 2
11 15 7 3
9 13 5 1
8 12 4 0
y
z
x
Variables w, x, y, z
$\overline{w}\,\overline{x}\,\overline{y}\,\overline{z} \rightarrow 0$
$\overline{w}\,\overline{x}\,\overline{y}\,z \rightarrow 1$
etc.

**Figure 2.9** Four-variable K map with miniterms.

In order to visualize the key ideas, the **Karnaugh map** (or K map) is used. This is a planar representation of the $n$-cubes given in Section 2.2.2. These maps preserve vertex adjacencies, and thus can represent cubes of different dimensions. Their limitation is that the number of variables which can be handled is restricted: up to four is easy and five just possible; for more than this the maps become voluminous and their use becomes prone to errors. A four-variable map for variables $w, x, y, z$ is given in Figure 2.9. The rows and columns bracketed by the variables are those for which the variables are true; a row or column with a variable unnamed corresponds to the case where that variable is false. Each square is associated with a minterm. These are given their decimal designations on the map in the figure. The layout of the variables ensures that a vertical or horizontal movement between any two squares, including those 'round the back', requires a change in value of only one variable. Each square thus corresponds to a vertex of a 4-cube.

A product term which has less than the maximum number of literals defines a square or rectangle on a K map. Some examples are shown in Figure 2.10. The smallest square possible is a minterm; the largest encloses the whole map and implies that the function value is always 1 (a tautology).

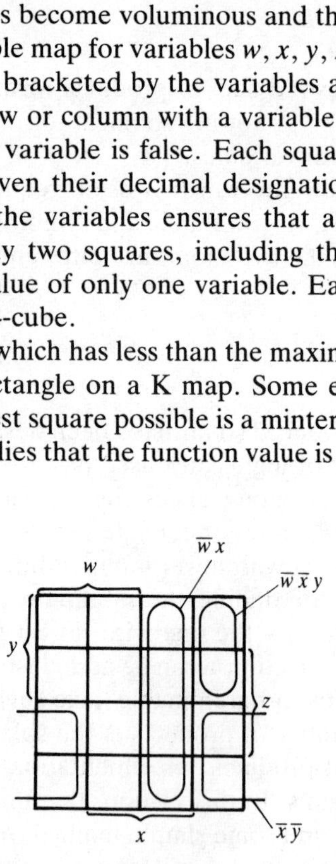
$\overline{w}\,x$
w
$\overline{w}\,\overline{x}\,y$
y
z
x
$\overline{x}\,\overline{y}$

**Figure 2.10** Examples of products.

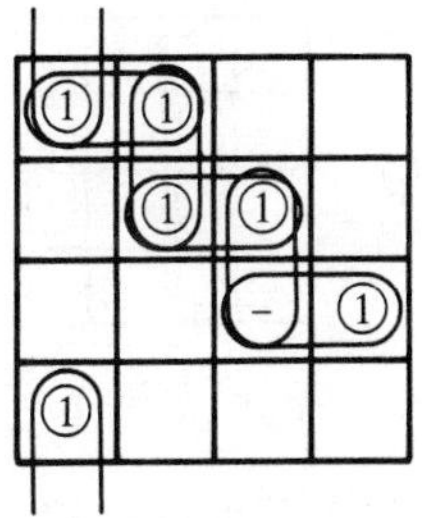
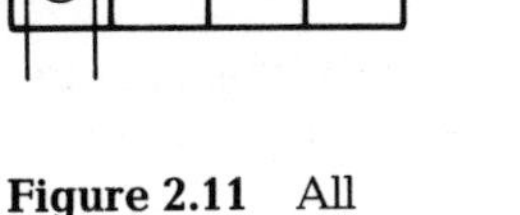

**Figure 2.11** All implicants of a function.

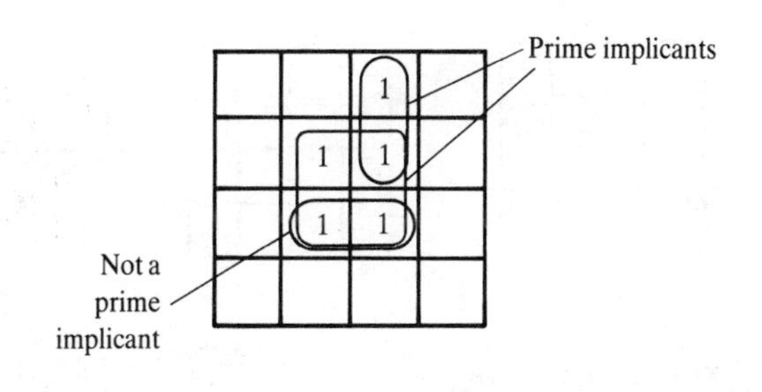


**Figure 2.12** Prime implicants.

A problem specification is transferred to a K map by filling in from the truth table those squares where the function is true with '1's and those where it is 'don't care' with '–'s.

An **implicant** of a function is any product term which implies the function, that is that if true implies that the function is true. All minterms are implicants. Figure 2.11 shows the K map of a four-variable function with all implicants enclosed. A **prime implicant** is an implicant which is not enclosed by any other implicant of the function. Figure 2.12 shows two prime implicants and one implicant which is not prime. The latter are obviously redundant, as all input combinations which make them true also make their enclosing implicant or implicants, and thus the function, true. The **complete sum** of a function is the sum of all of its prime implicants. Figure 2.13 shows a complete sum consisting of six prime implicants.

In general, the complete sum will contain prime implicants which are redundant – their job is done by a combination of other prime implicants. To reduce the number of prime implicants, and thus product terms, in the implementation, an **irredundant form** must be found. This is a set of prime implicants from which no prime implicant can be removed without changing the function. For the example of Figure 2.13 there are four irredundant forms. These are shown in Figure 2.14. A prime implicant which appears in every irredundant form is an **essential prime implicant**.

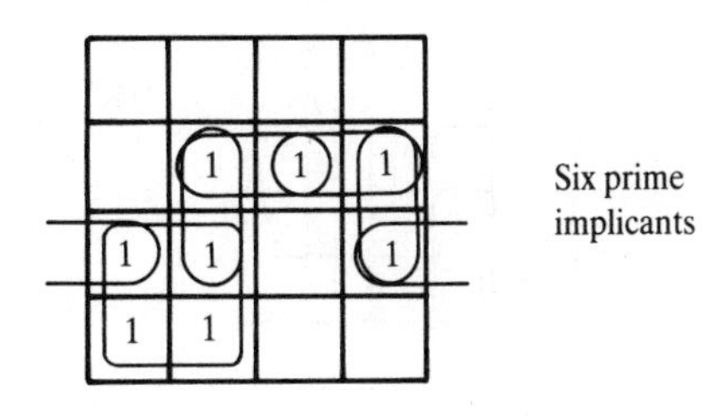


**Figure 2.13** A complete sum.

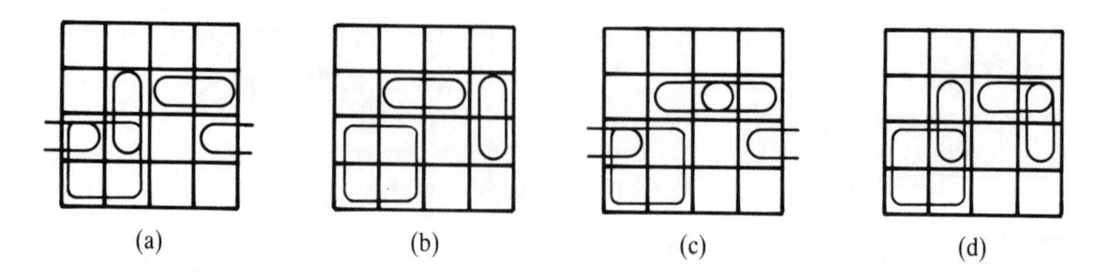

**Figure 2.14** Irredundant forms of Figure 2.13: (a) four prime implicants; (b) three prime implicants; (c) four prime implicants; (d) four prime implicants.

There is one such in the example, shown in Figure 2.15. A **minimal sum** (minimum cover) is one which contains the minimum number of prime implicants.

The minimization process can be summarized in the following steps:

(1) generate the complete sum (that is, find all prime implicants);
(2) find the essential prime implicants;
(3) find the minimal sum (that is, choose the other prime implicants).

This procedure can be performed manually on a K map for small numbers of variables. For larger numbers of variables other, more systematic, methods have to be used. These will be the subject of Chapter 4.

## 2.5 Finite state machines

It is now possible to move on to the representation and design of the sequential blocks of digital system – the parts whose behaviour depends on past as well as present inputs. The model used is the **finite state machine** (FSM).

In this ideal model time is assumed only to exist at discrete instants, at which inputs can change and new outputs can appear. The model is based purely on the behaviour of the block as seen from the terminals; we

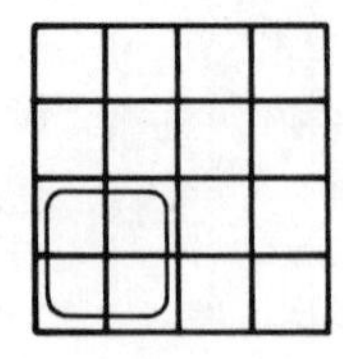

**Figure 2.15** Essential prime implicant of Figure 2.13.

are not concerned with the details of the implementation. This stage will be studied in Chapter 6.

If the input signal (not necessarily binary) at some instant is $X(t)$, let us assume that the machine's output is $Z(t)$. Because the machine has memory, this output will depend not only on the value of the input, but on the 'history' of the machine up to the present instant of time, $t$. Assume that this history, which takes account of all previous inputs to the machine, can be summed up in the quantity $H(t)$. Thus the machine output can be formally expressed as

$$Z(t) = \lambda[H(t), X(t)] \tag{2.2}$$

This relationship is not useful, however, because of the unlimited nature of $H(t)$; there are an infinite number of possible histories. The history that actually occurred determines the response $Z(t)$. However, if every input event that had ever occurred affected the machine's response, it would need an infinite memory. This obviously cannot be the case – in other words, a machine cannot distinguish all possible histories. There must thus be **equivalent** histories. Two histories, $H_1(t)$ and $H_2(t)$, are equivalent if two identically constructed machines $M_1$ and $M_2$ which have experienced these two histories produce the same outputs for the same sequence of inputs from time $t$. Histories can therefore be placed into a finite number of classes, each of which defines an **internal state**, $Y$, of the machine. Hence

$$Z(t) = \lambda[Y(t), X(t)] \tag{2.3}$$

defines how the output depends on the input and internal state. $\lambda$ is the **output function**.

The history at the next instant, $t + 1$, differs from the history at $t$ by only one term, that is $X(t)$. The state $Y(t + 1)$, therefore, can only depend on the previous state and the previous input, that is

$$Y(t + 1) = \delta[Y(t), X(t)] \tag{2.4}$$

$\delta$ is the **transition function**, or **next state function**. These two equations, 2.3 and 2.4, are a complete specification of the behaviour of a finite state machine. Given the present state and the future inputs, we can predict the response of the machine at any future instant. The elements of a finite state machine and their interconnection are shown in Figure 2.16. The internal state is assumed to be stored in a memory, which at instant $t + 1$ takes the value $Y(t + 1)$ – a **state transition**. The functions $\lambda$ and $\delta$ are combinational, as their outputs only depend on their current inputs, $Y(t)$ and $X(t)$. An alternative way of representing this machine is given in Figure 2.17, where the two functions are combined; this is possible because they have the same inputs. This form will be the one most frequently used in later chapters.

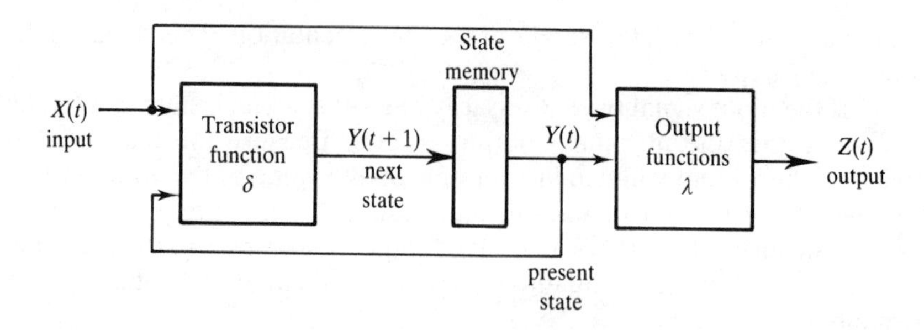


**Figure 2.16** FSM block diagram.

The behaviour of a finite state machine may be specified in tabular or graphical form. The **state table**, or **state transition table**, has the form shown in Figure 2.18. Along the top are listed all the possible input signals, or input states, and down the side all internal states. At each row and column intersection is given the next state and the present output. The table thus specifies the $\delta$ and $\lambda$ functions. In this example the signals were Boolean, but of course state tables can be set up using any digital signal type.

A graphical specification of the same machine is given in Figure 2.19. This is the **state diagram**, or **state transition diagram** (or graph). Each node corresponds to a state and each arc to a transition between states. On each arc is shown the input value which caused the transition and the value of the output generated. The machine described in Figures 2.18 and 2.19 is a serial adder, an FSM which can add two words bit by bit, starting at the least significant end. Two binary inputs are defined rather than one four-valued input to aid understanding of the function; this does not change the number of columns in the state table. The one item of information which

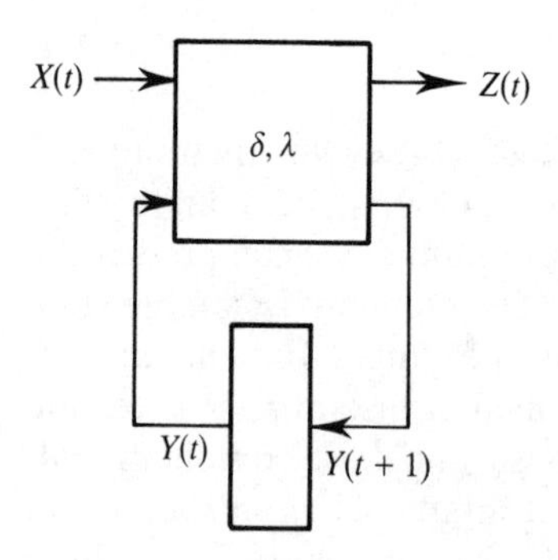


**Figure 2.17** Alternative form for FSM.

inputs $a, b$ : Boolean
state $c$ : Boolean
output $s$ : Boolean

| $c_i$ \ $a_ib_i$ | 0 0 | 0 1 | 1 0 | 1 1 |
|---|---|---|---|---|
| 0 | 0, 0 | 0, 1 | 0, 1 | 1, 0 |
| 1 | 0, 1 | 1, 0 | 1, 0 | 1, 1 |

$c_{i+1}, s_i$

**Figure 2.18** State table for serial adder.

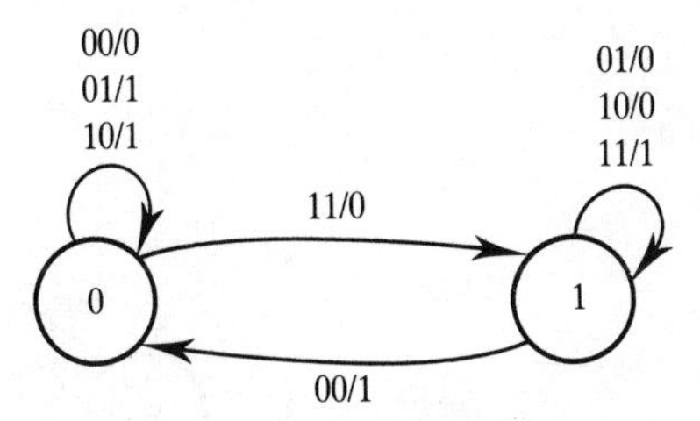


**Figure 2.19** State transition graph for serial adder.

has to be memorized between additions is the carry bit – this corresponds to the two-valued state, *c*.

As with combinational functions, an FSM can be incompletely specified. In this case one or more next state values or outputs may be 'don't care'. An unspecified next state implies that the input and state combination concerned cannot occur. This information can be useful when implementing the $\delta$ and $\lambda$ functions.

The FSM above has an output which depends at all times on both the state and the inputs. This is the so-called **Mealy machine**. An alternative form has the output dependent only on the state. This is the **Moore machine**. Figure 2.20 is the block diagram of a Moore machine, while Figures 2.21 and 2.22 show a state table and state transition diagram respectively. Notice that the outputs can be written on the state nodes now; only transitions are dependent on the input. Both models can be used to describe any FSM behaviour, and indeed both models are used in practice. The reasons for having the two alternatives will be explained in later chapters.

If combinational logic blocks and storage registers are viewed as degenerate FSMs (the first having no state memory or $\delta$ function, the second having only the state memory), then all digital systems can be viewed as networks of FSMs. However, it is not practical to specify all blocks with state tables or graphs. For example, an arithmetic processor may have a 16- or 32-bit register, implying $2^{16}$ or $2^{32}$ states and thus a massive table or diagram. The specification of such a machine would have to be in terms of the function performed on the data words. Another case

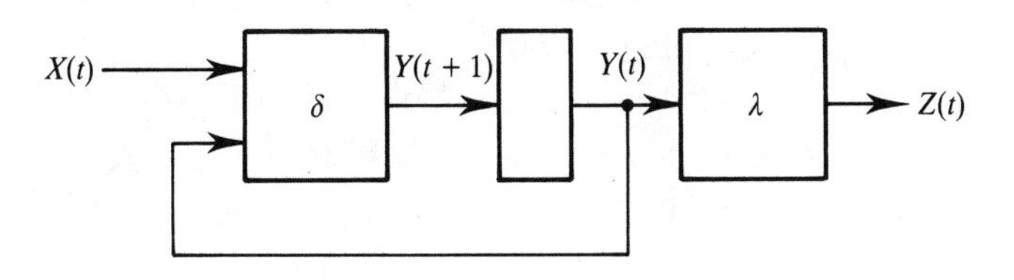


**Figure 2.20** Moore-type FSM.

| | |
|---|---|
| input | {0, 1} |
| state | {x, y, z} |
| output | {A, B} |

| | 0 | 1 | |
|---|---|---|---|
| X | Y | X | A |
| Y | Y | Z | B |
| Z | X | Z | A |

**Figure 2.21** Moore state table.

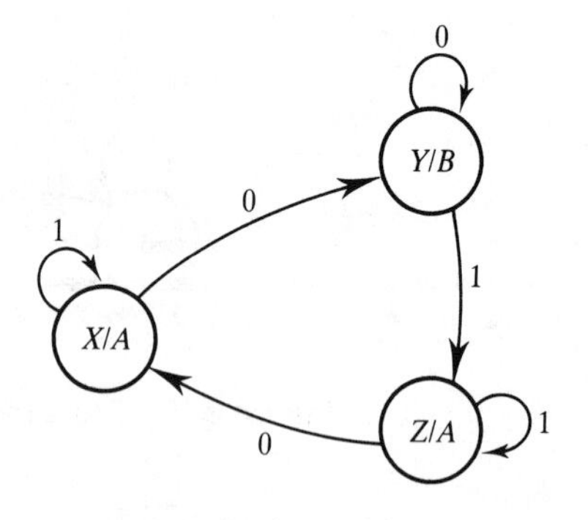


**Figure 2.22** Moore state transition diagram.

unsuitable for state table description is a memory. Here the number of states is astronomical, but the function is trivial. In this case, a structural description is the most practical. Controllers, however, do have to be specified by a state table or by some form of state transition notation, with the functions $\delta$ and $\lambda$ given by a listing of outputs and transitions.

## 2.6 The basic arithmetic circuits

Special techniques have been developed for the design of economical combinational networks for performing arithmetic operations. These are studied in more detail in Chapter 8, but the basics will be reviewed here. This section will look at addition and subtraction and demonstrate the usefulness of the exclusive OR gate.

The 1-bit **full adder** (Figure 2.23) has the truth table given in Table 2.7. The input bits are $a_i$ and $b_i$ and the sum is $s_i$. $c_i$ is the carry-in and $c_{i+1}$

**Table 2.7**

| $a_i$ | $b_i$ | $c_i$ | $s_i$ | $c_{i+1}$ |
|---|---|---|---|---|
| 0 | 0 | 0 | 0 | 0 |
| 0 | 0 | 1 | 1 | 0 |
| 0 | 1 | 0 | 1 | 0 |
| 0 | 1 | 1 | 0 | 1 |
| 1 | 0 | 0 | 1 | 0 |
| 1 | 0 | 1 | 0 | 1 |
| 1 | 1 | 0 | 0 | 1 |
| 1 | 1 | 1 | 1 | 1 |

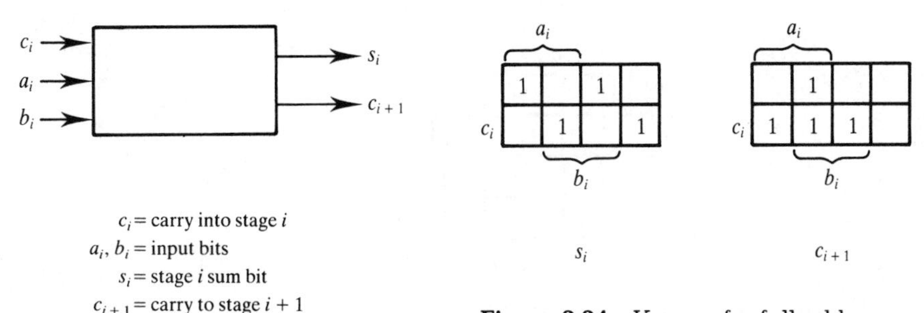


**Figure 2.24** K maps for full adder.

**Figure 2.23** Full adder.

(which is also a combinational output) is the carry-out. The K maps for the outputs $s_i$ and $c_{i+1}$ are shown in Figure 2.24.

At this point a brief digression will be made before continuing with the design of the adder. Notice the pattern of 1s on the map for $s_i$. The right-hand part is the mirror image of the left-hand part with the 1s and 0s interchanged. This implies that a relationship of the form

$$f = A\bar{x} + A\bar{x} \quad \textbf{(2.5)}$$

exists, where $x$ is the variable defining the two halves of the map, and $A$ is the function represented by the pattern of 1s. Now the equation above is the exclusive OR, that is

$$f = A \oplus x \quad \textbf{(2.6)}$$

the use of which halves the number of products required at the cost of an exclusive OR gate. If the pattern remaining still has this symmetry, another exclusive OR can be used, but at the cost of another level of gating. The $s_i$ map has this property (and, in general, a map with a 'checkerboard' pattern, like the parity function, can be implemented entirely with exclusive ORs). Figure 2.25 shows another map where an exclusive OR can be used, together with the resulting network. The number of products needed has been reduced from five to two.

Returning to the adder, an attempt will now be made to construct a network to add two words, based on single-bit adders. The simplest method is to string the full adders together by connecting the carry-out of one stage to the carry-in of the next, the **ripple carry** method. This is economical but slow as in the worst case the sum is not known until a carry signal has travelled from the least to the most significant bit of the adder. A faster network may be constructed by calculating the carry-in at each stage as shown in Figure 2.26, which is derived from the $s_i$ map of Figure 2.24. The $a_i \oplus b_i$ calculation is the same at every stage, requiring two products,

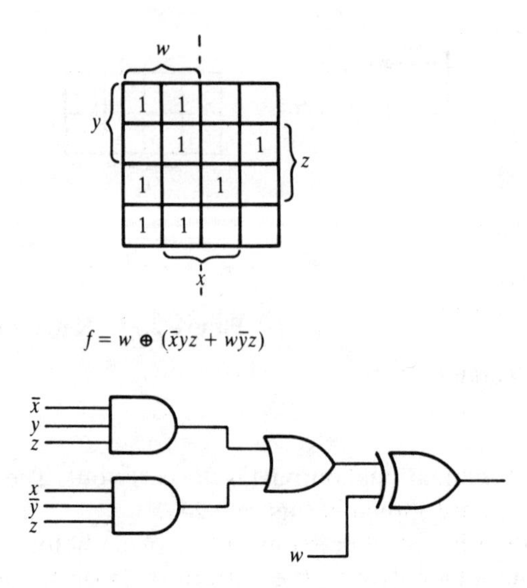


**Figure 2.25** Use of exclusive OR to reduce the number of products.

but the $c_i$ calculation is more complex, as it has to be evaluated at the same time as the carry-out from all previous stages, to avoid the 'ripple'. The equations may be derived by defining the signals $G_i$, which are true when a stage generates a carry, and $P_i$, which are true when a stage propagates the value of $c_i$ to $c_{i+1}$. There is then a carry-in to any stage if the previous stage is generating one or propagating one from its previous stage, that is

$$c_i = G_{i-1} + P_{i-1}c_{i-1} \tag{2.7}$$

This may be expanded recursively until the last term is $c_0$, the first carry-in. This is the principle of **carry lookahead**. By examining the truth table for

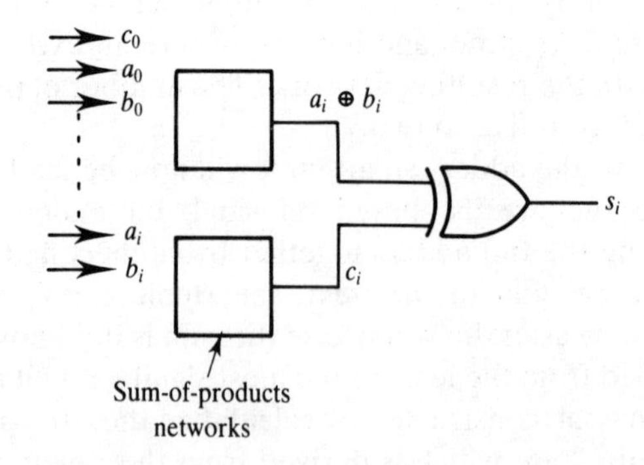


**Figure 2.26** Single stage of lookahead adder.

the full adder, it can be seen that

$$G_i = a_i \cdot b_i \quad \text{and} \quad P_i = a_i \oplus b_i \qquad \textbf{(2.8)}$$

The number of products required for calculating $c_i$ grows at each stage, the first few numbers being 1, 3, 7, 15, 31, . . . . Methods of reducing these will be studied in Chapter 8. The 'brute force' method of building a multiple-bit adder, writing down its complete truth table and attempting to minimize, would require many more products than this.

Two's complement subtraction is performed by the same network, except that one of the operands has to be made negative. This is performed by complementing all bits and adding a 1 at the least significant end. This procedure can be verified by applying it to the equation defining the two's complement encoding in Section 2.2.1. The 1 can most conveniently be inserted as a carry-in.

## 2.7 Documentation conventions

### 2.7.1 The need for conventions

Digital systems have to be documented at several levels, ranging from behavioural descriptions through to architectural block diagrams, logic diagrams and finally circuit diagrams. For each of these levels of description to fulfil its function, it must be consistent with adjacent levels and, at the same time, be comprehensible. Good documentation should make the function and mode of operation easy to determine. Universally accepted conventions do not yet exist for the higher levels, but standards for the lower levels are now widely agreed, if not yet used by the majority of designers. The remainder of this section will explain aspects of these standards which are relevant to this book.

### 2.7.2 Signal naming and logic diagrams

Binary-valued signals, or logic signals, can initiate actions, indicate conditions, or represent data. In almost all cases names must be given to logic signals. The name should be chosen to represent the condition or action in an obvious and consistent way, for example

| | |
|---|---|
| go, stop, read, write | (actions) |
| empty, full, timeout | (conditions) |
| lsb, address[7], data[3] | (data) |

Logic signals have two values (or states): true and false – 1 and 0. 1 is always true, 0 is always false. When an action is true, it is **asserted**. 'Active'

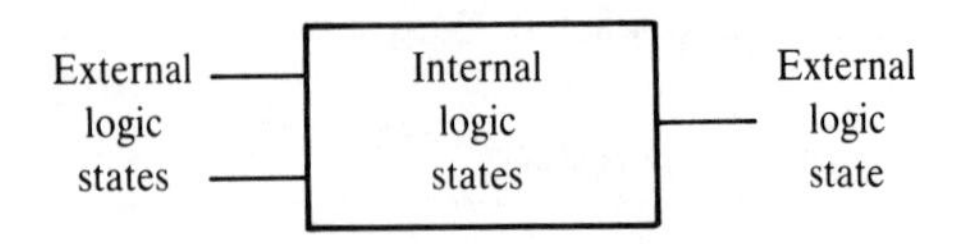


**Figure 2.27** Internal and external states.

can also be used to indicate a true condition. Thus 1, true, asserted, and active are equivalent terms for the signals above.

Occasionally, the complement of a signal is required. For example, $\overline{\text{alarm}}$ is a signal which is false when the condition alarm is true. This can cause confusion, however, as now the active or true *condition* is represented by a false, or 0, signal. Choosing a complemented signal name should therefore be avoided. When a signal has a dual function, it is possible to give alternative names, for example read/$\overline{\text{write}}$ causes reading to occur when it is true, and writing to occur when it is false.

**Pure logic diagrams**, or just **logic diagrams**, are a graphical way of showing the relationship between logical signals. They do not represent physical hardware. All signals have values 1 and 0, true and false. Figures 2.5–2.7 are logic diagrams. Signals are processed by logic elements, which perform their operations on **internal logic states**. These internal states are translated into **external logic states** at the element boundary, as shown in Figure 2.27. The signals on interconnections thus have values which are external logic states.

Negation is shown with the negation indicator, which can only exist at the boundary of a logic element (Figure 2.28). When this indicator is present, a 0 external state is translated into a 1 internal state, and vice versa. Without such an indicator, the internal and external states are equal. On a logic diagram, negation indicators should not appear at both ends of a signal line, as the two negations cancel.

### 2.7.3 Polarity conventions and circuit diagrams

Logic states are abstract objects – they have to be mapped onto physical quantities. The two physical states required are H and L, which in the commonest case are high and low voltages respectively. The logical

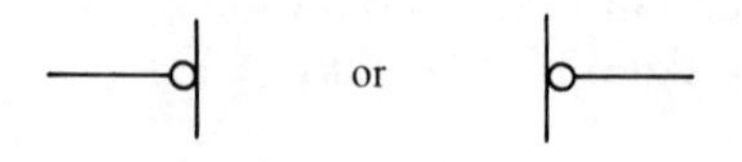


**Figure 2.28** Negation.

**Table 2.8**

| *Signal name* | *System condition* | *Signal* | *Logic state* | *Logic level* |
|---|---|---|---|---|
| alarm | alarm | true | 1 | H |
| | no alarm | false | 0 | L |
| $\overline{\text{alarm}}$ | alarm | false | 0 | L |
| | no alarm | true | 1 | H |

operations are performed by physical gates which have the same symbols as the logical operators.

There are three possible ways of mapping logic states to **logic levels**:

(1) 0 is always L, 1 is always H: **positive logic**;
(2) 0 is always H, 1 is always L: **negative logic**;
(3) the mapping varies from signal to signal.

The **polarity** of the signal indicates which mapping is to be used. In **single-polarity** systems all signals have the same polarity, positive or negative. The polarity only has to be indicated once on a diagram. In mixed polarity systems, each signal has to have its polarity indicated – this is the **direct polarity indication** method (it is not called 'mixed logic' in the current standards, a term which is now discouraged).

A **logic circuit diagram** is one in which the quantities existing on the interconnections are logic levels. It is the specification of an electrical circuit. In a positive logic system, a true signal is H, and a false signal is L; this is illustrated in Table 2.8. The signal alarm could be said to be **active high** (or asserted high), as the condition alarm corresponds to the H logic level. Conversely, $\overline{\text{alarm}}$ could be said to be **active low** (or asserted low).

In single-polarity logic circuit diagrams, the negation indicator is used to qualify the relationship between external logic levels and internal logic states (Figure 2.29). Thus they look just like logic diagrams, and they are in fact interchangeable.

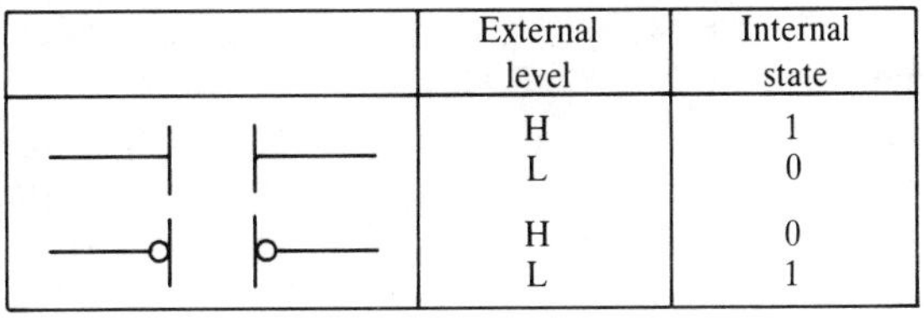

| | External level | Internal state |
|---|---|---|
| | H<br>L | 1<br>0 |
| | H<br>L | 0<br>1 |

**Figure 2.29** Levels and states in positive logic.

**Figure 2.30** Unwanted negation.

However, a problem arises when there is a limited choice of circuit elements, or when a signal has to be active low when it would be active high, or vice versa. An example of the former is shown in Figure 2.30. Here the desired AND gate is not available, so a NAND is used instead. However, now the output signal is $\bar{c}$, which is the complement of the signal required, This will require a change to the logic function later on in the circuit. In the second case, there are often electrical reasons why a signal must be active low, for example, in open-collector wired-OR busses. The only way we can indicate this in a single-polarity circuit diagram is to change the signal name to its complement. Thus, *the meaning of the signal name has been changed.* These problems can be overcome if each signal has a separate polarity indication because, with a single polarity, complementation and polarity are not separable.

In the direct polarity system, every signal has its polarity indicated, for example

alarm(H), alarm(L)

A condition can now be represented by four possible signal names, the two above plus

$\overline{\text{alarm}}$(H), $\overline{\text{alarm}}$(L)

Notice that alarm(H), $\overline{\text{alarm}}$(L) and alarm(L), $\overline{\text{alarm}}$(H) have identical mappings between conditions and logic levels. Alarm(H) could be called active high, and alarm(L) active low. However, what about $\overline{\text{alarm}}$(L) and $\overline{\text{alarm}}$(H)? We could stretch the definition and call these active high and low respectively, but these terms lose their directness in these cases. For this reason, the terms 'active high' and 'active low' should not be used with direct polarity indication.

In logic circuit diagrams with direct polarity indication, the polarity indicator is used in place of the negation 'bubble'. Figure 2.31 shows how it relates external levels to internal states. A signal with negative polarity connected to a terminal with a polarity indicator has logic states identical to the internal states, and vice versa. For example, all the circuits of Figure 2.32 are logically identical, even though four different electrical elements are required. Thus, with direct polarity indication, we can retain all logic operators and signal names from the logic diagram, adding polarity indications appropriate to the circuit elements chosen or available.

| | External level | Internal state |
|---|---|---|
| | H | 1 |
| | L | 0 |
| | H | 0 |
| | L | 1 |

**Figure 2.31** Levels and states with polarity indicator.

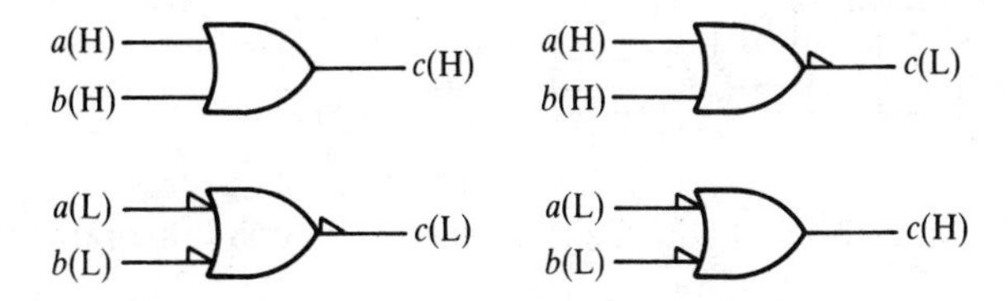


**Figure 2.32** Logically equivalent, circuits different.

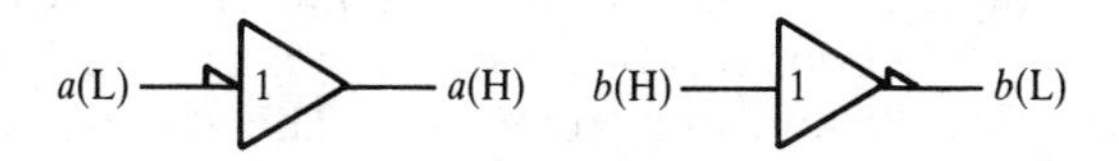


**Figure 2.33** Level shifters.

**Figure 2.34** Negation.

There is one problem, however. In Figure 2.33, the electrical inverter performs the **level shifting** operation if signal polarities are matched to terminal polarities. No logical function is performed. To perform negation, a signal name has to be reinterpreted, as shown in Figure 2.34. This is indicated by an optional vertical bar through the signal line where the negation occurs. A logical inversion without level shifting thus requires a level shifter and a signal name change.

Finally, Figure 2.35 shows how a logic diagram has been converted into a logic circuit diagram which uses direct polarity indication. The constraints were that $B$ was available only in negative polarity form and that only one type of gate circuit (positive NAND) was available. Notice that in the result all logical functions and negations are retained.

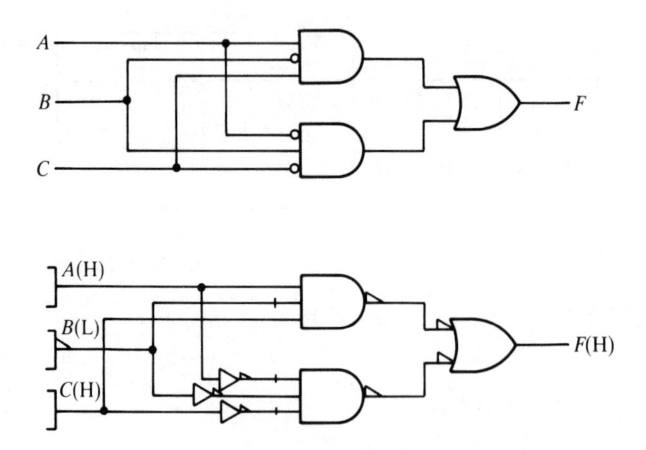


**Figure 2.35** Logic diagram and logic circuit diagram.

## SUMMARY

Certain encodings for digital signals are very commonly used, for example the two's complement code for numbers and the Gray code in state machines. Binary functions can be specified in a truth table or as sets of cubes defining on, off and don't care sets. The theorems of Boolean algebra can be used to manipulate Boolean functions and in particular to bring them into the sum-of-products or product-of-sums form. Networks of logic gates are a practical realization of Boolean functions. Boolean functions are minimized by choosing a minimal set of prime implicants. For functions of up to four variables, this can be performed on a K map. Sequential logic blocks are modelled as finite state machines, which can be specified either by state tables or by state diagrams. Two forms of finite state machine are used, the Moore and the Mealy. Arithmetic circuits are implemented most economically in special structures. The most common of these is the adder. Multiple-bit adders can be constructed from networks of single-bit adders and speeded up using carry lookahead. Designs can be documented as pure logic diagrams or as logic circuit diagrams. For the latter, the direct polarity indication method enables the same logic symbols to be used as in the logic diagram.

## BIBLIOGRAPHICAL NOTES

Comprehensive treatments of the fundamentals surveyed in this chapter can be found in Muroga (1979), Comer (1984), Mano (1984), Lewin (1985), Friedman (1986) and Unger (1989). The properties of FSMs are discussed in Minsky (1967).

A design methodology based on specification of three types of FSMs (logic, memory and arithmetic) called 'structured building blocks' is described by Burrows

(1986). Direct polarity indication is explained at length in Prosser and Winkel (1987) while recommended usage is given in IEEE (1986). New symbols for complex logic functions have now been standardized (IEEE, 1984; Kampel, 1986) and will be used in this book where applicable. The 'distinctive shape' gate symbols are no longer preferred but are more suitable than the recommended 'boxes' for use in complex programmable logic device diagrams.

## EXERCISES

**2.1** What range of numbers can be represented with the two's complement binary string

$$b_3b_2b_1b_0 . b_{-1}b_{-2}b_{-3}b_{-4}?$$

**2.2** How many different unit distance encodings are possible with 2-, 3- and 4-bit binary strings?

Show that it is always possible to find a unit distance encoding for a signal with an even number of values. (Hint: one approach is to use a K map.)

**2.3** Construct a truth table for a one-digit BCD adder with carry-in and carry-out signals, using don't cares. Express this as a list of cubes.

Generate minimal sum-of-products and product-of-sums expressions for each of the five outputs.

Can you find a way of using exclusive OR gates to reduce the number of logic gates required?

**2.4** Specify the finite state machines for the controllers of Exercises 1.4 and 1.5.

**2.5** Draw a logic network in sum-of-products form for the lookahead circuit of a 4-bit binary adder.

Redraw this using direct polarity indication. Is this an advantage?

CHAPTER 3

# Array Logic

---

**OBJECTIVES**

When you have completed studying this chapter you should be able

- to construct a diode matrix to realize a set of Boolean functions;
- to list the eight bussed cell combinations which can form a sum of products;
- to use a PLA to realize a set of Boolean functions, and possibly to use output negation and multiple-bit encoders to reduce the number of products required;
- to recognize sets of functions for which PAL-structured arrays are suitable;
- to understand the relationships which exist between memories, multiplexers and PLAs;
- to draw circuits for the distributed gate arrays of simple PLDs;
- to specify the function of a combinational PLD in tabular or equational form.

---

## 3.1 Introduction

In this chapter, the array structure which is the basis of most **programmable logic devices** (PLDs) will be studied. The term 'array logic', although very expressive, has now lost its distinct meaning in the noise of new terms that are continually being invented to distinguish yet more variations on the semicustom IC theme. However, it is kept here as a mark of respect to history; most of the fundamental structures and design techniques were invented when the term was well understood.

The simplest array logic structure, the diode matrix, will be introduced first, and it will then be shown how this can be generalized. From this model will be derived specific structures corresponding to the programmable logic components in use today, some of which are now moving back to a more general-purpose structure. The basics of the circuit technologies in use will be covered, and finally an introduction to the methods of specification of the function of a PLD will be given.

## 3.2 Principles

### 3.2.1 The diode matrix

The **diode matrix** is the simplest form of array logic structure. It is most easily understood by examining the operation of diode logic gates. A diode AND gate is shown in Figure 3.1. The behaviour shown in the table can be derived by considering just two cases:

(1) any input at a lower voltage than $V$ causes its diode to conduct resulting in the output also assuming this voltage (assuming ideal diodes with no forward voltage drop and no output loading), and

(2) when all inputs are at a voltage of $V$ or higher, the output will also be at $V$.

When interpreted in positive logic, this is the behaviour of an AND gate.

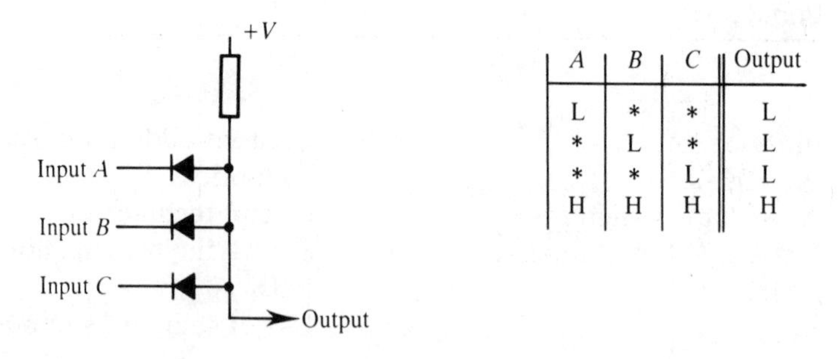


| A | B | C | Output |
|---|---|---|---|
| L | * | * | L |
| * | L | * | L |
| * | * | L | L |
| H | H | H | H |

**Figure 3.1** Diode AND gate (positive logic).

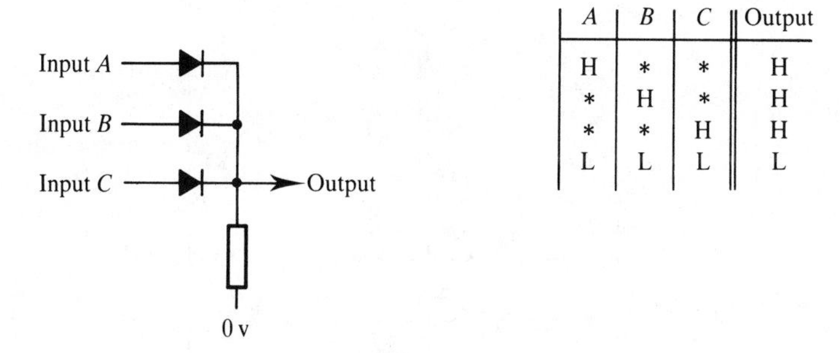


| A | B | C | Output |
|---|---|---|---|
| H | * | * | H |
| * | H | * | H |
| * | * | H | H |
| L | L | L | L |

**Figure 3.2** Diode OR gate (positive logic).

Figure 3.2 shows a diode OR gate. Here, the output will be high when one or more of the diodes are conducting, that is, when one (or more) of the inputs is at a voltage greater than zero (again assuming ideal diodes). The output will only reach zero when all the inputs are at a voltage of zero or lower. This circuit therefore acts as a positive OR gate.

A two-level diode logic circuit can be constructed by combining the two types of gate. Figure 3.3 is an example of this. This circuit can be redrawn as a matrix, as shown in Figure 3.4. The diode circuit of Figure 3.3 can thus be built as a uniform matrix in which all diodes are connected in the same direction at intersections. The array function is determined by diode placement and external connections. This is thus a simple example of **array logic**; the same matrix structure can be **personalized** or **programmed** to realize different logic functions.

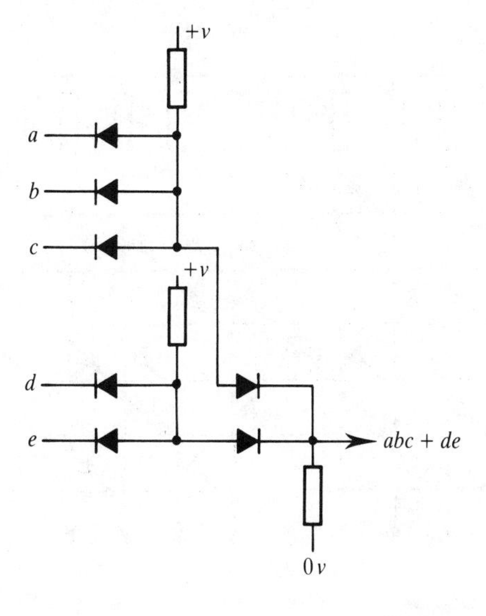


**Figure 3.3** Two-level diode logic.

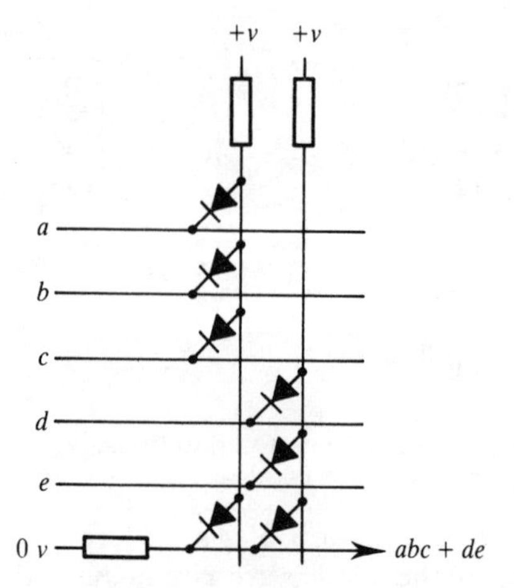


**Figure 3.4** The circuit of Figure 3.3 drawn as a diode matrix.

The dual of this circuit can be created by reversing all the diodes and the polarities of the supply voltages. The output would now be $(a+b+c) \cdot (d+e)$.

The diode matrix can be used to implement any sum-of-products (or product-of-sums) form, provided that the inputs are available in complemented form where required. Some examples of diode matrix circuits used in this way are shown in Figures 3.5–3.7.

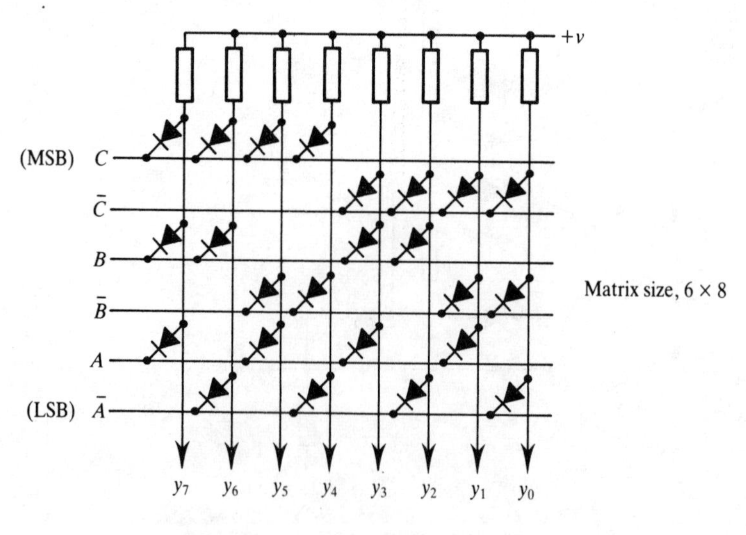


**Figure 3.5** A 3-line to 8-line decoder.

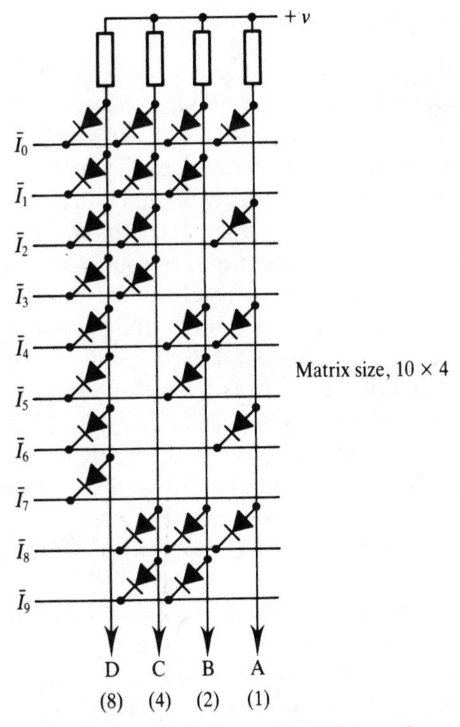


**Figure 3.6** A 10-line to BCD decoder.

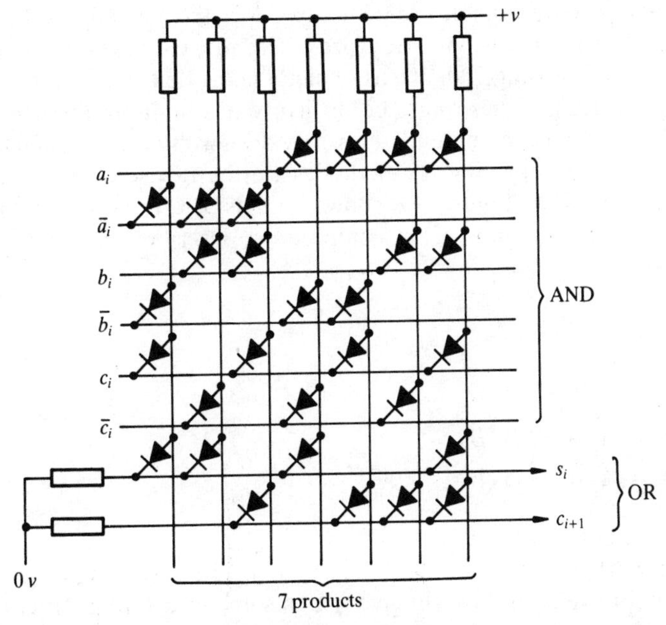


**Figure 3.7** Full adder.

### 3.2.2 Application of the diode matrix

Although the diode matrix is a very general component, it has very limited application in modern digital design. Firstly, the size of matrix is limited by the number of pins available in an IC package; with 14 pins, for example, $6 \times 8$ and $4 \times 10$ are two possible array sizes. Two-level circuits are wasteful of pins since the first-level product (or sum) lines are only used for the connection of resistors. (A 128-product matrix having internal resistors in a 48-pin package allowing 46 inputs and/or outputs was once available.) The second drawback is the forward voltage drop of the diodes. In the AND gate of Figure 3.1, for example, the low output voltage is higher than the lowest input voltage by the diode forward voltage drop, of the order of 0.7 V for silicon. The OR gate suffers from the same problem, except that here the output high voltage is reduced. The effect of these drops is to reduce the noise immunity of the input-to-output connection by this amount of 0.7 V. This is intolerable in a TTL system, whose noise immunity is 0.4 V. Therefore diode matrices have to be specially driven, or used with a logic family, such as CMOS, with a sufficiently high noise immunity.

Despite these limitations there are some applications where diode matrices are a suitable choice of component. These include simple encoders and decoders where no standard component is available, for example address recognition, and switch or discrete input encoding. One advantage is that, with suitable choice of load resistors, the power consumption can be low.

Fuse programmable diode matrix ICs have been available for a number of years in various array sizes. The reverse recovery times of the diodes are in the range 50–100 ns, which means that they are too slow for most applications. There may be difficulty in obtaining them nowadays, since they are not recommended for new designs by the manufacturers.

Networks requiring fewer diodes can be devised if more then two levels are allowed. Figure 3.8 shows an AND–OR–AND circuit which performs the function of a comparator described by the following equations:

$$
\begin{aligned}
f &= f_1 f_2 f_3 \\
f_1 &= \overline{A}_1 \overline{B}_1 + A_1 B_1 \\
f_2 &= \overline{A}_2 \overline{B}_2 + A_2 B_2 \\
f_3 &= \overline{A}_3 \overline{B}_3 + A_3 B_3
\end{aligned}
$$

This network requires 21 diodes instead of 56 for a two-level version. While multilevel matrices can give rise to some interesting structures, they are not economical or electrically practical in most cases.

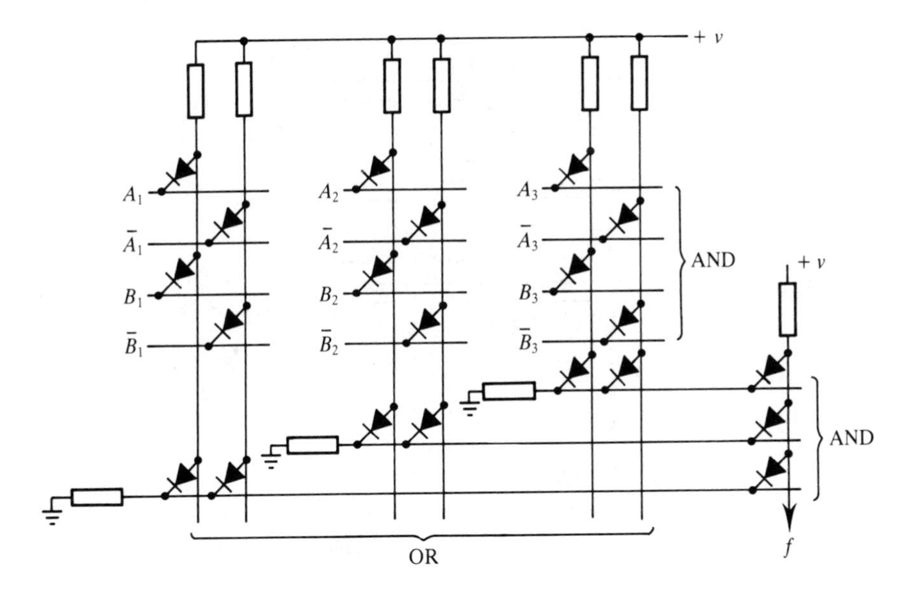


**Figure 3.8** Multilevel matrix.

### 3.2.3 A general model – the bussed cellular array

Before looking at the more complex PLDs, it will be shown how the array introduced above can be generalized as the **bussed cellular array**. With this model, we can discover just what is possible with array logic. Most PLDs invented were probably not conceived in this way, but they can all be shown to be special cases of this general form.

The structure of a bussed cellular array is shown in Figure 3.9. A bussed cellular array is a cellular array in which all cells in a row or column are connected in parallel to the same conductor. Signals can thus be transmitted the entire length or breadth of the array. In the conventional cellular array, a cell can only communicate with its neighbours. When the array is used combinationally, the bussed form has a potentially lower propagation delay since signals do not have to traverse strings of cells.

To determine the usefulness of such an array, the choices for cell functions must be enumerated. In the most general case, each cell can use either of the two busses to which it is connected as an input or an output. In the latter case, if other cells also drive the same bus, the wired-OR or wired-AND function is performed by the bus – which one results depends on the logical polarity and the cell output circuits. For example, the 'open collector' bus connection is a positive AND or a negative OR. In our model, the cells are imagined to be of the simplest possible type; they can only perform a single Boolean operation.

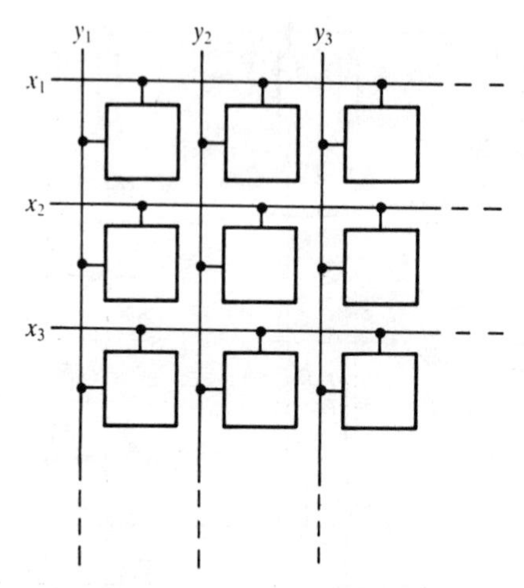


**Figure 3.9** Bussed cellular array.

The cell functions can be listed for the two cases of wired-OR and wired-AND outputs. These are given in Table 3.1. The signal notation is as shown in Figure 3.10 for a cell C. The signals appearing on the horizontal and vertical busses are $x$ and $y$ respectively. The signals which would appear on the busses without being driven by cell C, that is if C were disconnected, would be $\hat{x}$ and $\hat{y}$.

In a single array, both wired-OR and wired-AND busses can exist. Cells of types 1 and 10 can be ignored, as they have no effect on the busses to which they are connected. Certain combinations of cells placed in rows or columns can perform useful elementary operations. For example, a column of cells of types 2 and 3 can perform the AND of selected signals and their complements appearing on selected horizontal busses. An example of this is shown in Figure 3.11. A string of such cells can be thought of as a **distributed gate**. Similarly, cells of types 11 and 12 can perform vertical

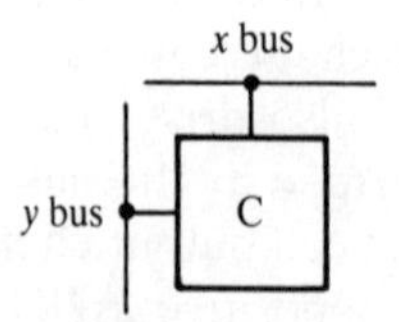


**Figure 3.10** Signal notation for a cell C.

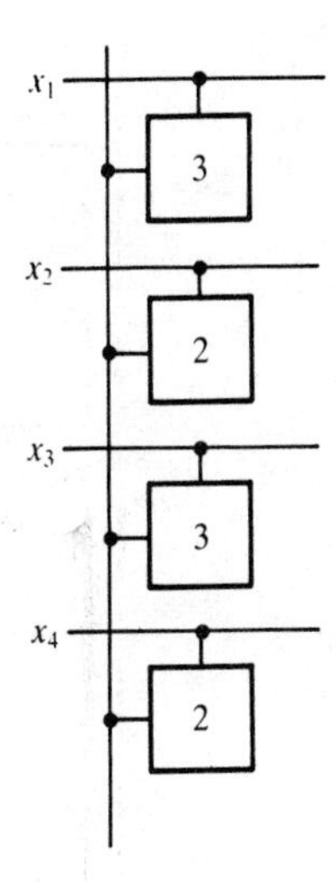


**Figure 3.11** Forming the AND of signals on horizontal buses: $y_1 = \overline{x}_1 x_2 \overline{x}_3 x_4$.

**Table 3.1** Possible cell functions.

| *Cell type* | *Signal on x bus* | *Signal on y bus* |
|---|---|---|
| *Outputs wire-ANDed* | | |
| 1 | $x = \hat{x}$ | $y = \hat{y}$ |
| 2 | $x = \hat{x}$ | $y = \hat{y} \cdot x$ |
| 3 | $x = \hat{x}$ | $y = \hat{y} \cdot \overline{x}$ |
| 4 | $x = \hat{x} \cdot y$ | $y = \hat{y}$ |
| 5 | $x = \hat{x} \cdot y$ | $y = \hat{y} \cdot x$ |
| 6 | $x = \hat{x} \cdot y$ | $y = \hat{y} \cdot \overline{x}$ |
| 7 | $x = \hat{x} \cdot \overline{y}$ | $y = \hat{y}$ |
| 8 | $x = \hat{x} \cdot \overline{y}$ | $y = \hat{y} \cdot x$ |
| 9 | $x = \hat{x} \cdot \overline{y}$ | $y = \hat{y} \cdot \overline{x}$ |
| *Outputs wire-ORed* | | |
| 10 | $x = \hat{x}$ | $y = \hat{y}$ |
| 11 | $x = \hat{x}$ | $y = \hat{y} + x$ |
| 12 | $x = \hat{x}$ | $y = \hat{y} + \overline{x}$ |
| 13 | $x = \hat{x} + y$ | $y = \hat{y}$ |
| 14 | $x = \hat{x} + y$ | $y = \hat{y} + x$ |
| 15 | $x = \hat{x} + y$ | $y = \hat{y} + \overline{x}$ |
| 16 | $x = \hat{x} + \overline{y}$ | $y = \hat{y}$ |
| 17 | $x = \hat{x} + \overline{y}$ | $y = \hat{y} + x$ |
| 18 | $x = \hat{x} + \overline{y}$ | $y = \hat{y} + \overline{x}$ |

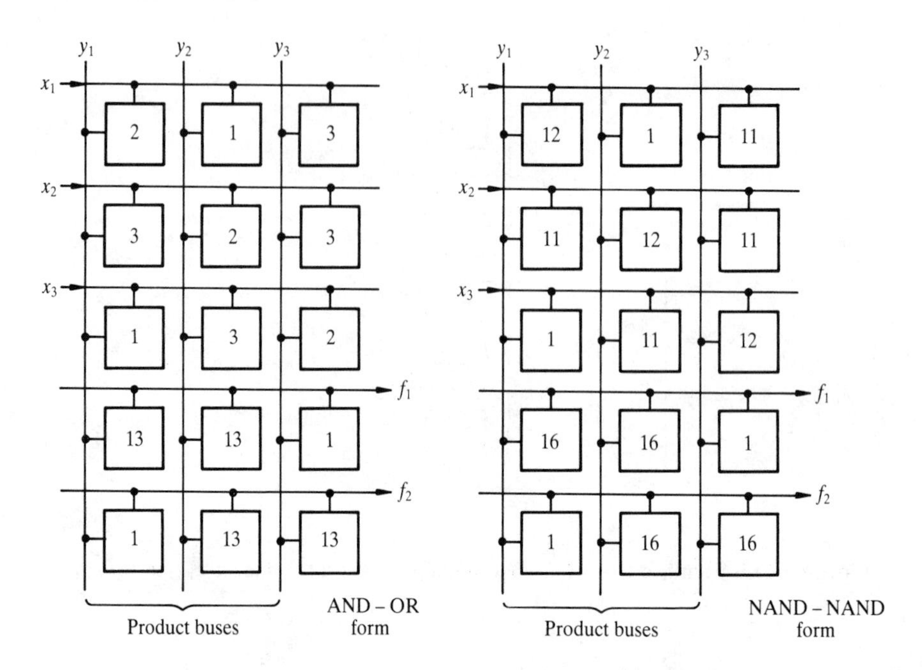


**Figure 3.12** Two equivalent sum-of-product arrays:

$$f_1 = x_1\bar{x}_2 + x_2\bar{x}_3$$
$$f_2 = x_2\bar{x}_3 + \bar{x}_1\bar{x}_2x_3.$$

ORs. Horizontal versions of these operations can be performed by cells of types 4 and 7, and 13 and 16, respectively.

Using these cell functions, an array can now be designed to realize a set of Boolean functions in sum-of-products or product-of-sums form. A simple example is given in Figure 3.12, where the AND–OR and NAND–NAND forms are illustrated. There are six other possible forms (AND–NOR, NAND–AND, OR–NAND, OR–AND, NOR–OR, NOR–NOR), all of which are possible with the array, with inputs entering either horizontally or vertically. Figure 3.13 shows the eight ways in which a sum of products can be implemented. There are eight more for the product of sums. Thus any sum of products or product of sums can be produced with only one cell type if inputs are available in both phases (that is in true and complemented form).

A shorthand notation is available for describing these arrays. The inputs to the distributed gates of a bussed cellular array are shown as crosses at the intersections of a matrix with the gate symbols at its edges, as shown in Figure 3.14. In a diode matrix, these crosses correspond to the

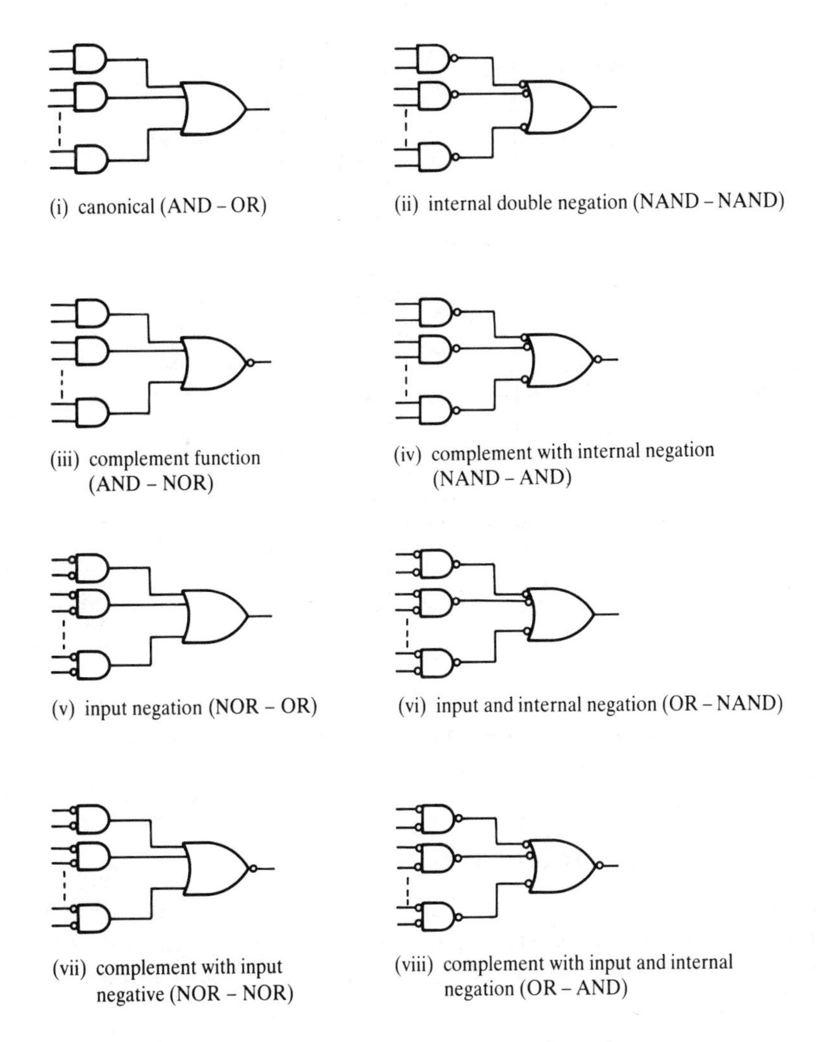


**Figure 3.13** The eight sum-of-products forms.

presence of diodes. The pattern of crosses is the **array personality**.

The other cell types have internal feedback and only two of them are useful. Cell types 6, 8, 15 and 17 can be shown to be unstable, cell type 5 is an unsettable flip–flop and cell type 14 is an unresettable flip–flop. The two useful types are 9 and 18, which are set–reset flip–flops. Rows and columns of type 9 or 18 cells can be constructed to provide combined logic and storage. They will not be considered further, however, as the sequential PLDs to be discussed in later chapters are built on different principles.

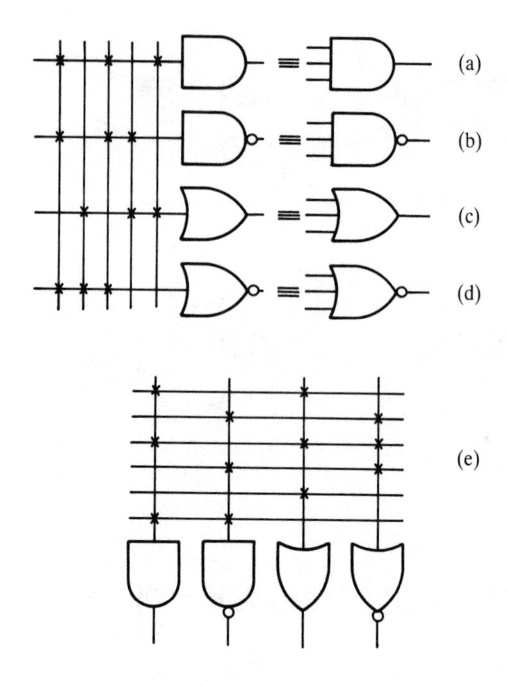


**Figure 3.14** Shorthand notation for distributed gates: (a) row of type 4 cells; (b) row of type 16 cells; (c) row of type 13 cells; (d) row of type 7 cells; (e) columns of cells of types 2, 12, 11 and 3.

## 3.3 Array logic structures

It is now only a short step to the general sum-of-products array with integral inverters for generation of any required complements of the inputs. This is the **programmable logic array** (PLA), shown in Figure 3.15

**Table 3.2**

| $a_i$ | $b_i$ | $c_i$ | $s_i$ | $c_{i+1}$ |
|---|---|---|---|---|
| 0 | 0 | 0 | 0 | 0 |
| 0 | 0 | 1 | 1 | 0 |
| 0 | 1 | 0 | 1 | 0 |
| 0 | 1 | 1 | 0 | 1 |
| 1 | 0 | 0 | 1 | 0 |
| 1 | 0 | 1 | 0 | 1 |
| 1 | 1 | 0 | 0 | 1 |
| 1 | 1 | 1 | 1 | 1 |

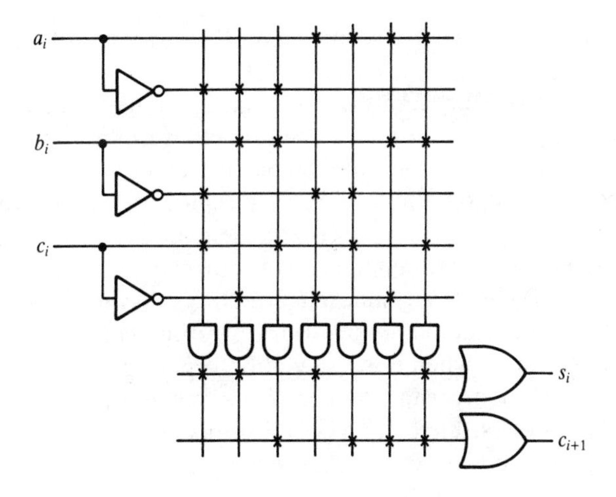


**Figure 3.15** Full adder PLA.

(in the shorthand notation) for the full adder example of Figure 3.7. An alternative method of specifying a PLA is with a **PLA table**. The table for the full adder is given in Table 3.2.

Note that this is exactly like a truth table. In this example every product term is a minterm, so there are no '*' entries in the AND part of the table. An '*' would mean that there were no '×'s on either intersection of the product line with the two input lines, or no diodes in the case of a diode matrix. The presence of both '×'s would mean that the product would be permanently 0 because one of the two inputs would always be 0. Thus an unused product line would have at least one such pair of '×'s. The four possible cases are shown in Figure 3.16. Unlike a truth table, a PLA table cannot have '–'s in the OR, or output, part, because a product line

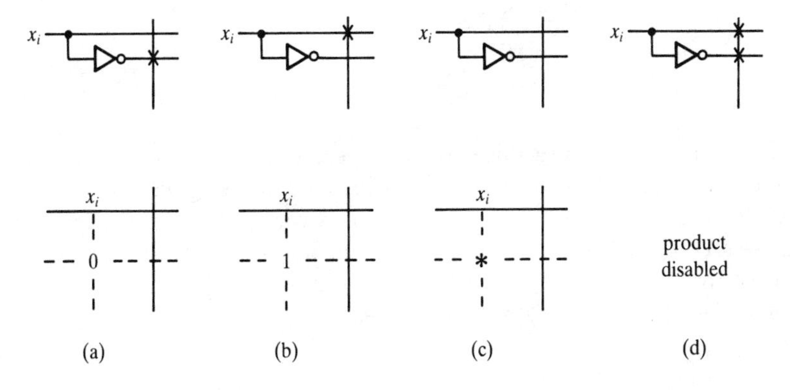


**Figure 3.16** The four possible ways in which an input can connect to a product line, and the corresponding PLA table entries.

can only be connected (1) or disconnected (0) to an output OR term; they cannot be left unspecified.

A saving in product terms is sometimes possible if the complement of a function is generated instead of the function itself. In the full adder example, if this is done for the carry-out signal, two products can be saved (this can be checked on the K maps of Figure 2.24). To restore the function, this output must now be complemented. To facilitate this, PLA circuits often include programmable output inverters, as shown in Figure 3.17. This is often indicated by an exclusive OR gate symbol, as this type of gate can act as a programmable inverter; when the control input is 0, no negation is performed, when it is 1, negation is performed.

Another economy can sometimes be made by a more complex encoding of the inputs. First, the general principle will be looked at, and then how it can be applied to the adder example. Consider the function

$$\begin{aligned} f(x_1, x_2, x_3, x_4) = {} & \bar{x}_1\bar{x}_2\bar{x}_3\bar{x}_4 + \bar{x}_1\bar{x}_2\bar{x}_3x_4 + \bar{x}_1\bar{x}_2x_3\bar{x}_4 \\ & + \bar{x}_1x_2\bar{x}_3\bar{x}_4 + \bar{x}_1x_2\bar{x}_3x_4 + \bar{x}_1x_2x_3x_4 \\ & + x_1\bar{x}_2\bar{x}_3\bar{x}_4 + x_1\bar{x}_2x_3x_4 + x_1x_2\bar{x}_3x_4 \\ & + x_1x_2x_3\bar{x}_4 \end{aligned} \quad (3.1)$$

These ten minterms can be reduced for PLA implementation to seven products (verify this with a K map):

$$\begin{aligned} f = {} & \bar{x}_1\bar{x}_3 + \bar{x}_1\bar{x}_2x_3\bar{x}_4 + \bar{x}_1x_2x_3x_4 + x_1\bar{x}_2\bar{x}_3\bar{x}_4 \\ & + x_1\bar{x}_2x_3x_4 + x_1x_2\bar{x}_3x_4 + x_1x_2x_3\bar{x}_4 \end{aligned} \quad (3.2)$$

If the inputs are now partitioned into two sets $(x_1, x_2)$ and $(x_2, x_3)$, and the sum of products is factorized with this in mind, the following is obtained from Equation 3.1:

$$\begin{aligned} f = {} & (\bar{x}_1\bar{x}_2 + \bar{x}_1x_2)(\bar{x}_3\bar{x}_4 + \bar{x}_3x_4) \\ & + (\bar{x}_1\bar{x}_2 + x_1x_2)(\bar{x}_3x_4 + x_3\bar{x}_4) \\ & + (\bar{x}_1x_2 + x_1\bar{x}_2)(\bar{x}_3\bar{x}_4 + x_3x_4) \end{aligned} \quad (3.3)$$

Each elementary term of this expression is a minterm of one of the sets of input variables, $(x_1, x_2)$ or $(x_2, x_3)$, which could be generated by 2-bit decoders. The expression for $f$ is now, however, a three-level expression: OR–AND–OR. It can be brought back to two levels by converting each sum of minterms in the parentheses into its equivalent product of max-terms. Thus the following is obtained:

$$\begin{aligned} f = {} & (\bar{x}_1 + \bar{x}_2)(\bar{x}_1 + x_2)(\bar{x}_3 + \bar{x}_4)(\bar{x}_3 + x_4) \\ & + (\bar{x}_1 + x_2)(x_1 + \bar{x}_2)(\bar{x}_3 + \bar{x}_4)(x_3 + x_4) \\ & + (\bar{x}_1 + \bar{x}_2)(x_1 + x_2)(\bar{x}_3 + x_4)(x_3 + \bar{x}_4) \end{aligned} \quad (3.4)$$

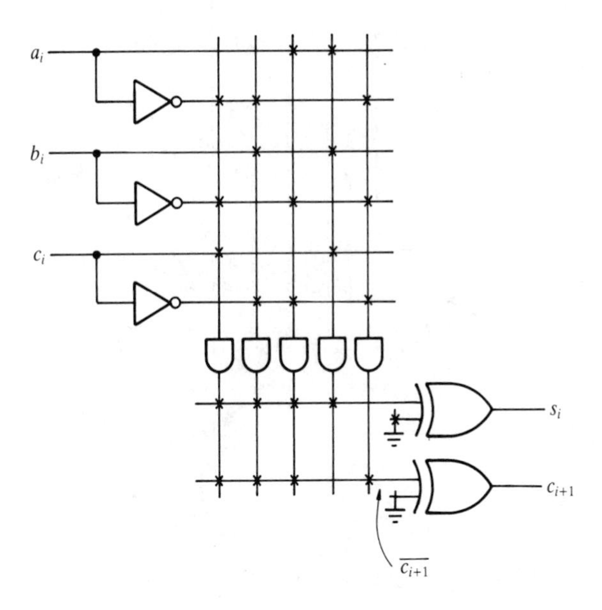


**Figure 3.17** Full adder with negation of $c_{i+1}$.

The expression now requires three products, each of which is made up from maxterms of $(x_1, x_2)$ and $(x_3, x_4)$. 2-bit decoders are required to generate the functions:

$$
\begin{array}{ll}
x_1 + x_2 & x_3 + x_4 \\
x_1 + \overline{x}_2 & x_3 + \overline{x}_4 \\
\overline{x}_1 + x_2 & \overline{x}_3 + x_4 \\
\overline{x}_1 + \overline{x}_2 & \overline{x}_3 + \overline{x}_4
\end{array}
$$

Returning now to the adder example, the number of products required can be reduced by partitioning the inputs into the sets $(a_i, b_i)$ and $(c_i)$. The two equations can be written as:

$$
\begin{aligned}
s_i &= (a_i\overline{b}_i + \overline{a}_i b_i)\overline{c}_i + (a_i b_i + \overline{a}_i\overline{b}_i)c_i \\
&= (\overline{a}_i + \overline{b}_i)(a_i + b_i)\overline{c}_i + (\overline{a}_i + b_i)(a_i + \overline{b}_i)c_i
\end{aligned} \tag{3.5}
$$

$$
\begin{aligned}
c_{i-1} &= (a_i\overline{b}_i + \overline{a}_i b_i)\overline{c}_i + \overline{a}_i\overline{b}_i \\
&= (\overline{a}_i + \overline{b}_i)(a_i + b_i)\overline{c}_i + (\overline{a}_i + \overline{b}_i)(\overline{a}_i + b_i)(a_i + \overline{b}_i)
\end{aligned} \tag{3.6}
$$

A 2-bit decoding of inputs $a_i$ and $b_i$ enables the adder equations to be programmed into a PLA with now only three products, as shown in Figure 3.18.

Logic networks for 1- and 2-bit decoders are shown in Figure 3.19.

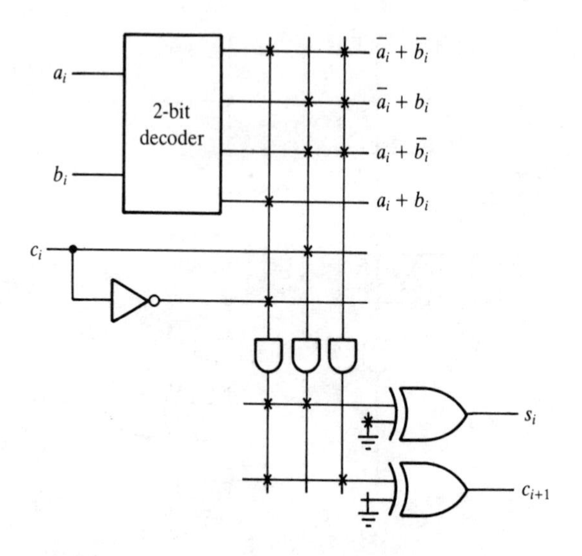


**Figure 3.18** Full adder with 2-bit decoder.

Table 3.3 shows the functions available by ANDing decoder outputs in a product term. The first column of the table indicates which decoder outputs are input to a product term (for example, '0000' is the case where no connection exists), the second shows the functions of the two inputs when using two 1-bit decoders, and the last shows those which can be produced with a 2-bit decoder.

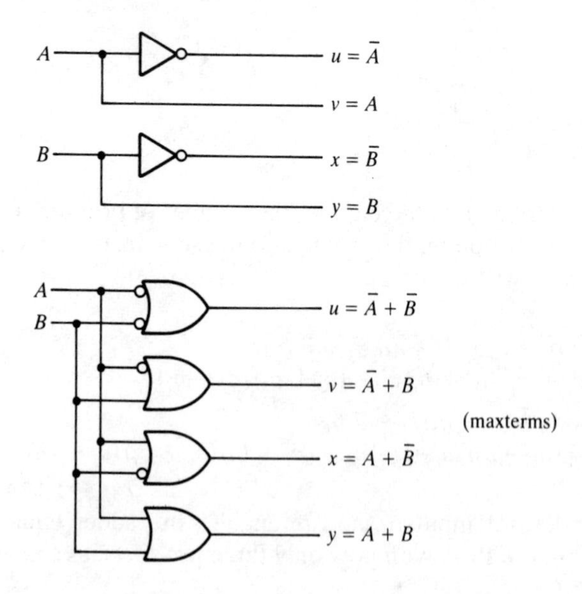


**Figure 3.19** Normal and 2-bit decoders.

**Table 3.3** Functions with 1- and 2-bit decoding.

| *UVXY* | *1-bit* | *2-bit* |
|---|---|---|
| 0000 | 1 | 1 |
| 0001 | $B$ | $A + B$ |
| 0010 | $B$ | $A + \overline{B}$ |
| 0011 | 0 | $A$ |
| 0100 | $A$ | $\overline{A} + B$ |
| 0101 | $AB$ | $B$ |
| 0110 | $A\overline{B}$ | $AB + \overline{A}\overline{B}$ |
| 0111 | 0 | $AB$ |
| 1000 | $\overline{A}$ | $\overline{A} + \overline{B}$ |
| 1001 | $\overline{A}B$ | $A\overline{B} + \overline{A}B = (A \oplus B)$ |
| 1010 | $\overline{A}\overline{B}$ | $\overline{B}$ |
| 1011 | 0 | $A\overline{B}$ |
| 1100 | 0 | $\overline{A}$ |
| 1101 | 0 | $\overline{A}B$ |
| 1110 | 0 | $\overline{A}\overline{B}$ |
| 1111 | 0 | 0 |

It is thus possible to generate any of the 16 possible functions of 4 variables and incorporate these into any product. These 16 functions correspond to all possible patterns of 1s in the rows of the K maps of Figure 2.24. With 2-bit decoding, the number of inputs to the array is the same as with normal encoding (that is, 4) and all of the original functions are available $(0, 1, A, B, \overline{A}, \overline{B})$. The AND array size is therefore guaranteed to be no larger with 2-bit encoding, and of course the hope is that it will be smaller, as in the example above. The disadvantage is that the design procedure loses its directness. For this reason 2-bit encoding is rarely seen in commercial PLAs. It is a difficult task to choose the optimal input partitioning in order to minimize the number of products. Further examples will be given in Chapter 8.

The degree of encoding may be expanded to sets of more than two variables and, in the limit, one set containing all of them. In this last case any function of the input variables can be generated by programming a single product line and, with $n$ product lines, the PLA becomes an $n$-bit **read-only memory**, as shown in Figure 3.20. Building the adder with full (3-bit) input encoding would require an array of size $8 \times 2$. By generating minterms (only one of which is active at a time) in the decoder instead of maxterms, there is a direct correspondence between the programming

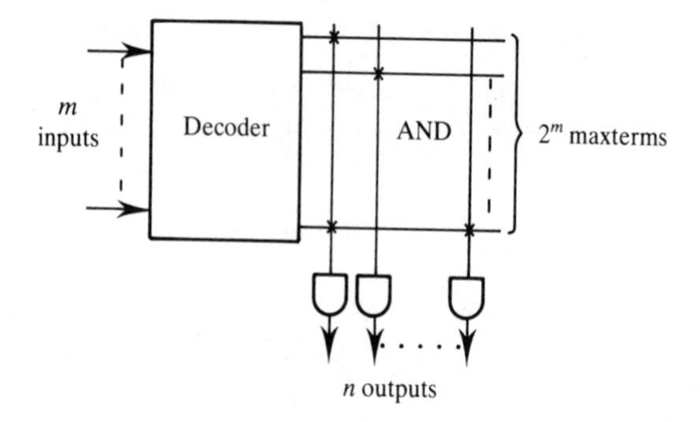


**Figure 3.20** Full decoding giving $2^m \times n$ bit read-only memory.

pattern and the contents of a memory array. These minterms address an OR array, instead of an AND array, whose rows are the data words of the memory (Figure 3.21).

It is interesting to study how the array size required depends on the size of the input decoders. This cannot be answered in general, as each type of function will have its own characteristics and there will be more than one way to partition the input bits for encoding. However, some general bounds can be calculated for the case of equally sized encoders. An example is given in Figure 3.22(a) for a 16-bit function. Here the maximum and minimum numbers of bits required in the AND array are shown. 2-bit encoding is no worse than 1-bit encoding, and can be better. Figure 3.22(b) shows the array size variation for the exclusive OR of 16 variables. Here it can be seen that 4-bit encoding is the most economical option.

The flexibility of PLA ICs can be increased by allowing some terminals (pins) to operate as either inputs or outputs, thereby increasing the range of application of the device. This is achieved by placing a three-state

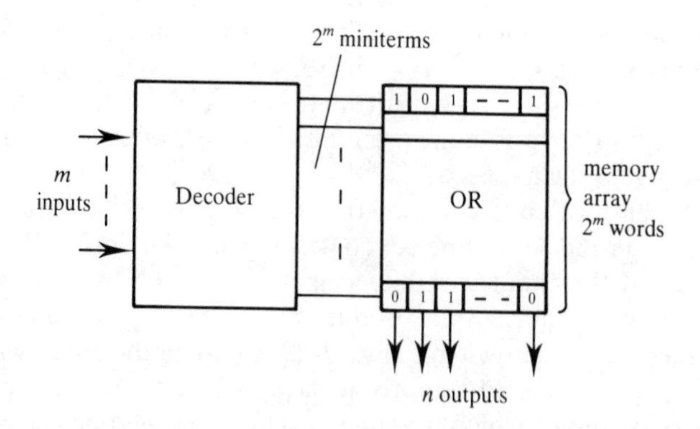


**Figure 3.21** Conventional form of read-only memory.

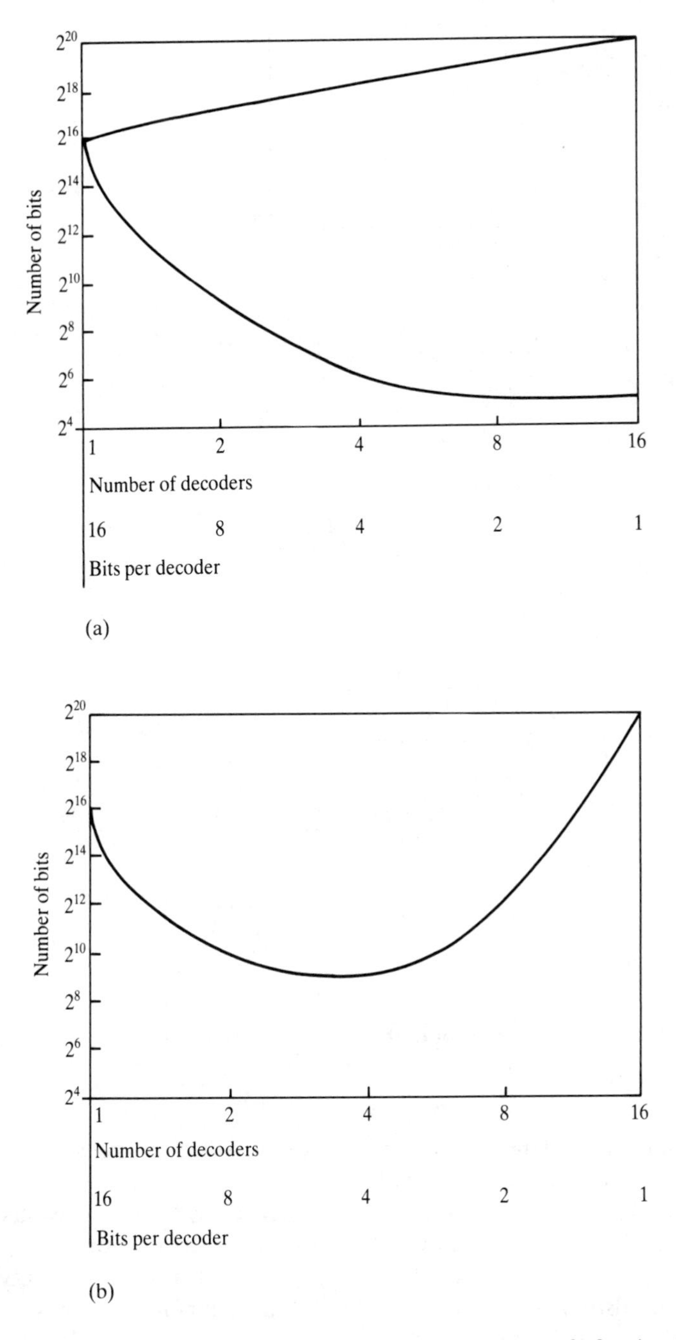


**Figure 3.22** (a) Maximum and minimum number of bits needed to implement any function of 16 variables as a function of decoder size. (b) Number of bits needed to implement the exclusive OR of 16 variables as a function of number of bits per decoder (From Fleisher and Maissel, 1975).

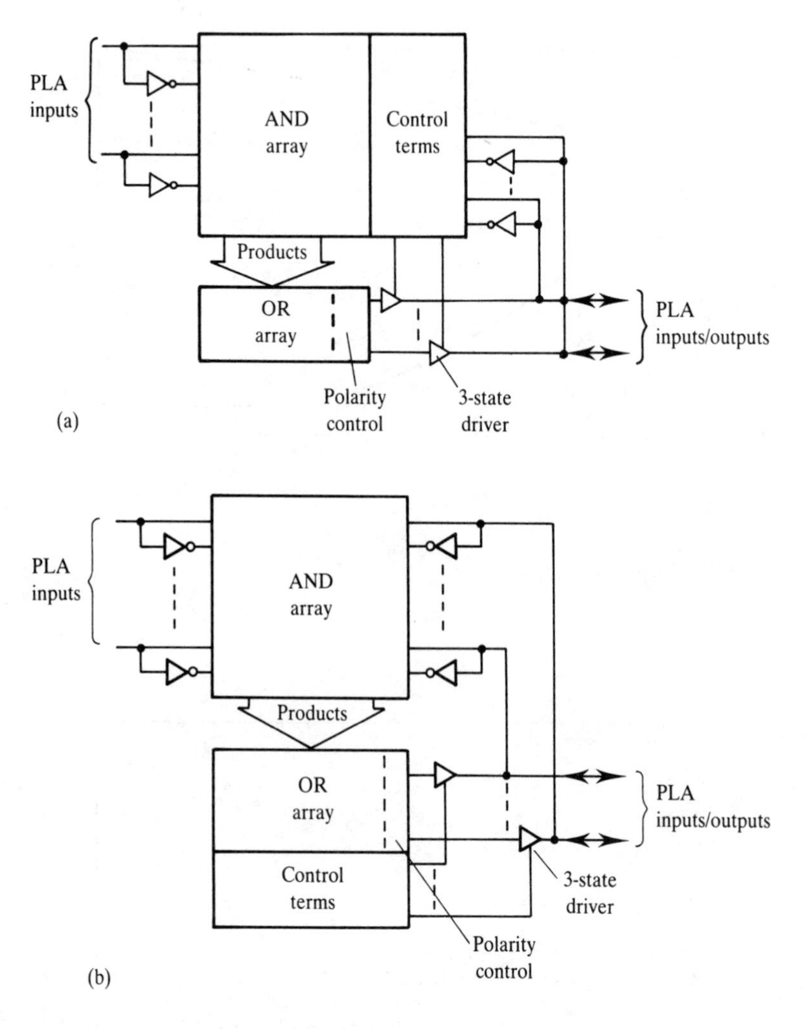


**Figure 3.23** (a) PLA with output control; (b) second form with control terms in OR.

(H, L, high impedance) driver at the outputs which can be controlled from within the PLA. In the simplest form, an extension to the AND array, the **control array**, generates additional product terms known as **control terms** (Figure 3.23(a)). If a control term is true, then the output driver which it controls is enabled and the terminal is an output from the OR array. These terminals also have a connection through decoders into the AND array to allow them to be used as inputs when their driver is disabled. A driver can be permanently enabled (the control term has no '×'s), permanently disabled, or sometimes enabled and sometimes disabled (control term realizes a product). In the latter case, the terminal is **bidirectional**. A

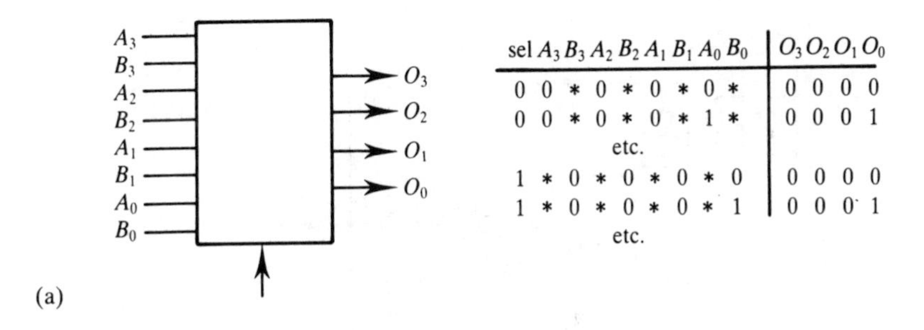


| sel | $A_3$ | $B_3$ | $A_2$ | $B_2$ | $A_1$ | $B_1$ | $A_0$ | $B_0$ | $O_3$ | $O_2$ | $O_1$ | $O_0$ |
|---|---|---|---|---|---|---|---|---|---|---|---|---|
| 0 | 0 | * | 0 | * | 0 | * | 0 | * | 0 | 0 | 0 | 0 |
| 0 | 0 | * | 0 | * | 0 | * | 1 | * | 0 | 0 | 0 | 1 |
| etc. | | | | | | | | | | | | |
| 1 | * | 0 | * | 0 | * | 0 | * | 0 | 0 | 0 | 0 | 0 |
| 1 | * | 0 | * | 0 | * | 0 | * | 1 | 0 | 0 | 0 | 1 |
| etc. | | | | | | | | | | | | |

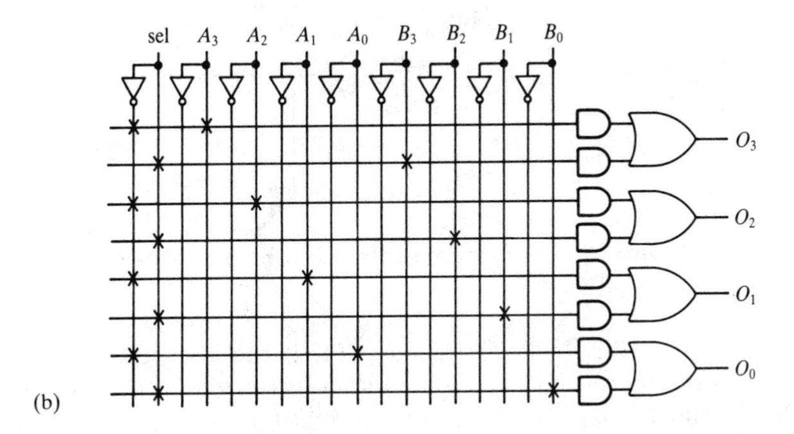


**Figure 3.24** (a) Multiplexer; (b) multiplexer array (PAL structure).

second form can be defined in which the driver controls come from an extension to the OR array, as shown in Figure 3.23(b). Controls can now be sum-of-products expressions rather than single-product terms.

An important economy is possible by making use of the fact that for many functions the OR array is not needed for the sharing of products between outputs. Figure 3.24 shows an example of such a function, a multiplexer. Such a function can be implemented by a PLA with only an AND array; the OR array has degenerated into a set of OR gates. The drawback is that the PLA is no longer universal, because a fixed allocation of products to OR gates has to be chosen. PLAs with this structure have become known as **PAL devices** or 'PALs', the name which is a trademark of Advanced Micro Devices Inc. (PAL denotes 'programmable array logic', a term which has no new intrinsic meaning. Although the term 'PAL' is a trademark, because it has achieved such widespread usage, it will be used in this book to denote all PLAs with a fixed OR array.) PLDs also exist with only an AND array, each output being a product. These devices are useful for recognizing words such as addresses or ranges of words and will be discussed in Chapter 5.

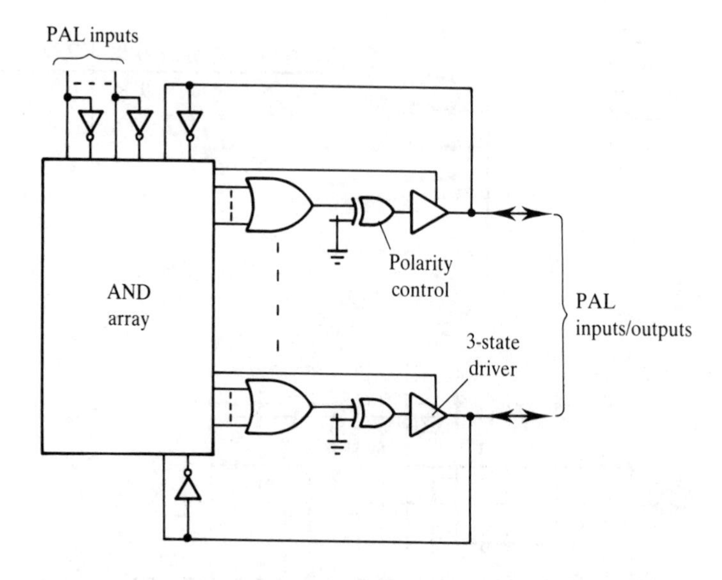


**Figure 3.25** PAL-structured PLA with output controls.

The flexibility of PAL-structured PLAs can also be enhanced by provision of controllable three-state output drivers, as shown in Figure 3.25. To simplify the diagram, the control terms are shown adjacent to each OR gate, and not collected together as in Figure 3.23. Polarity controls on each output are also a very useful feature in this type of device.

One further enhancement to PLAs needs to be mentioned. As shown in the previous chapter, the use of exclusive OR gates at the output of sums of products can produce economies in some applications. They are especially useful in arithmetic and counter circuits, as will be discussed in Chapter 8. Figure 3.26 shows how exclusive OR gates can be incorporated in this way into a PAL array.

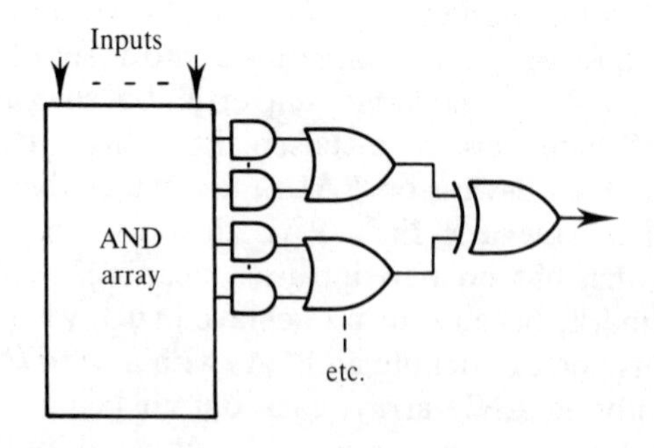


**Figure 3.26** AND–OR–XOR PAL structure.

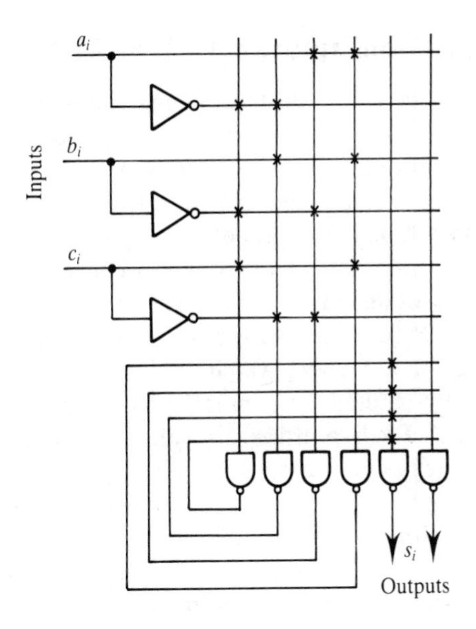


**Figure 3.27** 'Folded' NAND array device.

It is now possible to distinguish three classes of array logic device:

(1) the PLA with programmable AND and OR arrays,

(2) the memory with a programmable OR array, and

(3) the PAL with a programmable AND array.

One final form must be mentioned in this brief survey of array logic structures – the **multilevel array**. Recall from Figure 3.13 that, of the eight possible sum-of-products forms, there are two, (ii) NAND–NAND and (vii) NOR–NOR, which require only a single gate type. It is possible to make use of this fact by defining an array which realizes only one type of function (NAND or NOR), and which allows sums of products to be formed by feedback. Figure 3.27, in which the array is programmed to realize the sum output of a full adder, illustrates the principle. This type of array also allows multilevel logic to be realized directly without having to reduce it to a two-level sum of products, as is necessary with conventional PLAs and PALs. The structure is sometimes called a 'folded' array (a term which unfortunately conflicts with its conventional use; PLA folding in VLSI design is an optimization technique which reduces the area of a PLA by removing redundancy).

## 3.4 Is it a ROM, multiplexer, PAL or PLA?

Many array logic device variations have been proposed in the past 30 years, far more than have ever been commercially manufactured. Some have been available as products, but were soon withdrawn. On inspection, however, a lot of these structures can be related to each other. Some of these relationships will be explored below.

It is generally more effective from a circuit design point of view to build a ROM with split decoders rather than a single decoder, as in Figure 3.20. For example, Figure 3.28 shows an $m$-input ROM with $m/2$ input variables connected to a decoder which selects a row of the array, and the other $m/2$ inputs connected to a number of multiplexers equal to the number of outputs. Each multiplexer selects a column. The opposite extreme to the single decoder case is the single multiplexer case, shown in Figure 3.29 for a single output function. The ROM is now equivalent to a single multiplexer with $m$ 'select' inputs and $2^m$ 'data' inputs. Each data input is connected to a fixed value, 0 or 1, corresponding to the function value for the corresponding input combination.

These alternative ways of realizing a ROM can be formalized in the **Shannon expansion** of a Boolean function. Any function of $m$ variables, $f(x_1, x_2, \ldots, x_m)$, can be expressed in the following ways:

$$f(x_1,x_2,\ldots,x_m) = f(0,x_2,\ldots,x_m)\overline{x}_1 + f(1,x_2,\ldots,x_m)x_1 \tag{3.7}$$

$$\begin{aligned} &= f(0,0,x_3,\ldots,x_m)\overline{x}_1\overline{x}_2 \\ &\quad + f(0,1,x_3,\ldots,x_m)\overline{x}_1x_2 \\ &\quad + f(1,0,x_3,\ldots,x_m)x_1\overline{x}_2 \\ &\quad + f(1,1,x_3,\ldots,x_m)x_1x_2 \end{aligned} \tag{3.8}$$

$$\begin{aligned} &= f(0,0,0,x_4,\ldots,x_m)\overline{x}_1\overline{x}_2\overline{x}_3 \\ &\quad + f(0,0,1,x_4,\ldots,x_m)\overline{x}_1\overline{x}_2x_3 \\ &\quad + \ldots + f(1,1,1,x_4,\ldots,x_m)x_1x_2x_3 \end{aligned} \tag{3.9}$$

.

.

.

$$\begin{aligned} &= f(0,0,0,\ldots,0)\overline{x}_1\overline{x}_2\overline{x}_3\ldots\overline{x}_m + \ldots \\ &\quad + f(1,1,1,\ldots,1)x_1x_2x_3\ldots x_m \end{aligned} \tag{3.10}$$

Equation 3.7 has two terms on the right-hand side, Equation 3.8 has four, Equation 3.9 has eight, and so on until Equation 3.10, which has $2^m$. The functions $f$ which appear on the right-hand sides with some of their variables fixed are known as **residues** (or cofactors). These are the

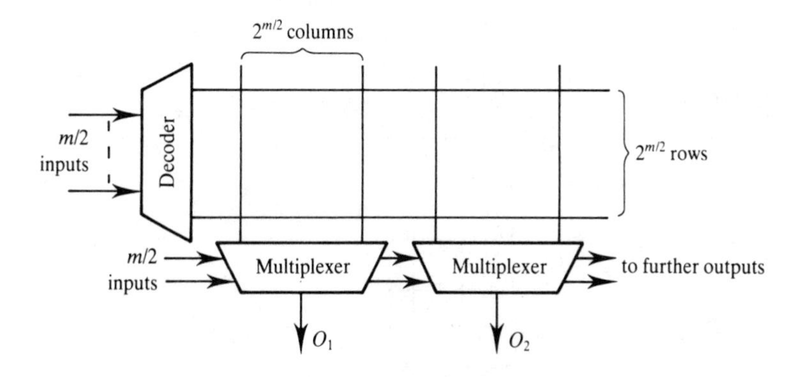


**Figure 3.28** ROM with split decoding.

multiplexer's data inputs in a ROM with split decoding. Equation 3.10 is the standard sum of minterms representation; the residues have values 0 and 1 and are the data inputs to the multiplexer of Figure 3.29. Figure 3.30 shows some expansions of a three-variable function and the equivalent ROM.

In the realization of a function with one of these structures it is likely that not every residue function line is required. For example, some residue functions may be zero and some may be repeated. In this case the multiplexer can be simplified – and in fact could be constructed as a sum-of-products array like that of a PAL device, as shown in Figure 3.31. A further optimization may be possible by modification of the decoder. By splitting the decoder into smaller decoders, it may be possible to handle

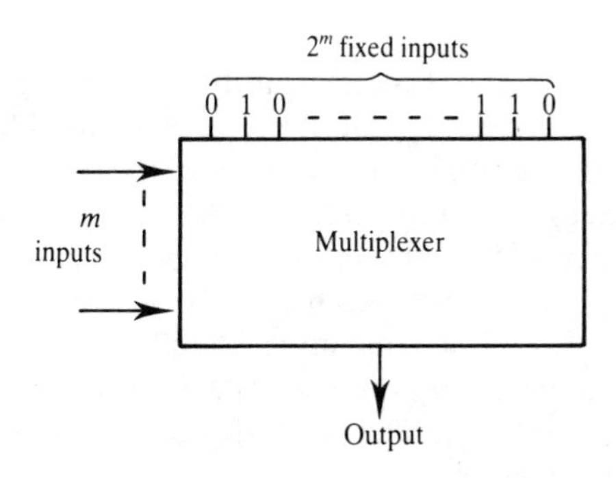


**Figure 3.29** ROM as a multiplexer.

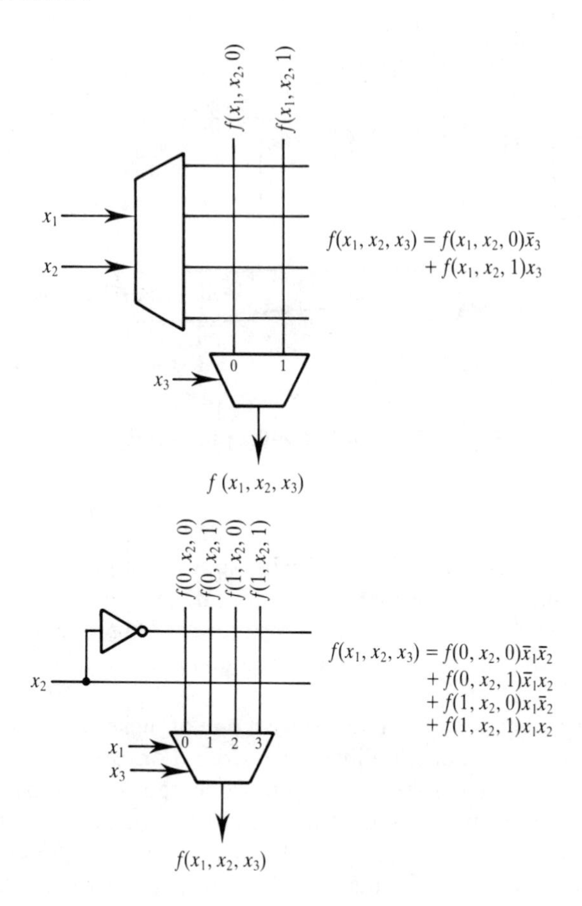


**Figure 3.30** Shannon expansion and ROMs.

more input variables without increasing the number of residue (product) lines. If 1-bit decoders are used, the structure becomes identical to that of a PAL device. Now, if multiple output functions are required, it can make sense to share products, thereby creating a PLA.

Two particular (now defunct) array logic devices can now be shown to be examples of this general scheme. IBM's 'writeable personalized chip' (WPC) is PAL-like but has more complex decoders (Figure 3.32). Raytheon's programmable multiplexer (PMUX) is like a ROM but with 1-bit decoders (Figure 3.33). The latter device was primarily intended for use in data path applications.

Thus array logic devices which may appear at first sight to be different are in fact members of the same family.

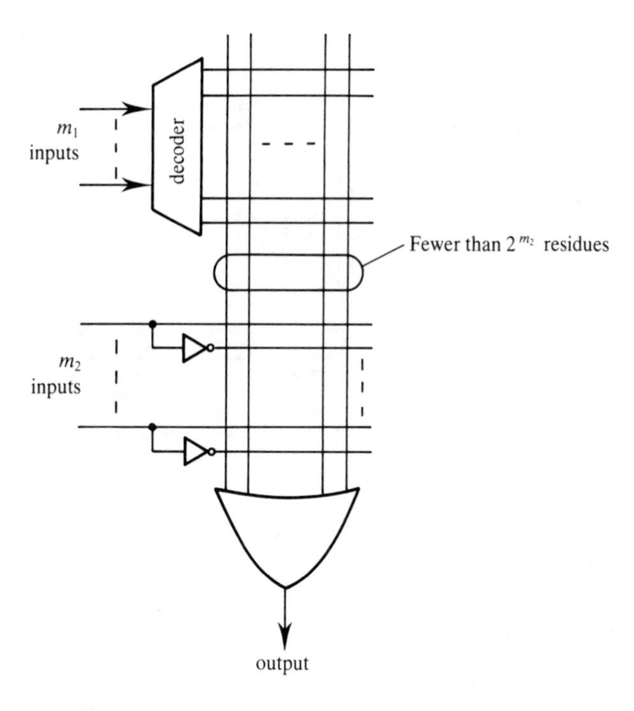


**Figure 3.31** ROM with optimized multiplexer.

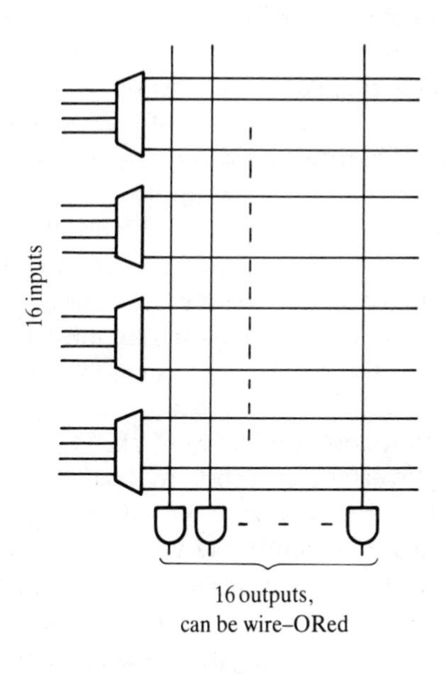


**Figure 3.32** The WPC.

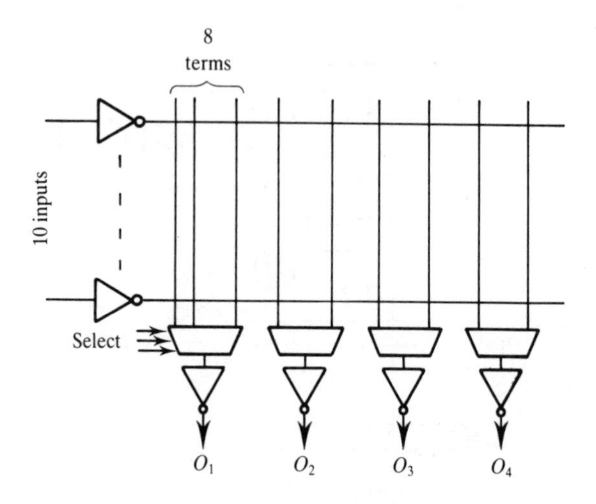


**Figure 3.33** The PMUX.

## 3.5 Content-addressable memories

The **content-addressable memory** (CAM), or associative memory (a term with a wider meaning), has a close relationship to the PLA. Figure 3.34 shows the simplest form of CAM. It is a memory array with a programmable address decoder, or directory, which stores key words, or **tags**, associated with each data word. To access a word the tag is presented to the directory, or **search array**, and any matches with stored tags enable reading from the data array. Access is thus by content (tag) rather than by location number, as is the case in a fully decoded memory. Multiple matches can be handled in different ways – one possibility is adding control logic to perform serial access of the multiple data words.

The similarity with the PLA should now be obvious. The search array corresponds to the AND array and the data array corresponds to the OR array. The difference is that read/write cells are now required at all matrix intersections, and some access control must be added. In fact, the PLA has been termed the read-only associative memory (ROAM) (or associative ROM (AROM)).

One of the commonest applications of CAMs in digital systems is for the control of two levels of memory in computer systems where the primary level has a faster access time than the secondary level, but is not large enough to hold all currently active programs and data. Processor operation is simplified if the two-level memory system has a single address space, that of the secondary level. The primary memory holds blocks of data from the secondary store together with a tag representing the most significant part of the address of each block stored. The most significant part of an address sent from the processor is matched with the tags stored

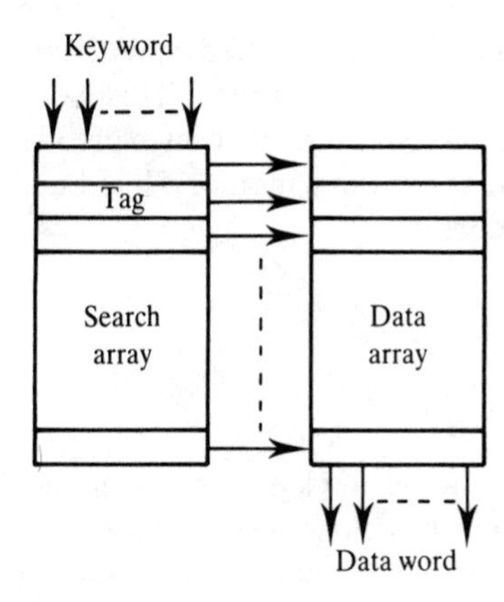


**Figure 3.34** Content-addressable memory.

in a CAM. If there is a match, the required block is in the primary memory and can be accessed rapidly. If not, a block has to be loaded from the secondary store, as shown in Figure 3.35. Many ways of operating this scheme have been devised; for details a computer architecture textbook should be consulted.

Another obvious application for CAM is reconfigurable logic. If a CAM is used as a PLA, then it is in principle possible to reload the CAM with new data defining a new logical function. For parts of a system used serially, this would seem to be practical. IBM investigated the use of such arrays as a general-purpose LSI technology in the late 1960s. Their hope was that one circuit type could implement all the logic of a computer. Their design of content-addressable module they called **functional memory**,

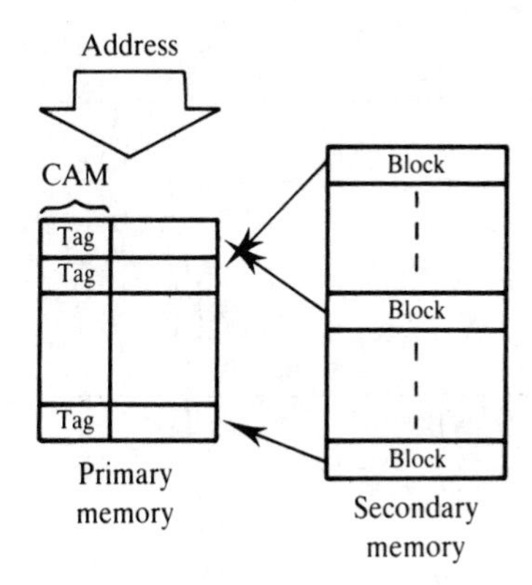


**Figure 3.35** CAM used for memory mapping.

which had combined search and data arrays, with control logic for sequencing the search, read and write operations. This work was eventually abandoned in favour of PLAs. Much of it, however, was valuable in the later PLA work. (The term functional memory has been used occasionally to mean PLA – this is incorrect.)

## 3.6 Circuit techniques

Modern programmable logic devices are not made from diode matrices; their circuit development has closely followed that of semiconductor memory technology in pursuit of the goals of the highest possible speed with the lowest possible power consumption. In this section some of the general principles of modern array logic circuitry will be sketched.

To produce logic matrices, distributed gates are required, for which any logic gate circuit which can be bussed is a candidate. This was shown to be possible for diode logic, leading to construction of the diode matrix. Two possible methods of constructing distributed gates with bipolar transistors are shown in Figure 3.36. Some of the highest speed arrays use ECL circuitry, and Figure 3.37 shows how ECL can be used in a PAL matrix. The multiple emitter transistor performs the function of the fixed OR, in the sum-of-products form of Figure 3.13(vi).

NMOS gate circuits can likewise be adapted; Figure 3.38 shows a distributed NOR. A problem with these arrays is that they consume power even when not switching and, when they do switch, high currents are required to change voltages rapidly in the highly capacitive arrays. Efforts

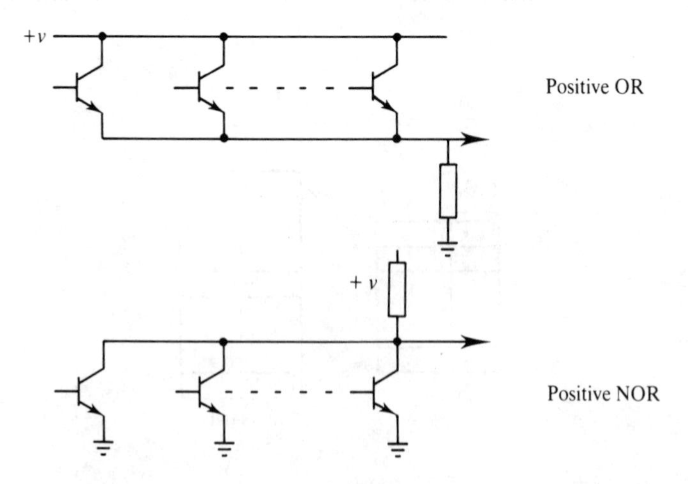


**Figure 3.36** Distributed gates with NPN transistors.

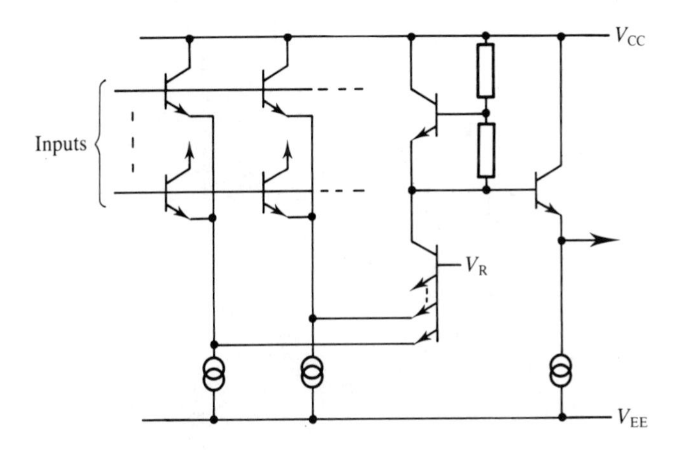


**Figure 3.37** ECL array (PAL structure).

have therefore been made to adapt existing low power techniques to arrays.

The use of static CMOS is not usually practical in the array application since a CMOS gate requires two dual logic networks, one with p-channel transistors and one with n-channel transistors. Both networks would have to be programmed to preserve the function and the zero static power consumption. However, dynamic logic techniques can be used, as only one of the two networks is required. Figure 3.39 illustrates one embodiment of the principle. Two additional transistors are required, a **precharge** p transistor, and an **evaluate** n transistor. To these a clock $\phi$ is fed. When $\phi$ is low, the output is connected to $V_{DD}$ and the bottom transistor is switched off. This is the precharge phase. When $\phi$ goes high, the output is disconnected from $V_{DD}$ and the evaluate transistor opens a path to ground. If the result of the NOR is H, then the output will remain

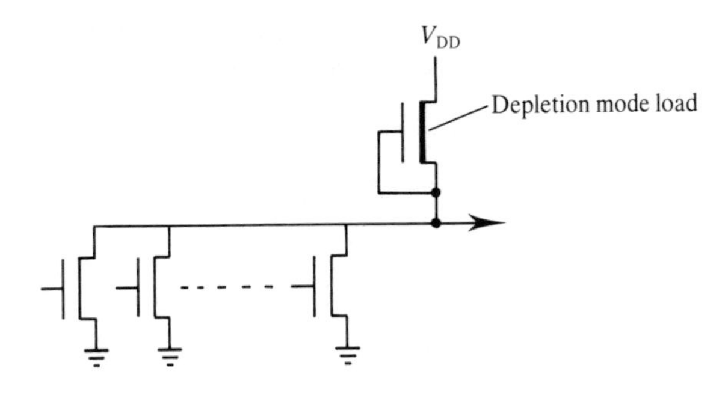


**Figure 3.38** NMOS distributed NOR.

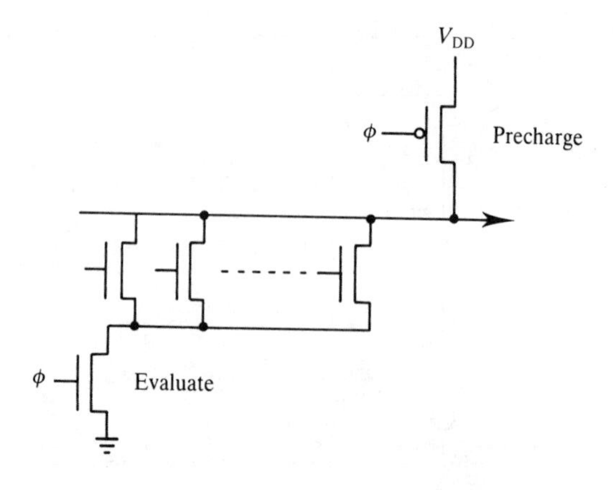


**Figure 3.39** Dynamic gate.

in its charged state, held up by the capacitance of the transistors and interconnector to which it is connected. If on the other hand the result is L then the output will discharge through the gate and the evaluate transistor. As in static CMOS there is no DC path from $V_{DD}$ to ground. The transistors can thus be made wide to increase switching speed.

A variation of this idea is used in 'zero static power' PLDs, devices which only consume appreciable power when switching. A combinational PLD can use dynamic logic if circuitry is added to detect input changes and to generate a clock signal. Figure 3.40 shows how such a circuit operates; any input change causes a pulse, $\phi$, to be generated (in practice, the MOS circuit would not be built with delay lines). In dynamic circuits, output latches must be provided to retain the output signals evaluated, so that the device appears to be static externally.

Various methods have been adopted for making arrays programmable by either the manufacturer or the user. Options available to the manufacturer include mask programming, in which the pattern on one of the photomasks is adapted according to the required array personality, and the opening of connections using a laser beam. User programmability has traditionally been enabled by the incorporation of fuses in series with each

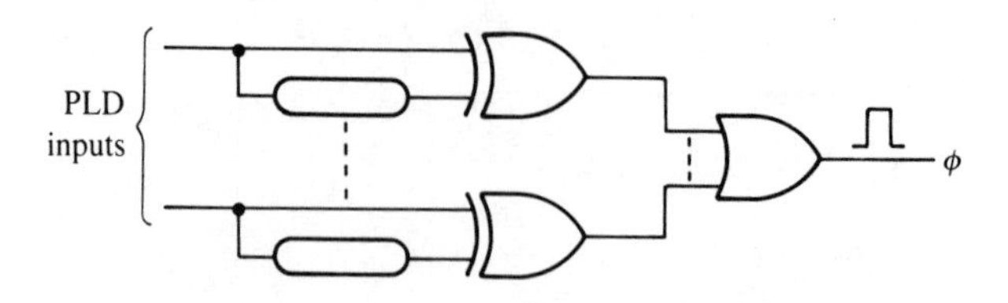


**Figure 3.40** Input transition detector.

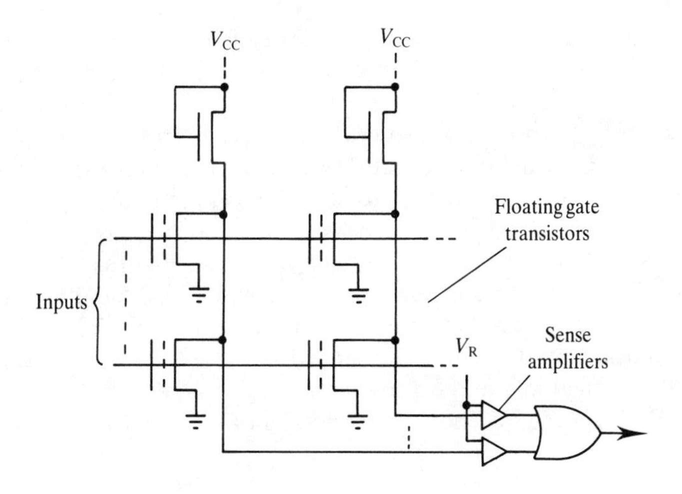


**Figure 3.41** Erasable PAL circuit.

diode or transistor or by building in transistors which can be broken down by avalanche-induced migration. In these cases, a device once programmed cannot be altered except by blowing more fuses. More recently, erasable memory technology has been adapted for use in programmable

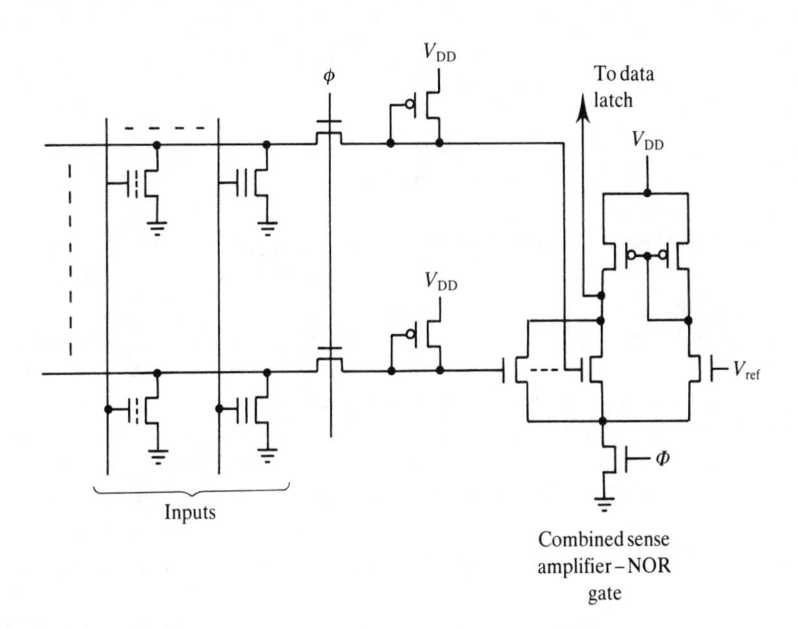


**Figure 3.42** Simplified EPLD circuit (NOR–NOR form) (after Wong *et al.* (1986)).

logic. Both ultraviolet (UV) and electrically erasable types are now produced. These devices have become known by the terms **EPLD** and **EEPLD**.

Figure 3.41 shows how an erasable PAL matrix can be constructed using transistors with 'floating gates' (which can retain charge) in the AND array. Floating gate cells are now used in some PLDs in preference to fuses even in non-erasable devices, because of the smaller area occupied by these cells and the improved reliability. Finally, Figure 3.42 shows (in simplified form) one possible circuit for a dynamic EPLD. When $\phi$ is low, the array output lines (the 'bit lines') precharge. This signal would be generated by a circuit like that of Figure 3.40. What has not been shown in any of these diagrams is the programming and input/output circuitry; in most PLDs this occupies more chip area than the logic array.

## 3.7 Specifying the function of a PLD

As with digital systems in general, PLDs can be specified in terms of their *behaviour* (what they do), or their *structure* (how their internal elements are wired together). It is preferable to design at the behavioural level wherever possible, but there are often cases where this option is not available or practical, as will be seen.

The most direct form of behavioural description for a combinational circuit is the truth table. For use as a PLD specification the unspecified entries (the '–'s) must first be removed from the output part, because all outputs must be assigned a value. For a PLA, the table maps directly onto the circuit; each line of the table defines a product term and a line of inputs into the OR array. In fact the modified truth table becomes a **PLA table**. Figure 3.43 is an example of a programming table for a typical PLA IC, which should be studied in conjunction with the PLA block diagram of Figure 3.23(a).

The table has spaces for specification of the output polarities and control array personality in addition to the logical sums of products. There are 32 product terms available, numbered from 00 to 31, each of which can be given a name. The inputs to the AND array are made up of exclusive inputs $I_0$–$I_7$, and bidirectional terminals (pins) $B_0$–$B_9$. If a signal appears in a product, then an 'H' is placed in the relevant square if it is uncomplemented, 'L' if it is complemented. An absent signal is denoted by '–' (this conflict of notation with '–' used for unspecified outputs is unfortunate). The second part of the product term line is used to specify the links into the OR array. 'A' ('active') is used for a connection, '·' for no connection. Notice that the outputs have the same name as the bidirectional inputs. To each output is attached an 'H' or 'L' to specify polarity. The control terms $D_0$–$D_9$ are specified beneath the products. There is one for each bidirectional signal. These are specified in the same way as products,

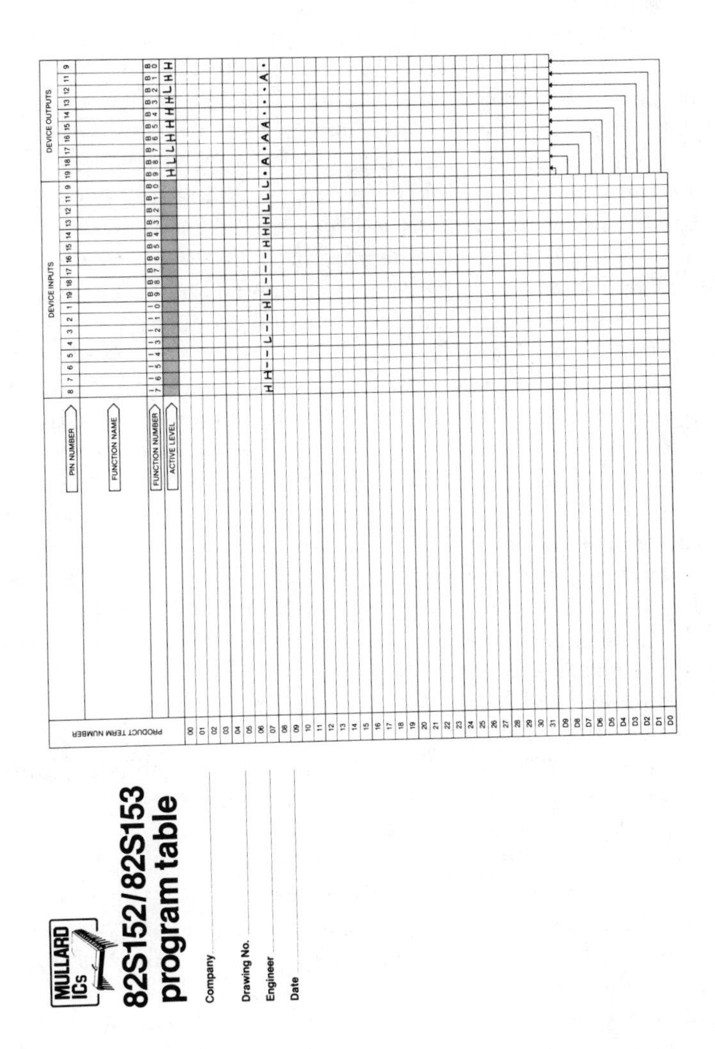


**Figure 3.43** PLA programming table.

and if a term is true then the output driver is enabled. Permanent outputs would have '–' in all positions of their control term, while permanent inputs would have '0' in all positions. '0' signifies that both the true and the complement parts of an input are connected, thus causing the term to be always false.

A completed PLA table may now be entered directly into a device programmer if this facility exists or into a CAD program which converts the information into a standard format readable by a programmer. (Most modern programmers conform to a data exchange format published by the JEDEC organization.) PLAs have the advantage that even fuse-programmable devices can be edited, provided that there are unused product terms. This is because in the unprogrammed state, when all fuses are present, products are held false because of the connection of both complemented and uncomplemented inputs. The inputs to the OR array will all be connected, but since the product lines will be giving zero outputs, this has no effect on outputs. To remove a product, the OR part of the line is made to contain only '·'s. A spare product may be brought into the function by simply programming it with the desired pattern.

However, even though this is a very natural way to specify the function of a PLA, it is too laborious and error prone for routine use. Higher level methods relying on more advanced CAD are necessary and will be introduced in later chapters.

ROM-implemented functions are also specified in the most direct way by a truth table. However, in addition to eliminating '–'s from the output part, any '*'s must be eliminated from the input part in order to form the minterms required. Memory truth tables can thus become very voluminous and cannot conveniently be dealt with by hand except for very small memories. CAD is required and a higher level method of specifying behaviour is essential.

A table equivalent to the PLA table has never been developed for PALs since from the time of their introduction a more convenient form of description has been offered. This is a description in terms of Boolean equations entered as text for processing by a conversion program, called PALASM ('PAL assembler'). In its pure form, this is a behavioural description. However, this input description and its derivatives also require device-specific structural information concerning, for example, built-in signals (such as output three-state enables) and gate structures (such as exclusive ORs). In fact, it is better to regard these simple assemblers as accepting purely structural information. In other words, each Boolean equation is an exact specification of product term fuse patterns, where additional features such as exclusive OR gates can be mapped directly into operators in equations. However, for the type of function for which PALs are best used, this form of description is very easy to use and in most cases the function is obvious from the specification. For example the multiplexer of Figure 3.25 would be described in PALASM as

```
O3 = sel * B3 + /sel * A3
O2 = sel * B2 + /sel * A2
O1 = sel * B1 + /sel * A1
O0 = sel * B0 + /sel * A0
```

(In PALASM, * means 'AND' and / means negation.) These very structured equation sets are typical of PAL applications. For PLAs, on the other hand, this is seldom the case. The ability to share products and type of application usually results in quite 'unstructured' Boolean descriptions. However, it is often possible to specify designs (particularly sequential ones) in a more abstract manner, thereby avoiding the problem of formulating the complex Boolean equations. Again, these methods will be discussed in later chapters.

PAL application examples often show device circuit diagrams with intact fuses marked with '×' (like Figure 3.24). In some cases, the patterns are revealing, but this method should never be used for specifying a function. The procedure is extremely error prone and allows no independent check of correctness.

As the number of PLD types multiplied the need arose for universal specification methods, that is methods which were, to the greatest possible extent, independent of a particular device structure (PLA, PAL, ROM, and so on) and manufacturer. At the same time, compiler techniques borrowed from computer programming languages were applied to PLD CAD software allowing more powerful language constructs. The characteristics and use of these more advanced languages will be discussed in Chapter 10.

A programmable logic CAD system must offer more than a language compiler if the complete design cycle is to be supported. At least the following facilities are needed;

(1) optimization to reduce resource requirements;
(2) ability to combine library designs;
(3) a simulator for verification of designs;
(4) a database of PLD characteristics;
(5) a method of generating test patterns.

Other more advanced facilities, such as automatic selection of the most suitable PLD and further forms of behavioural specification, are now becoming available.

Because of the variety of specification languages which exist, the approach in this book will be to use specification methods which are as general as possible and can be easily mapped into a given language. This is not difficult, as all the languages express the same types of information.

## 3.8 Use of standard symbols

Because each programmable logic application is unique, there is very rarely a predefined symbol available for use in logic and circuit diagrams. However, the IEEE standards do give certain rules and guidelines which can assist in the construction of symbols.

Firstly, logic internal to the PLD, that is that drawn within the symbol outline, must be drawn as a pure logic diagram. No polarity indicators must be used. Figure 3.44 is the logic diagram for a PLA of the type shown in Figure 3.23(b), having 8 inputs, 32 products, 4 outputs and 4 input/outputs. The qualifying symbols should be self-explanatory by comparing the two diagrams (the symbol ▽ indicates a three-state output). It is not possible to indicate the PLD personality on this type of diagram. These diagrams are only given in some manufacturers' data sheets, whereas all give the array diagrams used in this chapter. Which is preferred is a matter of personal taste. Diagrams such as these would not appear on a designer's schematic, where the internal structures of components are not shown. What is required is a means of annotating a rectangular outline in the most helpful manner.

In general, the qualifying symbol for a 'complex function', $\Phi$, should be used, together with a reference to supporting documentation, probably a table or some text in a formal specification language, as shown in Figure 3.45. Polarity indicators can be used at the external boundary of the symbol. Standard symbols are available for RAMs and ROMs, in which

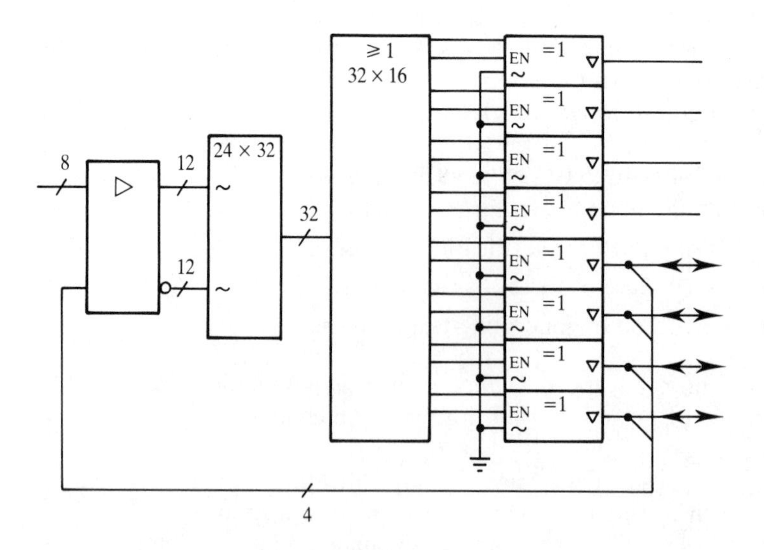


**Figure 3.44** Logic diagram of a PLA.

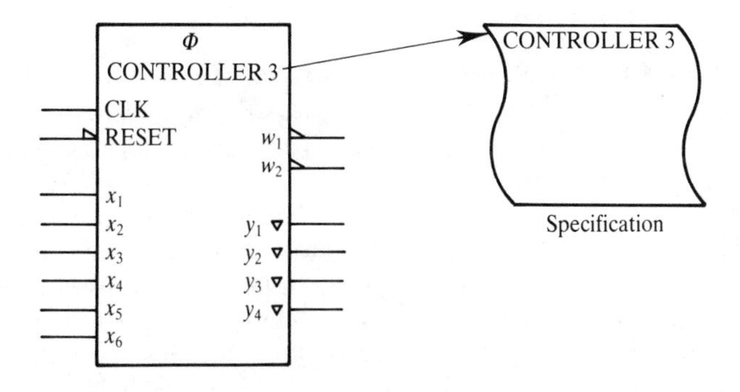


**Figure 3.45** Custom symbol for complex function.

inputs are assumed to be addresses. If it would be confusing to use one of these, then the complex function method can be used instead. For further guidance, the standards should be consulted.

---

## SUMMARY

The simplest form of array logic structure, which can be derived from diode–resistor gates, is the diode matrix. A diode matrix can realize any set of sum-of-products equations. However, it is not very useful in practice because it makes inefficient use of an IC package and has poor electrical properties. All array logic devices can be modelled as a bussed cellular array using cells selected from 18 possible types. There are eight ways of forming a sum of products using such cells. The most general PLD is the programmable logic array (PLA). The number of product terms required to realize a set of functions in a PLA can often be reduced by use of output negation and multiple-bit decoders. Internally controlled three-state output drivers can be used to vary the numbers of inputs and outputs, or to provide bidirectional terminals. A PLD with full decoding of inputs has the same logical form as a memory. A PLA without an OR array, which instead combines products in OR gates, is the most economical form for applications in which there are few (or no) shared products. This is the 'PAL' structure. ROMs, multiplexers and PLAs can all be shown to be related through the Shannon expansion. The content-addressable memory is a form of writeable PLA. For realization of array logic circuits, distributed gates are required. These can be built in all current technologies. Programming of PLD matrices can be done in many ways, but the most popular devices nowadays use erasable cells. Dynamic circuits, which only consume power when inputs change, are used in some PLDs.

---

## BIBLIOGRAPHICAL AND HISTORICAL NOTES

The general principles of diode matrices are covered in Wilkes (1956). The earliest descriptions of the use of diode matrices for logic are Brown and Rochester (1949) and Staff of the Harvard Computation Laboratory (1951). Applications are discussed in Guzeman (1972) and Uimari (1972). Typical data may be found in Harris Semiconductor (1984a). The 128-product diode matrix mentioned is described by Maggiore (1974). Chu (1962a) gives examples of multilevel matrices. The bussed cellular array model is due to Heutink (1974), and was extended in Bolton (1985a). PLA principles and multiple-bit encoding are given in Cook (1974) and Fleisher and Maissel (1975), from which Figures 3.21 and 3.22 are taken, and Sasao (1981). Representative early PLA references are Proebsting (1969), Henle *et al.* (1969), Wyland (1971), Carr and Mize (1972) and Mrazek and Morris (1973). A PLA with all the essential features of the PAL is described in Leininger (1970). The PAL was introduced in Birkner and Chua (1977), Monolithic Memories (1978) and Birkner (1978). ROM optimization is discussed in Tang (1971) and in Mitarai and Kuo (1975), the WPC in Fleisher *et al.* (1970), and the PMUX in Wyland (1978). Content-addressable memories are comprehensively treated in Kohonen (1980). The IBM functional memory work is described in Flinders *et al.* (1970) and Gardner (1971). An early transistor matrix is described in Bonn (1955), and a fuse-programmable matrix in Chow and Henrich (1957). An IC fuse-programmable diode matrix is described in Price (1962). The first fuse-programmable logic arrays (FPLAs) are described in Cavlan and Cline (1975) and Miles (1975). An ECL array is described in Millhollan and Sung (1985). Principles of MOS PLAs are covered in Glasser and Dobberpuhl (1985) and Weste and Eshraghian (1985). Circuit details of erasable PLDs are given in Cypress Semiconductor (1985), Patak *et al.* (1986), Wong *et al.* (1986) and Wahlstrom *et al.* (1988). Engeler *et al.* (1988) describe a CMOS static PLA which does not require series-connected transistors. A RAM-based PLA-structured device is described in Krug (1986). Application of the IEEE standards to PLDs can be studied in Texas Instruments (1988).

## EXERCISES

**3.1** Show how the diode matrix decoder of Figure 3.5 can be made into an eight-input multiplexer by adding one extra matrix row.

**3.2** Show that the sum and carry functions of a full adder are self-dual. Using this fact, modify the diode adder circuit of Figure 3.7 to produce an alternative implementation.

**3.3** Design a decimal (10 lines) to seven-segment character display decoder first using a PLA, and then a diode matrix requiring no more than 21 diodes. How many products would be required in a PAL implementation?

**3.4** Construct the equations for the carry-lookahead logic for a 4-bit adder. Compare a PLA and a PAL implementation. Which would be most efficient?

**3.5** For which type of function are ROMs the most suitable form of implementation?

**3.6** It is also possible to build folded arrays (see Figure 3.27) with distributed NORs. Show a programmed array which realizes a full adder. How does the total number of cross-points in this array compare with a PLA implementation (assuming no output negation and 1-bit decoders)?

**3.7** Suggest some possible applications for a writeable PLA.

CHAPTER 4

# Minimization

**OBJECTIVES**

When you have completed studying this chapter you should be able

- to determine when the application of a minimization technique is necessary for reduction of demand on PLD resources;
- to apply tabular methods for minimization of single- and multiple-output functions;
- to understand why these methods become impractical for large problems;
- to outline the type of heuristics used in modern minimizer programs;
- to apply a tabular method for detection of redundant function inputs.

## 4.1 Introduction

This chapter is concerned with the task of fitting a set of Boolean functions into a single programmable logic device. The **resources** of a PLD are the number of input and output pins, and the number of product terms available. If the set of functions to be implemented requires no more resources than the chosen device possesses, then there is no problem. If, on the other hand, a fit is not possible because of lack of resources, then an attempt must be made to reduce the resource requirements of the raw functions. This is the process of **minimization**.

At its simplest, this minimization is the reduction of obvious redundancies in the defining equations by application of the theorems of Boolean algebra. Also, De Morgan's theorem is useful when output inversion is programmable, as in the PLA of Figure 3.17; in some cases generating the complement of a function and then inverting it requires fewer product terms. Although algebraic methods can be extended to permit complete minimization, the majority of automatic methods are based on the processing of cubes.

Before looking at the workings of these methods, the 'classical' methods of function minimization, as they apply to PLAs, will be studied. These are methods which attempt to reduce the number of product terms required. As well as being essential background knowledge for any designer, they can be used as manual minimization procedures on small problems. The more advanced algorithms can be divided into two classes: those which are designed for efficient exact minimization of small to medium problems, and those which use heuristics to give an almost optimal solution of medium to large problems in a reasonable time. The majority of PLD minimization problems fall into the first category.

In some cases, there may be a more subtle redundancy built in to the problem definition – some inputs may not be necessary at all. A related set of minimization methods can be applied to the detection of redundant inputs.

For PAL-like devices, without an OR array, minimization is a collection of single-output problems; for PLAs it is a single multiple-output problem. Obviously, the former is a special case of the latter, but there do exist methods specially adapted to the PAL problem.

## 4.2 Systematic methods for exact minimization

### 4.2.1 Tabular method

This method, the **Quine–McCluskey method**, follows exactly the steps given in Section 2.4. It can be operated by hand and is useful for minimization problems too large to be conveniently handled by K maps.

**Table 4.1** List 1.

| | | | | |
|---|---|---|---|---|
| 0d | 0 | 0 | 0 | 0 |
| 1d | 0 | 0 | 0 | 1 |
| 5 | 0 | 1 | 0 | 1√ |
| 10 | 1 | 0 | 1 | 0√ |
| 7d | 0 | 1 | 1 | 1 |
| 11 | 1 | 0 | 1 | 1√ |
| 13d | 1 | 1 | 0 | 1 |
| 14 | 1 | 1 | 1 | 0√ |
| 15 | 1 | 1 | 1 | 1√ |

**Table 4.2** List 2.

| | | | | |
|---|---|---|---|---|
| 0d, 1d | 0 | 0 | 0 | * |
| 1d, 5 | 0 | * | 0 | 1 |
| 5, 7d | 0 | 1 | * | 1√ |
| 5, 13d | * | 1 | 0 | 1√ |
| 10, 11 | 1 | 0 | 1 | *√ |
| 10, 14 | 1 | * | 1 | 0√ |
| 7d, 15 | * | 1 | 1 | 1√ |
| 11, 15 | 1 | * | 1 | 1√ |
| 13d, 15 | 1 | 1 | * | 1√ |
| 14, 15 | 1 | 1 | 1 | *√ |

The first stage is to find all the prime implicants of the function, which must be specified as a list of minterms. For example, let us find the prime implicants of

$$f(x_1, x_2, x_3, x_4) = \sum(5, 10, 11, 14, 15) + d(0, 1, 7, 13)$$

The elements of the on and don't care sets are first partitioned into groups, in which the binary representations each have the same number of 1s. The group with the least number of 1s is placed at the top, followed by groups with increasing numbers of 1s. This is list 1 (Table 4.1).

The decimal minterm names are suffixed with a 'd' if they are members of the don't care set. The vectors in each group are now compared with those of the group below to find pairs which differ in only one bit position. For example 0d and 1d only differ in the last position. These two can be combined to form 000* which can be added to list 2 (Table 4.2). 1d and 5 from the second and third groups can be combined into 0*01 which forms the second group of list 2. Vector 5 is ticked to indicate that it has been combined with another. Vectors with labels which are all suffixed by 'd' are not ticked. All possible combinations are made and list 2 is filled, each time ticking off a 'used' on set vector in list 1. Note that vectors which can be combined have labels which differ by a power of 2.

List 3 (Table 4.3) is formed in a similar manner, except that vectors from list 2 can only be combined if they have an '*' in the same position.

**Table 4.3** List 3.

| | | | | |
|---|---|---|---|---|
| 5, 7d, 13d, 15 | * | 1 | * | 1 |
| 10, 11, 14, 15 | 1 | * | 1 | * |

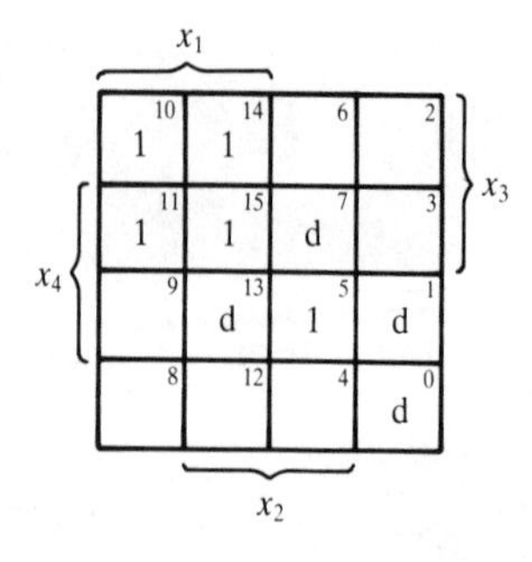


**Figure 4.1** Map of $\sum(5, 10, 11, 14, 15) + d(0, 1, 7, 13)$.

Notice that there are two ways of making each entry in list 3. For example, 10, 11, 14, 15 is the combination of 10, 11 with 14, 15 or 10, 14 with 11, 15. The list 3 vectors cannot be combined, and so the list-forming stage ends. The prime implicants can now be read from the lists. Entries which are not ticked and are not made up entirely of 'd' labels are the prime implicants of the function. In this case they are

1d, 5 5, 7d, 13d, 15 10, 11, 14, 15

or

$\bar{x}_1\bar{x}_3x_4$ $x_2x_4$ $x_1x_3$

The results can be checked on the K map of the function given in Figure 4.1.

The next stage is to find the smallest set of prime implicants which will cover the function. This can be done by setting up the **prime implicant table**. On such a table it is possible to indicate which minterms are covered by which prime implicants. The table for the example is given in Table 4.4.

It can be seen immediately that prime implicant $C$ is essential, as it is the only one which covers minterms 10, 11 and 14. This implicant also

**Table 4.4**

| | *Minterms* | | | | |
|---|---|---|---|---|---|
| *Prime implicants* | 5 | 10 | 11 | 14 | 15 |
| $A = \bar{x}_1\bar{x}_3x_4$ | × | | | | |
| $B = x_2x_4$ | × | | | | × |
| $C = x_1x_3$ | | × | × | × | × |

covers minterm 15, leaving minterm 5 as the only one uncovered. This may be covered by choosing either prime implicant $A$ or $B$, because in PLA minimization there is no need to choose implicants with the minimum number of literals. The minimal sum is therefore either

$$f = \bar{x}_1\bar{x}_3x_4 + x_1x_3$$

or

$$f = x_2x_4 + x_1x_3$$

For larger prime implicant tables, informal methods such as this are not sufficient; a more systematic approach is necessary. The second part of the Quine–McCluskey procedure consists of the following steps.

1. *Select essential rows*

Any column which contains a single '×' defines a row which corresponds to an essential prime implicant. Therefore mark the prime implicant as selected, delete the row, and tick off all minterms covered by this implicant. Also, delete all other '×'s in the columns of these minterms because their cover is now provided by the selected prime implicant. Do this for all essential prime implicants. When no more essential prime implicants can be found, application of the following steps should be attempted.

2. *Eliminate dominated rows*

A **dominated row** is a row which has '×'s in all the positions that another, dominating, row has them. This includes the case where the two rows are identical. Figure 4.2 illustrates such a pattern. The dominated row, C, can be eliminated because prime implicant C covers fewer minterms than A. Therefore A will always be a better choice than C as it covers those covered by C plus one other.

3. *Eliminate dominating columns*

A **dominating column** is a column that has '×'s in all the positions that another, dominated, column has them. This includes the case where the two columns are identical. Figure 4.3 illustrates such a pattern. Column 4 requires that rows A or C be selected, while column 6 requires that rows A, C or E be selected. Whenever column 4 is covered by some row, then

| | | | | | | | |
|---|---|---|---|---|---|---|---|
| A | | × | × | × | × | | × |
| B | × | | × | × | | × | |
| C | | × | | × | | | × |

**Figure 4.2** Row C dominated by row A.

| | | | | | 4 | | 6 | | 8 |
|---|---|---|---|---|---|---|---|---|---|
| A | | × | | | × | | × | | × |
| B | × | × | | × | | | | | |
| C | × | | | | × | × | × | | |
| D | | | × | | | × | | | |
| E | | | × | × | | | × | | |

**Figure 4.3** Column 6 dominates columns 4 and 8.

column 6 will also be covered. Column 6 therefore has no effect on row selection and can be eliminated. Column 4 can also be eliminated since it dominates column 8.

4. *Select secondary essential rows*
After application of steps 2 and 3, there may now be columns with a single '×', the others having been eliminated. The corresponding rows are now **secondary essential rows**. They are only essential because of the particular sequence of reductions applied; other sequences of reduction may give the result that one or more of these rows is not required in the minimal sum.

5. *Repeat steps 2, 3 and 4 in any order*
The reduction process continues until either all '×'s have been eliminated, or until no further reduction is possible. In the former case, the minimal sum has been found and the minimization is complete. In the latter case further steps are necessary.

A table from which no more rows and columns can be eliminated is called **cyclic**. Figure 4.4 is an example of such a table (of course, the column patterns can appear in any order). The so-called **Petrick method** is a solution to this problem. With this it is possible to enumerate all irredundant forms and from these to choose a minimal sum. The Petrick function, or prime implicant function, is a function which only has the value 1 when every column has at least one '×', that is all minterms are covered by at least one prime implicant. For the example of Figure 4.4, the Petrick

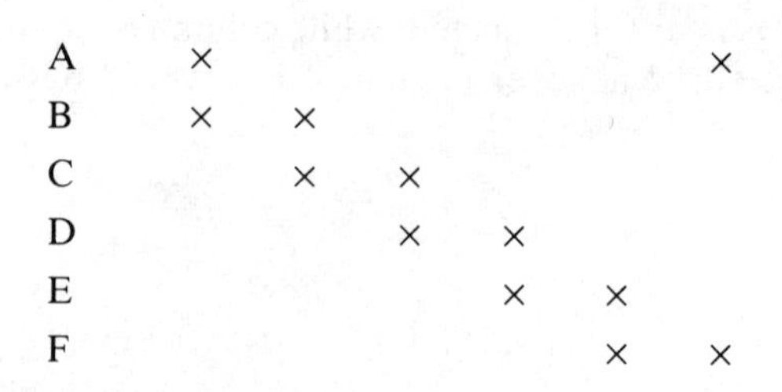

| | | | | | | |
|---|---|---|---|---|---|---|
| A | × | | | | | × |
| B | × | × | | | | |
| C | | × | × | | | |
| D | | | × | × | | |
| E | | | | × | × | |
| F | | | | | × | × |

**Figure 4.4** A cyclic table.

function is

$$p = (A + B)(B + C)(C + D)(D + E)(E + F)(F + A)$$

In words, this is 'all minterms are covered if either A or B is chosen, and either B or C is chosen, and either C or D is chosen, ...'. The right-hand side can be expanded and simplified to yield

$$p = ACE + BDF + ACDF + BCEF + ABDE$$

Each right-hand side term represents a choice of prime implicants. The two which would give minimal sums are A, C, E and B, D, F.

A method more suitable for automation, and which can form the basis of an algorithm, is the **branch-and-bound method**. The procedure is illustrated in Figure 4.5 for the cyclic table of Figure 4.4. At node 1, the choice is first made to delete row A. B and F are now secondary essential, but the reduced table is cyclic again. If the choice is now made at node 3 to delete C, row D is the only option. Thus a covering is B, D and F. If, on the other hand, the choice at node 3 was C, then the table is again cyclic. Thus another choice is necessary at node 6, yielding two solutions, B, C, D and F, and B, C, E and F. The effect of every choice can be explored to yield the full tree shown in the figure. Some of the solutions are not minimal, being included in others. The minimal solutions are underlined – notice that they are the same as those obtained with the Petrick method. Computational efficiency can be increased by **bounding** the search at paths which are not going to yield improved solutions. How this bounding is done is one of the keys to faster minimization algorithms.

The Quine–McCluskey procedure can be applied by hand to problems which have too many variables for K map solution, and which do not have too many minterms. A drawback of the method is that all of the minterms need to be listed. This can result in voluminous tables with many opportunities for human error.

The procedure described is useful for minimizing logic for devices with the PAL structure. For PLAs, an extension to the multiple-output case is necessary.

### 4.2.2 Minimization of multiple-output functions

The problem is to minimize jointly a set of $n$ functions each of $m$ inputs:

$$f_1(x_1, x_2, \ldots, x_m), f_2(x_1, x_2, \ldots, x_m), \ldots, f_n(x_1, x_2, \ldots, x_m)$$

It would be hoped that there will be some products in the implementation which can be shared between two or more of the functions. It is easy to

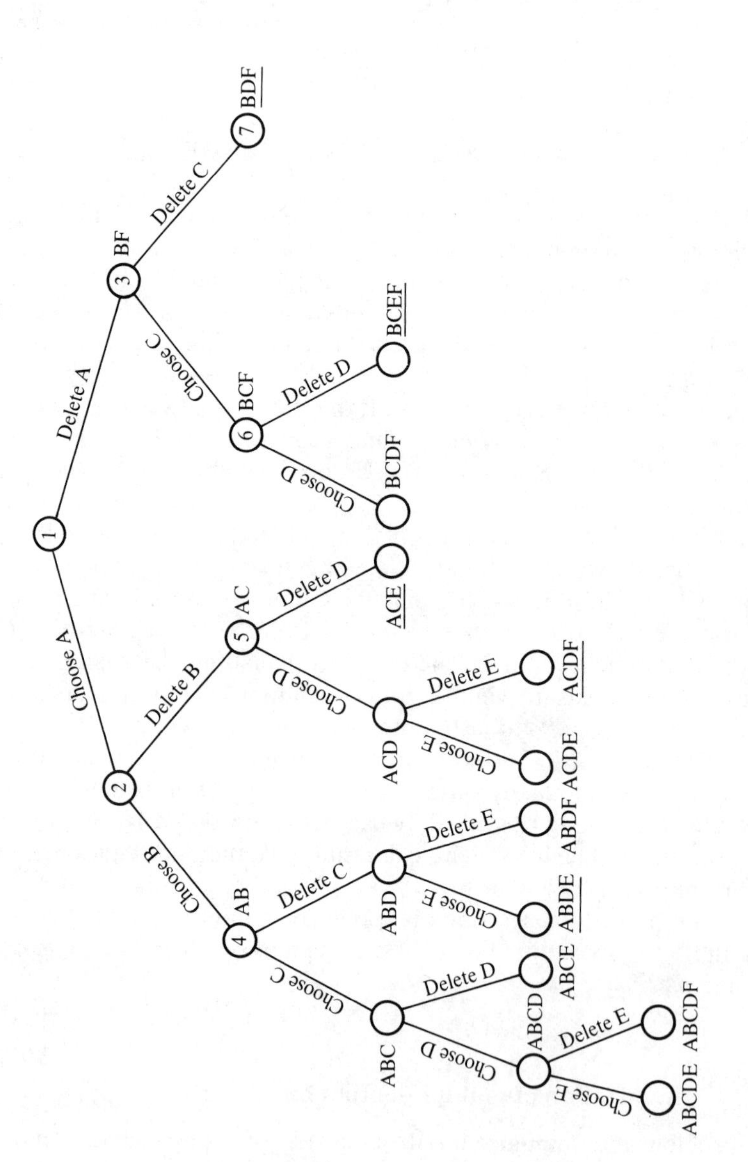


**Figure 4.5** Tree for the solution of the table of Figure 4.4.

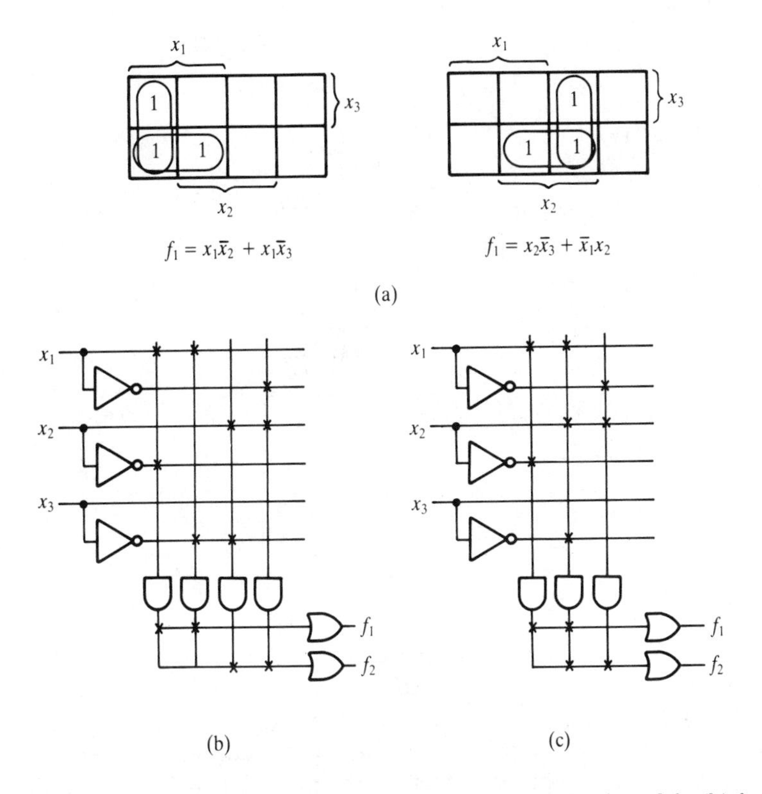


**Figure 4.6** Separate versus joint minimization: (a) maps for $f_1$ and $f_2$; (b) $f_1$ and $f_2$ minimized separately; (c) $f_1$ and $f_2$ minimized jointly.

demonstrate that treating the problem as $n$ single-output problems will not give the best result. For example, Figure 4.6 shows two functions which are first minimized separately; the PLA requires four products. If minimized jointly, the PLA requires only three products. The shared product is $x_1x_2\bar{x}_3$, which is not a prime implicant of $f_1$ or $f_2$. Thus knowledge of more than just the prime implicants of the separate functions is needed for multiple-output minimization.

To investigate what implicants are required for multiple-output minimization, let us look at the general form of a multiple-output function, shown in PLA form in Figure 4.7. If we assume that the implementation is minimal, then all products must correspond to prime implicants. If this were not so, then an input could be removed from a product without causing any change in any of the functions $f_1$–$f_n$. Minimized networks do not have redundant connections. Products feeding to a single output such as $p_1$ or $p_2$ must be prime implicants of their output functions, using the above argument. However, what about products which feed to two or more output functions? Product $p_3$, for example, contributes to both $f_1$ and

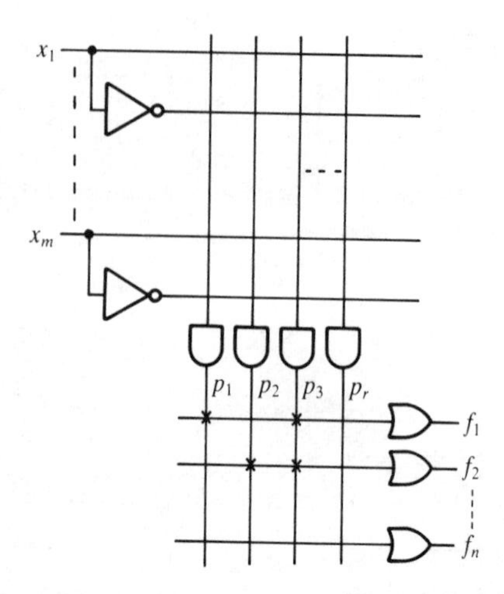


**Figure 4.7** Multiple-output function.

$f_2$. Since it is a prime implicant, then either $f_1$ or $f_2$, or both, must change if an input to $p_3$ is removed. The product, $f_1f_2$, will always change, but not necessarily both $f_1$ and $f_2$. $p_3$ is thus a prime implicant of $f_1f_2$. It is a **multiple-output prime implicant**. A multiple-output prime implicant is not necessarily a prime implicant of any of the individual output functions. For example, $x_1x_2\bar{x}_3$ of Figure 4.6 is a prime implicant of $f_1f_2$ but not of $f_1$ or $f_2$.

Thus, for minimization of $n$ functions, the prime implicants of $f_1$–$f_n$, and the prime implicants of all products of two or more functions must be determined. For $n$ functions, there are $2^n - 1$ of these types of prime implicants. The minimization process will be illustrated by using K maps to minimize the three functions of four variables given in Figure 4.8. (The map variables are omitted for clarity). Below the three basic maps are shown the maps for the function products; these may be derived directly by comparing minterm by minterm the appropriate maps in the line of maps above. All the multiple-output prime implicants are encircled. The problem now is how to choose the smallest set which will cover all three functions. It is obviously advantageous to choose implicants serving the largest number of functions as this allows maximal sharing of products. Thus, the search starts at the bottom of the set of maps. There are two prime implicants of $f_1f_2f_3$, labelled $A$ and $B$. These cover the minterms in the same squares in all the higher maps – these can therefore be changed into 'don't cares' before continuing the search. Moving up now to the map for $f_1f_2$, one more prime implicant is required, labelled $C$. The corresponding squares in the maps for $f_1$ and $f_2$ can now be converted to 'don't cares'. The process continues, with prime implicants $D$, $E$, $F$ and $G$ being selected. $H$ is a prime implicant of $f_3$, but it does not add any new 1s cover.

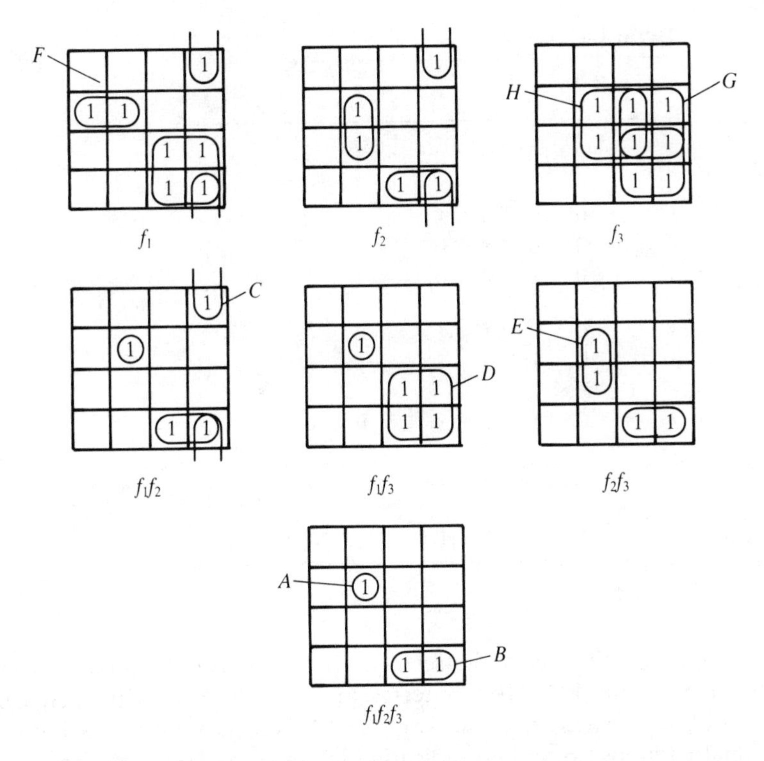


**Figure 4.8** Multiple-output minimization.

Notice that no prime implicants for $f_2$ are required. The minimal sums are thus:

$$f_1 = C + D + F \qquad f_2 = B + C + E \qquad f_3 = B/D + E/H + G$$

Notice that $A$ is not required as its job is done by $F$, $E$ and $H$. There are some choices in the cover of $f_3$. Either $B$ or $D$ can be chosen since they are both required elsewhere, but it does not make sense to choose $H$, as $E$ is already present. With this background, more systematic methods for finding the multiple-output minimal sum can now be examined.

The multiple-output prime implicants can be found by extending the tabular method. Using the same example, the functions to be minimized are

$$f_1 = \sum(0,1,2,4,5,11,15)$$
$$f_2 = \sum(0,2,4,13,15)$$
$$f_3 = \sum(0,1,3,4,5,7,13,15)$$

**Table 4.5** List 1.

| | | | | | $f_1$ | $f_2$ | $f_3$ | | |
|---|---|---|---|---|---|---|---|---|---|
| 0 | 0 | 0 | 0 | 0 | 1 | 1 | 1 | √ | |
| 1 | 0 | 0 | 0 | 1 | 1 | 0 | 1 | √ | |
| 2 | 0 | 0 | 1 | 0 | 1 | 1 | 0 | √ | |
| 4 | 0 | 1 | 0 | 0 | 1 | 1 | 1 | √ | |
| 3 | 0 | 0 | 1 | 1 | 0 | 0 | 1 | √ | |
| 5 | 0 | 1 | 0 | 1 | 1 | 0 | 1 | √ | |
| 7 | 0 | 1 | 1 | 1 | 0 | 0 | 1 | √ | |
| 11 | 1 | 0 | 1 | 1 | 1 | 0 | 0 | √ | |
| 13 | 1 | 1 | 0 | 1 | 0 | 1 | 1 | √ | |
| 15 | 1 | 1 | 1 | 1 | 1 | 1 | 1 | | *A* |

(minterms are labelled as in Figure 4.1). The first part of the table is set up as shown in Table 4.5. The minterms are listed in sets with increasing numbers of 1s in exactly the same way as in the single-output case, but now additional columns are added indicating in which functions the minterms are present. List 2 (Table 4.6) is now created by comparing minterms in

**Table 4.6** List 2.

| | | | | | $f_1$ | $f_2$ | $f_3$ | | |
|---|---|---|---|---|---|---|---|---|---|
| 0, 1 | 0 | 0 | 0 | – | 1 | 0 | 1 | √ | |
| 0, 2 | 0 | 0 | – | 0 | 1 | 1 | 0 | | *C* |
| 0, 4 | 0 | – | 0 | 0 | 1 | 1 | 1 | | *B* |
| 1, 3 | 0 | 0 | – | 1 | 0 | 0 | 1 | √ | |
| 1, 5 | 0 | – | 0 | 1 | 1 | 0 | 1 | √ | |
| 4, 5 | 0 | 1 | 0 | – | 1 | 0 | 1 | √ | |
| 3, 7 | 0 | – | 1 | 1 | 0 | 0 | 1 | √ | |
| 5, 7 | 0 | 1 | – | 1 | 0 | 0 | 1 | √ | |
| 5, 13 | – | 1 | 0 | 1 | 0 | 0 | 1 | √ | |
| 7, 15 | – | 1 | 1 | 1 | 0 | 0 | 1 | √ | |
| 11, 15 | 1 | – | 1 | 1 | 1 | 0 | 0 | | *F* |
| 13, 15 | 1 | 1 | – | 1 | 0 | 1 | 1 | | *E* |

**Table 4.7** List 3.

| | | | | | $f_1$ | $f_2$ | $f_3$ | |
|---|---|---|---|---|---|---|---|---|
| 0, 1, 4, 5 | 0 | – | 0 | – | 1 | 0 | 1 | *D* |
| 1, 3, 5, 7 | 0 | – | – | 1 | 0 | 0 | 1 | *G* |
| 5, 7, 13, 15 | – | 1 | – | 1 | 0 | 0 | 1 | *H* |

adjacent sets of list 1. When a new implicant is created the contents of the function columns are the bitwise ANDs of those of the two minterms. For example, implicant 0, 1 has 111 AND 101 = 101, indicating that this implicant is present in functions $f_1$ and $f_3$. A minterm is only ticked if the function column pattern is the same in one of the implicants formed from it. If the pattern is different, then some cover has been lost for at least one of the functions. Thus minterm 15 is not ticked because the pattern '111' does not appear in any of the implicants, including minterm 15. Any minterm combinations giving '000' in the function column are not valid implicants. For example 2, 3 and 3, 11 are not implicants of any of the functions. List 3 (Table 4.7) is created in the same manner. The unticked lines now correspond to multiple-output prime implicants. These are labelled *A*, *B*, *C*, *D*, *E*, *F*, *G*, *H* and are the same as those found manually in the K maps of Figure 4.8.

Selection of the best set of prime implicants can now proceed. An extended prime implicant table is now set up. There must be columns for

**Table 4.8** Multiple-output prime implicant table.

| | $f_1$ | | | | | | | $f_2$ | | | | | $f_3$ | | | | | | | |
|---|---|---|---|---|---|---|---|---|---|---|---|---|---|---|---|---|---|---|---|---|
| | 0 | 1 | 2 | 4 | 5 | 11 | 15 | 0 | 2 | 4 | 13 | 15 | 0 | 1 | 3 | 4 | 5 | 7 | 13 | 15 |
| A | | | | | | | × | | | | | × | | | | | | | | × |
| B | × | | | × | | | | × | | × | | | × | | | × | | | | |
| C | × | | × | | | | | × | × | | | | | | | | | | | |
| D | × | × | | × | × | | | | | | | | × | × | | × | × | | | |
| E | | | | | | | | | | | × | × | | | | | | | × | × |
| F | | | | | | × | × | | | | | | | | | | | | | |
| G | | | | | | | | | | | | | | × | × | | × | × | | |
| H | | | | | | | | | | | | | | | | | × | × | × | × |

the minterms of each function, which must all be covered, thus some minterms appear in more than one column. Table 4.8 is the multiple-output prime implicant table for our example. This table is treated in exactly the same way as the single-output table. Prime implicants $B$, $C$, $D$, $E$, $F$ and $G$ are essential and in fact provide a complete cover. The solution is thus the same as before. If the table was cyclic, or was reduced to a cyclic table, the methods already mentioned could be applied.

### 4.2.3 Computational problems

Programming the Quine–McCluskey algorithm directly will lead to a program which will execute rapidly for small problems. However, as the number of variables increases, memory usage and computation time will explode. The first part of the procedure requires all the minterms to be known so that they can be combined in every possible way to yield the prime implicants. The number of minterms of an $n$-variable function can be as large as $2^{n-1}$ (the parity function). Thus, for a 20-variable function, there could be up to half a million minterms. Also, the number of prime implicants can increase exponentially. For example, functions are known with numbers of prime implicants proportional to $3^n$. Another relationship known is that, for a function which can be expressed as a sum of $m$ product terms, the number of prime implicants is less than or equal to $2^m - 1$. The second part of the procedure is the covering problem. The general covering problem is currently thought to be **NP-hard**; in other words, the computation time for a solution is an exponential function of the size of the problem. Thus in the worst case, the time is proportional to $\exp[\exp(cm)]$, where $m$ is the number of product terms input and $c$ is a constant.

Hence, even if more efficient algorithms can be found for exact minimization, they will all eventually become impractical. One approach to finding solutions to NP-hard problems is not to insist on an exact solution, but to be satisfied with one which is almost optimal and obtainable in a reasonable time. This type of algorithm is based on heuristics, or rules which can be applied which are likely to improve the solution. A desirable feature of some such algorithms is that, the longer is the time spent on a solution, the better it is. Thus the amount of effort to be expended can be determined in advance.

A number of PLA minimization programs, both approximate and exact, some of which have gained a widespread usage, have been written in the last 15 years. There is not space to give descriptions of all of these, let alone to give full algorithmic details – this would require another book. However, in the following section, brief reviews of the methods used in a few of these programs are given. They have been chosen mainly because of their use in programmable logic design systems.

## 4.3 Some minimizer programs

### 4.3.1 MINI

**MINI** was developed in the early 1970s at IBM. It is the best known of the early heuristic minimizers. Versions of MINI are still in use.

The MINI program starts with a list of multiple-output implicants (cubes) defining the on and don't care sets of a set of functions. The objective is to minimize the number of cubes in the solution without regard to the number of inputs to each product, thus making it suitable for PLA minimization. The final solution is obtained from the initial solution by iterative improvement. The heuristics used are based on those which might be used in minimizing K maps. The minterms of the functions are not generated, and neither are all the prime implicants.

The algorithms are based on the cube description of Boolean functions. This allows covers to be described as lists of cubes; these can be processed according to simple rules to enable operations to be performed between cubes in a bit-by-bit manner. These operations range from the basic operations such as AND, OR and NOT to the more complex such as sharp products (#) which are more easily expressed as cube operations. There is not space here to describe in detail the algorithms used in MINI; only the general ideas are given.

The input cubes are first 'exploded' into a **disjoint cover**, one in which all cubes are mutually disjoint (that is, which contain no common minterms). The reasons for doing this are firstly to reduce any dependency on the way in which the problem is specified, and secondly because it allows more freedom for merging implicants. The explosion process relies on the **disjoint sharp** operation. The disjoint sharp of two cubes $A ⓓ B$ is a set of mutually disjoint cubes which covers $A\overline{B}$. The operation can also be performed between two covers expressed as lists of cubes. If $A = 1$, then $A ⓓ B$ is $\overline{B}$. If now $1 ⓓ \overline{B}$ is calculated, $B$ is available in disjoint form. Figure 4.9(a) shows the map for the implicants of a five-variable function after explosion.

The first process in the minimization cycle is **expansion**. Each implicant is enlarged by merging with others to its maximum size and any covered implicants are removed. Two or more cubes can be merged if a larger cube which is in the cover can be found to replace them. Before expansion, and the operations to follow, the cubes are first put into the 'best' order to maximize the effectiveness of the expansion. The procedure is analogous to circling prime implicants on a K map. The resulting implicants are in near-prime sizes, but some minterms may be covered unnecessarily. Figure 4.9(b) shows the result of expansion.

The second process is **reduction**. Here each implicant is reduced to the smallest possible size while still maintaining coverage of minterms. This operation 'trims' implicants to increase the probability of further merging

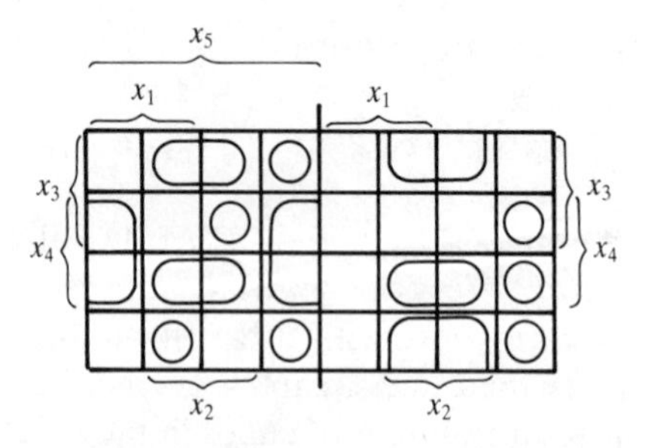


(a) Input function in disjoint form (12 implicants)

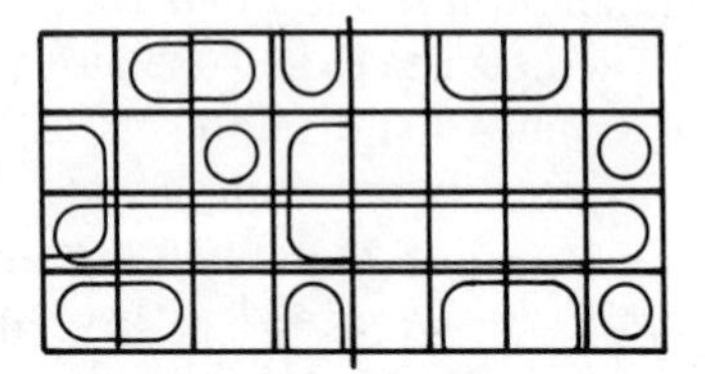

(b) After expansion (9 implicants)

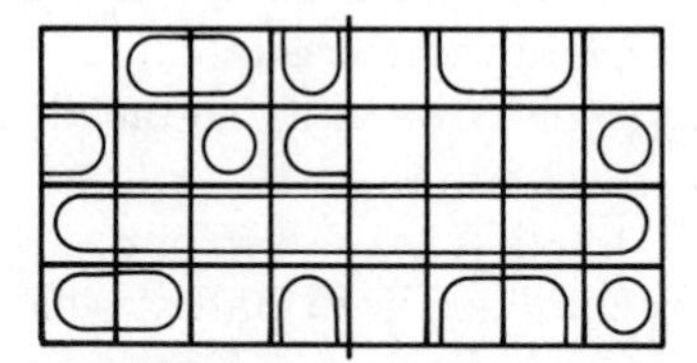

(c) After reduction (9 implicants)

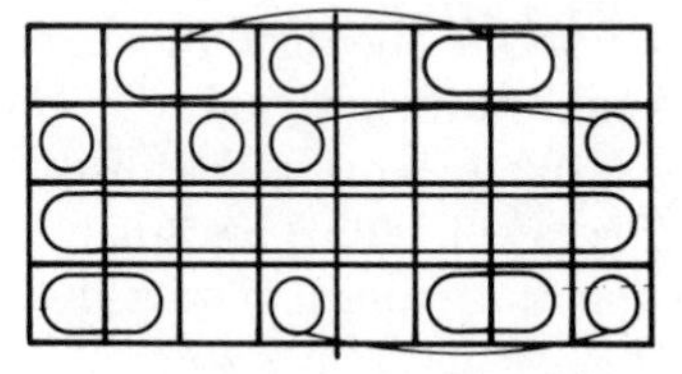

(d) After reshaping (9 implicants)

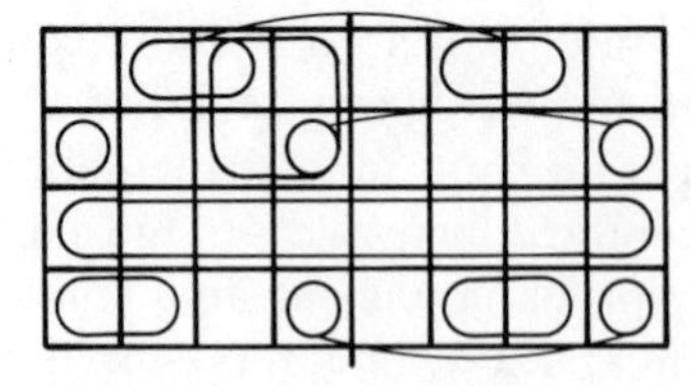

(e) After second expansion (8 implicants)

**Figure 4.9** Minimization of a five-variable function with MINI (from Hang *et al.* (1974))

and eliminates redundant implicants. Figure 4.9(c) shows the result of applying reduction.

The third process is **reshaping**. The procedure is to examine implicants in pairs to see whether they can be reshaped by reducing one and enlarging the other by the same set of minterms. The reshaped implicants are disjoint pairs. Figure 4.9(d) shows the new map. We are now ready for expansion again and the cycle repeats. The program stops when no further reduction is possible. In the example, only one more expansion needs to be applied to yield the result in Figure 4.9(e).

The MINI algorithms are described in terms of multivalued inputs, with Boolean inputs as a special case. The program is thus suitable for minimization of PLAs with partitioned inputs and multibit decoders.

### 4.3.2 PRESTO

**PRESTO** is also an algorithm based on iterative improvement rather than one which first generates prime implicants and then finds a cover for the output functions. It was developed by Svoboda shortly after MINI and has subsequently been improved by others. Because of its simpler nature, PRESTO requires less memory and time than MINI, but may not produce as good a result.

The input to PRESTO is an incompletely specified multiple-output function given as sums of products. Two sets of cubes are formed: *F*, which corresponds to the on set, and *FDC*, which corresponds to the union of the on and don't care sets. PRESTO attempts to minimize *F* by adding minterms from *FDC*. The two main operations are as follows:

(1) Try to expand each implicant in turn by eliminating input variables one by one. If the expanded implicant is still covered by *FDC*, then the literal is permanently removed.

(2) Try to reduce by eliminating each output variable in turn from each implicant. If the output is still covered, then that variable can be removed from the cube. If all the output variables are eliminated, then that implicant can be removed.

These two steps are repeated until there is no further reduction. The original PRESTO did not have a heuristic for choosing the order of product and variable testing, as does MINI. This limits the amount of reduction possible. The test for the function covering a product term can be done by checking all minterms, but this is not a very efficient operation. An improvement adopted in 'extended PRESTO' is to check for covering while progressively splitting implicants into minterm form (divide and conquer). Only in the worst case will a splitting proceed all the way to a minterm. More recent versions of PRESTO are POP and PRESTOL-II.

### 4.3.3 ESPRESSO-II

The ESPRESSO-II heuristic PLA minimizer was developed at IBM and the University of California, Berkeley, as a result of experiments with the MINI and PRESTO algorithms. It has become very widely used through its free distribution within the USA from Berkeley. It is also used in a number of programmable logic CAD packages, and has in fact replaced PRESTO in one of these.

ESPRESSO-II attempts to minimize the number of product terms and the number of connections in both the AND and the OR arrays. For programmable logic devices, with fixed array sizes, the latter minimization is not required. ESPRESSO-II is the best documented of the minimization programs; a book has been written by the developers describing the complete theory.

The main steps of ESPRESSO-II are as follows:

(1) Compute the off set by complementation (this is required in step (2)).

(2) Expand each implicant into a prime and remove those which are covered.

(3) Extract essential prime implicants and put them into the don't care set.

(4) Find the best irredundant cover so far.

(5) Reduce each implicant to a minimum essential implicant. The reduction order is chosen heuristically.

(6) Iterate (2), (4) and (5) until no further improvement is possible.

(7) Try reduction, expansion and irredundant cover once more using a different strategy ('lastgasp').

Procedures (1), (2) and (5) are also present in MINI, but more efficient algorithms are used. These are mainly based on the so-called 'unate recursive paradigm'. A unate function is a form in which only one of the two literals appears for each variable in the sum of products, for example

$$f = x_1\bar{x}_2 + x_1x_3 + \bar{x}_2x_3$$

To perform an operation such as tautology checking, reduction (step (5)) or complementation, the Shannon expansion (as defined in Section 3.4) is used to split the function representation repeatedly until unate cofactors are obtained. Very efficient methods can now be brought into play to perform the operations on the unate representations. Finally, the subresults are merged to form the required result. Heuristics are used to select the splitting variables and for merging.

## 4.4 Elimination of input variables

It may arise that a set of functions will not fit into a PLD because more inputs are specified than there are input pins available. Sometimes it is possible to modify the specification of the function by elimination of **redundant** input variables. Redundant input variables are inputs which can be removed without affecting the output functions. The process of detection and elimination of redundant variables will be illustrated by an example.

Table 4.9 is the truth table for four functions, $f_1$–$f_4$, of six variables $x_1$–$x_6$. The rows of the table have been partitioned into groups which have identical outputs.

It is now necessary to determine all the relations between input variables which distinguish between the partitions. For example, $x_2$, $x_3$ and $x_4$ are different in rows 1 and 4 and therefore can be said to distinguish between these rows, and thus the partitions $I_1$ and $I_2$. It is necessary to find the minimum number of input variables which can distinguish all partitions. The first step is to set up a **redundancy table**. This table has rows defined by the input variables and columns defined by all row pairs from different partitions. A '×' indicates that a row pair can be distinguished by a particular input variable. The redundancy table for our example is shown in Table 4.10.

This is the same type of covering table as the prime implicant table – the input variables are analogous to the prime implicants, and the row pairs to the minterms. The minimum set of the former must be chosen to cover the latter. The same rules can thus be applied for table reduction. In Table 4.10, many dominating columns can be removed; these are indicated with ticks. The reduced table is redrawn as Table 4.11.

The $x_1$ and $x_4$ rows can be eliminated as they are each dominated by two other rows, and column $S_{56}$ can be eliminated as it dominates column

**Table 4.9** Functions with redundant inputs.

| *Partition* | | $x_1$ | $x_2$ | $x_3$ | $x_4$ | $x_5$ | $x_6$ | $f_1$ | $f_2$ | $f_3$ | $f_4$ |
|---|---|---|---|---|---|---|---|---|---|---|---|
| $I_1$ | 1 | 0 | 1 | 0 | 0 | * | 1 | 1 | 0 | 1 | 0 |
| | 2 | 1 | 1 | 0 | 0 | 0 | 0 | 1 | 0 | 1 | 0 |
| | 3 | * | 1 | 0 | 1 | 0 | 1 | 1 | 0 | 1 | 0 |
| $I_2$ | 4 | 0 | 0 | 1 | 1 | * | 1 | 1 | 1 | 0 | 1 |
| | 5 | 1 | 0 | 1 | 1 | 0 | * | 1 | 1 | 0 | 1 |
| $I_3$ | 6 | 1 | 0 | 0 | 0 | 1 | 0 | 1 | 0 | 0 | 0 |
| | 6 | 0 | 1 | 1 | * | 1 | 0 | 1 | 0 | 0 | 0 |

**Table 4.10** Redundancy table.

| | ✓ | ✓ | ✓ | | ✓ | ✓ | | | | ✓ | ✓ | ✓ | ✓ | | | ✓ |
|---|---|---|---|---|---|---|---|---|---|---|---|---|---|---|---|---|
| | $S_{14}$ | $S_{15}$ | $S_{16}$ | $S_{17}$ | $S_{24}$ | $S_{25}$ | $S_{26}$ | $S_{27}$ | $S_{34}$ | $S_{35}$ | $S_{36}$ | $S_{37}$ | $S_{46}$ | $S_{47}$ | $S_{56}$ | $S_{57}$ |
| $x_1$ | | × | × | | × | | | × | | | | | × | | | × |
| $x_2$ | × | × | × | | × | × | × | | × | × | × | | | × | | × |
| $x_3$ | × | × | | × | × | × | | × | × | × | | × | × | | × | |
| $x_4$ | × | × | | | × | × | | | | | × | | × | | × | |
| $x_5$ | | | | | | | × | × | | | × | × | | | × | × |
| $x_6$ | | | × | × | × | | | | | | × | × | × | × | | |

$S_{27}$. Thus $x_1$ and $x_4$ are redundant. The table is now cyclic and can be solved with the aid of the Petrick function. Three solutions are possible: $\{x_2, x_3\}$, $\{x_3, x_5, x_6\}$ and $\{x_2, x_5, x_6\}$. The three reduced truth table input parts are shown in Table 4.12.

The number of product terms is not increased in this case. If there are lines where all outputs are unspecified, then these are not included in one of the partitions. However, in this case, it is possible that the number of products may increase when one or more inputs are removed. This is because the freedom to include parts of the off set in the cover may be reduced.

**Table 4.11** Reduced redundancy table.

| | $S_{17}$ | $S_{26}$ | $S_{27}$ | $S_{34}$ | $S_{47}$ | $S_{56}$ |
|---|---|---|---|---|---|---|
| $x_1$ | | | × | | | |
| $x_2$ | | × | | × | × | |
| $x_3$ | × | | × | × | | × |
| $x_4$ | | | | | | × |
| $x_5$ | | × | × | | × | × |
| $x_6$ | × | | | | | |

**Table 4.12** Reduced truth table input parts.

| | $x_2$ | $x_3$ | $x_3$ | $x_5$ | $x_6$ | $x_2$ | $x_5$ | $x_6$ |
|---|---|---|---|---|---|---|---|---|
| $I_1$ | 1 | 0 | 0 | * | 1 | 1 | * | 1 |
| | 1 | 0 | 0 | 0 | 0 | 1 | 0 | 0 |
| | 1 | 0 | 0 | 0 | 1 | 1 | 0 | 1 |
| $I_2$ | 0 | 1 | 1 | * | 1 | 0 | * | 1 |
| | 0 | 1 | 1 | 0 | * | 0 | 0 | * |
| $I_3$ | 0 | 0 | 0 | 1 | 0 | 0 | 1 | 0 |
| | 1 | 1 | 1 | 1 | 0 | 1 | 1 | 0 |

## SUMMARY

A PLD has a given set of logical resources. Any set of Boolean functions to be fitted into a PLD must not demand more resources than are available. The process of minimization attempts to reduce these resource requirements. Tabular methods, which can handle larger problems than can K maps, can be operated by hand for the exact minimization of both single- and multiple-output functions. Computation problems prevent their use as in computer-aided design programs, and heuristic methods which do not guarantee a minimal solution must be used. These methods generally do not first find all prime implicants and then select the best set, but combine these two steps. Sometimes it is possible to save input pins by detecting logically redundant inputs by application of a tabular procedure.

## BIBLIOGRAPHICAL NOTES

The classical methods for single- and multiple-output minimization are well covered in Muroga (1979), Lewin (1985) and McCluskey (1986). The adaptation of the Quine–McCluskey method for PLAs is shown in Kobylarz and Al-Najjar (1979). The relation for the number of prime implicants expressed as a function of the number of products comes from McMullen and Shearer (1986). Detailed descriptions of the algorithms used in named minimizer programs produced since 1974 may be found in the following: Hong *et al.* (1974) (MINI), Roth (1978, 1980) (SHRINK), Bricaud and Campbell (1978) (EMIN), Brown (1981) (PRESTO), Kang and vanCleemput (1981) (SPAM), Brayton *et al.* (1982) (ESPRESSO-I), Teel and Wilde (1982) (LOGMIN), Sasao (1983) (MINI-II), Martinez-Carballido and Powers (1983) (PRONTO), Brayton *et al.* (1984) (ESPRESSO-II), Poretta *et al.* (1984) (TAU), Biswas (1984) (CAMP), De Micheli *et al.* (1985) (POP), Bartolomeus and De Man (1985) (PRESTOL-II), van Laarhoven *et al.* (1985) (PHI-PLA), Agrawal *et al.* (1985) (MOM), Dagenais *et al.* (1986) (McBOOLE), Biswas and Gurunath (1986) (BANGALORE), Nguyen *et al.* (1987) (PALMINI), Rudell and Sangiovanni-Vincentelli (1987) (ESPRESSO-EXACT), and Wey and Chang (1988) (PLAYGROUND). Other recent papers on PLA minimization include Augin *et al.* (1978), Arevalo and Bredeson (1978), Kambayashi (1979), Li (1980), Grass and Thelen (1981), Gurunath and Biswas (1987), Caruso (1988), Wong and Ismail (1988), Perkins and Rhyne (1988) and Mathony (1989). The example used for input variable elimination is from Li (1980), after correction of errors.

## EXERCISES

**4.1** A five-input, single-output Boolean function is to be designed to detect all prime mumbers up to 31. Minimize the number of products required by applying the tabular procedure.

**4.2** Find all possible minimal forms of

$$f(x_1, x_2, x_3, x_4) = \sum(0, 1, 3, 16, 18, 19) + d(5, 7)$$

using the tabular method. Verify the solutions using a K map.

**4.3** It is required to implement a two-bit adder as a single sum-of-products network in a PLA, with inputs $a_1$, $b_1$, $a_0$, $b_0$, $c_{in}$, and outputs $c_{out}$, $s_1$, $s_0$. How many product terms are required?

**4.4** Can the number of inputs be reduced in the truth table of Table 4.13?

**Table 4.13**

| *Inputs* | | | | | *Outputs* | | |
|---|---|---|---|---|---|---|---|
| 0 | 1 | 0 | * | 0 | 1 | 1 | 1 |
| 0 | 1 | 0 | 0 | 1 | 0 | 1 | 0 |
| * | 0 | 1 | 1 | 1 | 1 | 0 | 0 |
| 1 | * | 0 | 0 | 1 | 0 | 1 | 0 |
| 1 | 0 | 0 | 1 | 0 | 1 | 0 | 0 |
| * | * | 1 | 0 | 0 | 1 | 1 | 1 |

# CHAPTER 5
# Combinational Logic with PLDs

**OBJECTIVES**

When you have completed studying this chapter you should be able

- to recognize when a ROM would be the most suitable PLD for a combinational logic application;
- to decide whether a PLA or a PAL-structured device is the most suitable for a given combinational logic application;
- to extend the number of products available by using extra levels of logic;
- to understand how decomposition of a combinational design problem can enable the use of multiple PLDs where no single one would have sufficient resources;
- to understand the data sheet timing parameters of combinational PLDs;
- to detect the presence of and if possible to cure hazards in combinational PLDs.

## 5.1 Introduction – choosing a part

In this chapter the task of implementing combinational logic in the different types of PLD available will be examined. It will be seen that each type of PLD has characteristics which make it suitable for some applications but not others; in fact there are some PLDs which have been designed with one very specific application in mind. However, even with the most suitable type of part, and minimization, the problem may demand more resources than a single PLD possesses. In this case we have to resort to a method of linking together two or more devices. Together with this we need to determine whether the timing constraints of the design can be met. Thus we must look at how the timing characteristics of PLDs are specified, so that we can estimate the performance of a design. Related to this is the topic of hazards – the underlying cause of output 'glitches'. These need to be understood so that we can predict their occurrence and, if necessary, correct or mask them.

It is often useful to have a measure of the capability of a PLD in terms of the number of simple logic gates it is able to replace. This is especially useful when making comparisons with gate arrays. For this reason manufacturers often quote the 'gate equivalence' of their PLDs. In a final section a critical look at the basis of these calculations will be provided.

## 5.2 ROMs for logic

The ROM is the most universal of all PLDs; an $m$-input, $n$-output ROM can implement any set of functions because every minterm is provided. However, because of this, a ROM is likely to be an inefficient implementation as few functions require such a large array. ROMs (or RAMs, the read/write devices of equivalent structure) are useful in the following situations:

(1) Where the problem is naturally specified in terms of a truth table which maps directly into the 'words' of a ROM, no processing of the specification or minimization is necessary. Also, the function can be modified word by word. This occurs in table look-up applications and microprogrammed controllers. In these cases it would be a positive disadvantage to destroy the structure of the problem by converting it into sums of products.

(2) The logic functions to be implemented require too many products for a PLA-based device. This is frequently the case with arithmetic functions (see Chapter 8).

(3) If a universal, rewriteable logic block is required, the product term demands cannot be predicted, and a RAM is often the only practical solution.

A good example of the first type of application is code conversion, where one binary code must be converted into another. If the output code is defined by a truth table, this directly becomes the specification for the memory contents. Interfaces to external devices often require code conversion of some kind; the internal representation of a signal has to be changed to that demanded by a peripheral, where the code either has been chosen for its special properties (for example, a Gray code, BCD), or is a standard (for example, the ASCII code). ROMs are particularly useful in function generation, where an arbitrary function $f(X)$ of the input (address), $X$, is required. Techniques for doing this will be studied in Chapter 8.

Another name which has been invented for ROMs is **programmable logic element** (PLE). This term is intended to signify the fact that a ROM is a general-purpose logic device, and not just a program or data store. A CAD program designed to speed up the programming of ROMs in this application named PLEASM (PLE assembler) is commercially available. This accepts equations describing Boolean and arithmetic relations between inputs and outputs, and converts them to truth tables for input to a PROM (PLE) programmer.

Memories suitable for logic are available in many different sizes and in various technologies and speed ranges. Propagation delays range from 10–15 ns for the fastest bipolar devices up to ten times this for the fastest of the large MOS devices. PROMs are available in non-erasable (fuse-programmable or 'one-time programmable' EPROM devices) or erasable forms (UV or electrically). Table 5.1 summarizes the range of memory sizes currently manufactured. These range in size from 64 bits ($16 \times 4$) to 1 Mbit ($128K \times 8$). 'Page-addressed' memories, and others intended for program storage and data path applications, are not included.

## 5.3 PLAs for logic

The structure of PLAs was introduced in Chapter 3. In this section their areas of application will be examined.

The general PLA is shown in Figure 3.23. The two-level logic is performed in the AND and OR arrays, where each product can be used in any output function, whose polarity is controllable. The PLA is thus also a universal logic component provided that the number of product terms is sufficient. The advantage over a ROM is that a much smaller array is required for a given number of inputs, since the minterms are not generated. For this reason PLAs are faster than the equivalent ROMs in the lower parts of Table 5.1. The smaller memories have similar speeds to PLAs. In addition, programming of the control array enables any output pin to be used as an input, thus allowing a PLA device to be used in various input/output configurations.

**Table 5.1** Commonly available memory formats.

| *Number of inputs* | *Number of words* | *Number of outputs* | | | |
|---|---|---|---|---|---|
| | | 1 | 4 | 8 | 16 |
| 4 | 16 | | × | | |
| 5 | 32 | | | × | × |
| 6 | 64 | | | | × |
| 7 | 128 | | | × | |
| 8 | 256 | × | × | × | |
| 9 | 512 | | × | × | |
| 10 | 1K | × | × | × | × |
| 11 | 2K | | × | × | × |
| 12 | 4K | × | × | × | × |
| 13 | 8K | | × | × | |
| 14 | 16K | × | × | × | |
| 15 | 32K | | | × | |
| 16 | 64K | × | × | × | × |
| 17 | 128K | | | × | |

There are applications where the number of products required is too great for standard PLAs, even after minimization. Most arithmetic functions fall into this category. On the other hand, there are many cases where a PLA is an 'overkill' and a simpler array could do the job. These reduced arrays will be discussed in the next section, where a PLA logic design example will be given.

By viewing a PLA as a memory with a programmable address decoder, a whole class of applications can easily be understood. These are situations where actions have to be taken when particular input combinations occur. For example, if it is required to 'patch' or overlay certain words in a program memory, a PLA can be used to recognize the addresses or address ranges to be patched and to substitute the new word. Figure 5.1 shows how the PLA is connected. Each line of the program table contains the address or range to be recognized and the word to be substituted, that is

| inputs (AND) | outputs (OR) |
|---|---|
| address | new data |

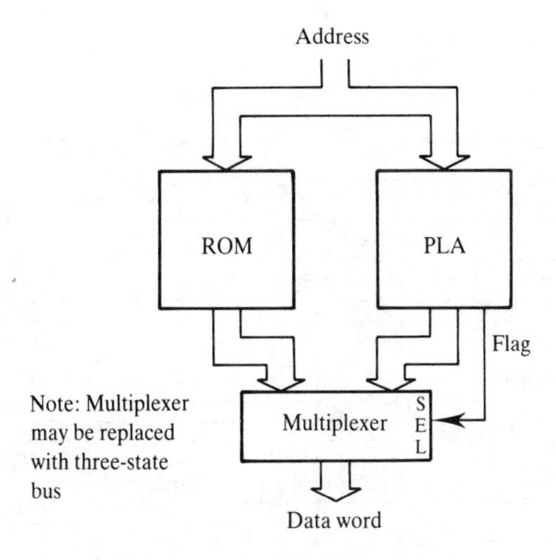


**Figure 5.1** PLA for memory patching.

One output, 'flag', is required to indicate the condition that an address has been recognized. This output is the OR of all products programmed; it will be asserted if any product is true. (A device called a 'field-programmable ROM patch', or FPRP, was once available for this application. The 'flag' output was permanently programmed and controlled the output three-state enable.)

Because of their universality, there is not a large number of PLA types available, and they do not become obsolete as rapidly as more specialized components (in fact, one of the first PLDs introduced, the PLS100 PLA, is still in production). The main developments have been in the manufacturing technology. The earliest field-programmable devices were slow (100 ns) bipolar fuse-programmable components. Their low speed in comparison with standard logic devices made them unattractive for many applications. This is no longer the case; fast CMOS erasable devices and very fast (20 ns) bipolar devices are now available. Table A.1 gives the main parameters of all the (at some time) commercially available PLA devices which have been produced. Figure 5.2 shows a typical PLA, a PLS173 device.

## 5.4 PAL devices for logic

### 5.4.1 Combinational PAL devices and applications

As explained in Chapter 3, a PAL device is a PLA with no OR array. Instead, it has a set of OR gates for combining partitions of the products (the PAL architecture is shown in Figure 3.25). For those applications

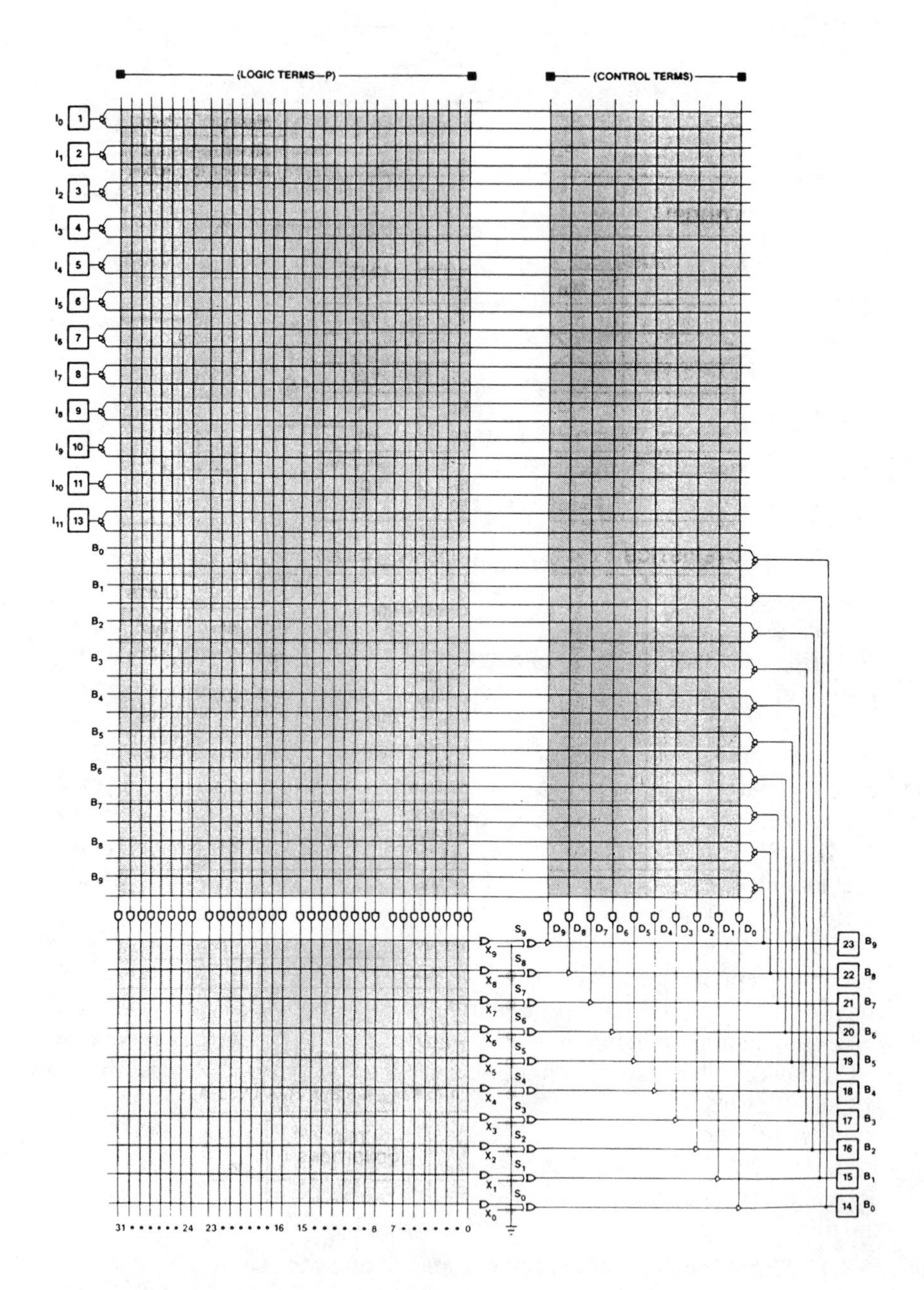


**Figure 5.2** PLS173.

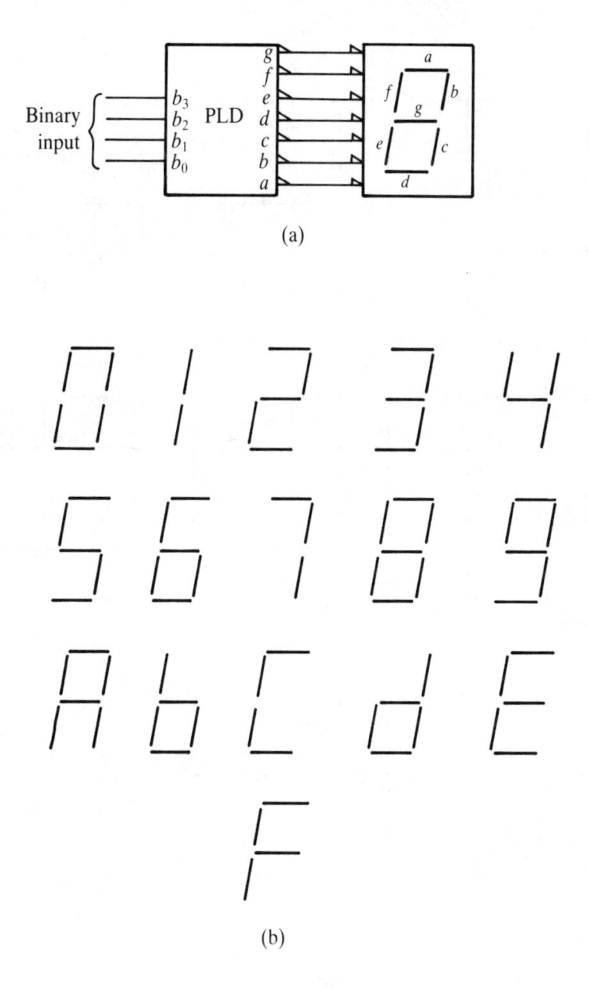


**Figure 5.3** Binary 7-segment decoder: (a) PLD as 7-segment decoder; (b) character formats. (Continues overleaf.)

where the product term sharing capability of the PLA is wasted, the PAL solution will generally be the more economical. It is also likely that the PAL device will have a smaller delay. To illustrate logic design with PALs, an example will be given. This will be followed with a PLA solution, so that the differences between the two types of device can be demonstrated.

The design example is a binary to 7-segment display decoder. Figure 5.3(a) is a block diagram of the problem; the PLD is required to convert a 4-bit binary input into seven signals each driving one of the segments of the display. These signals are of low polarity (power supply connections are not shown). Figure 5.3(b) shows the segment patterns required for each

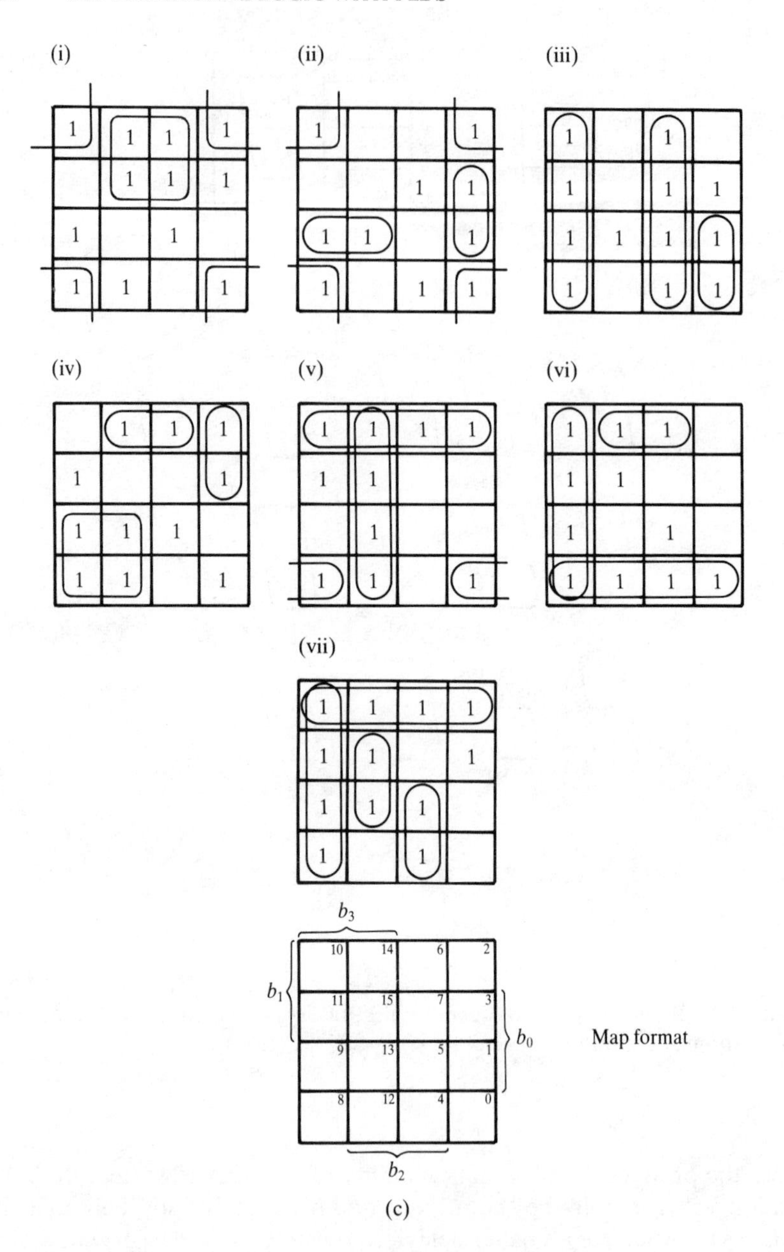


**Figure 5.3** (cont.) Binary 7-segment decoder: (c) K maps for outputs.

hexadecimal digit. From this specification, the truth table for the PLD can be directly produced. This is given in Table 5.2.

For PAL implementation, each of the outputs must be considered separately, since product terms cannot be shared. A K map for each output

**Table 5.2** Truth table for binary to 7-segment decoder.

| Input | | | | Output | | | | | | |
|---|---|---|---|---|---|---|---|---|---|---|
| $b_3$ | $b_2$ | $b_1$ | $b_0$ | $a$ | $b$ | $c$ | $d$ | $e$ | $f$ | $g$ |
| 0 | 0 | 0 | 0 | 1 | 1 | 1 | 1 | 1 | 1 | 0 |
| 0 | 0 | 0 | 1 | 0 | 1 | 1 | 0 | 0 | 0 | 0 |
| 0 | 0 | 1 | 0 | 1 | 1 | 0 | 1 | 1 | 0 | 1 |
| 0 | 0 | 1 | 1 | 1 | 1 | 1 | 1 | 0 | 0 | 1 |
| 0 | 1 | 0 | 0 | 0 | 1 | 1 | 0 | 0 | 1 | 1 |
| 0 | 1 | 0 | 1 | 1 | 0 | 1 | 1 | 0 | 1 | 1 |
| 0 | 1 | 1 | 0 | 1 | 0 | 1 | 1 | 1 | 1 | 1 |
| 0 | 1 | 1 | 1 | 1 | 1 | 1 | 0 | 0 | 0 | 0 |
| 1 | 0 | 0 | 0 | 1 | 1 | 1 | 1 | 1 | 1 | 1 |
| 1 | 0 | 0 | 1 | 1 | 1 | 1 | 1 | 0 | 1 | 1 |
| 1 | 0 | 1 | 0 | 1 | 1 | 1 | 0 | 1 | 1 | 1 |
| 1 | 0 | 1 | 1 | 0 | 0 | 1 | 1 | 1 | 1 | 1 |
| 1 | 1 | 0 | 0 | 1 | 0 | 0 | 1 | 1 | 1 | 0 |
| 1 | 1 | 0 | 1 | 0 | 1 | 1 | 1 | 1 | 0 | 1 |
| 1 | 1 | 1 | 0 | 1 | 0 | 0 | 1 | 1 | 1 | 1 |
| 1 | 1 | 1 | 1 | 1 | 0 | 0 | 0 | 1 | 1 | 1 |

function can thus be constructed as a first stage in finding the smallest number of products for each output function. (This is practical since in this design there are only four input variables.) The maps are given in Figure 5.3(c). Essential prime implicants larger than minterms have been encircled. There is no reason to attempt to cover the remaining minterms with larger terms, since this serves only to reduce the number of literals, which is of no benefit in PAL (or PLA) design. The number of products required for each output is thus as follows:

$$a, 6;\ b, 5;\ c, 5;\ d, 6;\ e, 4;\ f, 5;\ g, 5\ (\text{total}, 36)$$

Thus a PAL device with at least six products per output is required. Also, it should have low output polarity. Referring to Table A.2, where the small PAL devices are listed, the following devices could meet these requirements (obsolete devices excluded):

16L8 16LD8 16P8 18P8 EPL16P8

It is possible to produce a design requiring fewer products by generating the complement of each function and using a PAL device with high output polarity. That fewer products are needed is likely because the maps contain more 1s than 0s. In fact, the numbers of products required are

$$\bar{a}, 4;\ \bar{b}, 4;\ \bar{c}, 3;\ \bar{d}, 4;\ \bar{e}, 3;\ \bar{f}, 4;\ \bar{g}, 3\ (\text{total}, 25)$$

For this solution, a PLD with at least four products per output and high polarity is required. The following devices are suitable candidates:

16H8 16HD8 16P8 18P8 EPL10P8 EPL16P8

The architecture chosen (and the speed–power option and/or technology) will depend on factors such as cost, power consumption and company preference. In this application, speed is unlikely to be a factor. Some of the 24-pin PAL devices listed in Table A.3 would also meet the functional requirements, but would not be utilized efficiently.

The design will now be repeated, but using a PLA. In fact, the design already exists, because the truth table of Table 5.2 can be used directly as a PLA pattern. 16 products are required if high output polarities are chosen, but only 15 if low polarities are chosen. The reason for this reduction is that the outputs for character '8' are all 1s; with low polarity, no product is required to be active to generate this pattern. So, even without minimization, many fewer products are required than with either PAL solution. A suitable PLA can be selected from Table A.1.

This problem is one that easily fits into a PAL device, but is obviously of the type more suited to a PLA. A larger design of this type may exceed the product term capability of a PAL device, but still easily fit into a PLA. Problems which are best suited for PAL implementation are those with little potential for shared products. These appear most often in the less 'random' parts of a digital system, especially in parallel data paths. An extension to the decoder design will be given in Section 5.5.

Tables A.2 and A.3 list about 50 different combinational PAL architectures. Why are so many required? The reasons are historical. The first PAL devices had no bidirectional pins (and therefore a fixed number of inputs and outputs), fixed output polarities, and a limited total number of product terms. To serve many applications, therefore, a set of devices was required. With improvements in technology, it became possible to manufacture more flexible devices which were 'supersets' of the simpler components. For example, the 16L8 device can be configured to replace the fixed configuration 10L8, 12L6 and 14L4 devices. With programmable polarity, even fewer devices are needed. For example, the 18P8 (shown in Figure 5.4) can replace all devices above it except the 16C1; it could be termed a 'generic' device. The EPL devices, which have programmable output cells, as shown in Figures A.1 and A.2, can replace all the devices in Table A.2 and in addition realize functions impossible with any other device. There are still reasons for using the simpler devices, however; they

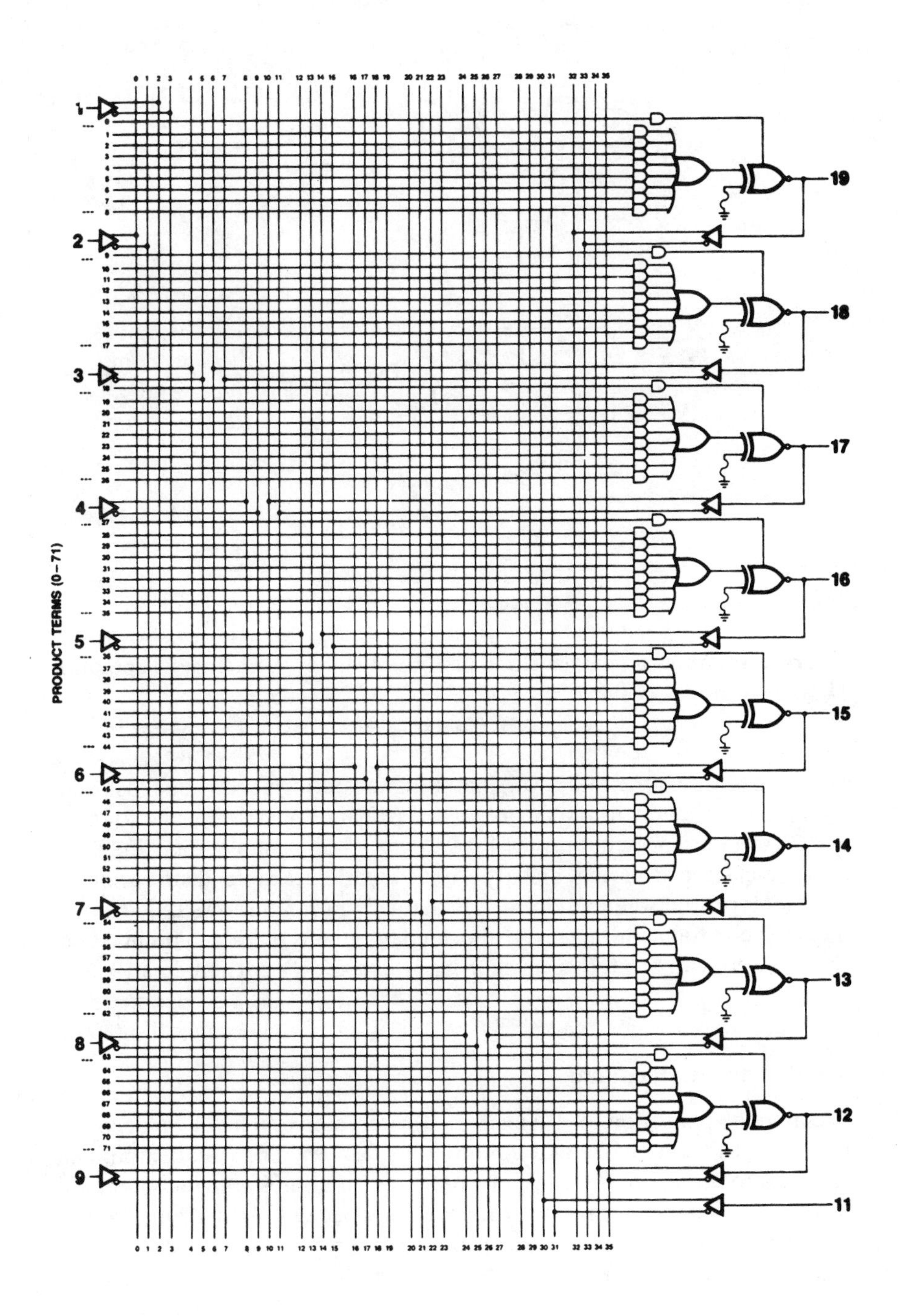


**Figure 5.4** 18P8.

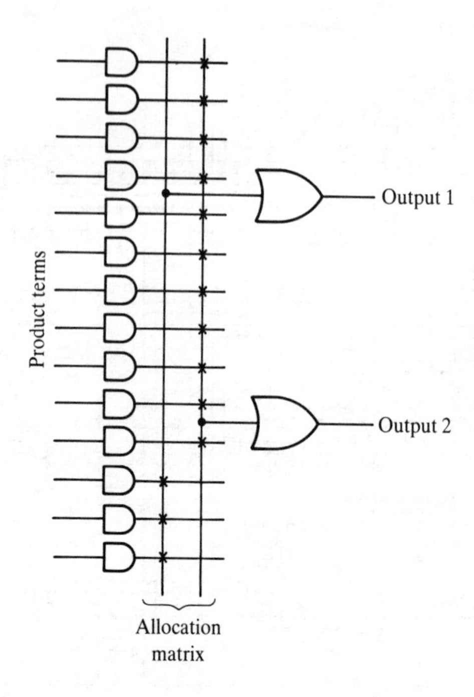


**Figure 5.5** Product term steering in PAL steering (3 products→output 1, 11 products→output 2).

are generally cheaper and available in higher performance versions. Similar arguments apply to the devices listed in Table A.3.

A feature present in some PAL devices (for example, 16SP8, 20S10) is **product term steering**. This permits a more flexible distribution of product terms between adjacent OR gates. Figure 5.5 shows the arrangement. Each product term can be allocated to either OR gate. This must not be confused with product term sharing, which is only possible in a PLA.

### 5.4.2 Address decoding

A common application for PALs in microcomputer systems is the decoding of addresses for memory and input/output devices. The decoders may be required to recognize either single addresses or address ranges. To recognize a single address, only one product term is needed. A single term is also adequate for decoding some ranges, as may be seen from Table 5.3 (for example, a range of length 2 starting at an address ending in 0, or a range of length 4 starting at an address ending in 00, etc.). A number of simple PLDs have been produced specifically for this application, and are listed in Table A.4. These devices (with the exception of one which is obsolete)

**Table 5.3** Number of products required for decoding address ranges.

| *Length of range* | *Starting address* | *Number of products* |
|---|---|---|
| 1 | All | 1 |
| 2 | ..0 | 1 |
| | ..1 | 2 |
| 3 | All | 2 |
| 4 | ..00 | 1 |
| | ..10 | 2 |
| | ...1 | 3 |
| 5 | ..00, ..11 | 2 |
| | ..01, ..10 | 3 |
| 6 | ..00, ..10 | 2 |
| | ..11, .001 | 3 |
| | ..101 | 4 |
| 7 | All | 3 |
| 8 | ..000 | 1 |
| | ..100 | 2 |
| | ...10 | 3 |
| | ....1 | 4 |
| 9 | ..000, ..111 | 2 |
| | ..011, ..100 | 3 |
| | ...01, ...10 | 4 |
| 10 | ..000, ..110 | 2 |
| | .010, .100, .111 | 3 |
| | .011, .0001, .0101 | 4 |
| | .1001, .1101 | 5 |
| 11 | .000, .101, .110, .111 | 3 |
| | .001, .010, .011, .100 | 4 |
| 12 | ..000, ..100 | 2 |
| | ..010, ..110 | 3 |
| | .101, .111, .0001, 0011 | 4 |
| | .1001, .1011 | 5 |
| 13 | ...00, ...11 | 3 |
| | .101, .110, .0001, .0010 | 4 |
| | .1001, .1010 | 5 |

**Table 5.3** (cont.) Number of products required for decoding address ranges.

| *Length of range* | *Starting address* | *Number of products* |
|---|---|---|
| 14 | ...00, ...10 | 3 |
| | ...11 | 4 |
| | ..101, .0001 | 5 |
| | .1001 | 6 |
| 15 | All | 4 |
| 16 | .0000 | 1 |
| | .1000 | 2 |
| | ..100 | 3 |
| | ...10 | 4 |
| | ....1 | 5 |

have single products which feed directly to outputs. For the decoding of ranges which require more than a single product, one of the PAL devices listed in Table A.2 or A.3 should be used.

## 5.5 Multilevel logic

The vast majority of PLDs are inherently two-level logic devices, and are best used in this way. However, it is sometimes necessary to use more than two levels within a single device to overcome resource limitations, but at the cost of additional delay. Figure 5.6 shows how a sum of products can be expanded by using an extra pair of levels. Here two four-product units have been cascaded to produce a seven-product unit. This type of connection is only possible with PAL-type devices; indeed, it would never be

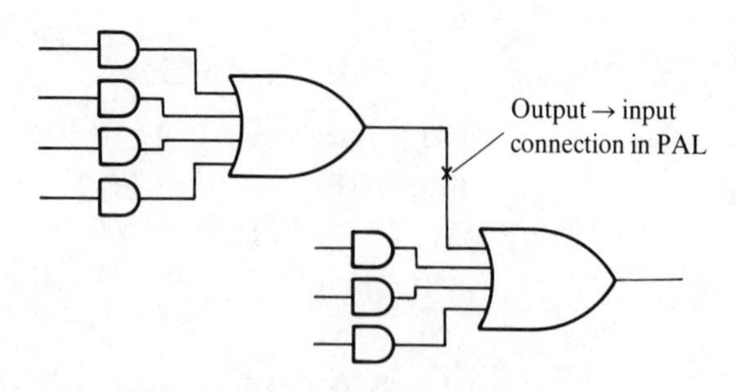


**Figure 5.6** Product term expansion.

**Table 5.4** Truth table for BCD to 7-segment decoder.

| Input | | | | *a* | *b* | *c* | *d* | *e* | *f* | *g* | |
|---|---|---|---|---|---|---|---|---|---|---|---|
| 0 | 0 | 0 | 0 | 1 | 1 | 1 | 1 | 1 | 1 | 0 | |
| 0 | 0 | 0 | 1 | 0 | 1 | 1 | 0 | 0 | 0 | 0 | |
| 0 | 0 | 1 | 0 | 1 | 1 | 0 | 1 | 1 | 0 | 1 | |
| 0 | 0 | 1 | 1 | 1 | 1 | 1 | 1 | 0 | 0 | 1 | |
| 0 | 1 | 0 | 0 | 0 | 1 | 1 | 0 | 0 | 1 | 1 | |
| 0 | 1 | 0 | 1 | 1 | 0 | 1 | 1 | 0 | 1 | 1 | |
| 0 | 1 | 1 | 0 | 1 | 0 | 1 | 1 | 1 | 1 | 1 | |
| 0 | 1 | 1 | 1 | 1 | 1 | 1 | 0 | 0 | 0 | 0 | |
| 1 | 0 | 0 | 0 | 1 | 1 | 1 | 1 | 1 | 1 | 1 | |
| 1 | 0 | 0 | 1 | 1 | 1 | 1 | 1 | 0 | 1 | 1 | |
| 1 | 0 | 1 | 0 | 1 | 0 | 0 | 1 | 1 | 1 | 1 | Display 'E' |
| 1 | 0 | 1 | 1 | 1 | 0 | 0 | 1 | 1 | 1 | 1 | Display 'E' |
| 1 | 1 | 0 | 0 | 1 | 0 | 0 | 1 | 1 | 1 | 1 | Display 'E' |
| 1 | 1 | 0 | 1 | 1 | 0 | 0 | 1 | 1 | 1 | 1 | Display 'E' |
| 1 | 1 | 1 | 0 | 1 | 0 | 0 | 1 | 1 | 1 | 1 | Display 'E' |
| 1 | 1 | 1 | 1 | 1 | 0 | 0 | 1 | 1 | 1 | 1 | Display 'E' |

necessary in a PLA, since all products are available to all outputs. The cost of doing this is a doubled propagation delay and the wasting of two pins (one output and one input), except in two special cases:

(1) 'folded' PLDs (see Section 3.3), and
(2) PLDs whose output cells allow internal feedback as well as an external input to the associated pin (see Table A.7).

The 7-segment decoder design of Section 5.4.1 will now be extended to illustrate the usefulness of multilevel logic. The design will be adapted to perform BCD to 7-segment decoding. The truth table for the new function is given in Table 5.4.

The difference between this table and Table 5.2 is that, for inputs greater than 9, 'E' for 'error' must be displayed. The seven functions could be processed in the same manner as before for PAL or PLA implementation. However, when using a PLA, the number of products may be reduced by using the property of the truth table that 'E' is the output only if none of the others is produced. So, if this condition can be recognized, one product rather than six may be used to generate the 'E' output. Figure 5.7 shows how this is done. An extra OR term is connected to the products

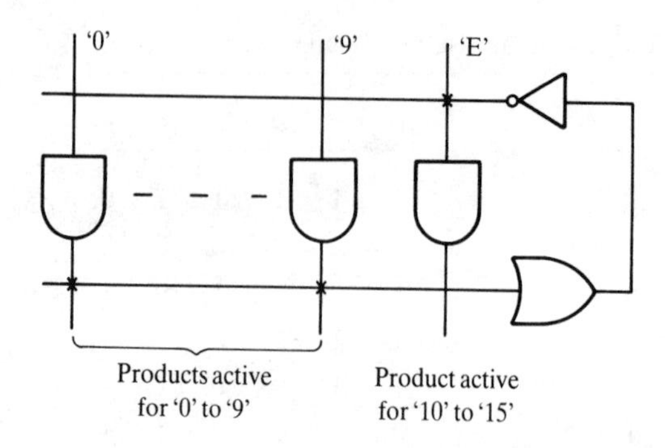


**Figure 5.7** Feedback term for exception detection.

which detect '0'–'9'; if none of these is asserted, then this term will have a '0' output. This can now be negated and fed back to activate a single product term connected into the OR array in such a way that the segments lit give the 'E' pattern. Using an OR term in this way to detect exceptions is often useful, especially in sequential circuit design. In fact, as will be seen in the next chapter, some sequential PLAs have this loop built in. Again, the cost of using it is an additional delay, although in this example it is of no consequence.

Many arithmetic functions can *only* be implemented economically (that is, with a reasonable number of products) with multilevel logic. The parity function is a good example of this. This function generates a true output when an odd number of inputs are true. The complement of the function generates a true output when an even number of inputs are true. The K map for such a function (of any number of variables) has a 'checker-board' pattern – one which has a 1 in every other square. A map like this cannot be minimized since there are no adjacent minterms. The number of minterms in an $n$-input parity function is $2^n/2$.

Parity functions can be decomposed into a multilevel tree of smaller parity functions. This decomposition can continue until the smallest parity function – the exclusive OR gate – is reached. This property is used to enable the larger parity functions to be implemented in PLAs. For example, a nine-input parity function requires 256 minterms – the only element which could implement this directly is a memory, but the function can be decomposed into a tree of three-input parity functions, as shown in Figure 5.8. Each three-input parity function requires four products. Thus, feeding back the intermediate variables enables this function to be realized in a PLA with 12 inputs, 4 outputs and 16 products, at a cost of 2 delays. In Chapter 8 it will be shown that there are other ways of realizing this type of function with specialized PLDs.

The 'folded' array of Figure 3.27 is able to implement multilevel logic directly. The fixed internal feedback paths prevent the wastage of

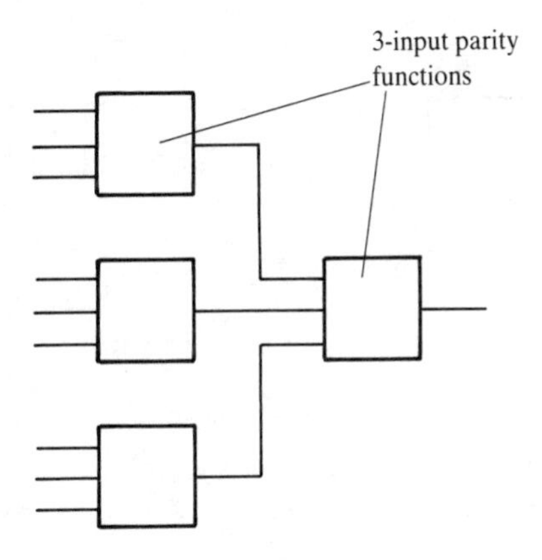


**Figure 5.8** Decomposition of nine-input parity function.

pins and reduce delay since these feedback signals do not have to pass through input and output buffers. This type of device is particularly suitable for integrating combinational logic which is designed in clusters of a few gates, some of which may have local feedback and be interconnected by signals which are not required externally. This style of design is often seen in the 'glue logic' surrounding microprocessor devices and their peripherals. The multilevel PLDs available are listed in Table A.9.

## 5.6 Using multiple devices

### 5.6.1 Decomposition

It is sometimes the case that a set of combinational functions cannot be made to fit into any single PLD. The only solution is to **decompose** the problem in such a way that the requirement can be met by a network of two or more PLDs each implementing a part of the problem. Decomposition is a large topic in its own right – here we will only look at the basic ideas and then at some practical techniques for use with PLDs.

The general problem is shown in Figure 5.9. The set of functions to be implemented requires a logic block with $M$ inputs, $N$ outputs and $R$ product terms. The design task is to design a network which will perform this task using PLDs with a maximum of $m$ inputs, $n$ outputs and $r$ products, where at least one of the following is true:

$$m < M, n < N, r < R$$

The classical methods of decomposing a function are shown in Figure 5.10. These are all 'disjunctive' forms, in which the inputs are

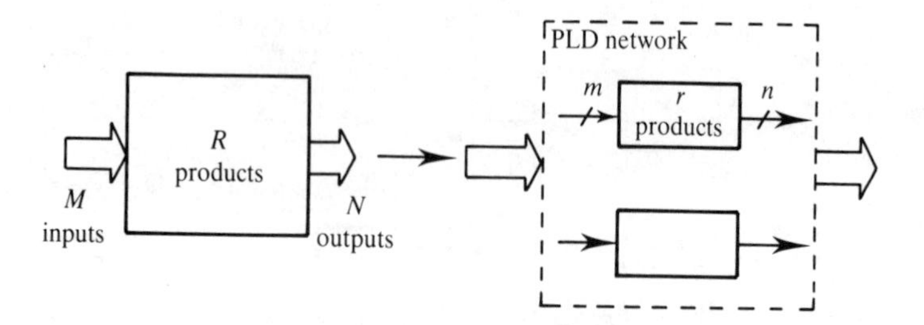


**Figure 5.9** The decomposition problem.

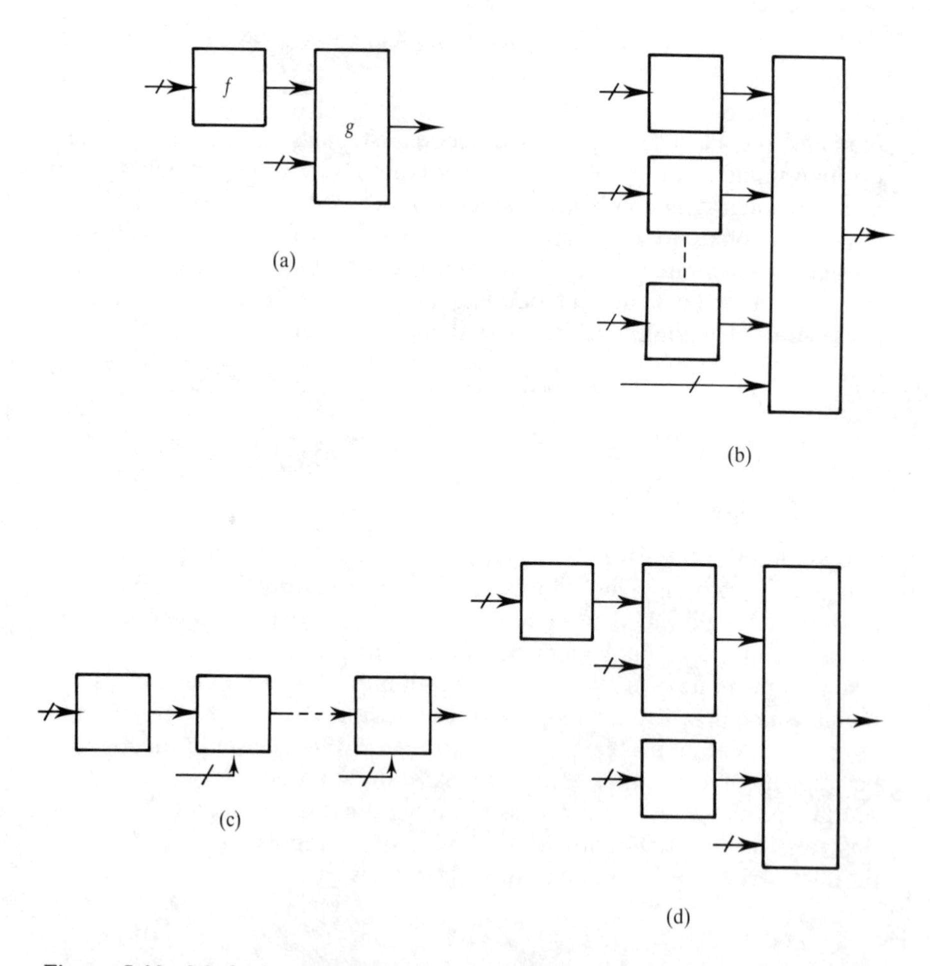


**Figure 5.10** Methods of decomposition: (a) simple disjunctive decomposition; (b) multiple disjunctive decomposition; (c) iterative disjunctive decomposition; (d) complex disjunctive decomposition.

partitioned into disjoint sets, in other words there is no sharing of inputs between blocks (non-disjunctive forms allow an input to be fed to more than one block). Many methods have been devised for developing such decompositions where one is possible. However, for multiple output functions and PLA blocks (which themselves have multiple outputs, in general), most of these are of little practical use. With the increasing interest in the synthesis of multilevel logic in VLSI design, there is a renewed interest in decomposition, and some efficient algorithms applicable to larger problems are appearing. Here some simple decomposition methods useful for PLA networks will be presented.

### 5.6.2 Product term expansion

It is sometimes the case that a PLD has enough input and output pins but too few products for the problem. In a PAL device, if only a few outputs have this problem, and there are spare input and output pins, then the solution of Figure 5.6 can be adopted. For open-collector output PLAs (now less common, unfortunately) the connection shown in Figure 5.11 can be used. Here each output requires more products than can be provided by a single PLA. Simple wired-OR connection of output pins achieves the expansion. For the wired-OR to work, all output polarities must be low, and of course external pull-up resistors must be used.

Product term expansion is not so straightforward when three-state PLAs (the more common kind) are used, because outputs on different devices cannot now drive simultaneously. A method which may occasionally be useful is shown in the following example. The problem is to

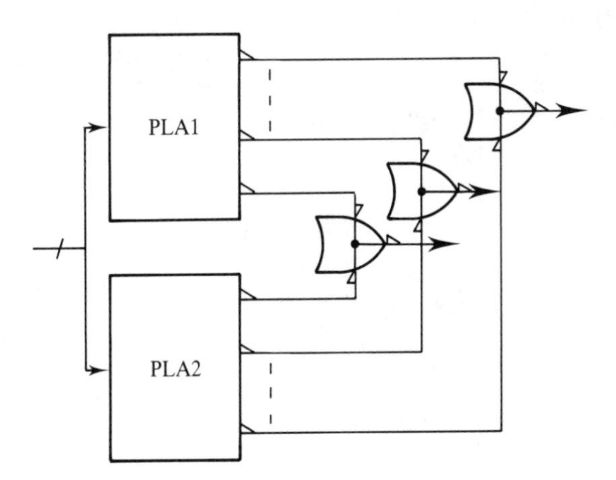


**Figure 5.11** Product term expansion with open-collector PLAs (pull-up resistors not shown).

**Table 5.5** A squaring function.

| *Input* | | | | *Output* | | | | | | | | *Product* |
|---|---|---|---|---|---|---|---|---|---|---|---|---|
| $I_3$ | $I_2$ | $I_1$ | $I_0$ | $F_7$ | $F_6$ | $F_5$ | $F_4$ | $F_3$ | $F_2$ | $F_1$ | $F_0$ | *number* |
| * | * | * | 1 | 0 | 0 | 0 | 0 | 0 | 0 | 0 | 1 | 0 |
| * | * | 1 | 0 | 0 | 0 | 0 | 0 | 0 | 1 | 0 | 0 | 1 |
| * | 1 | 0 | 1 | 0 | 0 | 0 | 0 | 1 | 0 | 0 | 0 | 2 |
| * | 0 | 1 | 1 | 0 | 0 | 0 | 0 | 1 | 0 | 0 | 0 | 3 |
| * | 1 | 0 | 0 | 0 | 0 | 0 | 1 | 0 | 0 | 0 | 0 | 4 |
| 0 | 1 | * | 1 | 0 | 0 | 0 | 1 | 0 | 0 | 0 | 0 | 5 |
| 1 | 0 | * | 1 | 0 | 0 | 0 | 1 | 0 | 0 | 0 | 0 | 6 |
| 1 | 0 | 1 | * | 0 | 0 | 1 | 0 | 0 | 0 | 0 | 0 | 7 |
| 1 | 1 | * | 1 | 0 | 0 | 1 | 0 | 0 | 0 | 0 | 0 | 8 |
| 0 | 1 | 1 | * | 0 | 0 | 1 | 0 | 0 | 0 | 0 | 0 | 9 |
| 1 | 0 | * | * | 0 | 1 | 0 | 0 | 0 | 0 | 0 | 0 | 10 |
| 1 | * | 1 | * | 0 | 1 | 0 | 0 | 0 | 0 | 0 | 0 | 11 |
| 1 | 1 | * | * | 1 | 0 | 0 | 0 | 0 | 0 | 0 | 0 | 12 |

implement Table 5.5 (in which the output is the square of the input) in two PLAs with only ten product terms. Minimization has been performed, which accounts for the 'don't cares' in the input part. There are 13 product terms.

The approach is to segment the table by choosing an input variable which is 0 in one subtable and 1 in the other. Products including this variable are divided into two disjoint sets; it is impossible for products in both sets to be active simultaneously. For a product in which the segmenting variable is 'don't care', a copy must be put into each set. The sets can be selected by driving the PLA 'chip enable' pins by the segmenting variable and its complement. The connection is shown in Figure 5.12. By choosing

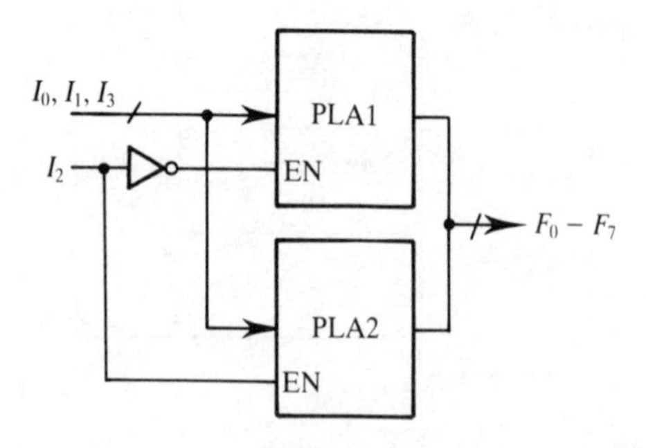


**Figure 5.12** Product term expansion with three-state PLAs.

**Table 5.6** Squaring function – first subtable.

| *Input* | | | | *Output* | | | | | | | | *Product* |
|---|---|---|---|---|---|---|---|---|---|---|---|---|
| $I_3$ | $I_2$ | $I_1$ | $I_0$ | $F_7$ | $F_6$ | $F_5$ | $F_4$ | $F_3$ | $F_2$ | $F_1$ | $F_0$ | *number* |
| * | 0 | * | 1 | 0 | 0 | 0 | 0 | 0 | 0 | 0 | 1 | 0r |
| * | 0 | 1 | 0 | 0 | 0 | 0 | 0 | 0 | 1 | 0 | 0 | 1r |
| * | 0 | 1 | 1 | 0 | 0 | 0 | 0 | 1 | 0 | 0 | 0 | 3 |
| 1 | 0 | * | 1 | 0 | 0 | 0 | 1 | 0 | 0 | 0 | 0 | 6 |
| 1 | 0 | 1 | * | 0 | 0 | 1 | 0 | 0 | 0 | 0 | 0 | 7 |
| 1 | 0 | * | * | 0 | 1 | 0 | 0 | 0 | 0 | 0 | 0 | 10 |
| 1 | 0 | 1 | * | 0 | 1 | 0 | 0 | 0 | 0 | 0 | 0 | 11r |

**Table 5.7** Squaring function – second subtable.

| *Input* | | | | *Output* | | | | | | | | *Product* |
|---|---|---|---|---|---|---|---|---|---|---|---|---|
| $I_3$ | $I_2$ | $I_1$ | $I_0$ | $F_7$ | $F_6$ | $F_5$ | $F_4$ | $F_3$ | $F_2$ | $F_1$ | $F_0$ | *number* |
| * | 1 | * | 1 | 0 | 0 | 0 | 0 | 0 | 0 | 0 | 1 | 0r |
| * | 1 | 1 | 0 | 0 | 0 | 0 | 0 | 0 | 1 | 0 | 0 | 1r |
| * | 1 | 0 | 1 | 0 | 0 | 0 | 0 | 1 | 0 | 0 | 0 | 2 |
| * | 1 | 0 | 0 | 0 | 0 | 0 | 1 | 0 | 0 | 0 | 0 | 4 |
| 0 | 1 | * | 1 | 0 | 0 | 0 | 1 | 0 | 0 | 0 | 0 | 5 |
| 1 | 1 | * | 1 | 0 | 0 | 1 | 0 | 0 | 0 | 0 | 0 | 8 |
| 0 | 1 | 1 | * | 0 | 0 | 1 | 0 | 0 | 0 | 0 | 0 | 9 |
| 1 | 1 | 1 | * | 0 | 1 | 0 | 0 | 0 | 0 | 0 | 0 | 11r |
| 1 | 1 | * | * | 1 | 0 | 0 | 0 | 0 | 0 | 0 | 0 | 12 |

input $I_2$, Tables 5.6 and 5.7 result. Each has fewer than ten products. Notice the repeated terms, labelled 'r' in each table. Obviously, it is sensible to choose a segmenting variable with as few 'don't care' entries in its column as possible, to minimize the number of repeated product terms.

This method can be extended by choosing two or more segmenting variables and decoding these to derive the enable signals.

### 5.6.3 Input expansion

The problem here is that the set of functions to be implemented requires a PLD with more input pins than are available. One solution is identical to the last solution mentioned in the previous section – a subset of input

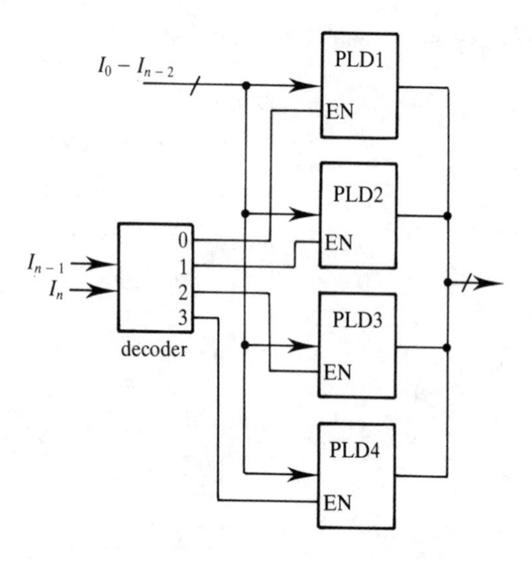


**Figure 5.13** Input expansion using decoder.

variables is removed and fed instead to a decoder which generates enable signals for parallel PLDs. A four-PLD system is shown in Figure 5.13. This method is most often seen for memory expansion, where the requirement is to expand the address space of a memory bank while retaining the word size. Because there cannot be any shared product terms in this latter case (memories generate minterms) partitioning the truth table is straightforward. An alternative way of performing this type of expansion is to use the segmenting variables to control an output multiplexer instead of a decoder, but this is likely to be a more expensive option. (Compare this paragraph with Section 3.4.)

A second method of reducing the number of module inputs required is **input encoding**. This form of decomposition corresponds to that shown in Figure 5.10(a). A subset of input variables is encoded by block f in order to reduce its size. This is possible if less than the maximum number of combinations of these variables is needed to define the on set of the function to be realized. For example, it may be required to realize a multiple output function with 27 inputs, but only 16-input PLDs are available. On examining the truth table it is determined that 16 of these variables have 31 or fewer combinations which result in at least one of the outputs becoming true. These 16 variables can therefore be encoded into 5. These 5, with the remaining 11, can be input into a second PLD, as shown in Figure 5.14. The reason why 32 ($2^5$) combinations of the 16 selected variables cannot be encoded is that the last code is required for 'all other combinations of the 16' which define the off set. Systematic methods of detecting this type of decomposition are known as column partitioning,

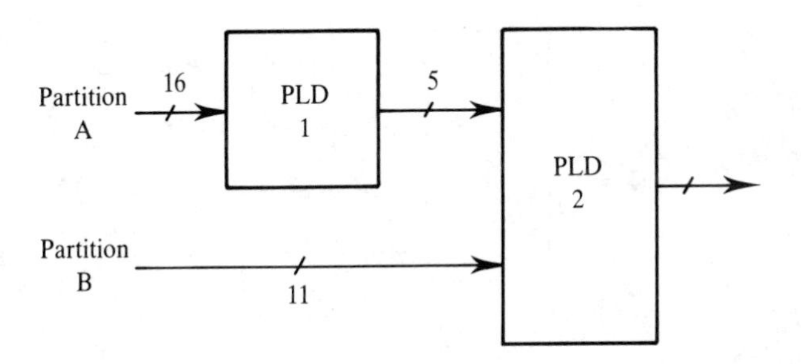


**Figure 5.14** Input encoding.

that is the truth table columns are allocated to partitions which contain rows with a limited number of combinations.

The bibliographical notes at the end of this chapter refer to sources of algorithms for input expansion. It is also worth trying to detect redundant inputs, perhaps by using the method of Section 4.4.

### 5.6.4 Output expansion

The problem to be solved here is that of realizing a set of functions greater in number than the number of outputs provided in the PLDs available. This problem is most simply solved by connecting the required number of devices in parallel, as shown in Figure 5.15. This is equivalent to an arbitrary partitioning of the output columns of the truth table. In memory arrays, this is 'word expansion' (generally used together with the address expansion of Section 5.6.3).

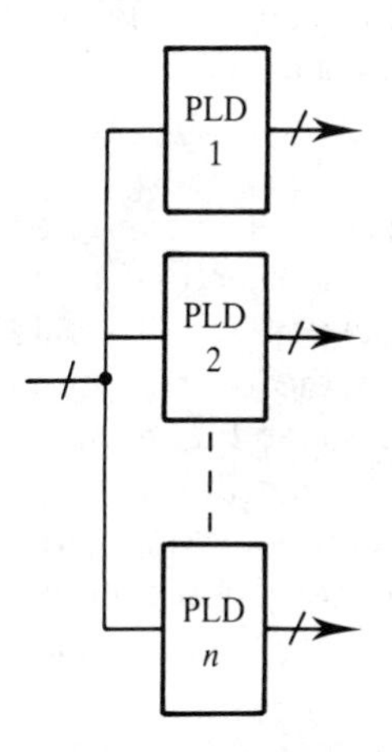


**Figure 5.15** Output expansion.

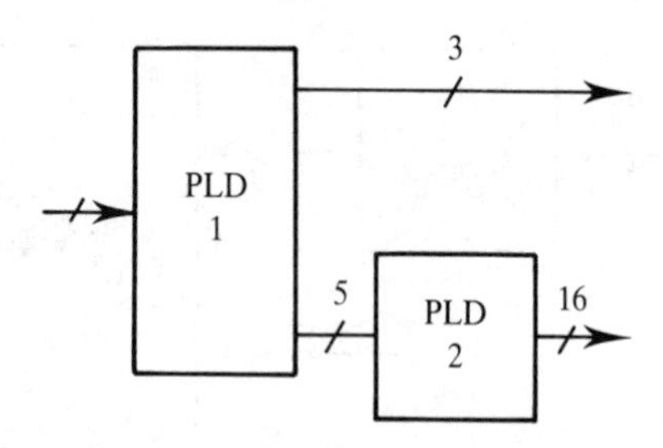


**Figure 5.16** Output coding.

A technique which may be economical, if the function set allows it, is **output coding**. The principle is illustrated in Figure 5.16. In this example, it is observed from the truth table that 16 of the outputs occur in 32 or fewer combinations, including '0 . . . 0'. They can thus be arbitrarily encoded into 5 bits, which are generated by PLD 1, and then decoded into the original 16 by PLD 2. PLD 2 may often be an inexpensive PROM device.

Again, more formal algorithms have been developed for output expansion. See the bibliographical notes for an example.

Input and output encoding may also serve to reduce product terms while sometimes also saving input and/or output pins. Development of algorithms for achieving this is currently an active field of research for application to the optimization of the area of custom PLA networks.

### 5.6.5 Trees

The decompositions discussed so far have depended on the properties of the functions to be implemented. In this section, some general-purpose decompositions will be introduced. These are techniques for constructing PLD networks which will realize any function within the input/output limits of the network.

First we need to recall the Shannon expansion given in Equations 3.7–3.10. These show that any function can be implemented with a multiplexer with $n$ control inputs (where $n = 1, 2, 3, 4, \ldots$). $n$ of the input variables are connected to the control inputs, and the $2^n$ residues are connected to the data inputs (see Figure 3.29). If $n$ is equal to the number of function input variables, then the residues are constant values. If $n$ is equal to one less than the number of input variables, then the residues are 0, 1, $x_i$ and $\overline{x}_i$, where $x_i$ is any one of the input variables. A multiplexer may thus be thought of as an $m$-input **universal logic module** (ULM), as shown in Figure 5.17.

If it is required to realize an $m$-variable function with smaller ULMs, then a ULM tree can be constructed, by generating the residues at

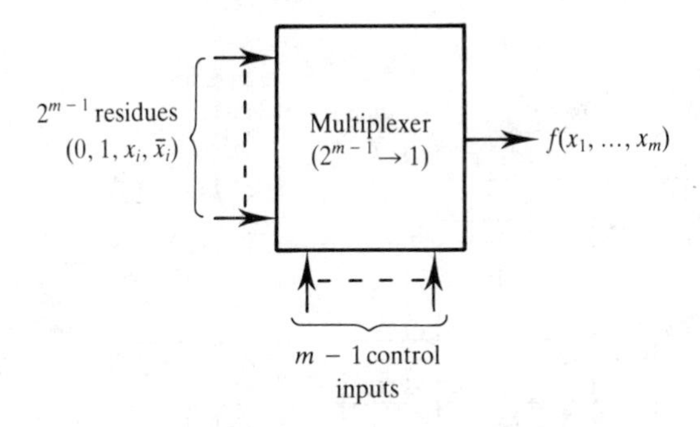


**Figure 5.17** *m*-variable ULM.

each level with ULMs at the previous level. The residues at the first level will be 0 and 1, or 0, 1, $x_i$ or $\bar{x}_i$. The general scheme is illustrated in Figure 5.18, for three-variable ULMs. Notice that at each stage two input variables are consumed. This type of structure soon becomes uneconomical because of the exponential growth in module numbers at each level. Minimization techniques must be applied to reduce the number of modules used (however, now, of course, the network is no longer universal).

The ULM tree building technique can be extended to the realization of multiple output functions with the use of PAL devices. A PAL may be used to implement more than one multiplexer, as shown in Figure 5.19,

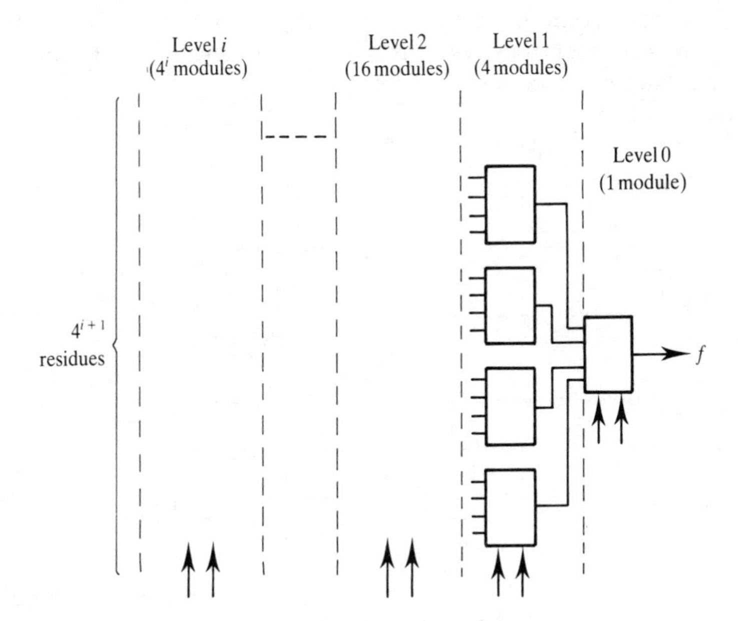


**Figure 5.18** ULM tree.

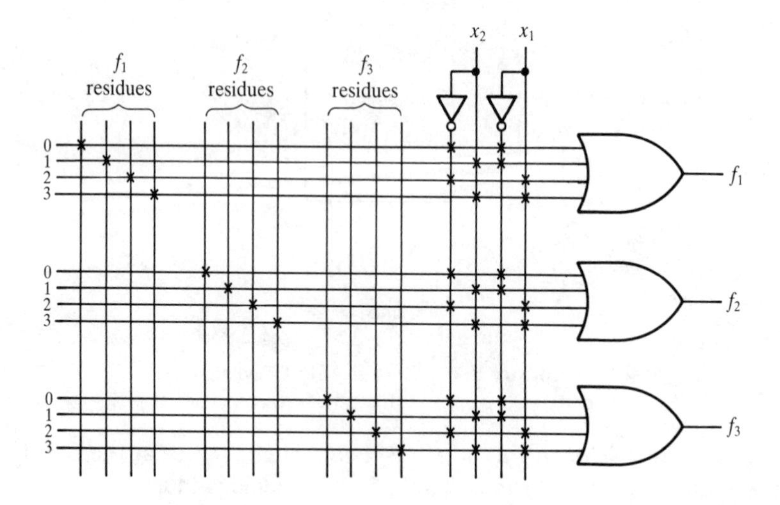


**Figure 5.19** Three ULMs in PAL device.

where three multiplexers are shown in the same array. PALs programmed in this way may be used to construct universal trees, as shown in Figure 5.20. Here, PLDs of the first level are uniquely programmed; there is no need to continue the ULMs to higher levels if such PLDs can be programmed to generate the residues. Thus an 18-input, 3-output function is realized with 14-input devices at the first level. This method can thus be viewed as another form of input expansion.

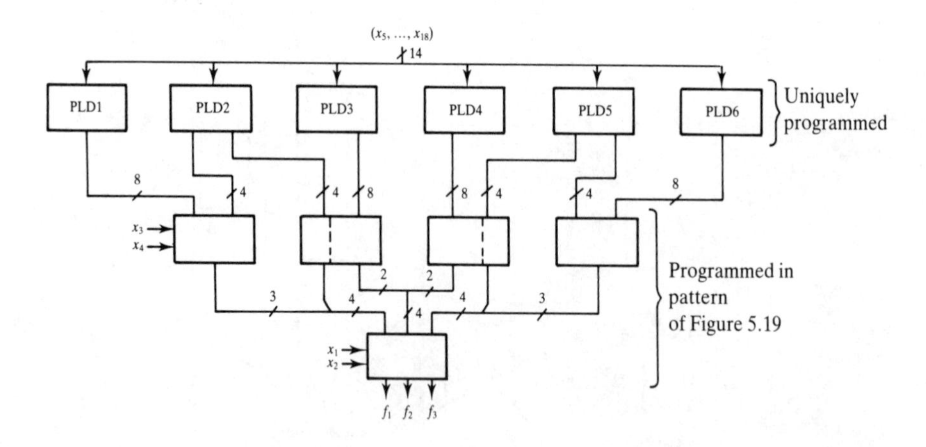


**Figure 5.20** 18-input 3-output tree.

## 5.7 Timing

### 5.7.1 Timing parameters

Estimation of the dynamic performance of a combinational PLD or network requires a knowledge of the timing parameters of the devices. These are simply specified for combinational devices – the two parameters of interest are the propagation delay and the output enable/disable time. Figure 5.21 shows how these delays are measured. For a specified load, supply voltage ($V_{CC}$), and ambient temperature, the response is measured to a defined input waveform. The delays are measured by relating the input and output waveforms. In device data sheets, 'typical' and 'worst-case' figures are given for these parameters. The typical figures should be ignored, as there is no guarantee that a given device will meet every one of these.

The origins of the two types of delay are shown in Figure 5.22. The **propagation delay**, or logic delay, $t_{PD}$ (unfortunately, there are not yet standard abbreviated symbols for timing parameters accepted by all manufacturers), is the delay between a device input change and a consequent output change (in a memory device, this is referred to as the **address access time**, $t_{AA}$). The **output enable delay**, $t_{OE}$, is the delay between a signal change at an input pin and a three-state output driver changing from the high impedance to the active state. Conversely, the **output disable delay** is the time between an input change and an output moving into the high impedance state. There are two types of enable/disable delay: one where there is a dedicated 'enable' pin, the other where the output driver is controlled by a product term.

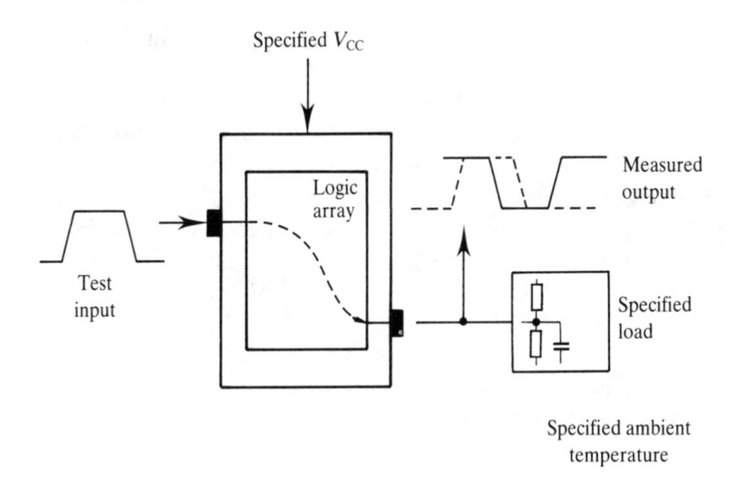


**Figure 5.21** Delay measurement.

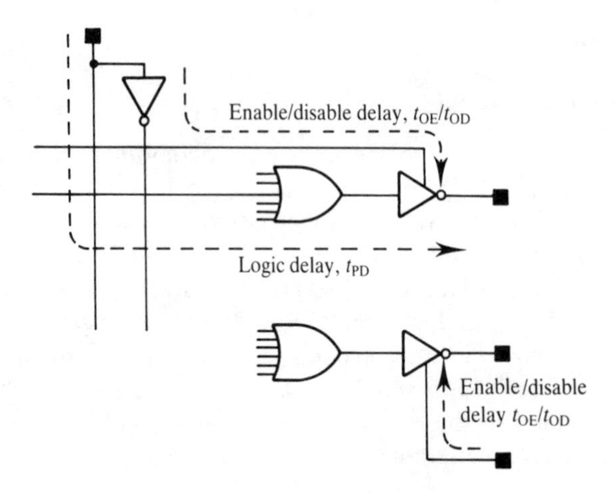


**Figure 5.22** Combinational PLD delays.

In any given device, all delays of a given kind will be different, depending on which input/output pin combination is selected for the measurement. The worst-case figures given in the data sheet will refer to the combinations giving the largest delay. However, an important rule which should never be forgotten is that no assumptions must be made about the actual values of a delay. In particular, no two delays should ever be considered equal. Unfortunately, one figure hardly ever given in data sheets is the minimum propagation delay, that is, the time before which it is guaranteed an output cannot change. Knowledge of this parameter is sometimes useful in sequential machine design, as will be seen later.

The standard waveforms for delay definition in TTL-compatible devices are given in Figure 5.23. Figure 5.23(a) shows the definitions for rise and fall times for a signal transition: this is the time for the signal to move between the 10% and 90% levels, or vice versa. Rise times for test inputs are usually specified in data sheets. Figure 5.23(b) shows the waveform relevant to propagation delay measurement. The input signal has levels of 0 and 3 V. Time measurements are referenced to the points where the waveforms cross a threshold, $V_T$, of 1.5 V. (The maximum input 'low' voltage for a TTL-compatible device is 0.8 V, and the minimum input 'high' voltage is 2 V). The propagation delays from the same input, an output moving from 'high' to 'low' and from 'low' to 'high', will in general be different. The data sheet worst-case value should refer to the larger of these figures. The waveform in Figure 5.23(c) refers to the measurement of enable and disable times.

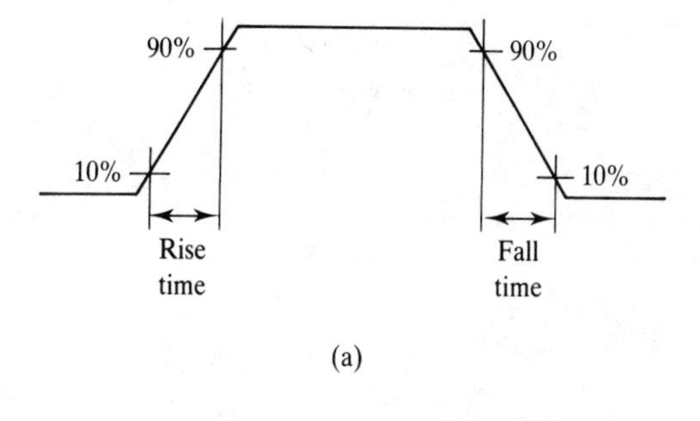


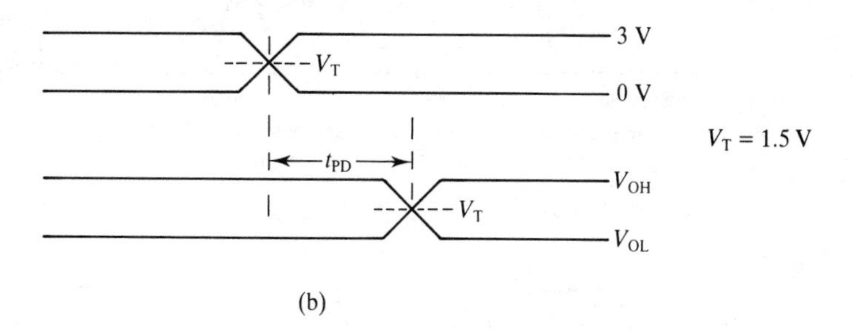


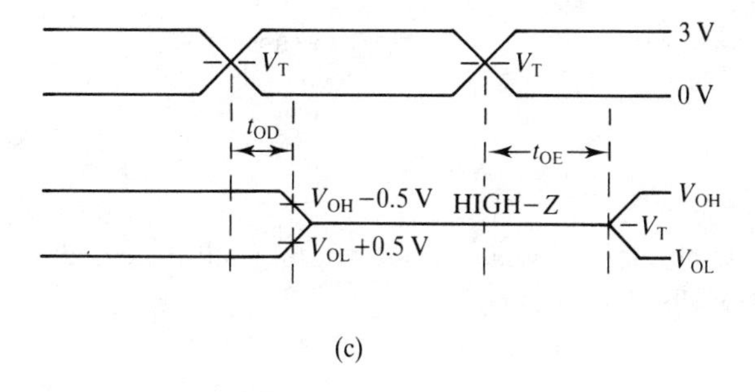


**Figure 5.23** Input/output waveforms: (a) rise and fall times; (b) propagation delay; (c) enable/disable delays.

### 5.7.2 Hazards

This section is concerned with an important aspect of the transient behaviour of combinational circuits. A combinational circuit is said to contain a **hazard** if, in response to a change of one or more inputs, an output momentarily assumes an incorrect value. There are different ways

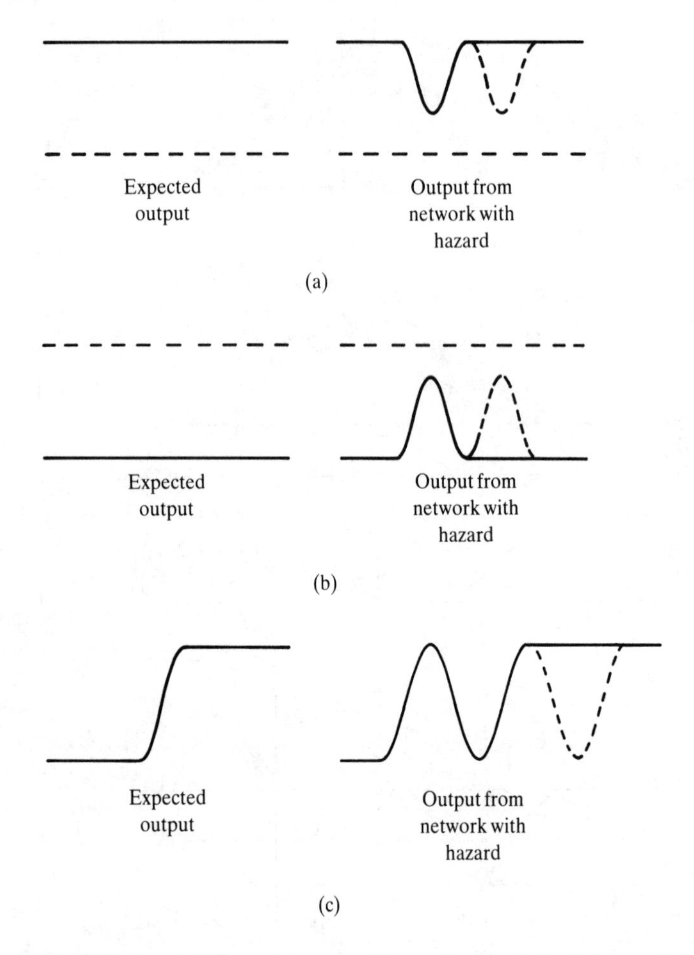


**Figure 5.24** Effects of different types of hazard: (a) static 1-hazard; (b) static 0-hazard; (c) dynamic hazard.

in which an output can misbehave. Firstly, if there are two input states which both cause a particular output to be 1, then a transition between them which causes the output to become 0 briefly implies that the circuit has a **static 1-hazard**. This is shown in Figure 5.24(a). A **static 0-hazard** causes the output to become 1 momentarily, as shown in Figure 5.24(b). The effect of a dynamic hazard is multiple transitions of an output signal where only one is required (Figure 5.24(c)). In all cases there are one or more short pulses, or 'glitches'. (A 'glitch' is merely a term for a very narrow pulse. Glitches can arise for reasons other than hazards.) These glitches may sometimes be undesirable, especially in sequential circuit designs where they can prevent correct operation. It is therefore important to be aware of the presence of hazards in critical combinational logic blocks

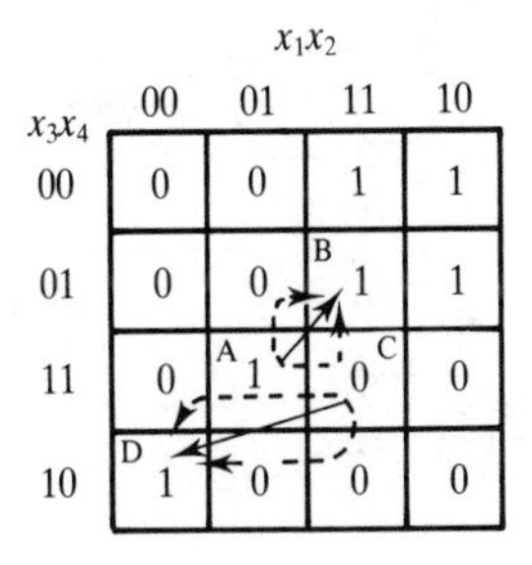


**Figure 5.25** Map illustrating function hazard.

and of techniques for their elimination. The effects of hazards will be discussed in later chapters.

The hazard classification above was based on the output waveforms. This can be further refined by distinguishing two causes of hazards: non-simultaneity of input transitions, and unequal delays within the logic network itself.

When an input transition involves two or more bit changes, it is impossible to guarantee that these will be simultaneous; the transition therefore is equivalent to a sequence of transitions each with a single bit change. If this sequence can cause output glitches, then there is a **function hazard**. This is illustrated by the K map of Figure 5.25. Consider first the transition from square A to square B, that is $0111 \rightarrow 1101$, which both define the output to be 1. The transition requires changes in $x_1$ and $x_3$. Since these two signals cannot change simultaneously, there will be an intermediate state of either 0101 or 1111, depending on which variable changes first. Since these input states cause the output to be 0, there is a function static 1-hazard for this transition. Similar examination of the transition from C to D ($1111 \rightarrow 0010$) will reveal the presence of a function dynamic hazard. Function hazards are a property of the logic function alone; they do not depend on the implementation. Thus no change to the structure of the circuit can eliminate a function hazard. However, if there is an upper limit to the time between input bits changing during a transition (that is, they are 'almost simultaneous'), the logic block may not be able to respond rapidly enough to produce output glitches large enough to reach a logic threshold. Some rules of thumb for deciding whether this is the case are given in Section 9.5.

Hazards arising in the structure of the combinational logic are known as **logic hazards**. Logic hazards are defined for single-input bit changes and can, in general, be eliminated. The simple sum-of-products circuit of Figure 5.26 will be used to illustrate the origin of a logic hazard. Consider the one-bit change input transition from A to B. By referring to the map it can be seen that the output is 1 for both states, but that a different implicant is responsible; the cover must therefore 'switch'

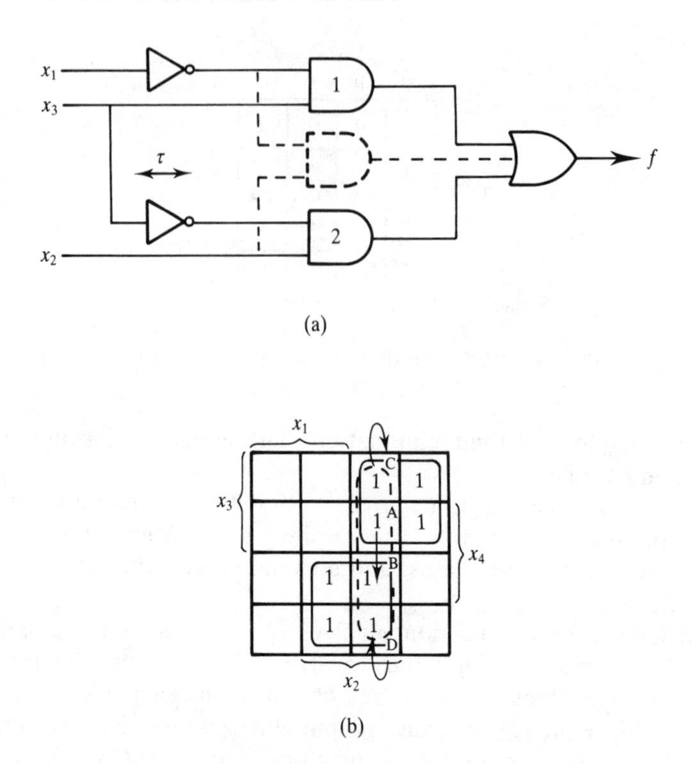


**Figure 5.26** Circuit with logic hazard: (a) network; (b) map.

between these two implicants. The input transition is $x_3$: $1 \rightarrow 0$, which will first cause the output of AND gate 1 to become 0. Because of the delay $\tau$ of the lower inverter, the output of AND gate 2 will not yet be 1. Therefore there is the possibility that the output $f$ will become 0 momentarily during the transition – a logic static 1-hazard. The transition C to D is identical.

Logic static 1-hazards are easy to detect. A single bit transition which causes the cover to change between implicants is a potential logic static 1-hazard. The rule suggests the cure: eliminate 'gaps' on the map between adjacent parts of implicants. In the example of Figure 5.26, this is done by adding the implicant $\overline{x}_1x_2$. This is shown dotted in the figure. The network is now no longer minimal, as the new term is logically redundant. There is also now a testing problem, as will be shown in Section 10.5.

Fortunately, in sum of products networks, logic static 0-hazards and logic dynamic hazards cannot arise. These statements can be easily justified. First, consider the case of static 0-hazards. The only type of transition which could give rise to this hazard is shown in Figure 5.27(a). For a glitch to occur, a product term such as that in Figure 5.27(b) would have to be present. Such a product is clearly redundant. Therefore this type of hazard should never occur. In the case of a logic dynamic hazard, the same

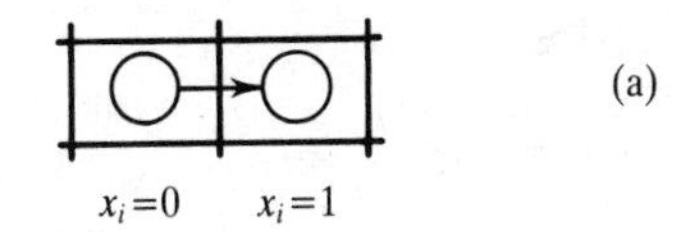


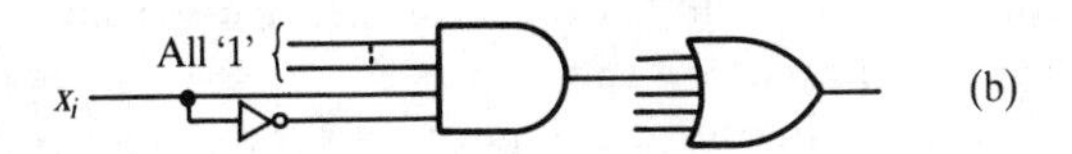


**Figure 5.27** Logic static 0-hazard in sum of products: (a) transition; (b) necessary product.

reasoning applies; a redundant product including both $x_i$ and $\bar{x}_i$ as input would have to be present. Since the PLA family of devices is based on sums of products, we do not have to consider these types of logic hazard in designs.

It is possible to detect the logic hazards present in a PLD design by looking for certain patterns in the fuse map. The condition for a logic static 1-hazard is that a single input variable change causes one product to become inactive and another to become active. Two such products (product 1 and product 2) are shown in Figure 5.28(a); the input whose change

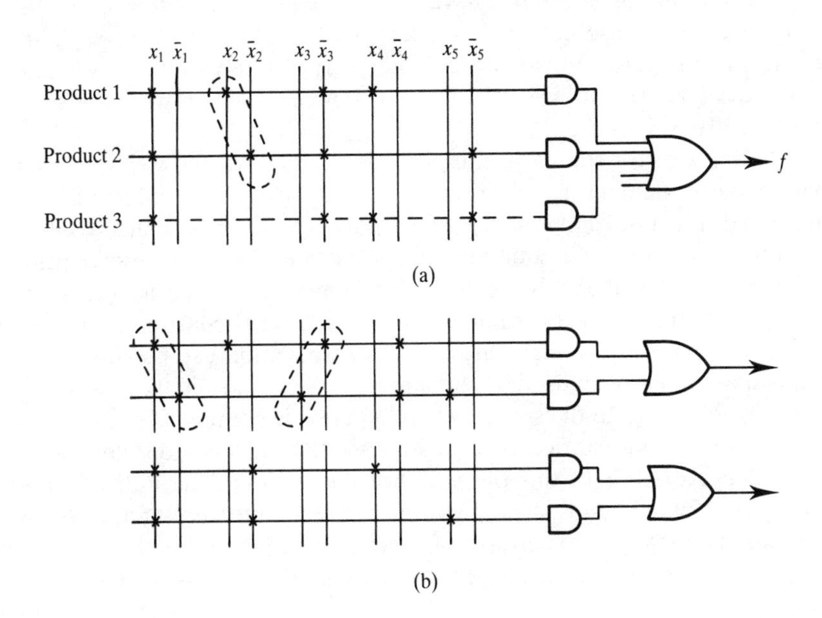


**Figure 5.28** Fuse maps for hazard detection: (a) hazard and its cure; (b) no hazards present.

can cause a hazard is $x_2$. The cure is to add an extra term which is always true during the changeover. This is the AND of the two terms, and is shown as product 3. Figure 5.28(b) shows product pairs which cannot cause logic hazards. In these cases no single variable change can cause the cover to switch from one product to the other. These patterns can be checked in both PLA and PAL devices. With PLAs the sets of products which feed to each output must be examined. Since these can overlap, some products may have to be examined more than once.

Hazard detection in multilevel networks is a longer procedure, as all three types of logic hazard can occur. In addition, hazard removal is more difficult. Standard procedures exist for this, but the best general advice is not to use multilevel logic where glitches can be a problem. The same applies to memory devices. These have inbuilt hazards which cannot be removed.

## 5.8 The gate equivalence of PLDs

In the past, PLDs were promoted by their manufacturers on their ability to replace at least three or four, and sometimes more, SSI or MMI standard components. Increasing array sizes, however, have led to their being compared with gate arrays in complexity. Therefore it is becoming more common for PLDs to have a 'gate equivalence' figure on their data sheet. How useful are these figures? It is difficult to give a direct answer, as the gate equivalence depends very strongly on the application; some designs will utilize the PLD resources efficiently, others very inefficiently.

The basis for comparison most widely adopted is a CMOS gate array whose basic element is a two-input NAND gate. The question to be answered is thus: 'how many two-input NAND gate cells would be required to perform the same function as a given PLD?' The most optimistic calculation which can be performed assumes that every product term is required, and that every input and feedback term contributes to every product term. Even though this degree of utilization can be shown to be impossible, it has been used by some manufacturers to show a device in the best possible light. In the space available here it is not possible to do justice to this topic, but suffice it to mention that, in real designs, a gate equivalence of 10% of this figure is not uncommon. The utilization efficiency possible depends strongly on the PLD architecture and, as devices become more dense, expansion of a simple PLA-based architecture will result in increasing inefficiency. (A new type of PLD, the **programmable gate array**, not considered in this book, can be much more accurately specified in terms of equivalent gates owing to its gate-array-like structure.)

## SUMMARY

For the implementation of blocks of combinational logic, the three major PLD structures, ROMs, PLAs and PALs, each have particular advantages. ROMs are useful where the specification has a word-structured format or where a large number of products is present. PLAs are the most flexible type since all products may be shared. However, many applications do not require this and more economical, and often faster, PAL-structured devices are the best choice. Use of feedback enables the number of products to be increased, but at the cost of extra delay. Decomposition, or the splitting of a problem into a network of smaller problems, can sometimes help when no single PLD can be found with enough resources to handle the task alone. Detecting other than simple decompositions is a task for automated methods. The performance limits of a combinational PLD design can be determined by correct use of data sheet values, and the possibility of glitches due to hazards can be determined by examination of the fuse map. Often hazards cannot be eliminated and therefore the effect of the glitches which may occur must be considered in the system design.

## BIBLIOGRAPHICAL NOTES

Many publications, appearing mostly in the early 1970s, describe methods of using ROMs in digital systems. A few representative examples are Krausener (1971), Monolithic Memories (1971) and Mitchell (1977). PLEs and PLEASM are covered in Monolithic Memories (1984). A good source of PLA applications is Philips (1985). The FPRP is described in Cavlan (1977). The best recent source of PAL device applications is Advanced Micro Devices (1988). The binary to 7-segment decoder example is based on Wong (1985b). The parity detector example is from Signetics (1985b). Applications of folded arrays can be found in Signetics (1988). Decomposition theory is covered in Curtis (1962), McCluskey (1986) and Bibilo and Yenin (1987). Only a sampling of the available PLA decomposition methods has been presented (this topic is particularly popular in the Soviet Union). The simpler methods are presented in Peatman (1980). Cavlan (1976) gives examples particularly suitable for PLA application. The method of column partitioning is described (with an error) and a program is given in Almaini (1986). Another algorithm for input encoding is described in Bul (1980). A method for input and product expansion is given in Novikov (1980). Shvartsman (1981) gives an algorithm for output expansion. A decomposition algorithm related to the input partitioning and decoding methods of Section 3.3 is presented in Kuo *et al.* (1988). Algorithms for input and output encoding for product reduction are described in Devadas *et al.* (1988) and Saldanha and Katz (1988). ULM minimization techniques are covered in Almaini (1986), and the extension to PLAs is in Novikov (1977), from where the example was taken. Questions of universality of networks of programmable elements are examined in Aleksander (1978). Hazards are covered in Friedman (1986), and in more detail in McCluskey (1986). The use of fuse maps for hazard detection is described in Ptasinki (1982) and Streicher (1985). Gate equivalence is discussed in Hild (1984) and Hartmann (1984).

## EXERCISES

**5.1** The truth table in Table 5.8 is to be realized in a single PLD. What size ROM would be required, and how many products would be required for PLA and PAL implementations? How would the most suitable PLD be selected?

**5.2** How many products are required for decoding the following address ranges?

(1) 01011001 – 01011010

(2) 10010111 – 10110001

(3) 10000000 – 11111111

**5.3** Draw circuit diagrams for an 8-bit adder using ROMs in the following ways:

(1) a single ROM;

(2) four ROMs using ripple carry;

(3) two ROMs using ripple carry;

(4) configuration (1) speeded up with a carry-lookahead ROM.

**Table 5.8**

| *Inputs* | | | | | | | | | | | | *Outputs* | | | | |
|---|---|---|---|---|---|---|---|---|---|---|---|---|---|---|---|---|
| 0 | 0 | 0 | 0 | 0 | 0 | 1 | 1 | 0 | 0 | 1 | 0 | 0 | 0 | 1 | 1 | 0 |
| 1 | 0 | 0 | 0 | 0 | 0 | 0 | 0 | 0 | 1 | 0 | 0 | 1 | 1 | 1 | 0 | 0 |
| 1 | 1 | 0 | 0 | 0 | 0 | 0 | 0 | 1 | 0 | 0 | 0 | 1 | 1 | 0 | 0 | 1 |
| 0 | 0 | 0 | 0 | 0 | 1 | 1 | 0 | 0 | 0 | 0 | 0 | 1 | 0 | 0 | 0 | 0 |
| 1 | 0 | 0 | 0 | 0 | 0 | 0 | 0 | 0 | 0 | 0 | 1 | 1 | 1 | 1 | 1 | 1 |
| 0 | 0 | 1 | 1 | 1 | 0 | 0 | 0 | 0 | 0 | 0 | 0 | 0 | 0 | 0 | 1 | 1 |
| 1 | 1 | 1 | 1 | 1 | 1 | 1 | 1 | 1 | 1 | 1 | 1 | 1 | 1 | 0 | 0 | 0 |
| 0 | 1 | 0 | 0 | 0 | 1 | 1 | 0 | 0 | 0 | 0 | 1 | 0 | 1 | 1 | 1 | 0 |

In each case calculate the total memory size and the number of stages of delay. Which is the most efficent solution measured in terms of 1/(delay × number of bits)? How does this change for a 16-bit adder? How could the efficiency measure be made more accurate?

**5.4** The 18P8 PAL (Figure 5.4) has a maximum of eight products per output. Show how this can be raised to 16 by using the output enable control terms. What condition must be satisfied by the products in such a solution?

**5.5** A simple pattern recognition system has as input the elements of a 4 × 4 matrix with values 'black', 'white' and two shades of grey. The output of the recognizer is to be 1 if the matrix contains patterns with one white element surrounded by eight black elements, and 0 otherwise.

Design the combinational logic for the recognizer. First give a description of the function as a truth table containing high level signals. Show how this function can be realized with two 20-input, 3-output PLAs of the PAL structure. How many product terms are required in each device?

**5.6** Design a 4-bit shifter. This combinational logic device has seven data inputs, D0–D7, and four data outputs Y0–Y3. The function control inputs, I0 and I1, determine the number of places the input data is to be shifted. Table 5.9 defines the operation of the circuit. Select the most suitable type of PLD and specify its personality in the most compact way.

**5.7** The truth table in Table 5.10 specifies a priority encoder; the outputs F2–F0 indicate the highest input which is a 1, and output $X$ is 0 when no input is 1. What is the minimum number of products required for this function? Choose the smallest PLDs from Appendix A which could implement this function.

**Table 5.9**

| *I1* | *I0* | *Y3* | *Y2* | *Y1* | *Y0* |
|---|---|---|---|---|---|
| 0 | 0 | D6 | D5 | D4 | D3 |
| 0 | 1 | D5 | D4 | D3 | D2 |
| 1 | 0 | D4 | D3 | D2 | D1 |
| 1 | 1 | D3 | D2 | D1 | D0 |

**Table 5.10**

| *I7* | *I6* | *I5* | *I4* | *I3* | *I2* | *I1* | *I0* | *F2* | *F1* | *F0* | *X* |
|---|---|---|---|---|---|---|---|---|---|---|---|
| 1 | * | * | * | * | * | * | * | 1 | 1 | 1 | 1 |
| 0 | 1 | * | * | * | * | * | * | 1 | 1 | 0 | 1 |
| 0 | 0 | 1 | * | * | * | * | * | 1 | 0 | 1 | 1 |
| 0 | 0 | 0 | 1 | * | * | * | * | 1 | 0 | 0 | 1 |
| 0 | 0 | 0 | 0 | 1 | * | * | * | 0 | 1 | 1 | 1 |
| 0 | 0 | 0 | 0 | 0 | 1 | * | * | 0 | 1 | 0 | 1 |
| 0 | 0 | 0 | 0 | 0 | 0 | 1 | * | 0 | 0 | 1 | 1 |
| 0 | 0 | 0 | 0 | 0 | 0 | 0 | 1 | 0 | 0 | 0 | 1 |
| 0 | 0 | 0 | 0 | 0 | 0 | 0 | 0 | 0 | 0 | 0 | 0 |

**5.8** The six-input parity function can be decomposed into two or three levels in many different ways. Show as many of these as you can find. If this function is to be implemented in a folded array, which decomposition results in the smallest array size?

**5.9** Are there any logic hazards in the following function?

$$f = a \cdot c + \bar{a} \cdot c \cdot d + a \cdot b \cdot \bar{c}$$

If so, how can these be removed? Illustrate the solution on a fuse map. Show some possible function hazards. Can these be removed?

CHAPTER 6

# Synchronous Machines and PLA-Based Sequencers

**OBJECTIVES**

When you have completed studying this chapter you should be able

- to recognize the synchronous and asynchronous Mealy and Moore forms of the synchronous sequential machine;
- to specify a finite state machine using a PLA or PLS table;
- to use the timing parameters of a sequencer PLD to calculate operating limits;
- to specify the behaviour of a finite state machine with flowcharts and the equivalent textual notation;
- to convert these specifications into the combinational logic for the next state and output functions; and to perform this for *D*, *S–R*, *J–K* and *T* flip–flop implementations;
- to understand the problems caused by asynchronous inputs and outputs and the limited cures available;
- to perform limited hand minimization to reduce the number of product terms in a design;
- to use the complement array of a sequencer to reduce products.

## 6.1 Introduction

In Section 2.5, the principles of finite state machines were reviewed. In this chapter the design of synchronous finite state machines (or just 'state machines'), and in particular sequential controllers implemented with PLAs, will be examined.

When designing the parts of digital systems which perform sequential tasks – those whose behaviour depends on their past as well as their present inputs – it will be discovered that two types can be distinguished. Both, of course, contain the elements essential to all sequential circuits, combinational logic and memory, but the difference lies in the way these are structured.

On the one hand there are sequential blocks which have a regular, repetitive internal structure; their combinational logic and memory can be partitioned into 'slices' which have very similar functions and a regular intercommunication (Figure 6.1(a)). Blocks of this type are mainly found

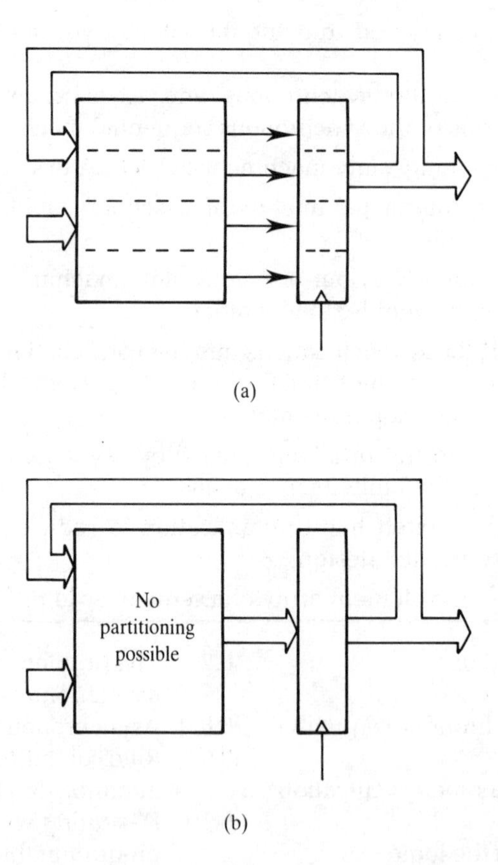


**Figure 6.1** (a) Functional block with partitioned logic; (b) functional block with irregular logic.

in the parts of a system which store, route and process data – registers of various types, ALUs, shifters, and so on. The memory in these applications is most often required to store intermediate results, as for example in a data pipeline. PAL devices, with their groups of logical product terms each devoted to a single output, are ideal for efficiently creating functions such as these.

On the other hand there are sequential blocks whose structure cannot be partitioned into a pattern of similar single-bit stages. This type of functional block is usually found in those parts of the system which perform sequencing and controlling tasks. Here, no regular circuit structure results – just a block of very 'random' logic feeding a row of flip–flops (Figure 6.1(b)). The most suitable element for creating this more general type of machine is the PLA-based **sequencer**. In a sequencer the logical terms are not partitioned and therefore devoted to particular memory elements or outputs; the designer is free to optimize the logic of the whole sequential machine as a single entity. In addition to this, many sequencers have special features which add to their usefulness in controller applications.

Of course, PAL devices can be used for these less structured applications as well, and are quite suitable for the smaller ones. Even though their structure is not optimal for controllers, simple and fast circuits can often be designed. However, for more complex applications, sequencers are usually the best choice. Use of PAL devices for state machines will be studied in the following chapter.

## 6.2 The sequencer

Before going into details, let us first look at the structure of a sequencer, as shown in Figure 6.2. The three major parts are the two logic arrays, the AND array and the OR array (which constitute a PLA), and the row of

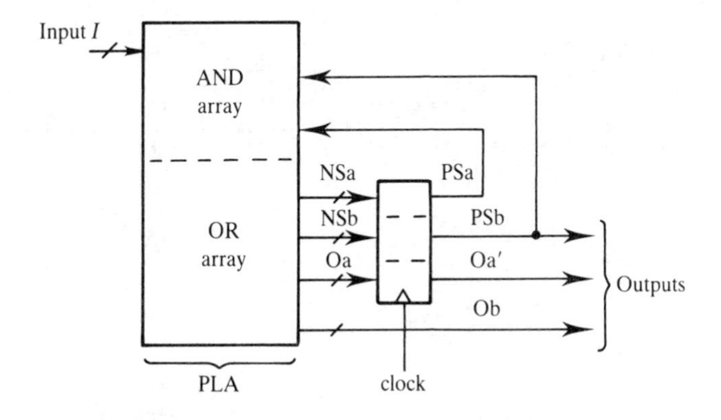


**Figure 6.2** Sequencer generic structure.

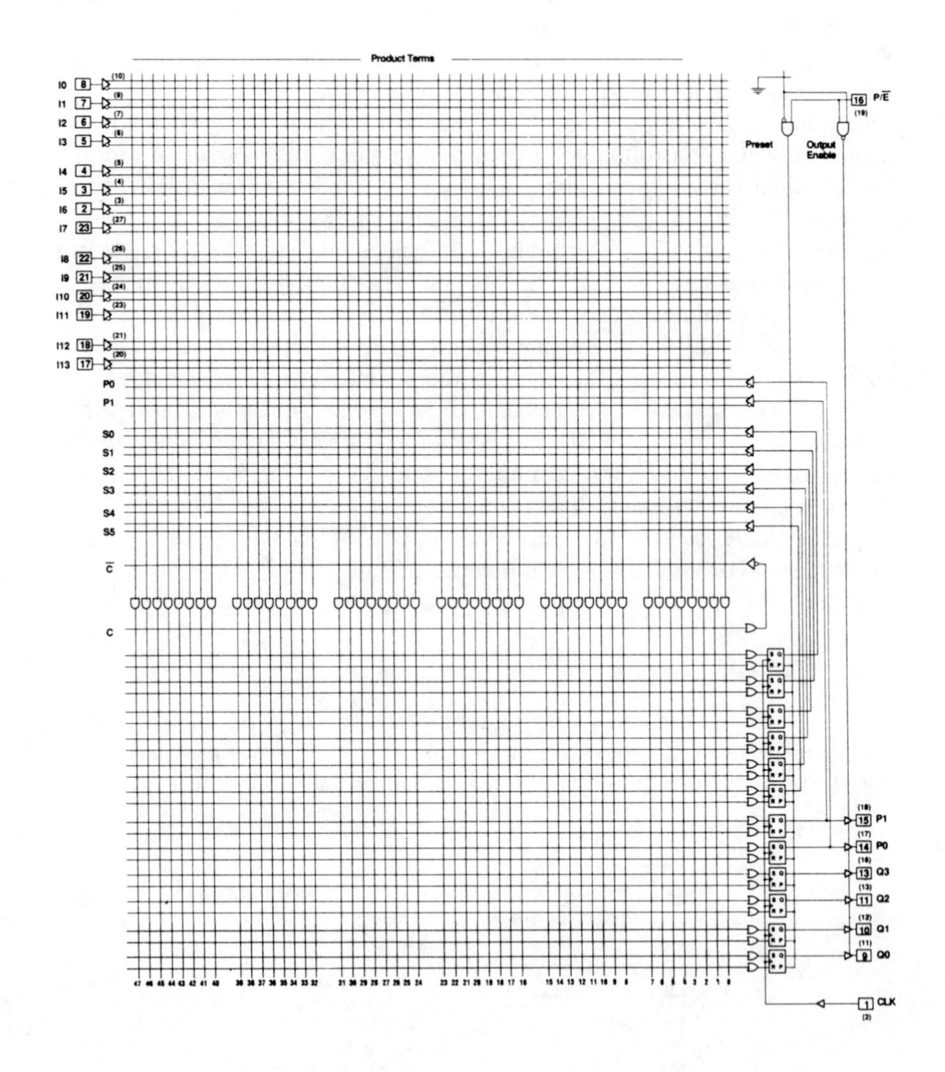


**Figure 6.3** PLS 167.

clocked flip–flops. The outputs, which are produced by the OR array, feed either directly to the pins (Ob) or to flip–flop inputs (NSa, NSb and Oa). The flip–flop outputs are fed back either into the AND array (PSa and PSb) or to pins (PSb and Oa′). The sequencer primary inputs to the AND array are labelled *I*. Not every sequencer will have all of these paths in its structure. Sequencers can be characterized by the number of inputs, number of product terms, number of flip–flops and number of outputs. The sequencer family of devices is listed in Table A.5.

Figure 6.3 shows a typical sequencer, the PLS 167. The AND array can produce up to any 48 logical products of the device inputs and their complements, and of the variables fed back internally from a group of the flip–flops, and their complements. The product terms are fed into the OR array which is able to combine these in any desired manner to produce outputs which become the excitation inputs to the flip–flops. An excitation may be only a single product or, in the extreme, a sum of all 48 products. A single product can serve as an input to more than one OR term. These two arrays thus form a PLA. An important addition to the PLA is the complement array, introduced in Section 5.5. This additional OR line is first complemented and then taken back into the AND array where it becomes an extra input. As will be seen later, this feature can save many products because of the possibility of multiple use in a single design.

The flip–flops have a common clock line. In this device, all are of the *S–R* type, which will be shown to have particular advantages in sequencer applications. The flip–flops are connected in one of three ways:

(1) Their outputs are fed back internally to the AND array. They are thus 'buried', as they have no access to pins (PSa in Figure 6.2).

(2) Their outputs are both fed back into the AND array and connected to pins (PSb in Figure 6.2).

(3) Their outputs are connected directly to pins (Oa′ in Figure 6.2).

Finally, in this particular device, there is a pin (number 16) which can be programmed by the designer to be used in one of two ways. In 'output enable' mode the pin can be used to control the three-state outputs, and in 'preset' mode it can be used to preset asynchronously all the flip–flops. The first mode is useful when the outputs are connected to a bus, and the second allows a particular step of the control sequence to be unconditionally selected. Even if this pin is used for output enable an additional power-on preset feature ensures that the sequencer starts in a defined state.

In Chapter 2 the tabular form of description for a state machine used was the state table, or state transition table (Figure 2.18). This type of table is not suitable for specifying practical machines in which there is a large number of inputs, since each input combination defines a column of the

**Table 6.1** PLS table for serial adder.

| *Inputs* | | *Present state* | *Next state* | *Output* |
|---|---|---|---|---|
| $a_i$ | $b_i$ | $c_i$ | $c_{i+1}$ | $s_i$ |
| 0 | 0 | 0 | 0 | 0 |
| 0 | 1 | 0 | 0 | 1 |
| 1 | 0 | 0 | 0 | 1 |
| 1 | 1 | 0 | 1 | 0 |
| 0 | 0 | 1 | 0 | 1 |
| 0 | 1 | 1 | 1 | 0 |
| 1 | 0 | 1 | 1 | 0 |
| 1 | 1 | 1 | 1 | 1 |

table. With 10 inputs, for example, there would have to be $2^{10}$ columns. A more suitable format is the **PLA table** (or **PLS table**) which, as well as being more compact, has a very close relationship to the hardware structure of a sequencer.

Table 6.1 is the PLS table for the same serial adder of Figure 2.19. Here there is only one column for each input instead of one for each input combination. These columns together with the 'present state' column define inputs to the combinational logic whose outputs are the next state and machine output. The PLA table is therefore just the truth table for this logic. As with truth tables the economy comes if some input entries can be made 'don't care'. A single 'don't care' compresses two lines into one, two 'don't cares' in a row compress four into one, and so on. 'Don't cares' arise frequently in sequencer applications, as will be seen.

This FSM has an output which depends on both the state and the input, like the one shown in Figure 2.16, and is thus a Mealy machine. In fact there are six ways of using the sequencer, three of which implement Moore machines and three Mealy. It is important to be aware of these forms, especially when using CAD tools for the synthesis of state machines. First, let us look at the Mealy forms.

The standard Mealy form is shown in Figure 6.4, where the signals are labelled as in Figure 6.2 to indicate which registers and outputs are used. The register outputs PSa and PSb are fed back into the array and define the present state. The PLA implements two functions, the transition function, which produces the next state flip–flop inputs, NSa and NSb, and the output function, which produces the machine output Ob. This is the **asynchronous Mealy form**. The Oa′ and PSb outputs are not used.

An alternative Mealy form is shown in Figure 6.5. Here the outputs are passed through a register and thus do not respond immediately to input

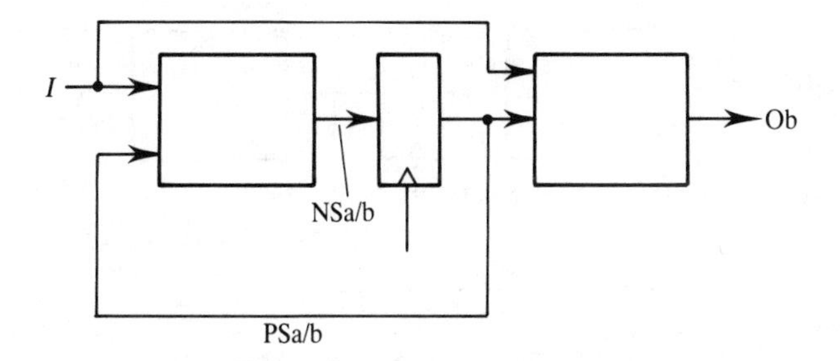


**Figure 6.4** The asynchronous Mealy form.

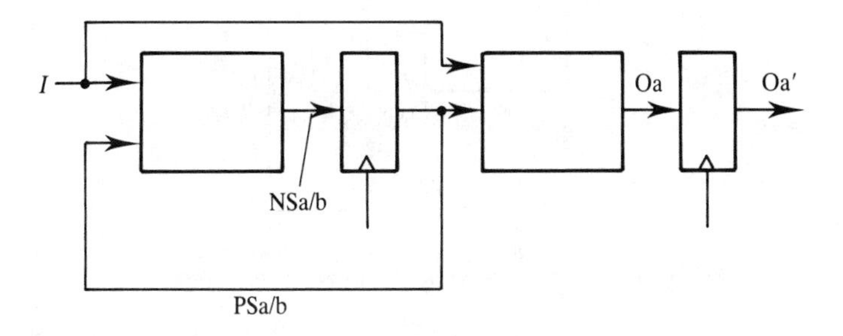


**Figure 6.5** The synchronous Mealy form.

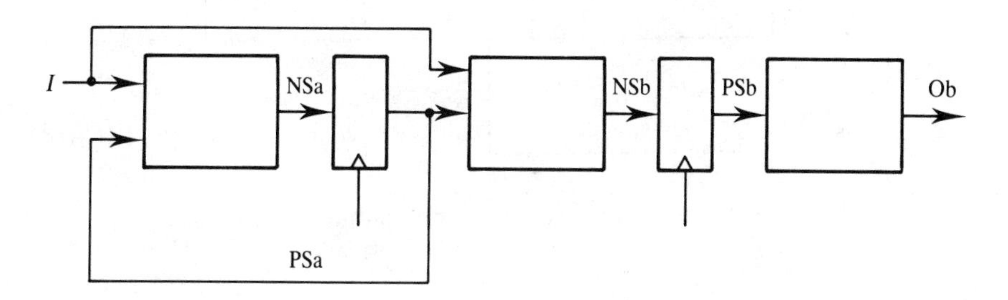


**Figure 6.6** A Mealy form equivalent to that of Figure 6.4.

changes. This is the **synchronous Mealy form**. The third form, shown in Figure 6.6, is really a variation of the asynchronous Mealy form of Figure 6.4. The second register can be considered to be part of the state register, and the first two logic functions can be merged. It will not therefore be used again.

The standard Moore form is given in Figure 6.7. Here the output Ob depends only on the present state PSa and PSb. This is the **asynchronous Moore form**. The **synchronous Moore form** is shown in Figure 6.8. Here the output is a direct state output. The third Moore form, shown in Figure 6.9,

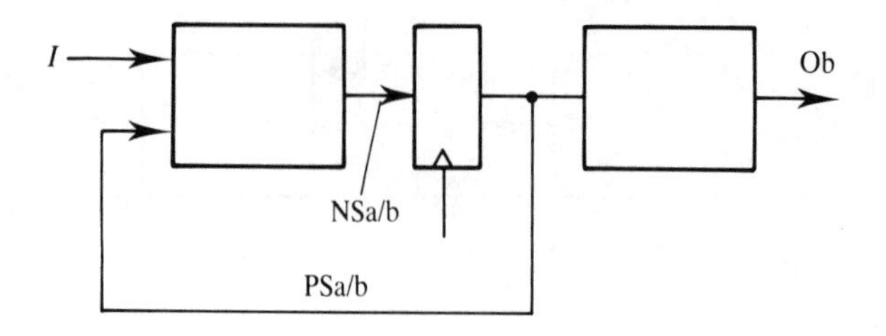


**Figure 6.7** The asynchronous Moore form.

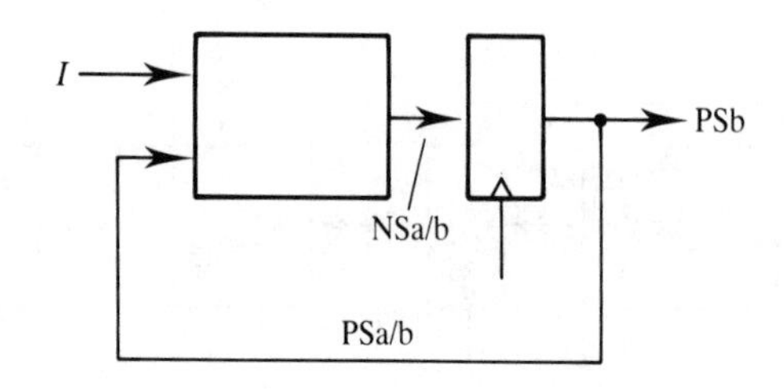


**Figure 6.8** The synchronous Moore form.

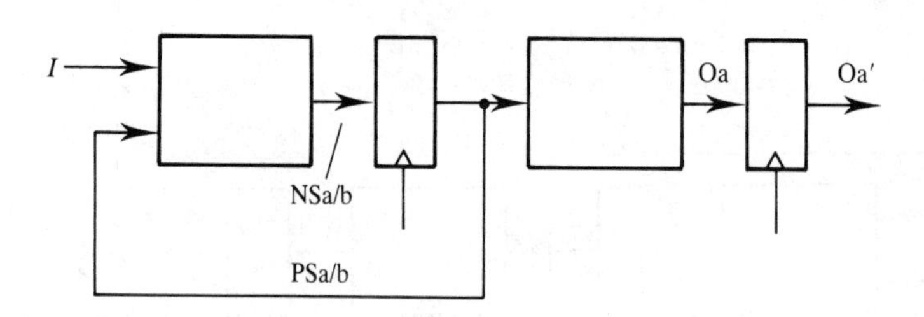


**Figure 6.9** A Moore form equivalent to that of Figure 6.8.

is again just a variation, this time of Figure 6.8. The output Oa′ can be considered to be part of the state and the two logic blocks can be merged.

Although these forms have been described separately, a single sequencer is able to realize a machine which combines them, provided that the required paths exist in the sequencer. For example, both Moore and Mealy outputs are possible and in both synchronous and asynchronous forms. The PLS 167 shown in Figure 6.3 does not have the Ob outputs, and thus cannot implement the asynchronous forms.

In both of the Moore forms and in the asynchronous Mealy form, outputs occur in the state in which they are named in the state transition diagram. This is because they are combinational functions of the state (and inputs in the Mealy case). Thus state transition diagrams such as those of Figures 2.19 and 2.22 can be used. However, the synchronous Mealy

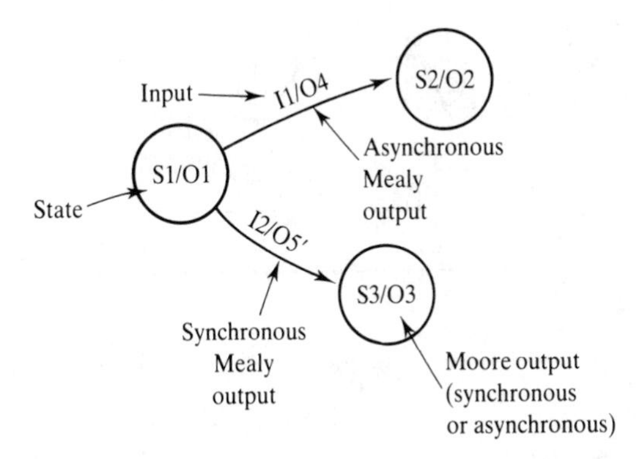


**Figure 6.10** State transition diagram labelling for different output types.

machine is different. Here the output does not appear in the state in which it is named as it first goes into a register. It appears in the next state; it is a **delayed** output. This fact is indicated on the state transition diagram by appending a '' ' to the output symbol. Figure 6.10 illustrates all the possibilities on a state transition diagram.

## 6.3 The synchronous sequential circuit

If a clock signal is used to trigger the state transitions of an FSM it is a **synchronous sequential circuit**, where the clock is connected to all the state and output flip–flops. Edge-triggered flip–flops allow a state change to occur on the rising edge of the clock. Figure 6.11 shows a block diagram of such a circuit. Two cycles of its operation are shown in Figure 6.12.

There are two regions in each cycle: the **stable region**, when all signals are steady, and the **transition region**, when the machine is changing state and signals are unstable. The active clock edge causes the flip–flops

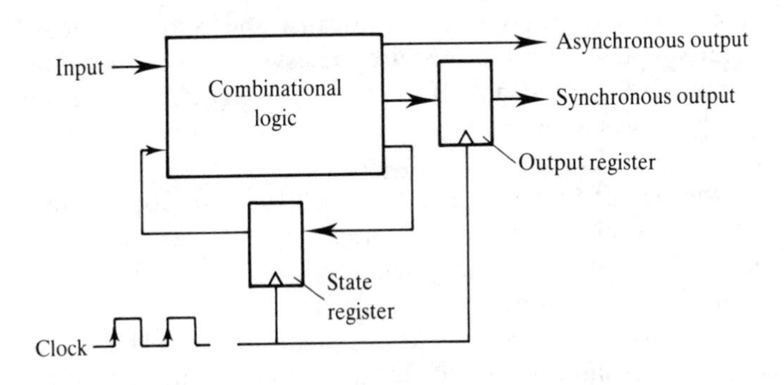


**Figure 6.11** Synchronous sequential circuit.

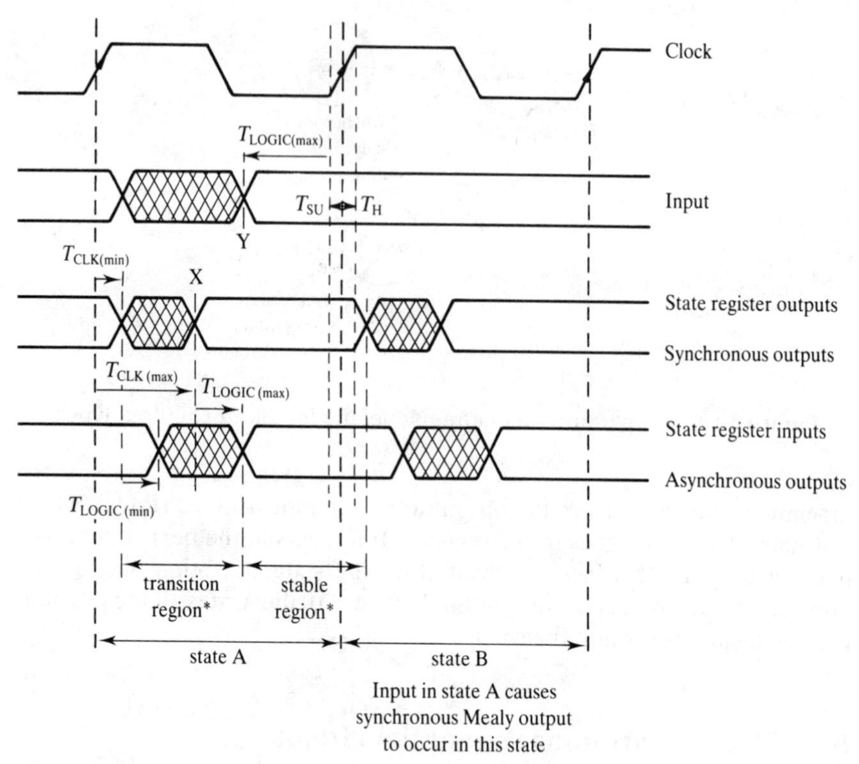


**Figure 6.12** Two cycles of a synchronous sequential circuit.

to load the value of the new state which has been set up at their inputs. At a time equal to the minimum value of $T_{CLK}$ after this, the present state and output flip–flop outputs will start to change to their new values. After a time equal to the maximum value of $T_{CLK}$ (specified in the data sheet) has elapsed, the last flip–flop output will be stable. Ignoring input changes for the moment, the state register changes cause the combinational logic to start to evaluate new outputs which are the asynchronous machine outputs and the inputs to the flip–flops. If the propagation delay of the logic array is $T_{LOGIC}$, then the stable period will start at a time equal to the sum of the maximum values of $T_{CLK}$ and $T_{LOGIC}$.

For the circuit to operate reliably, all the flip–flop inputs must be stable at the corresponding flip–flops no later than the minimum **flip–flop set-up time**, $T_{SU}$, before the next active clock edge. If one of the inputs changes after this threshold, then the next state or synchronous output could be stored incorrectly and the circuit malfunctions. This is a **transition race**. To avoid transition races, the clock period, $T_P$, must be greater than the sum of the two maximum propagation delays and the set-up time of the flip–flops. This determines the minimum clock period and hence the maximum clock frequency, $f_{MAX}$, of the circuit. There is another constraint which must be obeyed for correct operation – the flip–flop inputs must be held steady for a time at least equal to the flip–flop **hold time**, $T_H$. This means that the sum of the minimum propagation delays of the flip–flops and logic must be greater than the hold time, a constraint which is nearly always met in practice.

It has been assumed so far that the input becomes stable early enough in the cycle for its timing implications to be ignored. However, if it changes later than $T_{CLK(max)}$ after the active clock edge, the transition region will be extended. The latest allowable time for an input change, unless special precautions are taken, is $T_{LOGIC(max)} + T_{SU}$ before the next active clock edge. The problem of asynchronous inputs will be considered in Section 6.7.

The asynchronous outputs will also have an unstable period in each cycle, again as a result of the unequal propagation delays of the state flip–flops and logic. Even if a particular output bit is not required to change in a state transition, a glitch may occur because of a hazard in the logic. If the outputs must not suffer from glitches and multiple transitions, the only universal cure is to resynchronize them with an output register, in other words, to convert them into synchronous outputs.

## 6.4 State machine specification methods

The state machines which can be implemented by a PLS can be quite complex – up to 16 inputs and dozens of states are possible. Before beginning a design the best method of specifying it must be carefully considered. Although the state transition diagram can always be used, it is not always the most convenient method. Here some alternatives and the conversion of these into PLS tables will be examined.

State transition diagrams can be made more compact by writing on the transitions not the input values which cause the transition, as in Figures 2.19 and 2.22, but a Boolean expression defining the input combination or combinations which cause this transition. For example, in Figure 6.13, some transitions have been shown for a machine with inputs START, $X_1$ and $X_2$. In the transition between states 1 and 2, the inputs $X_1$ and $X_2$ are ignored (that is they are 'don't cares') and thus do not appear on the diagram. This saves space and makes the function more obvious.

There can be a problem with this method if you are careless, however. The state transitions in Figure 6.14 show what can happen. There are three input combinations, $I_0I_1I_2I_3$ = 1011, 1101 and 1111, which make both $\overline{I_0}\overline{I_2} + I_3$ and $I_0I_1 + I_0I_2$ true. Since transitions to two next states are impossible in a conventional state machine, this is an error in specification. Either it must be guaranteed that these input combinations never occur, or

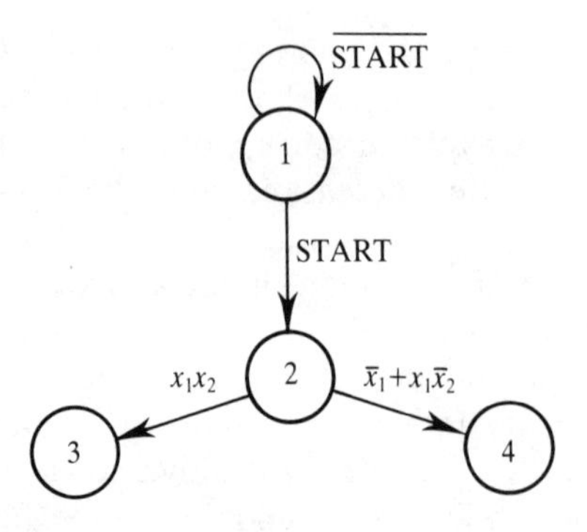


**Figure 6.13** State diagram with mnemonics.

the transition conditions must be modified. In this example, changing $I_0I_1 + I_0I_2$ to $(I_0I_1 + I_0I_2)\bar{I}_3$ would solve the problem.

Another popular notation is based on flowcharts. It was developed by Thomas Osborne at Hewlett-Packard and popularized by Christopher Clare in the book *Designing Logic Systems using State Machines*. In this notation, states are represented by rectangular boxes, and alternative state transitions are selected by strings of diamond-shaped decision boxes. The use of these symbols is shown in Figure 6.15. Each path through the decision boxes from one state to another defines a particular combination or set of combinations of the input variables. A path does not have to include all input variables, thus accommodating 'don't cares'. These decision trees take more space than the expressions would, but in most practical designs state machine controllers only test a small subset of the input variables in each state and thus the trees are quite manageable. Also, the chain of decisions often mirrors the designer's way of thinking about the actions of the controller. It is important to note that these tests are not

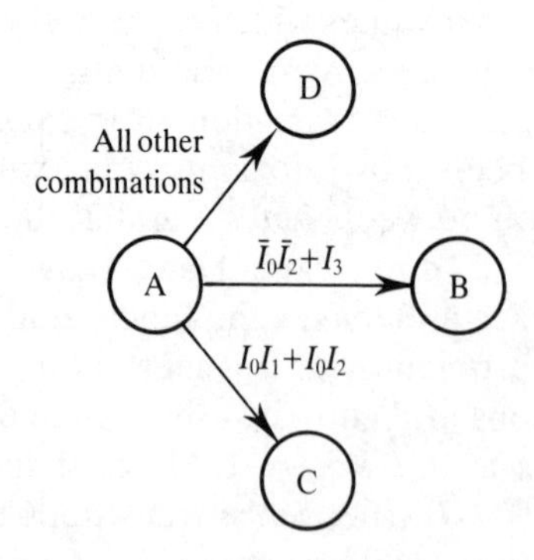


**Figure 6.14** State diagram with conflict.

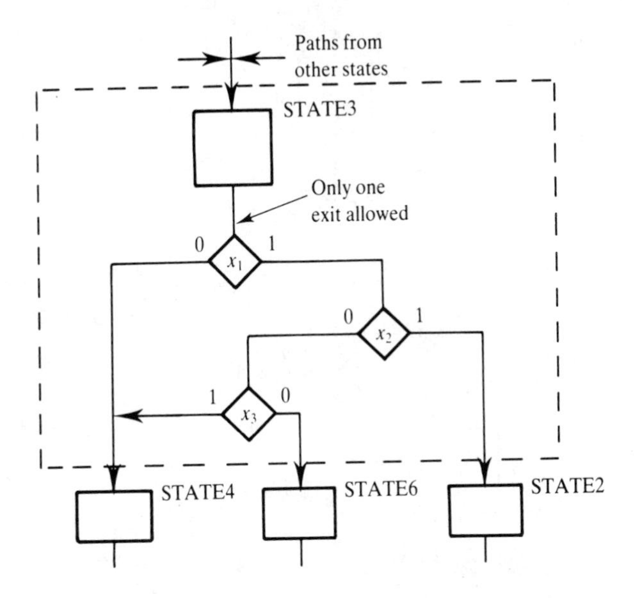


This is equivalent to:

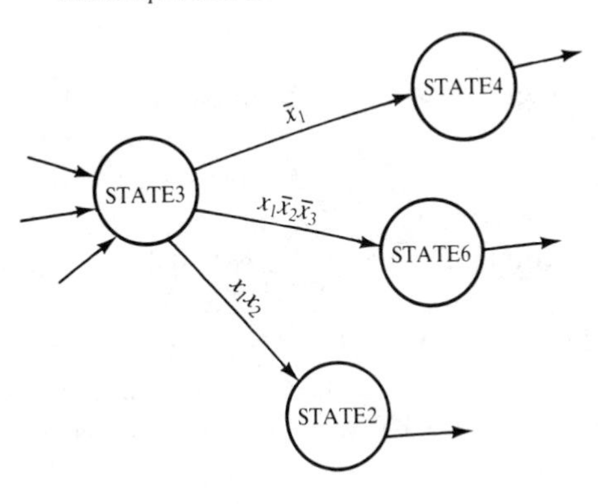


**Figure 6.15** Flowchart method of representing states and transitions.

performed sequentially in the sequential circuit; all are performed in parallel by its state transition logic. (Because of their similarity with program flowcharts, and the algorithmic way of thinking that this encourages, state machine flowcharts are sometimes referred to as 'algorithmic state machine' charts, or **ASM** charts.)

A benefit of this method of specifying transitions is that the problem of Figure 6.14 can be avoided. Such a conflict would be impossible as one path cannot diverge to define paths to two states. The transitions of Figure 6.14 would be drawn as in Figure 6.16.

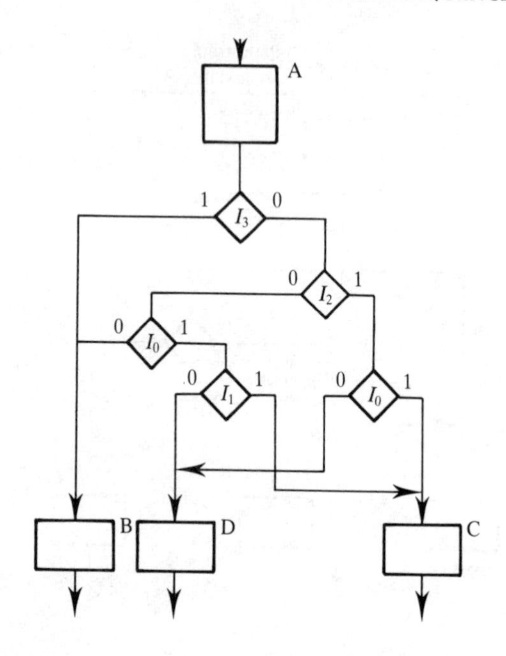


**Figure 6.16** Flowchart version of Figure 6.14.

Where there is no danger of conflicts, because of multiple next states being defined, this flowchart-like notation can be compacted by allowing more complex decisions. Expressions can be tested, as shown in Figure 6.17(a), or multiple branches from a decoding box, as in Figure 6.17(b). In the second case it is convenient to group the set of binary inputs into a vector, and to branch on different values of this vector.

Exactly the same information can be expressed in words, for example by using the construct IF... THEN to describe a path through the tree. Thus, for the flowchart of Figure 6.16, we can write, in the syntax of the 'AMAZE' state machine language,

IF [$I_3$ + /$I_3$*/$I_2$*/$I_0$] THEN [B]
IF [/$I_3$*$I_2$*$I_0$ + /$I_3$*/$I_2$*$I_1$*$I_0$] THEN [C]
IF [/$I_3$*$I_2$*$I_0$ + /$I_3$*/$I_2$*/$I_1$*$I_0$] THEN [D]

where '/' means negation, and '*' means AND.

Because all combinations of the inputs are taken into account, we can eliminate the last 'IF' and replace it with 'ELSE', meaning 'all the other combinations not defined'. Thus the last line can be replaced by

ELSE [D]

As well as saving time in writing down the specification, the 'ELSE' can be implemented directly in the sequencers, as will be shown later.

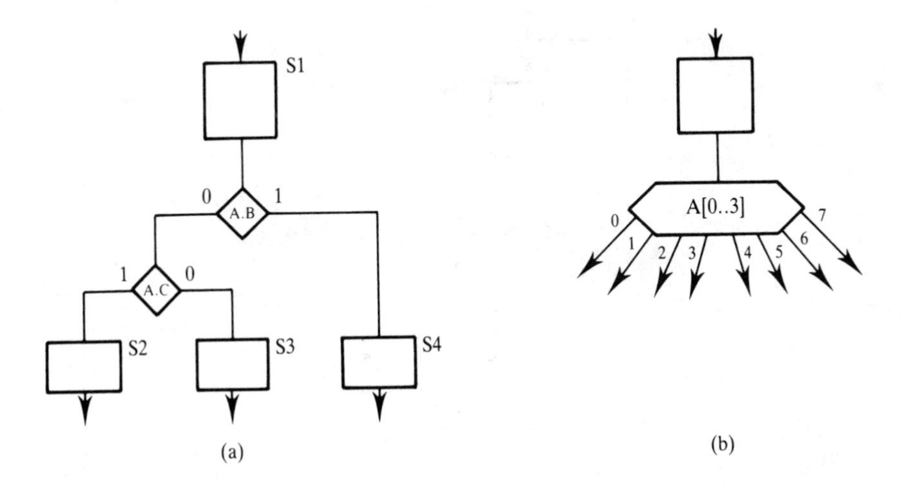


**Figure 6.17** More compact forms: (a) testing expressions; (b) multiway branch.

Since both Moore and Mealy machines can be constructed using sequencers, it is necessary to look at the specification of outputs for both types of design. Moore machine outputs are easily specified, as they can just be appended to the state label. The method of Figure 2.22 can be used with state diagrams, while with flowcharts Moore outputs are listed in the state boxes. These are asserted immediately the machine enters the state in which they are encountered. Figure 6.18 is an example of a flowchart which has Moore outputs. In text form, the second part of this diagram can be expressed as:

WHILE [STATE2]
  IF [$X_1$*$X_2$] THEN [STATE3]
  IF [/$X_1$ + $X_1$*/$X_2$] THEN [STATE4] (*or* ELSE [STATE4])
WHILE [STATE3] : [$Y_1$*$Y_3$]
. . .
WHILE [STATE4] : [$Y_2$]
. . .

Mealy outputs are added to the text after lines defining the transitions. Synchronous Mealy outputs, which are delayed by one state, are also represented in the textual form by appending '' to the Mealy output symbols.

Mealy, or conditional, outputs are indicated on flowcharts by using a specially shaped box, as shown in Figure 6.19. There may be several of these on the paths leaving a state. Again, registered, or synchronous Mealy, outputs may be indicated by ''.

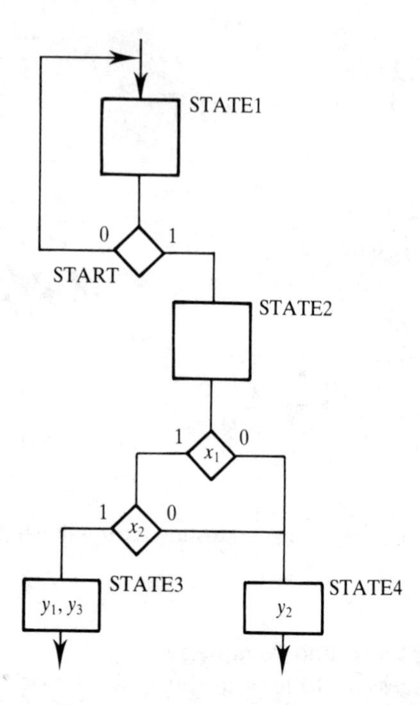


**Figure 6.18** Flowchart with Moore outputs.

The three methods of specification, state diagrams, flowcharts and text, are all equivalent and interchangeable, as they all describe the same behaviour and hardware structure. Each style has its own particular advantages. Flowcharts are convenient for small problems where there are not

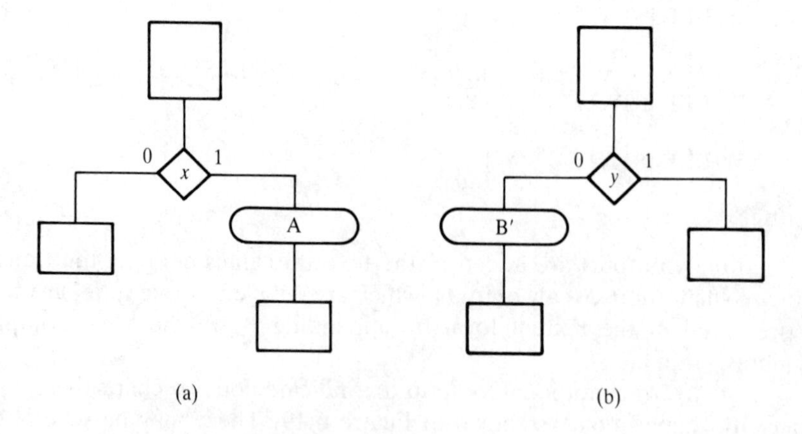


**Figure 6.19** Conditional (Mealy) outputs in a flowchart: (a) combinational (asynchronous); (b) registered (synchronous).

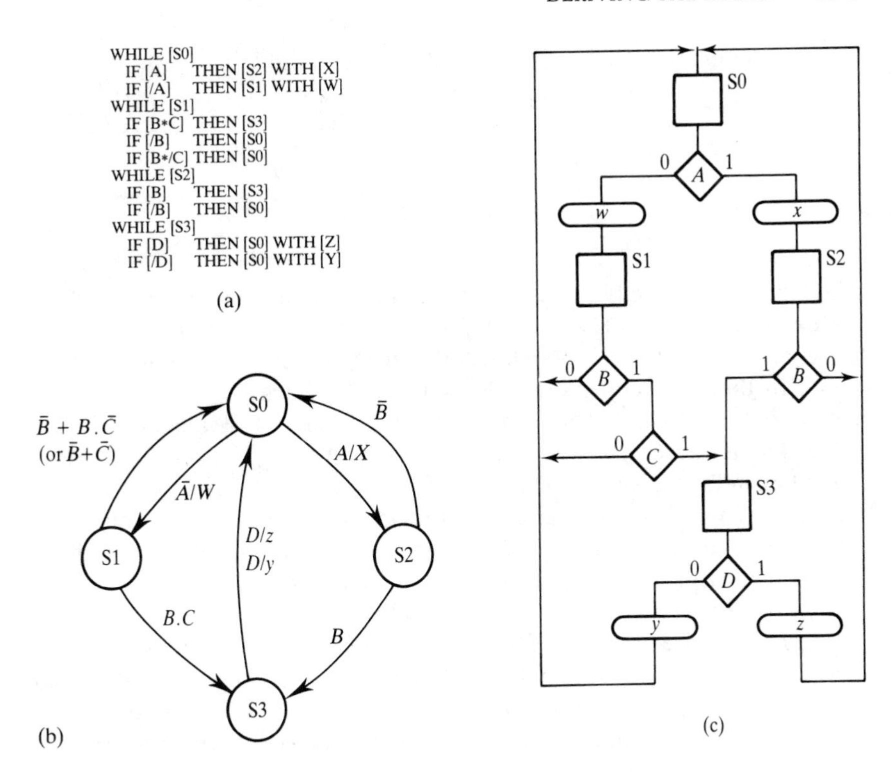


**Figure 6.20** Three forms of state machine description: (a) text; (b) state transition diagram; (c) flowchart.

more than about ten states and where up to two or three inputs or input expressions are tested in each state. For larger problems than this, they can become ungainly. State transition diagrams are more compact for problems where state transitions depend on many inputs, as the transition conditions are written directly on the transition arrows. Also, they make more efficient use of the page since transitions can be drawn in any direction. Text can also be used directly for a state machine design, and this may be the first choice for those with a software orientation. Either form of diagram can be readily converted into text for entry into a logic compiler (alternative forms of textual description are discussed in Chapter 10). The three forms may be directly compared by studying the example of Figure 6.20.

## 6.5 Deriving the logic

These state machine descriptions must now be converted into a definition of the combinational logic required to implement the transition and output functions. For this the PLS table, whose format is given below, is used.

| inputs | | | present state | | | next state | | | outputs | | |
|---|---|---|---|---|---|---|---|---|---|---|---|
| I0 | I1 | ... | PS0 | PS1 | ... | NS0 | NS1 | ... | O0 | O1 | ... |
| | | | | | | | | | | | |

The table defines the two functions which produce the outputs and the next state. Both functions share the inputs 'present state' and 'inputs'. Each possible path between two states, a **link path**, becomes a line in the PLS table. In the serial adder example of Table 6.1, each link path was completely defined by both inputs and thus there were no 'don't cares' in the table. This is unusual, however, as in most sequencer applications link paths do not include every input. This gives rise to 'don't cares' and fewer lines in the table. The collection of all link path lines is a complete definition of the combinational logic required. The following example illustrates all three forms of description and shows how the PLS table is generated.

The machine's function is shown in Figure 6.20. The inputs are $A$, $B$, $C$ and $D$, the state names are S0, S1, S2 and S3 and the outputs are $W$, $X$, $Y$ and $Z$. To construct the PLS table, a **state assignment** is necessary. This is an assignment of a different binary code to each state. Guidelines for doing this will be given later, but for now the assignment is chosen arbitrarily as follows:

S0: 00 S1: 01 S2: 10 S3: 11

With the two state variables $P$ and $Q$, the PLS table is as shown in Table 6.2.

**Table 6.2**

| *Path number* | *Input* | | | | *Present state* | | *Next state* | | *Output* | | | |
|---|---|---|---|---|---|---|---|---|---|---|---|---|
| | *A* | *B* | *C* | *D* | *P* | *Q* | *P'* | *Q'* | *W* | *X* | *Y* | *Z* |
| 1 | H | – | – | – | L | L | H | L | L | H | L | L |
| 2 | L | – | – | – | L | L | L | H | H | L | L | L |
| 3 | – | H | H | – | L | H | H | H | L | L | L | L |
| 4 | – | L | – | – | L | H | L | L | L | L | L | L |
| 5 | – | H | L | – | L | H | L | L | L | L | L | L |
| 6 | – | H | – | – | H | L | H | H | L | L | L | L |
| 7 | – | L | – | – | H | L | L | L | L | L | L | L |
| 8 | – | – | – | H | H | H | L | L | L | L | L | H |
| 9 | – | – | – | L | H | H | L | L | L | L | H | L |

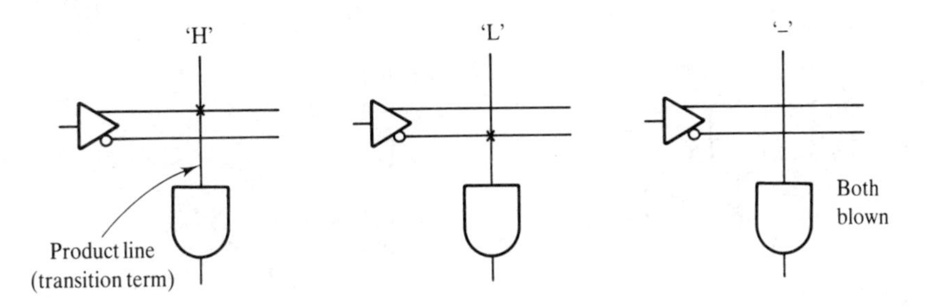


**Figure 6.21** Input connection alternatives.

This is now a complete description of the combinational logic of the state machine. The number of lines in the table is equal to the number of links between states in the flowchart. Notice that this is not the same as the number of lines in the state transition diagram as lines 4 and 5 of the table can be shown as one arc.

The PLS table can be related directly to the programming of a PLS. Each line corresponds to a product term where the 'input' and 'present state' parts define which signals are part of this product. The AND array thus requires nine product terms and inputs $A$, $B$, $C$, $D$, $P$, $Q$. The 'H', 'L' and '–' entries corespond to the connections to a product term shown in Figure 6.21. (A fourth case '0' exists, in which both fuses are intact. This is the state of the virgin device and is not used by the designer.)

A product becomes active (or is 'satisfied') when two conditions are fulfilled:

(1) the machine is in a particular state, and

(2) the inputs are present in a combination which defines a transition from this state.

For this reason, the product terms in a PLS are known as **transition terms**. As the circuit moves from state to state, new transition terms become active as others become inactive. In the example above, only one transition term is active at a time, but in minimized designs more than one can be active at the same time, as will be seen later.

Each transition term is routed into the PLS's OR array where it defines a pattern of next state bits and outputs. Figure 6.22 shows how the 'H' and 'L' entries in the second part of the PLS table define the connections in the OR array.

In this section, it has been implicitly assumed that the PLS has $D$-type flip–flops in its state register. However, there are advantages in using other types, as will now be shown.

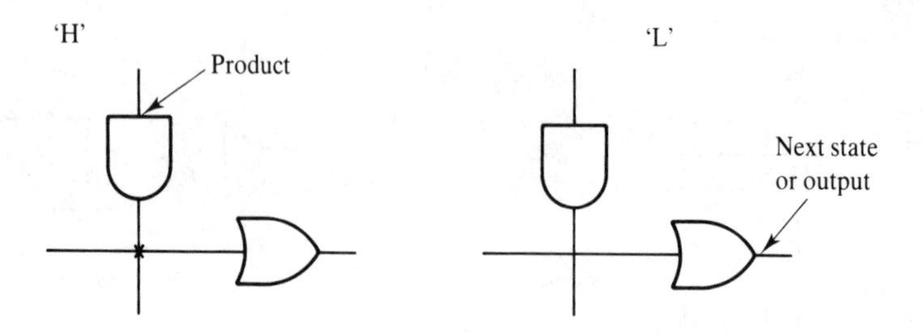


**Figure 6.22** OR array connections.

## 6.6 Using different flip–flop types

If there was a way in which product terms could be used to define only changes in state variables, in general fewer transitions would be needed. With $D$ flip–flops every state variable which is 1 in the next state requires a product, even if is 1 in the present state. For example, let us look at the effect of using $S$–$R$ flip–flops, the type used in the most popular sequencers. The behaviour of a clocked $S$–$R$ flip–flop (Figure 6.23) can be described by its **excitation table**, shown in Table 6.3.

This table shows what $S$ and $R$ inputs are needed for all possible transitions of the flip–flop's $Q$ output. For the 0 to 1 and 1 to 0 transitions there is only one possible pair of inputs, ($S = 1$, $R = 0$), and ($S = 0$, $R = 1$). For each of these a single transition term is needed – that which defines the 1 input. The 0 to 0 and 1 to 1, or 'hold', transitions are different. For these there is a 'don't care' entry. This is because the transitions can be viewed in two ways: 0 to 0 is 'reset' or 'do nothing', 1 to 1 is 'set' or 'do nothing'.

The three possible OR array connections to the $S$ and $R$ lines in a PLS are shown in Figure 6.24. 'H' indicates that the transition term is connected to the $S$ input, 'L' indicates that it is connected to the $R$ input, and '–' indicates that the term is not connected at all to this flip–flop. Thus the four transitions can be created as shown in Table 6.4.

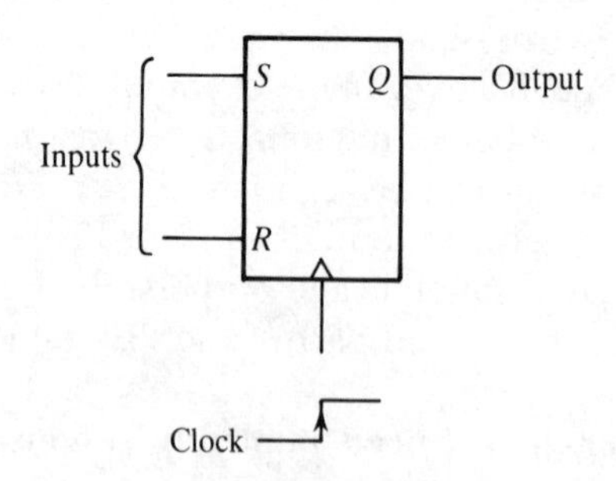


**Figure 6.23** Clocked $S$–$R$ flip–flop.

**Table 6.3**

| *Present state* | | *Next state* | *Inputs S* | *R* |
|---|---|---|---|---|
| 0 | → | 0 | 0 | – |
| 0 | → | 1 | 1 | 0 |
| 1 | → | 0 | 0 | 1 |
| 1 | → | 1 | – | 0 |

**Table 6.4**

| *Present state* | | *Next state* | *Table entry* |
|---|---|---|---|
| 0 | → | 0 | – or L |
| 0 | → | 1 | H |
| 1 | → | 0 | L |
| 1 | → | 1 | – or H |

The PLS table now has one additional entry possible, '–' in the 'next state' and 'output sections'. (The fourth possibility, '0', indicating that both fuses are intact, is the state of the virgin device. This cannot be used in a design as the transition term would create the illegal condition $S = R = 1$ when active.)

The result of this extra possibility is that 'hold' transitions, like that in Figure 6.25, can be 'free' in a sequencer which has *S–R* flip–flops – no transition term is required. This may be seen in the two lines of the PLS table corresponding to the two link paths shown (Table 6.5).

The first path, corresponding to the first line in the table, is a transition back to the same state. No change is thus required in any of the state variables, so '–' entries can be used. The first line has only '–' entries in the OR array part of the table – the transition term is not connected and this line can be eliminated altogether. This is a logic minimization which can be done immediately when converting the flowchart or state diagram into a PLS table. The second path is to a different state. This does require a term as some state variables have to change.

The notation previously used for indicating outputs is inconvenient when using sequencers with outputs stored in *S–R* flip–flops. Since outputs, like state variables, are naturally held unless required to change, specifications can be shortened if only output changes are indicated. This is

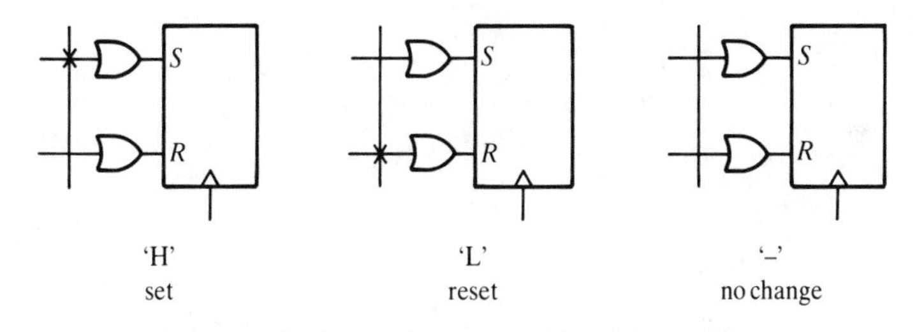


**Figure 6.24** OR array connections with *S–R* flip–flops.

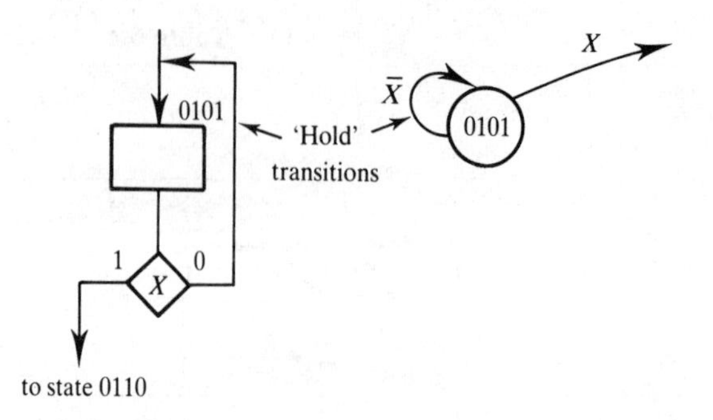


**Figure 6.25** 'Hold' transitions.

**Table 6.5**

| *Inputs* X | *Present state* | *Next state* | |
|---|---|---|---|
| L | LHLH | ---- | |
| H | LHLH | --HL | new state is 0110 |

illustrated in the flowchart of Figure 6.26. Here the output *A* changes every cycle if input *X* is true, otherwise it remains set.

'Hold' state transitions are only free if no output changes are required. Thus, 'hold' transitions such as that shown in Figure 6.27 do require a transition term even though there is no state change, because an output change is possible. The lines of the PLS table are given in Table 6.6.

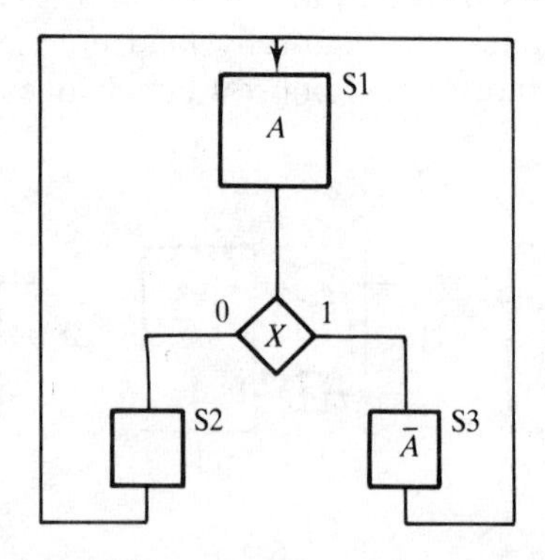


**Figure 6.26** Output notation with *S–R* output register. Output *A* is set in S1, reset in S3, held in S2.

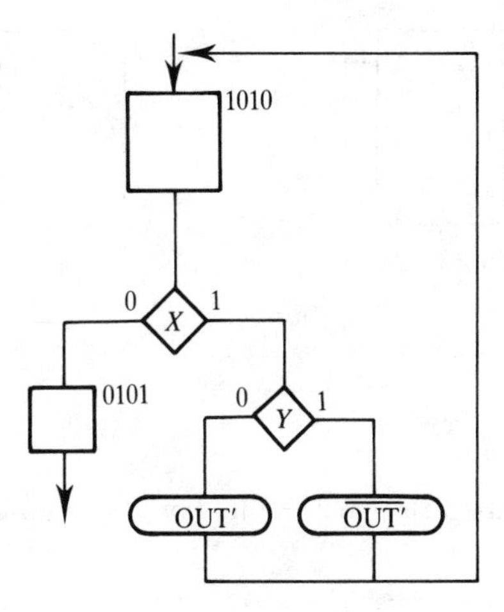


**Figure 6.27** 'Hold' transitions which are not 'free'.

The two hold transitions require transition terms because OUT can switch its value.

Further possibilities for logic minimization will be studied in Section 6.8.

Another type of flip–flop found in sequencers is the *J–K* flip–flop (Figure 6.28(a)). The excitation table for this flip–flop is shown in Table 6.7. Comparing this with the excitation table for the *S–R* flip–flop, it can be seen that there are additional 'don't care' entries. This is because the input state $J = 1$, $K = 1$ is allowed, and causes a 'toggling' action, that is a change of output state. The use of this type of flip–flop thus gives further scope for product term saving. The final type of flip–flop, available as a programmable option in some PLDs, is the *T* (or toggle) flip–flop. This flip–flop has only one input (see Figure 6.28(b)), and the excitation table shown in Table 6.8.

Selecting which type of flip–flop to choose is not simple, but most often there is no choice, the PLD being chosen for other reasons. Where there is a choice, sequencing and counting types of state machine will

**Table 6.6**

| *Inputs* X | Y | *Present state* | *Next state* | *Output* OUT | |
|---|---|---|---|---|---|
| L | – | HLHL | LHLH | – | new state 0101 |
| H | H | HLHL | –––– | L | |
| H | L | HLHL | –––– | H | |

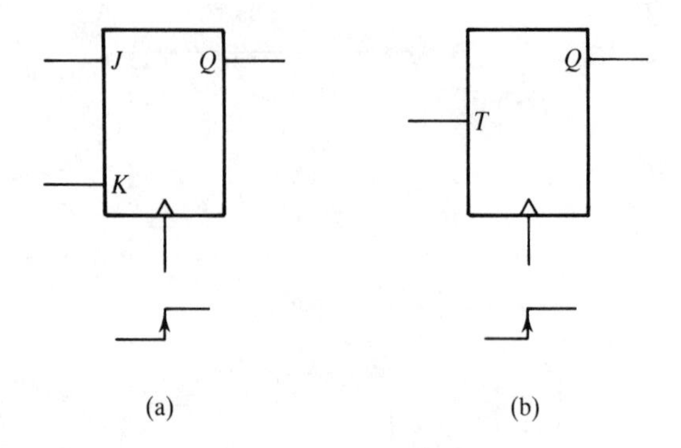


**Figure 6.28** (a) $J$–$K$ flip–flop; (b) $T$ flip–flop.

**Table 6.7**

| *Present state* | | *Next state* | *Inputs* $J$ | $K$ |
|---|---|---|---|---|
| 0 | → | 0 | 0 | – |
| 0 | → | 1 | 1 | – |
| 1 | → | 0 | – | 1 |
| 1 | → | 1 | – | 0 |

**Table 6.8**

| *Present state* | | *Next state* | *Input* $T$ |
|---|---|---|---|
| 0 | → | 0 | 0 |
| 0 | → | 1 | 1 |
| 1 | → | 0 | 1 |
| 1 | → | 1 | 0 |

probably use least products with $J$–$K$ or $T$ flip–flops. However, a comparison can only be carried out by doing a complete and minimized design with each option – a task for CAD tools.

## 6.7 The problem of asynchronous inputs

The timing of the inputs to a synchronous state machine is often beyond the control of the designer – they may be random, such as sensor or keyboard inputs, or they may come from another synchronous system which has an unrelated clock. In either case no assumptions can be made about the times when inputs can or cannot arrive. This fact causes problems of reliability which cannot be completely eliminated, but only reduced to acceptable levels. Let us first see what the problem is.

Figure 6.29 shows two possible transitions from state S1 (code 00) either back to itself, or to state S2 (code 11). Which transition is taken depends on input variable $A$ which is asynchronous with respect to the clock. The transition term defining the state change has connections to the $S$ inputs of both state flip–flops (assuming that $S$–$R$ flip–flops are being

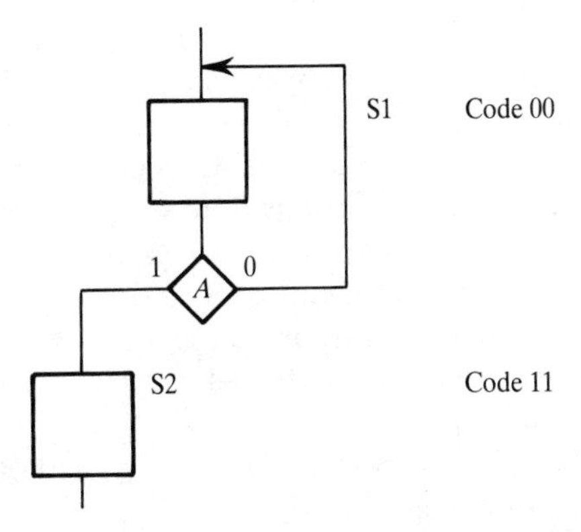


**Figure 6.29** Asynchronous input causing race.

used) as both state variables must be set. This term is activated by the asynchronous input, which can appear in any part of the clock cycle. The instant when the flip–flop inputs are steady is $T_{\text{LOGIC}}$ (defined in Figure 6.12) after the input is stable. However, $T_{\text{LOGIC}}$ will not be identical for both flip–flop input signals, giving rise to the possibility that only one will cause its flip–flop to set. This is shown in Figure 6.30. Here, one of the signals has changed inside the flip–flop's 'ambiguity window' defined by $T_{\text{SU}} + T_{\text{H}}$. This will cause the sequence to jump to states 01 or 10, both undefined transitions. This type of erroneous behaviour is termed an **input**

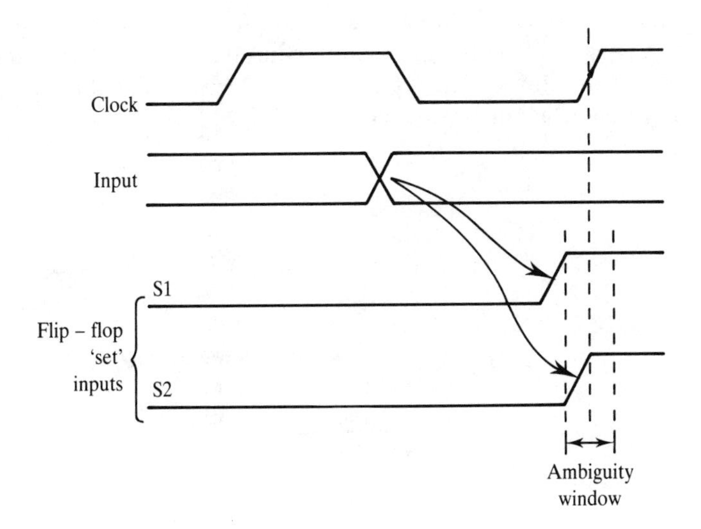


**Figure 6.30** Flip–flop input S2 changing in an ambiguity window.

**race**. Even if the two values of $T_{LOGIC}$ are very close, the ambiguity windows of the different flip–flops in the sequencer will not be identical.

In this example, a solution to the problem is to change the state assignment so that only one state variable depends on the asynchronous input. Thus the 11 code must be changed to 01 or 10. Now, with only one unsynchronized flip–flop input, only two possibilities exist: the input occurs in time to cause the transition, or it does not, in which case no transition occurs. An erroneous transition is not possible. In the case of a late input, the machine will respond to it one cycle later, provided that the input is of sufficient duration.

The same problem arises when outputs depend on an asynchronous input. Consider the following transition:

| *Inputs* | *Present state* | *Next state* | *Outputs* |
|---|---|---|---|
| ---H- | HHHLLL | -----H | HL-- |

Assume that the active input is asynchronous. The state transition will occur without error, as only a single state variable has to change. However, it is also required that two outputs must change. It is possible that the transition takes place but one or both of the outputs do not change because their flip–flop inputs have not settled in time. This **output race** thus has the same cause as an input race. To prevent input or output races, any transition which depends on an asynchronous input must have only one non-'–' entry in the next state and none in the output positions.

The situation shown in Figure 6.31, where a single asynchronous input determines which one of two next states is to be selected, can be dangerous. It is not a safe thing to do in sequencer designs, as more than one state variable must change when moving from state S1 to state S2 or S3. A race can thus occur. This type of decision can be made safe, however, when designing state machines with PAL or discrete logic where

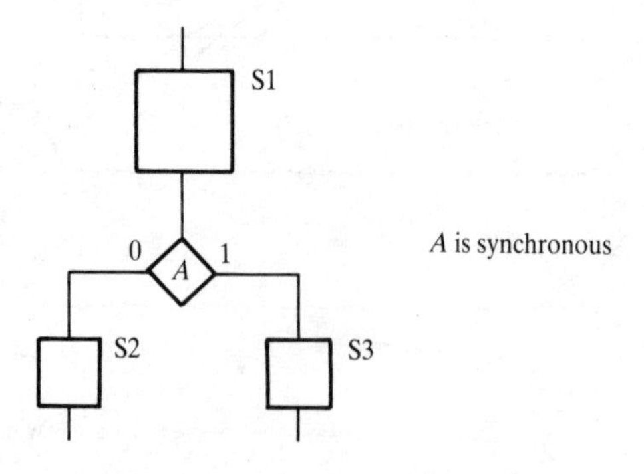


**Figure 6.31** An unsafe decision for any state assignment.

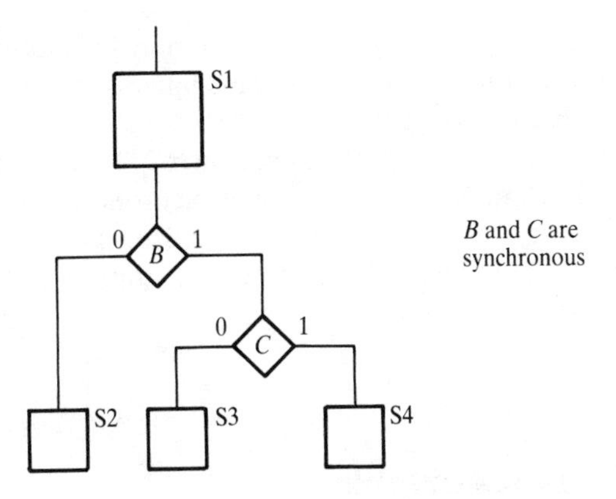


**Figure 6.32** Another unsafe construct for any state assignment.

separate sums of products are used to define each state variable. If state codes which differ in only one position are chosen for S2 and S3, the next state variables which are identical – all but one of them – are defined by product terms which do not depend on the asynchronous input. In a sequencer, because it is based on a PLA, all next state variables in a link path are defined by the same product (transition) term. Thus all next state variables depend on the asynchronous input.

What happens when a transition depends on more than one asynchronous input? If the input changes are independent, then it is not possible to find a state assignment which will prevent erroneous operation. Figure 6.32 shows such a situation where the transitions from state S1 depend on asynchronous inputs *B* and *C*.

The outcome of all this is that there is very little that can be done to handle asynchronous inputs without severely constraining the design of the state machine. The only way to have complete freedom in the use of inputs as decision variables is to convert them into synchronous inputs. This can be done by allocating a flip–flop to each input as shown in Figure 6.33. These synchronizing flip–flops are clocked by the sequencer clock, and may even be the sequencer's own internal flip–flops. This solution will be illustrated later.

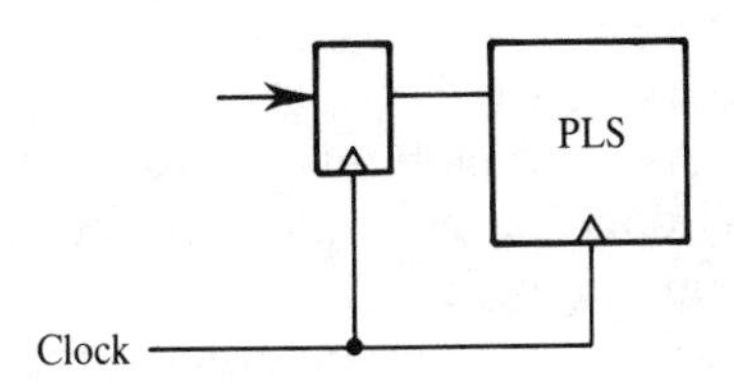


**Figure 6.33** Synchronizing an input.

Asynchronous inputs of short duration may be captured by using an *S–R* latch in front of the synchronizer. This latch is set by the input signal and reset by a sequencer output.

However, even with input synchronizers, there is still a chance of erroneous state machine behaviour. If an asynchronous input changes level during the ambiguity window of its synchronizer flip–flop, the flip–flop may enter a **metastable state**. This important topic will be discussed in Section 9.6.

## 6.8 Asynchronous outputs

Where there are asynchronous outputs, that is, outputs which do not come directly from a register, another type of problem can arise. Asynchronous outputs are present in the asynchronous Mealy and Moore forms of Figures 6.4 and 6.7. In these cases, the outputs Ob are generated by part of the logic array. In the Mealy form, the machine inputs enter this logic, and in the Moore form it has only the machine state as input.

Asynchronous outputs can have glitches during state transitions, even if the output is defined as a constant value, as shown in Figure 6.34. If these outputs are fed to other synchronous machines driven by the same clock, or if the following circuitry is insensitive to short pulses, the problem can be ignored. However, if one or more of these outputs is used as a clock, set or reset signal, good design practice demands that they be glitch free.

Let us first look at the Moore form of Figure 6.7. The output logic could contain both function and logic hazards. Function hazards cannot, of course, be removed. Since this type of hazard can cause glitches when there are multiple input changes, a state assignment with only a single state variable change at each transition can eliminate these. This problem is sometimes referred to as an **output race**. However, even with single state variable changes, logic hazards may still be present. These can be removed, as was shown in Section 5.7.2, and thus the outputs can be made entirely glitch free. If these cures are not possible, then all that can be done is to remove the symptoms, the glitches, rather than the causes, the hazards. One possibility is to synchronize the output with a register fed with the machine clock. We now have the synchronous Moore form of Figure 6.9. This of course has the effect of delaying the appearance of the outputs by one cycle. Another method of masking glitches is to enable the asynchronous outputs only during stable periods. This requires an extra external input to the output logic.

It is important to be aware of the form of the implementation arising from particular flowchart constructs when looking for output glitches. For example, the behaviour of the output *A* in Figure 6.35 would appear at first

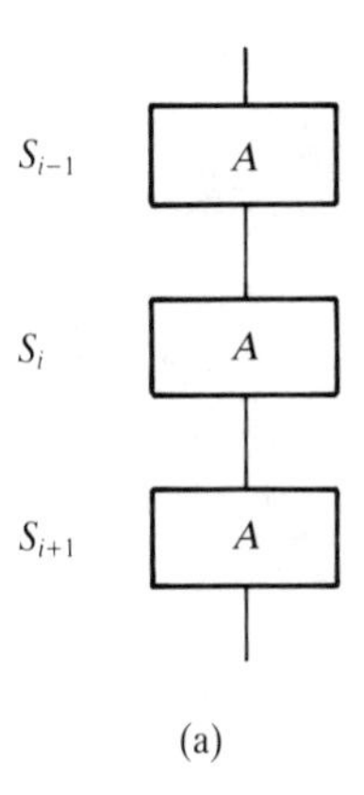


(a)

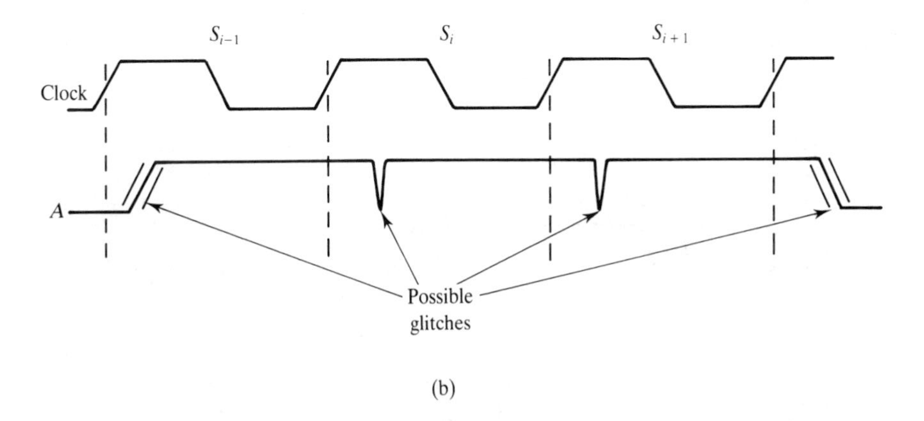


(b)

**Figure 6.34** Asynchronous Moore outputs with glitches.

sight to be the same in cases (a) and (b), being true for the duration of state $S_i$. However, Figure 6.35(a) is the synchronous Mealy form, and Figure 6.35(b) the asynchronous Moore form, which is susceptible to output glitches.

With the asynchronous Mealy form (Figure 6.4), there is the additional problem of the inputs, *I*, feeding into the output logic. Unless the behaviour of the inputs is constrained, there is nothing that can be done about hazards in the output logic. If the inputs are asynchronous, it cannot be guaranteed that they will not change at the same time as state variables. Therefore, the only general solution in this case is to synchronize both the inputs and the outputs.

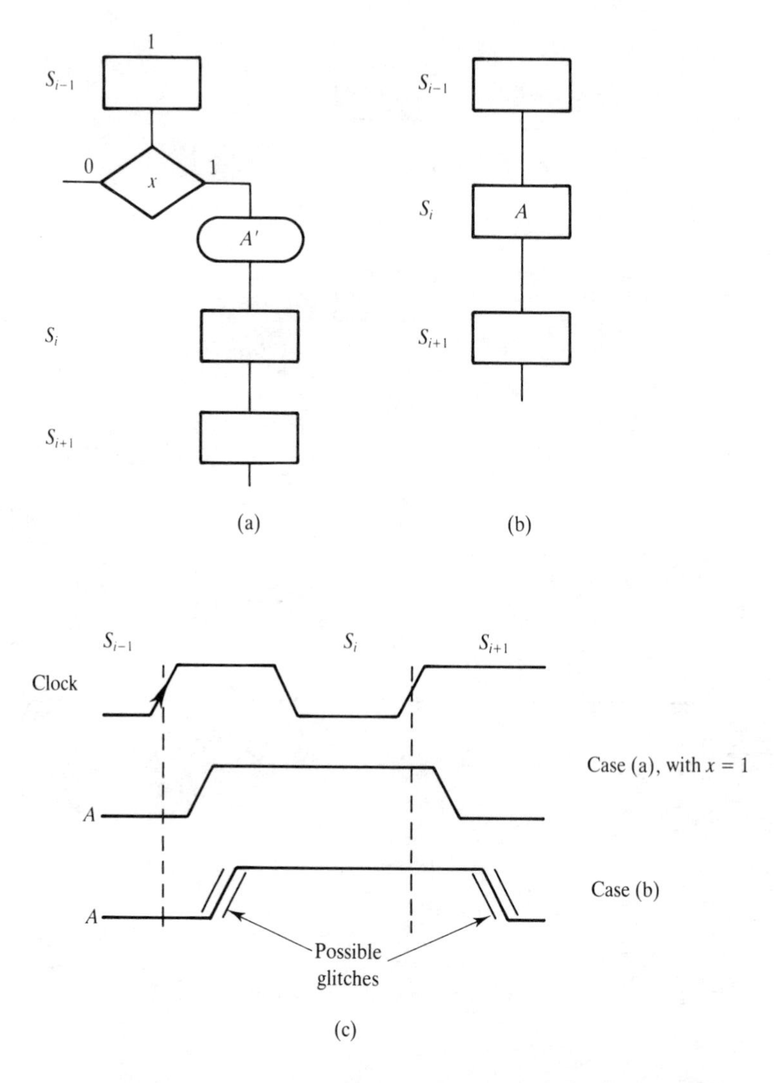


**Figure 6.35** Synchronous Mealy and asynchronous Moore forms.

Even if glitches are not a problem, asynchronous inputs can cause incorrect outputs lasting longer than the typical duration of a glitch. Figure 6.36(a) shows where this can happen. The transition from state S1 is selected by asynchronous input $X$. On the link path to state S2, there is the asynchronous (conditional) output $A$. The timing diagram, Figure 6.36(b), shows the problem which could occur. At the end of state period S1, $X$ is steady at 0 and so the transition is to state S3. However, during state S1, $X$ changed value, causing the asynchronous output to follow. The only cures for this are either to redesign the flowchart or to synchronize the input.

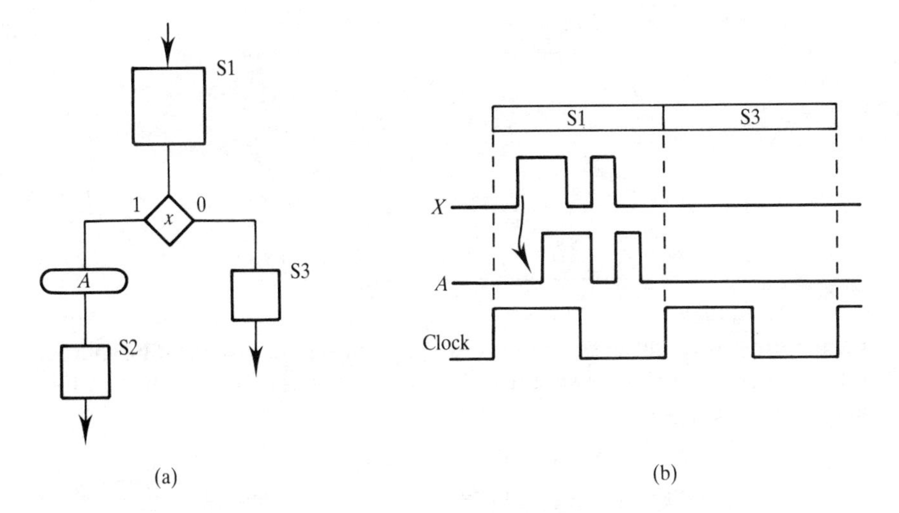


**Figure 6.36** Asynchronous input causing erroneous asynchronous output: (a) flowchart; (b) timing diagrams.

## 6.9 Rules of thumb for minimization

It is often possible to reduce sufficiently the number of transition terms needed in a design without having to resort to the use of minimizer programs, which are not always available. For example, look at the state transitions of Figure 6.37. There are four link paths, but one of them is a 'hold' and therefore requires no term. The three terms obtained from the flowchart are (assuming $S$–$R$ flip–flops) as shown in Table 6.9. Each of

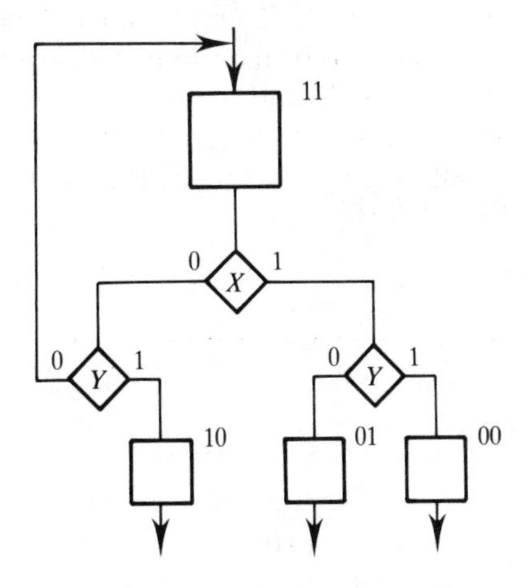


**Figure 6.37** Four link paths requiring only two terms.

**Table 6.9**

| *Term number* | *Inputs X* | *Y* | *Present state* | *Next state* |
|---|---|---|---|---|
| 1 | L | H | HH | –L |
| 2 | H | L | HH | L– |
| 3 | H | H | HH | LL |

these terms has a different 'next state' part, and so no two can be merged into one. However, if we split term 3 into two terms, both of which will be active together,

| | | | | |
|---|---|---|---|---|
| 3a | H | H | HH | –L |
| 3b | H | H | HH | L– |

then something can be done. Because the input $X = Y = 1$ satisfies both of these terms, the next state will be 00 as required. However, now there are some terms with identical 'next state' entries, 1 and 3a with '–L', and 2 and 3b with 'L–'. Both of these pairs differ in only one position in the left half of the table. They can therefore be combined thus:

| | | | | |
|---|---|---|---|---|
| 1 and 3a | – | H | HH | –L |
| 2 and 3b | H | – | HH | L– |

Three terms have been reduced to two. In the transition to state 00, both terms will be active.

It is sometimes possible to reduce the number of terms required by choosing a suitable state assignment. Figure 6.38 is an example of where this can be done. Here two states, S1 and S2, have link paths which go to the same next state, S3, have identical outputs, and are defined by identical input conditions. If the states S1 and S2 are given adjacent assignments, that is assignments which differ in only one bit position, then the two paths can be realized with only a single term. In the table, terms 1 and 2 are replaced by term 3 (Table 6.10).

**Table 6.10**

| *Term number* | *Input X* | *Present state* | *Next state* | *Outputs A* | *B* |
|---|---|---|---|---|---|
| 1 | H | LLL | HHH | H | H |
| 2 | H | LHL | HHH | H | H |
| 3 | H | L–L | HHH | H | H |

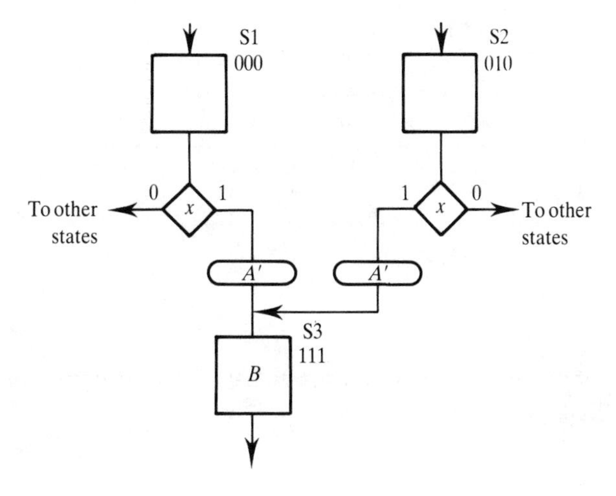


**Figure 6.38** Paths with identical next states, outputs and input conditions.

This rule can be extended to cases where more than two states have paths to the same state with the same outputs and under the same input conditions. Provided that adjacent assignments are given, then only one term is needed.

Where a counting sequence is required, this can be implemented very economically – an $n$-bit counter has $2^n$ transitions, but only requires $n+1$ of the sequencer's transition terms. The example in Table 6.11, a 3-bit binary counter, shows why. Now terms 1, 3, 5 and 7 can be combined, as they have the same next state and are adjacent – that is, the combinations LL, LH, HL, HH appear in the same position in all. Also, terms 2 and 6 can be combined. The reduced table is shown in Table 6.12. The

**Table 6.11**

| *Term number* | *Present state* | *Next state* |
|---|---|---|
| 1 | LLL | --H |
| 2 | LLH | -HL |
| 3 | LHL | --H |
| 4 | LHH | HLL |
| 5 | HLL | --H |
| 6 | HLH | -HL |
| 7 | HHL | --H |
| 8 | HHH | LLL |

**Table 6.12**

| *Terms* | *Present state* | *Next state* |
|---|---|---|
| 1, 3, 5, 7 | --L | --H |
| 2, 6 | -LH | -HL |
| 4 | LHH | HLL |
| 8 | HHH | LLL |

**Table 6.13**

| *Term number* | *Present state* | *Next state* |
|---|---|---|
| *i* | ---------L | ---------H |
| *i* + 1 | --------LH | --------HL |
| *i* + 2 | -------LHH | -------HLL |

pattern can be extended to counters of any size. For example, the first few terms for a 10-bit counter are shown in Table 6.13.

## 6.10 Designing with the programmable logic sequencer

### 6.10.1 The program table

Each sequencer type has its own program table format which holds complete information on the pin usage and application program. For example, the design of Table 6.14 is entered onto a table for the PLS105 device. This table is only used where the design is entered manually. If a CAD package is used, then this information will be created by the compiler. However, the table is useful for learning about and experimenting with sequencer designs. Also, it is possible to manipulate sequencer programs at the 'hardware level' in ways which are not possible with the more rigid CAD languages.

The PLS105 table has provision for input and output signal pin allocation and naming, and a line for each of the 48 possible transition terms. The entries used in the transition term lines are as follows:

| **AND** (input, present state) | | **OR** (next state, output) |
|---|---|---|
| H | true input/state bit | set |
| L | complemented | reset |
| – | don't care | no change |

A comment may be appended to each term to aid documentation of the design. An additional column permits definition of the complement array. Three symbols are used in this column: 'A', '.' and '–'. Their use will be explained shortly.

Finally, a space is allocated for a statement of the mode of the preset/enable pin. 'H' indicates preset, 'L' indicates output enable.

For sequencers with *J–K* flip–flops, the additional symbol '0' is used in the OR array part to denote both inputs connected to the product line.

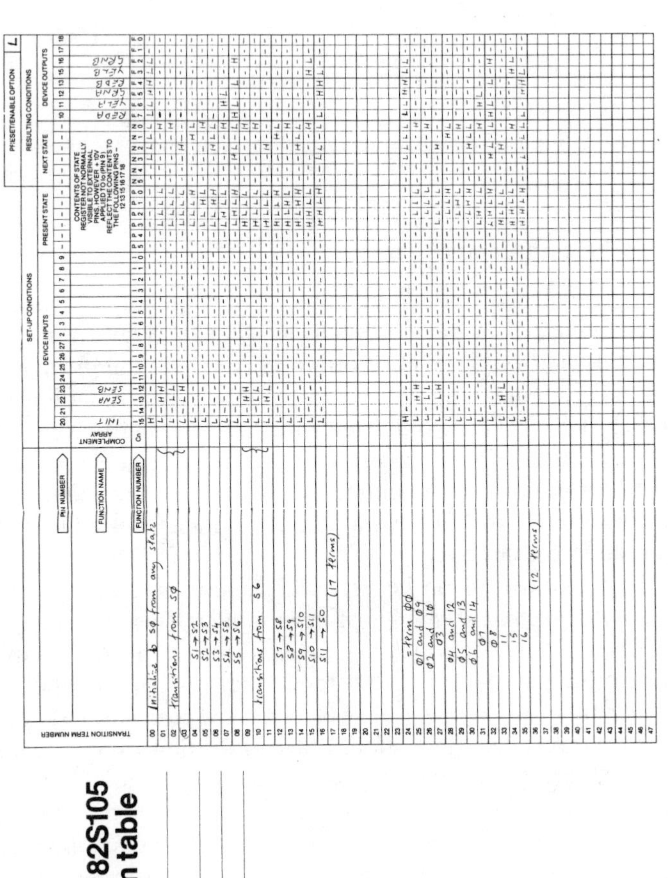

Table 6.14 Traffic signal controller program table.

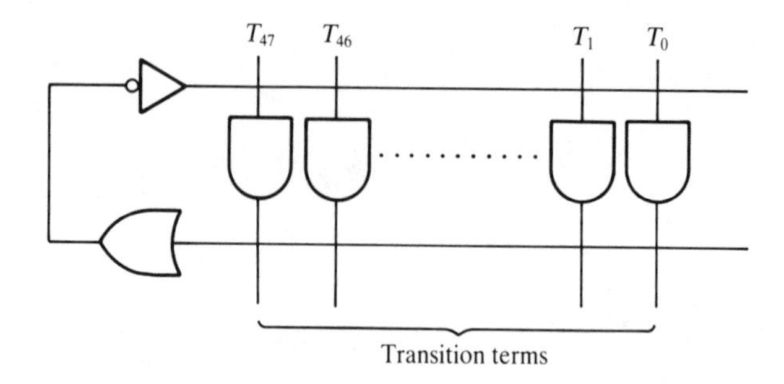


**Figure 6.39** Connection of the complement array.

### 6.10.2 The complement array

The complement array is a feature unique to sequencers. Figure 6.39 shows how it is connected into the sequencer's PLA. It is an extra OR line, that can have inputs from any set of products, which is complemented and fed back as an additional input line to the products. This input line will be true if none of the products connected into the OR line is true. Figure 6.40 shows the three possible configurations of the array at each transition term line. This information is appended to each line in the programming table. (A fourth state '0', inactive, with both fuses intact is used to represent the state of the virgin device.)

To see how this can be used, let us look at some examples. Every reliable state machine design must have some means of escape from illegal states. These are states which are defined by any unused combinations of the state bits; there will be such states whenever the number used in the state machine is not a power of two. If for any reason the sequencer lands in one of these states there should be a transition to a known state. The complement array can perform this task very efficiently. Whenever the machine is in an undefined state, no product will be active, since the products are defined by legal machine states and input combinations. This condition can be detected by connecting every transition term used to the

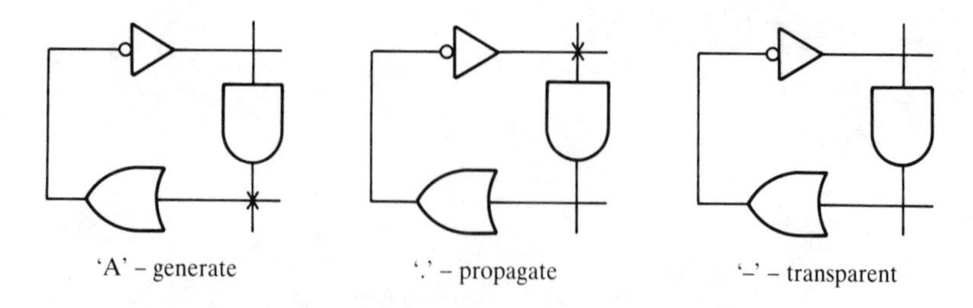


**Figure 6.40** Complement array configurations.

**Table 6.15**

| *Cn* | *Inputs* | *Present state* | *Next state* | |
|---|---|---|---|---|
| . | ----- | ---- | LLLH | transition to 0001 |
| A | -H-LL | LHHH | --LL | normal transition |
| A | L---H | LHLL | H--- | another normal transition |
| | | . | | |
| | | . | | |
| | | . | | |

complement array OR line and feeding the complement of this into a new transition term defining the transition to the known state. In Table 6.15, entry to an illegal state will cause an unconditional transition to state 0001.

To have performed this without the complement array, in most cases more than a single term would have been required. Another use of the complement array which saves terms is in the implementation of 'ELSE' transitions. Figure 6.41 shows a set of transitions from state Sa which are enabled by three combinations of inputs *A*, *B*, *C* causing transitions to states S0, S1 and S2. All other combinations cause a transition to state Sx. Without the complement array, the terms required are as shown in Table 6.16.

Thus four terms, representing all the 'exceptions', are required for the single transition to state Sx. However, these terms can be thought of as 'not the transitions to S0 or S1 or S2'. This is where the complement array can be used again. The table now becomes that shown in Table 6.17.

The four last terms have been compressed into one. Whenever one of the three defined input combinations does not occur in state Sa, there will be no signal ORed into the complement array, thereby activating the

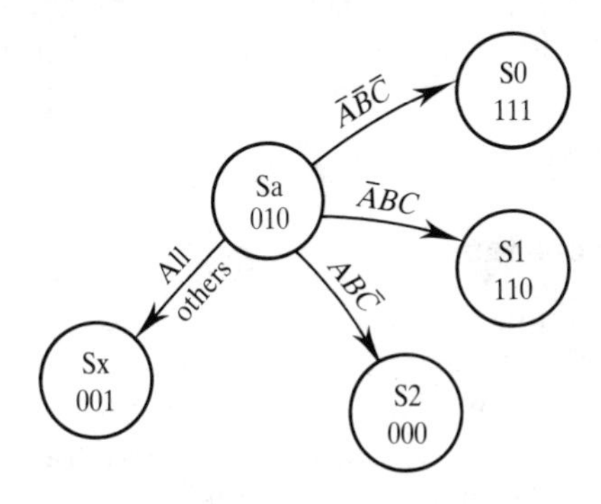


**Figure 6.41** Transitions with an 'exception .

**Table 6.16**

| *Cn* | *A* | *B* | *C* | *Present state* | *Next state* | |
|---|---|---|---|---|---|---|
| – | L | L | L | LHL | H–H | |
| – | L | H | H | LHL | H–– | |
| – | H | H | L | LHL | –L– | |
| – | H | – | H | LHL | –LH | path to state Sx |
| – | – | L | H | LHL | –LH | |
| – | H | L | – | LHL | –LH | |
| – | L | H | L | LHL | –LH | |

**Table 6.17**

| *Cn* | *A* | *B* | *C* | *Present state* | *Next state* | |
|---|---|---|---|---|---|---|
| A | L | L | L | LHL | H–H | |
| A | L | H | H | LHL | H–– | |
| A | H | H | L | LHL | –L– | |
| . | – | – | – | LHL | –LH | path to state Sx |

fourth term and causing a transition to Sx. The same array can be used in other states too, since the propagated signal is ANDed with the present state code. Therefore all 'exceptions' or 'ELSEs' can be realized with one term per state.

The penalty for using the complement array is an increased logic array propagation delay, and thus a reduced maximum operating frequency. The reason for this is that two passes through the array are required before those products with complement array inputs can settle.

### 6.10.3 Asynchronous inputs

As mentioned in Section 6.7, spare internal sequencer flip–flops can be used to synchronize asynchronous inputs. If a state register flip–flop is used, it would be programmed as shown in Table 6.18. The input is $X$, and state flip–flop 0 is used as the synchronizer. If there was no spare state flip–flop, an output flip–flop could be used and wired externally to another input.

**Table 6.18**

| Input<br>*X* | Present<br>state<br>210 | Next<br>state<br>210 | |
|---|---|---|---|
| L | --- | --L | |
| H | --- | --H | |
| – | LLL | HH– | transition from 00 to 11 enabled by $\overline{X}$ |

The asynchronous preset, when used, has to be treated as an asynchronous input to a state machine. This is illustrated in Figure 6.42 where an asynchronous preset pulse is shown together with the clock. The problem arises when the preset signal is released. Before release, all flip–flops are in the '1' state. If the preset is released at least $T_{SPR}$ before the next clock edge, all flip–flops will operate. This cannot be guaranteed, however, as the preset is asynchronous. Therefore this set-up time is bound to be violated occasionally. In this case, not all flip–flops will respond to the clock after release. If the transition from the reset state requires more than one flip–flop to change, then an incorrect transition is possible. To avoid this, any transitions out of the reset state must change only one state bit.

### 6.10.4 A design example – a traffic signal controller

A controller is required for traffic signals on an intersection between two one-way streets (Figure 6.43). Two traffic sensors give outputs SENA and SENB to determine the sequence. The six outputs control each signal lamp. The signal INIT initializes the sequence. The controller block diagram is shown in Figure 6.44 and the state transition diagram for the controller is given in Figure 6.45. Note that only output changes are specified, as *S–R* flip–flops will be used in the implementation.

The design requires 3 inputs, 12 states (and therefore 4 state bits), and 6 outputs. The state sequences (S1, S2, S3, S4 and S7, S8, S9, S10) are

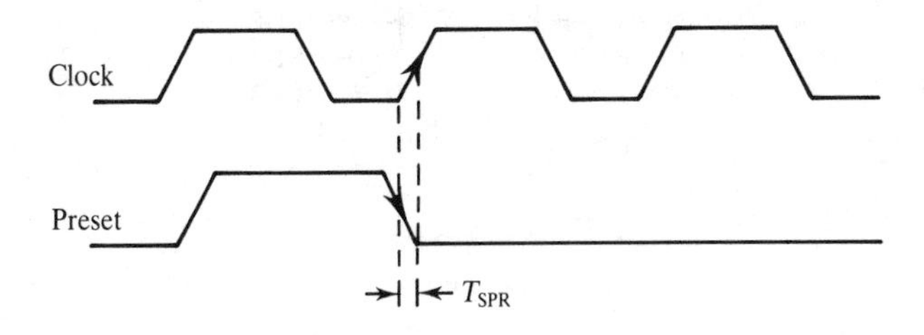


**Figure 6.42** Asynchronous preset.

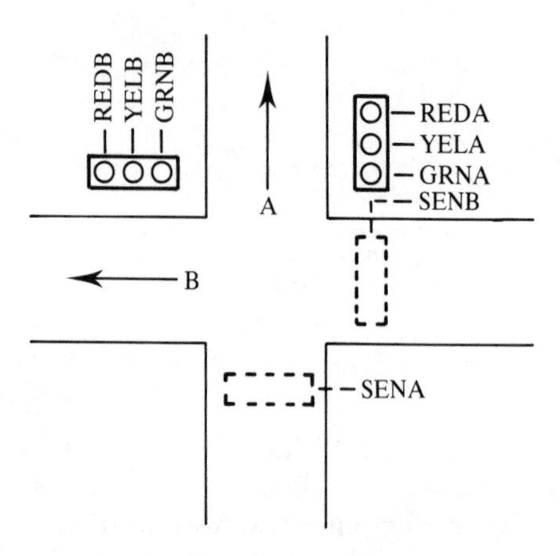


**Figure 6.43** Traffic intersection.

used to provide delays. The design easily fits into any of the available sequencers, provided that no more than 48 transition terms are required. A PLS105 is chosen here. The first step is to allocate signals to pins. This was done as shown on the program table (Table 6.14). The following state assignment is used:

| | | | | | |
|---|---|---|---|---|---|
| S0: 0000 | S1: 0001 | S2: 0010 | S3: 0011 | S4: 0100 | S5: 0101 |
| S6: 1000 | S7: 1001 | S8: 1010 | S9: 1011 | S10: 1100 | S11: 1101 |

With this assignment, the transitions can be entered directly onto the program table. 17 terms are required. The state assignment was chosen to enable minimization by noting the similarity between the left-hand and right-hand halves of the state diagram. Codes differing in one position were chosen for states having similar positions in the sequence. The result is shown in the lower part of the table (of course this could not coexist with the upper part). The combination of terms results in only 12 terms being

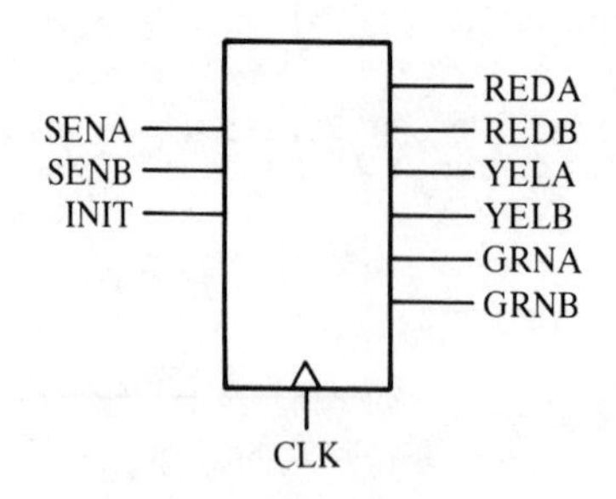


**Figure 6.44** Traffic signal controller.

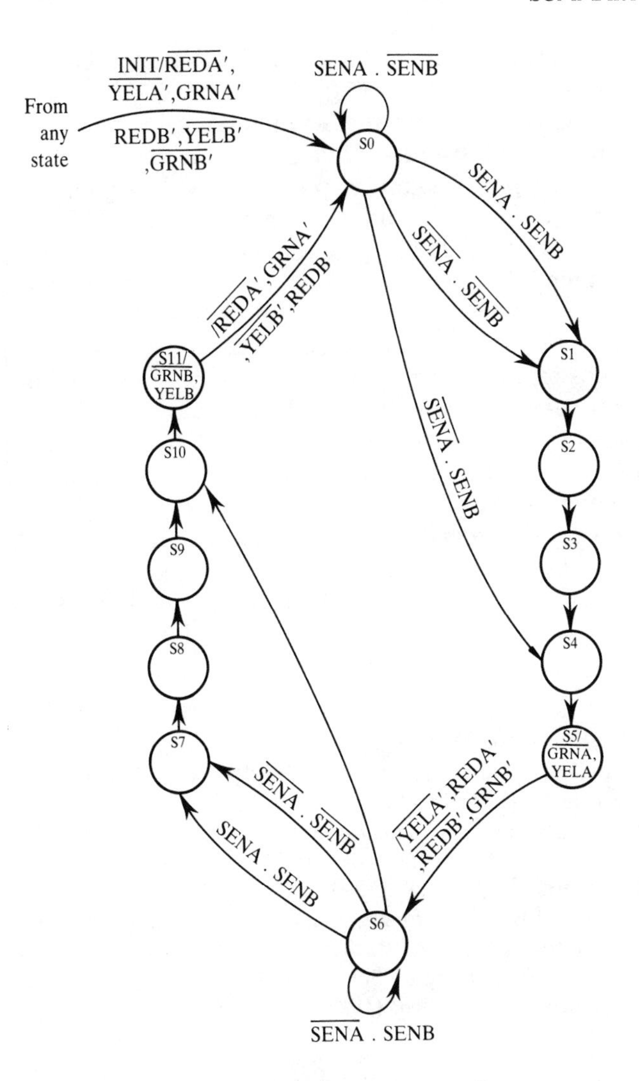


**Figure 6.45** Traffic signal controller.

required. Of course, if the sequencer is not to be put to any other use, there is no need for this minimization.

## SUMMARY

Digital systems contain synchronous sequential blocks whose combinational logic has no regular structure and are thus a suitable PLA application. Controllers and sequencers are in this category. Synchronous sequential machines may be categorized into the synchronous and asynchronous variants of the Mealy and Moore forms. All types can occur in designs. A PLD containing a PLA and a set of clocked flip–flops is a sequencer. The behaviour of a synchronous machine can be specified in a PLA (or PLS) table, which is also a direct statement of the sequencer personality. The timing parameters of a sequencer's PLA and flip–flops enable the maximum clock frequency to be calculated. State machine flowcharts, or their textual equivalents, are a very convenient way of specifying the behaviour of a controller. They may be converted in one step into a PLS table. Use of *S–R* and *J–K* flip–flops can often save product terms and can be handled with modified PLS tables. Asynchronous inputs cause problems which can only be partially overcome by state assignment. Input synchronization is usually the best way of handling them. Asynchronous outputs, in both Mealy and Moore forms, can cause glitch problems as a result of hazards. These again cannot always be cured by state assignment. Where the number of products only just exceeds the PLD capacity, hand minimization by combining terms may be adequate. The complement array, present in some sequencers, can reduce numbers of product terms at the cost of a lower clock rate.

## BIBLIOGRAPHICAL NOTES

The fullest range of sequencers and applications is described in Signetics (1986); the AMAZE state machine specification notation is described in Signetics (1984). State machine flowcharts are fully explained in Clare (1973); the first half of Green (1986) is a modern restatement. Other textbooks which have sections on state machine flowcharts are Fletcher (1980), Wiatrowski and House (1980), Comer (1984) and Roth (1985). Treatment of asynchronous inputs in PLDs is covered more fully in Bolton (1987). The traffic signal controller example is adapted from the PAL design in Monolithic Memories (1986). An example of 'hardware-oriented' sequencer design is Britt (1986).

## EXERCISES

**6.1** A sequencer has the following timing parameters:

set-up time, input to clock = 40 ns
set-up time, input to clock, with complement array = 70 ns
propagation delay, clock to output = 20 ns

What is the maximum frequency of operation with and without the complement array?

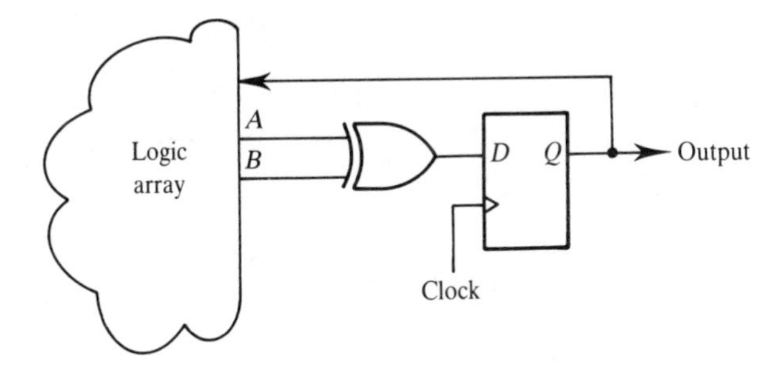


**Figure 6.46**

**6.2** Draw flowcharts for the following state machines with inputs $A$ and $B$:

(1) a serial adder, and

(2) a serial comparator with outputs $A > B$, $A = B$ and $A < B$.

In each case the data enters least-significant bit first. Show how a third synchronous input can be used to delimit words, and modify the flowcharts to include it.

**6.3** Describe the priority encoder of Exercise 5.7 as a flowchart. If this decision network was used to select from eight next states, what is the minimum number of products which would be required?

**6.4** When would a state transition diagram be a more suitable form of specification for a state machine than a flowchart? What could be the dangers?

**6.5** Some PLDs contain flip–flops which are wired as shown in Figure 6.46. Show how the signals $A$ and $B$ can be defined such that the flip–flop appears to be of the $J$–$K$ type. (First look at how it can be converted to the $T$ type.)

**6.6** A sequential circuit is required which continuously generates the waveform shown in Figure 6.47. Design a synchronous state machine which produces this waveform directly from the output logic without resynchronization. No glitches due to hazards must appear in the output signal.

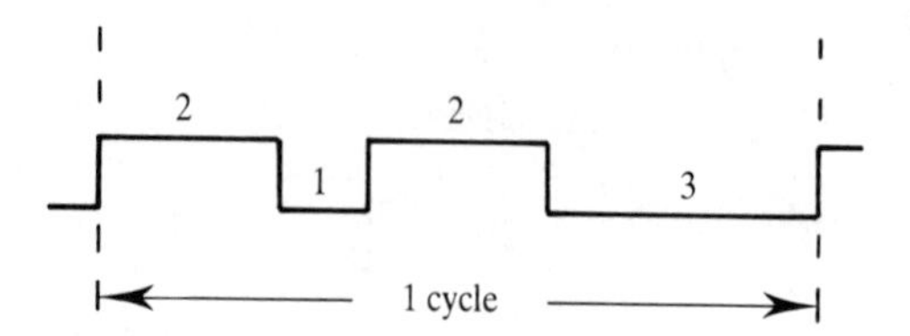


**Figure 6.47**

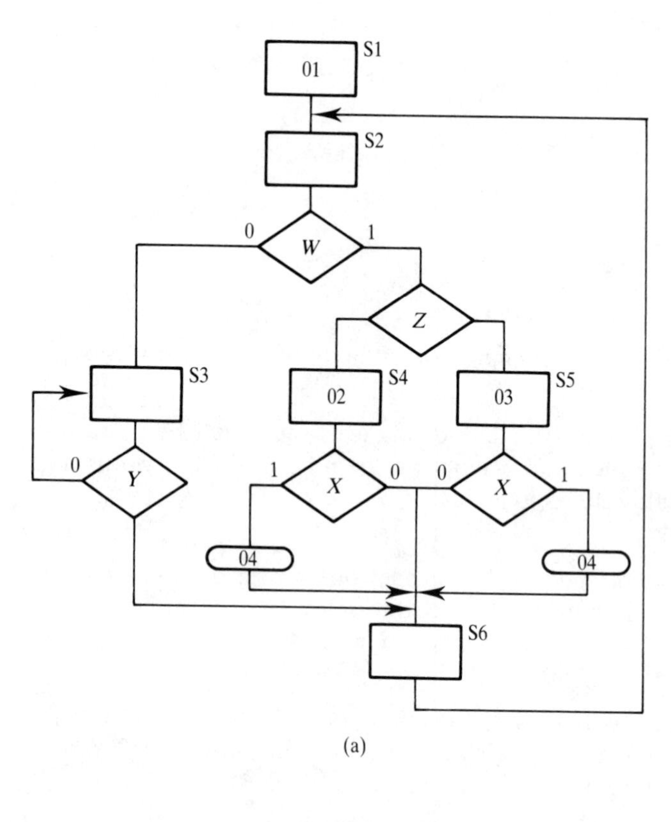


(a)

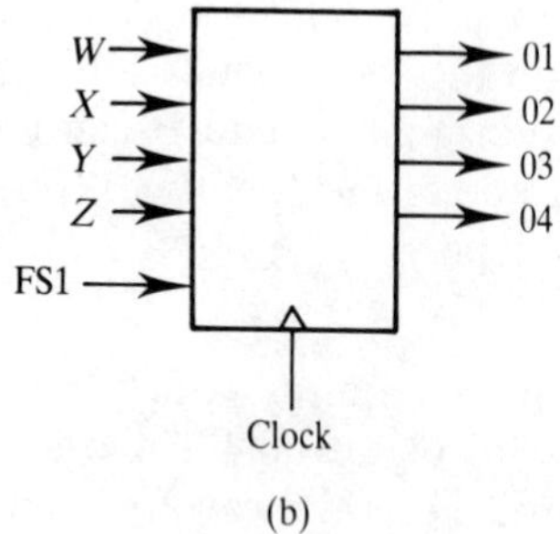


(b)

**Figure 6.48**

**6.7** A noise filter for a serial data receiver is to be designed. The filter has access to a clock running at 16 times the serial data rate, and to the serial data stream. An output, 'noise flag', is to be generated whenever there is an isolated sample (either 1 or 0) in the input data.

(1) Design a state machine for the filter which examines three adjacent samples and generates the output 'noise flag' when noise is detected (four states are required).

(2) Draw a PLA table for an implementation.

(3) Is there a hazard in the output logic? Can it be removed, and if so, how?

**6.8** Figure 6.48 is the specification of a state machine which is to be constructed with a PLA and three *D* flip–flops. The flip–flops have both asynchronous preset and clear inputs.

The machine is asynchronously forced into state S1 whenever input FS1 is asserted. All the inputs *W*, *X*, *Y* and *Z* are asynchronous with respect to the clock.

Draw a block diagram and produce a state assignment for this machine. The state assignment should be such as to attempt to minimize the logic and to avoid possible timing problems. (Remember that transitions to state 000 are free.)

Are there any insoluble timing problems? If so, suggest a design change.

**6.9** Draw the flowchart for a counter which counts in the sequence 0, 1, 2, 3 . . . and resets after reaching 3, 7, 11 or 15 depending on the state of two inputs *X* and *Y*. Show how, in a sequencer implementation, the number of products required can be reduced by using the complement array.

**6.10** What would be the advantages of a sequencer with two complement arrays?

CHAPTER 7

# Further Topics in State Machine Design

---

**OBJECTIVES**

When you have completed studying this chapter you should be able

- to understand the difficulties and limitations of applying manual methods of state reduction and state assignment;
- to design and minimize manually state machines implemented in PAL-structured devices;
- to design more compact state machine flowcharts through the use of subroutines;
- to apply some simple decompositions for overcoming the resource limitations of a PLD;
- to design parallel controllers using linked state machines.

---

## 7.1 Introduction

In the last chapter, the basic concepts in state machine specification and implementation with sequencers were covered. In this chapter some further state machine design and optimization methods and the use of other PLD types, which can sometimes lead to more efficient implementations, will be looked at. In addition, the design of ensembles of communicating state machines, and methods of placing them into the same PLD, will be studied.

## 7.2 State reduction

For every finite state machine specified by its input/output behaviour, in theory there exists a state diagram or table which has the minimum possible number of states. To utilize the state flip–flops in a PLD most efficiently, a state machine design should have the smallest possible number of states (unless the number of states in the reduced version does not bring the number below the next lowest power of 2). Therefore it may pay to reduce the number of states in a design by applying a state reduction technique. 'May' is appropriate rather than 'will' because it cannot be guaranteed that the reduced version will require fewer product terms – it may indeed require more. Also, the larger the state machine, the less is likely to be gained by state reduction. Since each additional state bit used doubles the number of states possible, a large reduction in states may be necessary to save one state register bit.

When doing the initial sketch of a state machine specification, it is not unusual to produce a design with more states than necessary. For example, where different outputs must be generated in response to sets of input conditions, the first attempt may lead to a construction like that in Figure 7.1(a). Here the inputs are tested sequentially in states S1, S2 and S3, and the outputs *X* and *Y* are state outputs. However, provided that the input and output timing constraints allow it, all of this can be done in state S1 through the use of conditional outputs, as shown in Figure 7.1(b); the decisions are performed in parallel. Another form of reduction is sometimes possible by sharing states. For example, in Figure 7.2(a) the states Sa and Sb do identical tasks, except that in one case input *C* is true, and in the other it is false. They may therefore be combined into state Sab provided that an additional decision box is inserted to ensure that the two next states can be entered appropriately. To do this reduction, the behaviour of the inputs must be known – it could not be done by considering the flowchart in isolation.

It is difficult to formalize this type of procedure; effective state reduction depends on a good understanding of the problem, and in fact some reductions only become possible through minor changes to the specification, as in the example of Figure 7.1. Of course, as in all PLD minimization procedures, if the resources of the PLD are adequate, there

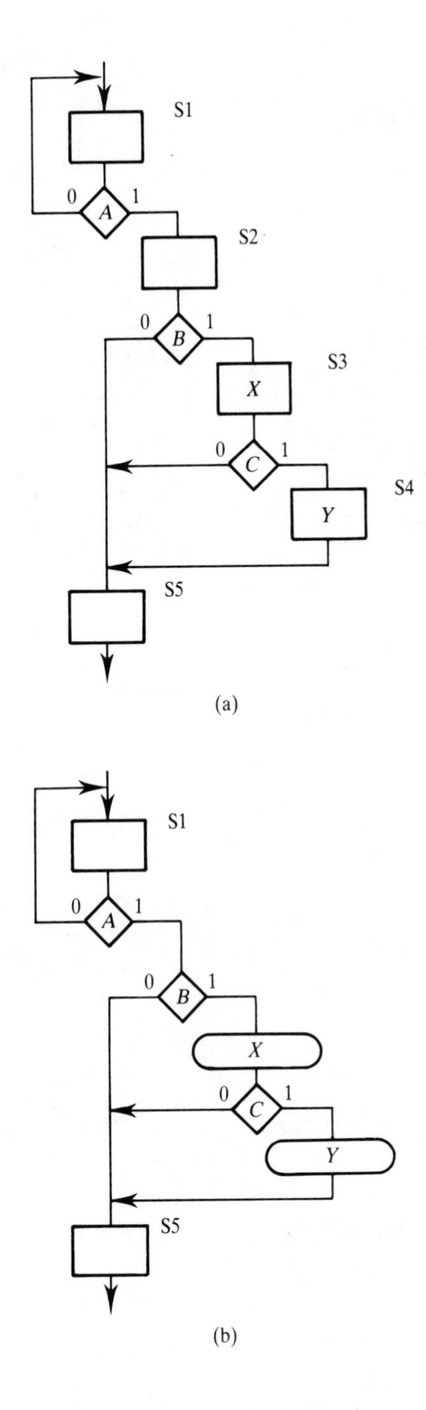


**Figure 7.1** State reductions through use of conditional outputs: (a) original version; (b) reduced version.

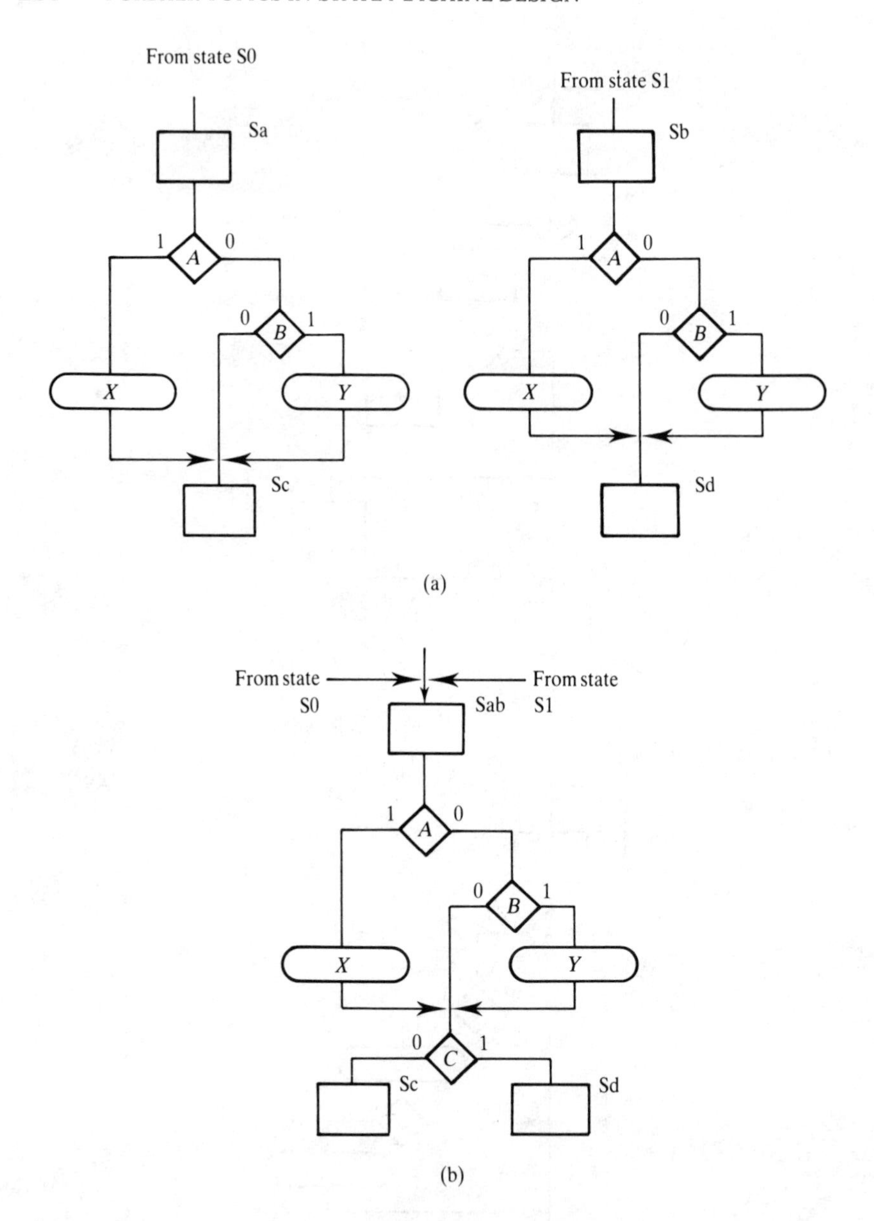


**Figure 7.2** State reduction through state sharing: (a) original version; (b) reduced version.

is no point in a further reduction. Similarly, it is only necessary to reduce sufficiently to allow a fit.

Formal methods do exist for state reduction, but are of doubtful value in practice. These procedures take a state machine design, and produce as a result an exactly equivalent state machine with fewer states, if reduction is possible. They rely on the detection of **equivalent states**, that is, states which have identical outputs and transitions to next states which are also equivalent. For machines with many inputs, these methods become very inefficient and impractical to apply manually.

## 7.3 Using other types of PLD for state machines

### 7.3.1 Sequencers with 2-bit decoders

In Section 3.3 it was shown how 2-bit input decoding could reduce the number of products required for implementing a set of functions in a PLA. The same idea can be applied to sequencers to yield the structure of Figure 7.3, where the inputs are decoded two bits at a time. Table 7.1, which is an extension of Table 3.2, shows what PLS table entries are now possible.

**Table 7.1** Sequencer table entries with 1- and 2-bit input decoding of variables $A$ and $B$.

| *UVXY* | *1-bit* | | *2-bit* | |
|---|---|---|---|---|
| | *Function* | *Table* | *Function* | *Table* |
| 0000 | 1 | -- | 1 | -- |
| 0001 | $B$ | –H | $A+B$ | PP |
| 0010 | $\overline{B}$ | –L | $A+\overline{B}$ | PN |
| 0011 | 0 | –0† | $A$ | H– |
| 0100 | $A$ | H– | $\overline{A}+B$ | NP |
| 0101 | $AB$ | HH | $B$ | –H |
| 0110 | $A\overline{B}$ | HL | $A=B$ | EE |
| 0111 | 0 | H0† | $A \cdot B$ | HH |
| 1000 | $\overline{A}$ | L– | $\overline{A}+\overline{B}$ | NN |
| 1001 | $\overline{A}B$ | LH | $A \oplus B$ | UU |
| 1010 | $\overline{A}\overline{B}$ | LL | $\overline{B}$ | –L |
| 1011 | 0 | L0† | $A \cdot \overline{B}$ | HL |
| 1100 | 0 | 0–† | $\overline{A}$ | L– |
| 1101 | 0 | 0H† | $\overline{A} \cdot B$ | LH |
| 1110 | 0 | 0L† | $\overline{A} \cdot \overline{B}$ | LL |
| 1111 | 0 | 00 | 0 | 00 |

$U$, $V$, $X$ and $Y$ are defined in Figure 3.19.
† Equivalent to 00.

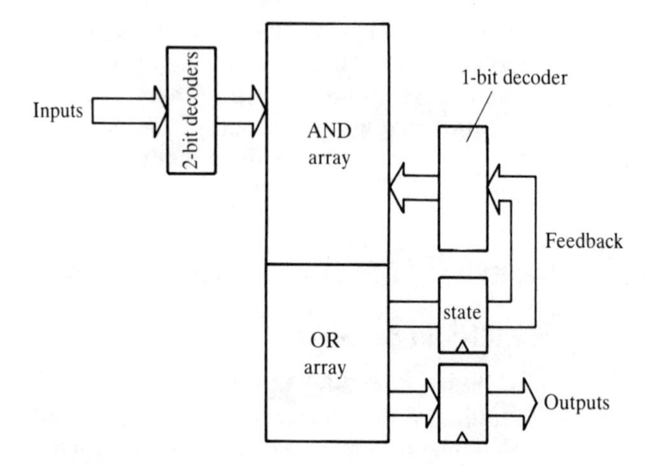


**Figure 7.3** Sequencer with 2-bit input decoding.

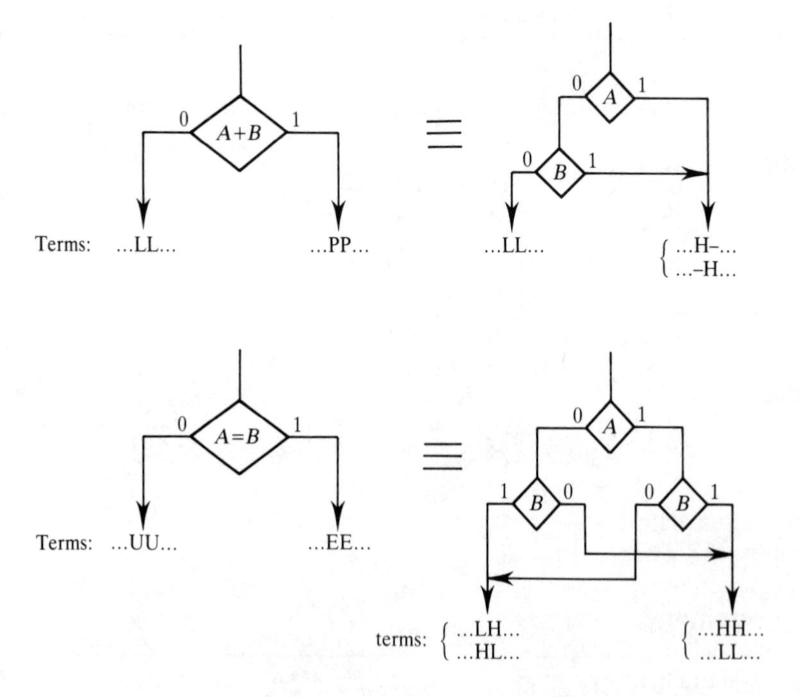


**Figure 7.4** Flowchart decisions with 1- and 2-bit decoding.

There are six new cases:

$$A + B \qquad A + \overline{B} \qquad \overline{A} + B \qquad A = B \qquad \overline{A} + \overline{B} \qquad A \oplus B$$

These have the table entries:

PP PN NP EE NN UU

The use of these entries can save product terms as shown in the examples of Figure 7.4. In Figure 7.4(a) three link paths are replaced by two, and in Figure 7.4(b) four are replaced by two.

The feedback terms from the state flip–flops in Figure 7.3 are fed through the usual 1-bit decoders, because the table entries for 'present state' only need to be 'H', 'L' and '–' for each state bit.

Although such sequencers are not difficult to use, they have not been widely offered as standard parts by the semiconductor firms. They have, however, been used internally by computer manufacturers.

### 7.3.2 PAL-type devices

Although PLA-based sequencers are the most natural devices to use for state machine controller applications, there are often circumstances where PLDs with the PAL architecture are not too difficult to use and may be the most economical solution. For example, small state machines which need to operate with a high clock frequency can most economically be implemented with a PAL device. Also, many of the larger PLDs have the PAL architecture, that is they have groups of products which are dedicated to particular outputs or internal registers (these devices are listed in Table A.10).

With PAL devices, the simple transformation from flowchart to PLA or PLS table via link paths breaks down; an intermediate logic design stage is necessary. This is because the product terms for each output have to be designed separately. No longer does a single link path necessarily map into a single product. These points will become clear in the following design example.

The machine to be designed is a clock generator for a system which requires two glitch-free clock signals and two related level signals. It is driven by a master clock and is controlled by four inputs. Figure 7.5 shows these signals on a block diagram, always the first thing to be drawn. The inputs are synchronized. Note that the polarity of each signal is given. The clock generator can be specified as a state machine, and it is required to implement the design in a registered PAL device. One of the devices from Table A.6 or A.7 would therefore be suitable. Before being able to draw the state machine flowchart, however, it is necessary to know what type or types of flip–flop are used for registered output storage. In registered PAL

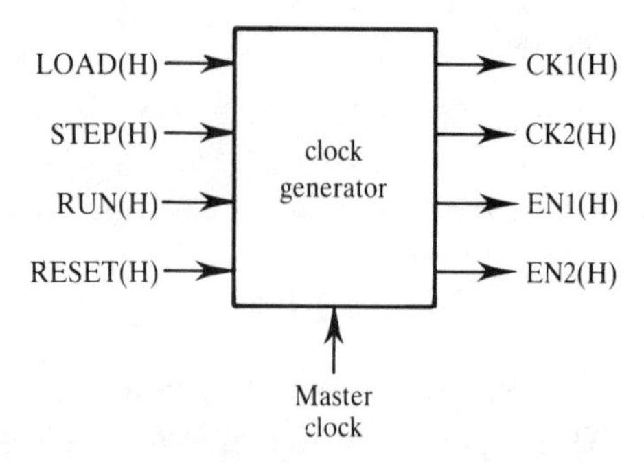


**Figure 7.5** Clock generator I/O signals.

devices, *D* flip–flops are used. In the sequencer designs of the last chapter, we assumed *R–S* or *J–K* flip–flops when drawing flowcharts. One rule has to be changed when using *D* flip–flops: since registered outputs do not by default remain in their previous state after clocking, every '1' output bit must be defined by an active product. Thus registered outputs must be named in a state or conditional output box whenever they are active, in fact just like asynchronous outputs. A further implication of using *D* flip–flops is that 'hold' transitions are not now free; all apart from the transition from '0 . . . 0' to '0 . . . 0' require at least one product to be active.

The flowchart for the clock generator is given in Figure 7.6. It is to be implemented in a 16R4 PAL device, illustrated in Figure 7.7. There are

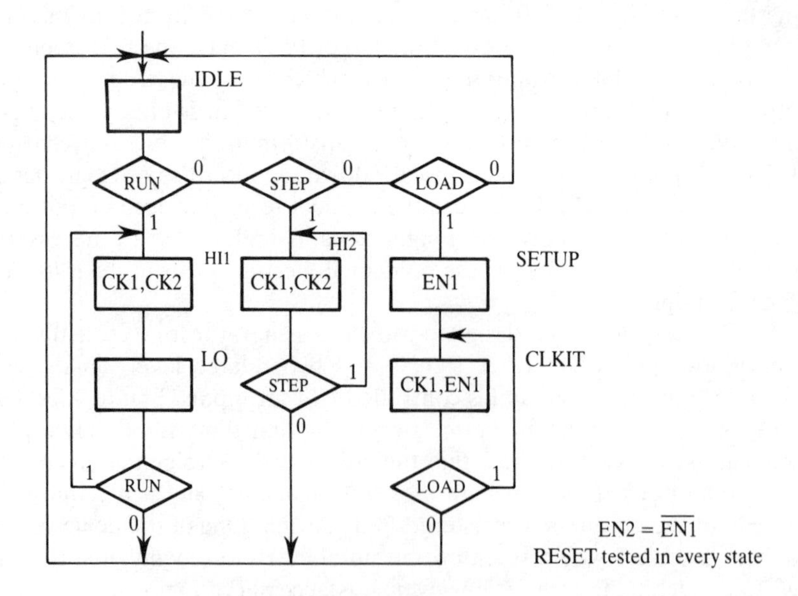


**Figure 7.6** Clock generator flowchart.

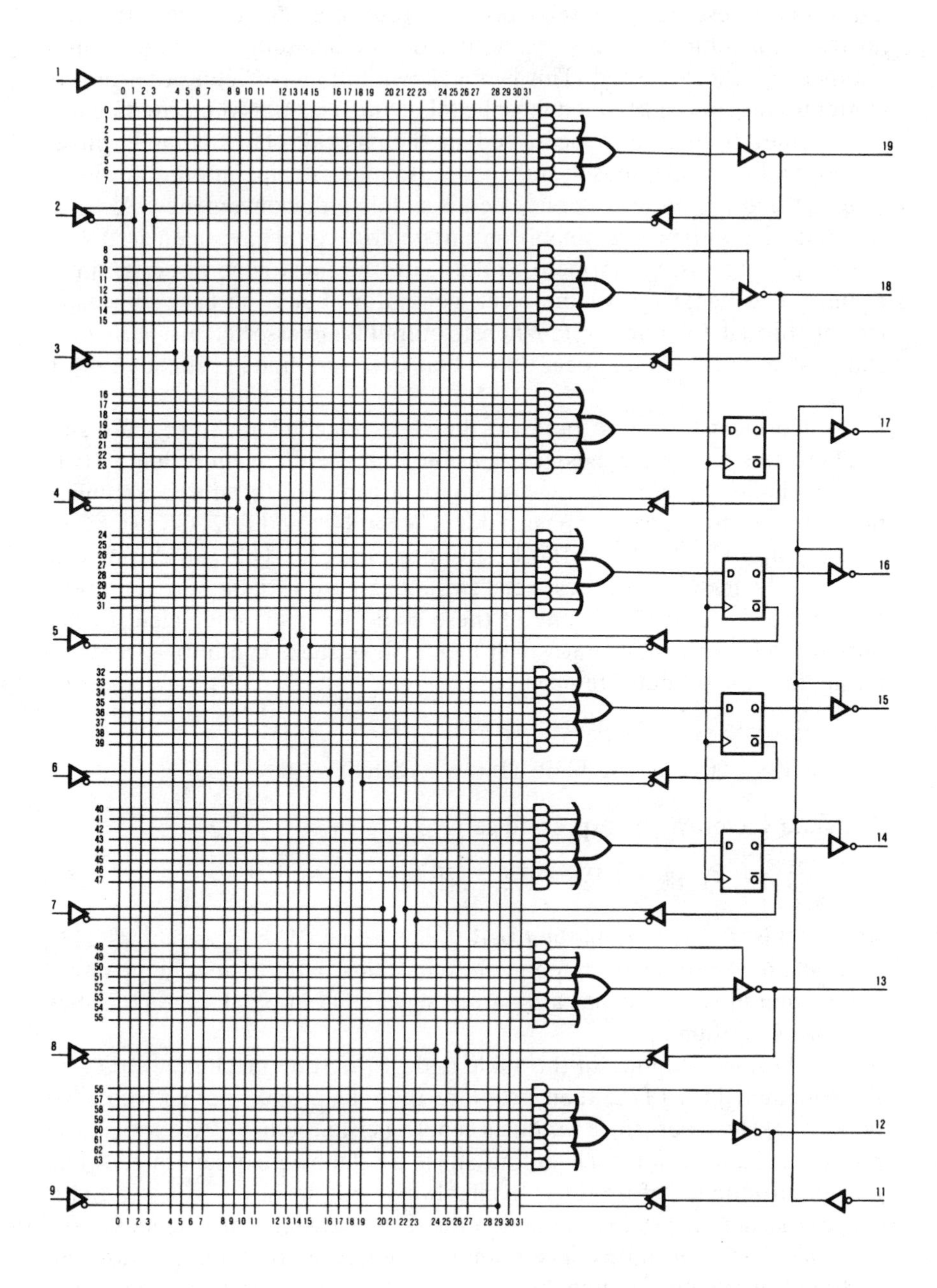


Figure 7.7 16R4 PAL device.

two additional important points to note about this device: firstly it has no independent reset pin, and secondly all outputs are negated. Since there is no reset function, this must be designed into the state machine as just another input to be tested. This is not shown in Figure 7.6 in order not to clutter up the flowchart, but it must be taken into account when creating the PLA table. It must also be tested in the 'illegal' states, that is those corresponding to the unused state codes, to allow escape into a safe state. The fact that the outputs are negated is simply an inconvenience. A more recent device with programmable output polarity could have been used, but the simpler one is chosen here to illustrate the most general design procedure. The behaviour of the clock generator should be easy to see by tracing through the flowchart. When an output is not asserted in a particular state its name does not appear. Note that EN2 is defined as the inverse of EN1.

The next step is to perform the state assignment. Since CK1 and CK2 must be free of glitches, it is sensible to make them equivalent to two state variables. Looking at the flowchart, it can seen that three combinations of these two signals appear: $CK1 \cdot CK2$ in HI1 and HI2, $CK1 \cdot \overline{CK2}$ in CLKIT, and $\overline{CK1} \cdot \overline{CK2}$ in IDLE, LO and SETUP. Thus, to distinguish between the members of these sets, two more state variables are required. It would also be helpful if one of these could be made equivalent to the output EN1. An assignment which meets all of these conditions, remembering that the outputs are negated, is:

| | | |
|---|---|---|
| IDLE: 1110 | HI1: 0010 | LO: 1111 |
| HI2: 0011 | SETUP: 1100 | CLKIT: 0100 |

The state vector can be expressed as

$$S3 \cdot S2 \cdot S1 \cdot S0 = \overline{CK1} \cdot \overline{CK2} \cdot \overline{EN1} \cdot S0$$

where S0 is a state variable not tied to an output. The PLA table (Table 7.2) can now be set up by mapping flowchart link paths to lines in the table. Notice that all signal names are purely logical and internal – the polarities have been subsumed.

There are 13 lines in this table and, if the state machine were to be implemented in a PLA, then no more than 13 product terms would be necessary. However, since products cannot be shared in a PAL device, the products required for each output must be determined separately. The maximum number of products available per output in the 16R4 is eight. Hence the sum-of-products equation for each next state variable must have no more than eight terms. The number required before minimization can be found simply by counting the number of 1s in each output column of the PLA table. Column NS3 has seven, and column NS0 has three; no minimization is necessary for these functions. However, NS2 has nine and NS1 has ten. For the design to fit, these must be reduced to eight or less.

**Table 7.2** PLA table for clock generator.

| *Inputs* | | | | *State* | | | | *Next state/outputs* | | | |
|---|---|---|---|---|---|---|---|---|---|---|---|
| *RUN* | *STEP* | *LOAD* | *RESET* | *S3* | *S2* | *S1* | *S0* | *NS3* | *NS2* | *NS1* | *NS0* |
| * | * | * | 0 | * | * | * | * | 1 | 1 | 1 | 0 |
| 0 | 0 | 0 | 1 | 1 | 1 | 1 | 0 | 1 | 1 | 1 | 0 |
| 1 | * | * | 1 | 1 | 1 | 1 | 0 | 0 | 0 | 1 | 0 |
| 0 | 1 | * | 1 | 1 | 1 | 1 | 0 | 0 | 0 | 1 | 1 |
| 0 | 0 | 1 | 1 | 1 | 1 | 1 | 0 | 1 | 1 | 0 | 0 |
| * | * | * | 1 | 0 | 0 | 1 | 0 | 1 | 1 | 1 | 1 |
| 1 | * | * | 1 | 1 | 1 | 1 | 1 | 0 | 0 | 1 | 0 |
| 0 | * | * | 1 | 1 | 1 | 1 | 1 | 1 | 1 | 1 | 0 |
| * | 1 | * | 1 | 0 | 0 | 1 | 1 | 0 | 0 | 1 | 1 |
| * | 0 | * | 1 | 0 | 0 | 1 | 1 | 1 | 1 | 1 | 0 |
| * | * | * | 1 | 1 | 1 | 0 | 0 | 0 | 1 | 0 | 0 |
| * | * | 1 | 1 | 0 | 1 | 0 | 0 | 0 | 1 | 0 | 0 |
| * | * | 0 | 1 | 0 | 1 | 0 | 0 | 1 | 1 | 1 | 0 |

If this minimization is to be done by hand, there is a type of K map which greatly simplifies the procedure. This is the method of **map-entered variables**, or infrequently used variables. It is useful where the independent variables can be divided into two classes: frequently and infrequently used. In state machine design, the state variables generally fall into the former category, and the input variables into the latter. The method will be introduced by applying it to the minimization of the functions NS2 and NS1. Before setting up the maps, the variable RESET must be considered. This is neither a state variable nor an infrequently used variable as no 'don't cares' appear in its column. To prevent problems in applying the method, it can fortunately be eliminated by noting that its entry is '1' in every row but the first. Hence new variables NS2′ and NS1′ can be defined, where

$$\mathrm{NS2} = \overline{\mathrm{RESET}} + \mathrm{RESET} \cdot \mathrm{NS2}'$$
$$\mathrm{NS1} = \overline{\mathrm{RESET}} + \mathrm{RESET} \cdot \mathrm{NS1}'$$

(or $\mathrm{NS2} = \overline{\mathrm{RESET}} + \mathrm{NS2}'$, $\mathrm{NS1} = \overline{\mathrm{RESET}} + \mathrm{NS1}'$).

Now variable-entered maps for NS2′ and NS1′ can be drawn, and are shown in Figure 7.8. Each square corresponds to a combination of the

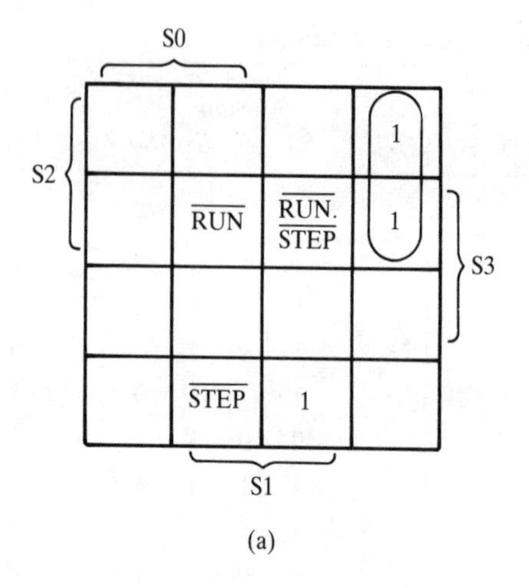


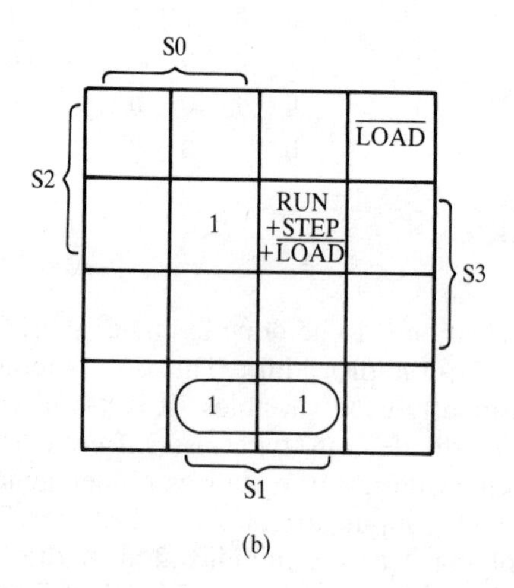


**Figure 7.8** Variable-entered map for NS2′ and NS1′: (a) variable-entered map for NS2′ (NS2 = $\overline{\text{RESET}}$ + RESET.NS2′); (b) variable-entered map for NS1′ (NS1 = $\overline{\text{RESET}}$ + RESET.NS1′).

state variables. For those squares corresponding to states used, an expression is entered defining the input conditions which make the output variable true. Where all of the inputs are 'don't care', a '1' is entered. Seven-variable maps have thus been compressed into four-variable maps. In the map for NS2′, two minimizations are possible. Firstly, two lines of the table have been compressed into the square marked '$\overline{\text{RUN}} \cdot \overline{\text{STEP}}$', and two '1's can be encircled. The number of products for NS2 is thus five plus the one required for $\overline{\text{RESET}}$. Similarly, from the map for NS1′, the number is six plus one. The state machine can thus fit into a 16R4 PAL.

The final equations are as follows:

$$\begin{aligned}
\mathrm{NS3} = {} & \overline{\mathrm{RESET}} + \mathrm{S3}\cdot\mathrm{S2}\cdot\mathrm{S1}\cdot\overline{\mathrm{S0}}\cdot\overline{\mathrm{RUN}}\cdot\overline{\mathrm{STEP}}\cdot\overline{\mathrm{LOAD}} \\
& + \mathrm{S3}\cdot\mathrm{S2}\cdot\mathrm{S1}\cdot\overline{\mathrm{S0}}\cdot\overline{\mathrm{RUN}}\cdot\overline{\mathrm{STEP}}\cdot\mathrm{LOAD} + \overline{\mathrm{S3}}\cdot\overline{\mathrm{S2}}\cdot\mathrm{S1}\cdot\overline{\mathrm{S0}} \\
& + \mathrm{S3}\cdot\mathrm{S2}\cdot\mathrm{S1}\cdot\mathrm{S0}\cdot\overline{\mathrm{RUN}} + \overline{\mathrm{S3}}\cdot\overline{\mathrm{S2}}\cdot\mathrm{S1}\cdot\mathrm{S0}\cdot\overline{\mathrm{STEP}} \\
& + \overline{\mathrm{S3}}\cdot\mathrm{S2}\cdot\overline{\mathrm{S1}}\cdot\overline{\mathrm{S0}}\cdot\overline{\mathrm{LOAD}} \\
\mathrm{NS2} = {} & \overline{\mathrm{RESET}} + \mathrm{S2}\cdot\overline{\mathrm{S1}}\cdot\overline{\mathrm{S0}} + \mathrm{S3}\cdot\mathrm{S2}\cdot\mathrm{S1}\cdot\overline{\mathrm{S0}}\cdot\overline{\mathrm{RUN}}\cdot\overline{\mathrm{STEP}} \\
& + \mathrm{S3}\cdot\mathrm{S2}\cdot\mathrm{S1}\cdot\mathrm{S0}\cdot\overline{\mathrm{RUN}} + \overline{\mathrm{S3S2}}\cdot\mathrm{S1}\cdot\mathrm{S0} \\
& + \overline{\mathrm{S3}}\cdot\overline{\mathrm{S2}}\cdot\mathrm{S1}\cdot\mathrm{S0}\cdot\overline{\mathrm{STEP}} \\
\mathrm{NS1} = {} & \overline{\mathrm{RESET}} + \overline{\mathrm{S3}}\cdot\mathrm{S2}\cdot\overline{\mathrm{S1}}\cdot\overline{\mathrm{S0}}\cdot\overline{\mathrm{LOAD}} \\
& + \mathrm{S3}\cdot\mathrm{S2}\cdot\mathrm{S1}\cdot\overline{\mathrm{S0}}(\mathrm{RUN} + \mathrm{STEP} + \overline{\mathrm{LOAD}}) \\
& + \mathrm{S3}\cdot\mathrm{S2}\cdot\mathrm{S1}\cdot\mathrm{S0} + \overline{\mathrm{S3}}\cdot\overline{\mathrm{S2}}\cdot\mathrm{S1} \\
\mathrm{NS0} = {} & \mathrm{S3}\cdot\mathrm{S2}\cdot\mathrm{S1}\cdot\overline{\mathrm{S0}}\cdot\overline{\mathrm{RUN}}\cdot\mathrm{STEP}\cdot\mathrm{RESET} \\
& + \overline{\mathrm{S3}}\cdot\overline{\mathrm{S2}}\cdot\mathrm{S1}\cdot\overline{\mathrm{S0}}\cdot\mathrm{RESET} + \overline{\mathrm{S3}}\cdot\overline{\mathrm{S2}}\cdot\mathrm{S1}\cdot\mathrm{S0}\cdot\mathrm{STEP}\cdot\mathrm{RESET}
\end{aligned}$$

NS3 and NS0 have not been minimized. These equations can now be directly entered into an assembler program such as PALASM.

In the above example, it was not possible to illustrate a further aspect of the method of map-entered variables – the ability to encircle squares with identical expressions. These are treated just like '1's for the purposes of encirclement. However, note that dissimilar expressions cannot be drawn together to define a larger implicant. (There is another step defined which allows already-encircled '1's to be combined with map-entered variables. This is not necessary with PLDs, as it only reduces the number of literals in a product.)

The method is not of much use for PLA designs, as here the minimization problem is one of multiple outputs. In all but easy cases, however, a minimizer program would be the best option.

## 7.4 Re-using states

### 7.4.1 Subroutines

Where identical sequences are required in different parts of a state machine flowchart, the documentation can be simplified by defining subroutines – common sequences which can be entered from any part of the flowchart, and which transfer control back to the point from which it was called.

The task is to construct a state machine which has a common sequence which can be entered from any point of the main sequence (Figure 7.9). There are two ways to approach the problem. The first technique is to assign the states of the main sequence and the subroutine to two partitions of the state vector, as shown in Figure 7.10(a). Transitions

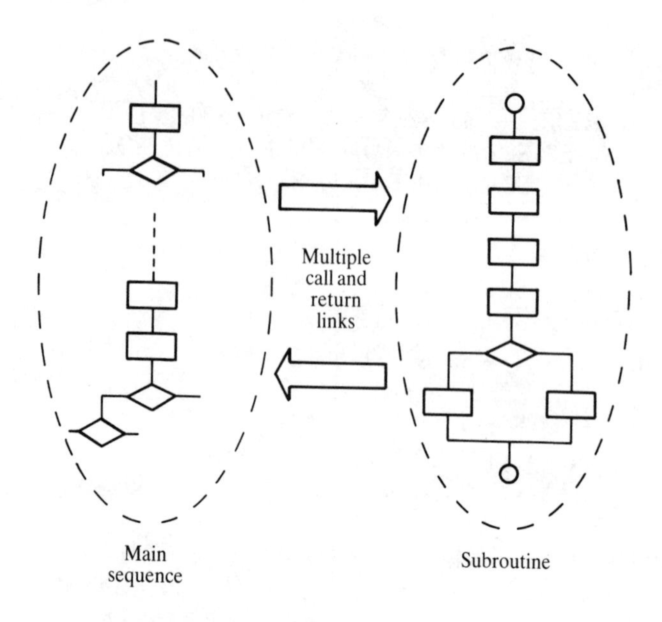


**Figure 7.9** State machine with subroutine.

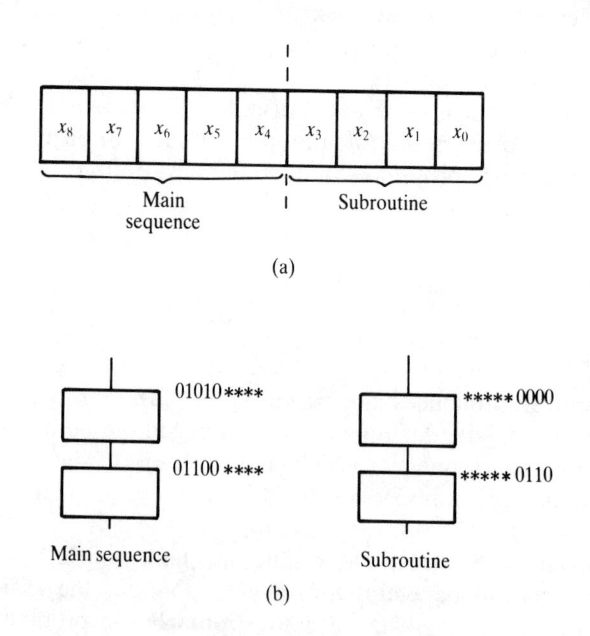


**Figure 7.10** State vector partitioning: (a) partitioned state vector; (b) state assignment.

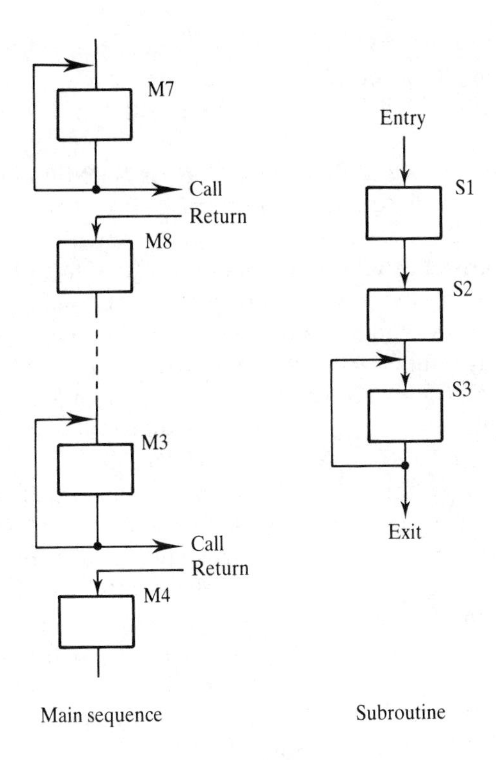


**Figure 7.11** Subroutine linkage with partitioned state vector.

entirely within the main sequence therefore must treat the subroutine state variables as 'don't cares' and vice versa, as can be seen in Figure 7.10(b).

Thus no transition terms in the main sequence would include $X_0$ to $X_3$, and no terms in the subroutine would include $X_4$ to $X_8$. However, for transfer of control between the two parts, two new rules must be applied. The transfer mechanism is shown in Figure 7.11.

The subroutine has three states, S1, S2 and S3, an entry point and a return point. Two calling points are shown in the main sequence, one at state M7 and one at state M3. When the main sequence reaches state M7, two things must happen: the main sequence must be halted, and control must be passed to S1 of the subroutine. The main sequence and the subroutine cannot be active, that is making state transitions, at the same time. At the return point, a transition is made back to the main sequence at the state following the call and the subroutine ceases activity at its last state. Consider now what transition terms are required. When the main sequence reaches M7, it must pause, while the term M7 causes the subroutine to move to state S1. At the end of the subroutine, another pause occurs and the term S3 · M7 forces the next state M8 in the main sequence. Similarly, the call from M3 requires the term M3 and the return requires S3 · M3.

This technique will only work if *J–K* or *S–R* flip–flops are used in the state register, as these require no terms to be active for the pauses in states M7, M3 and S3. If terms were required for these transitions, then conflicts would arise at the call points when next states of both S1 and S3 would be demanded, and at the return point, when next states of M7 and M8 (or M3 and M4) would be demanded. Some other conditions must also be respected. Any output asserted in the pausing states (M7, M3) must not conflict with another specification of the same signal in the subroutine, and vice versa for state S2. Secondly, the subroutine should initialize in state S3.

Application of this method will not save any state variables or product terms; the main benefit is clearer documentation. Nested subroutines are possible if the state vector is split into more than two partitions. Recursion (a subroutine calling itself) is not possible.

A second method of creating subroutines is to use part of the state register for 'flags', bits which can be set and tested by the state machine as if they were connected to inputs and outputs. The condition of these bits is used to indicate the point where the call occurred, and thus can be tested to enable a return to the required state. Figure 7.12(a) shows the extended state register, and Figure 7.12(b) illustrates how the calling mechanism works in the case where the subroutine is called from four different points of the main sequence. At the call, the flag bits *A*, *B* are set to one of the four possible patterns, and the branch is made to the subroutine entry state. At the return, the flag bits are tested to determine which branch to take back to the main sequence.

The second method requires the overhead of the flag bits, whose function is taken by the paused calling state in the first method. However, no conflicts between outputs can arise, and *D* flip–flops can be used.

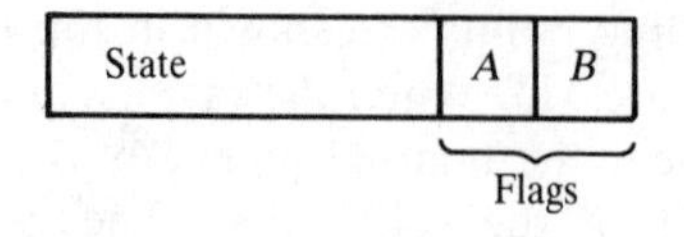


**Figure 7.12** (a) Extension of state register.

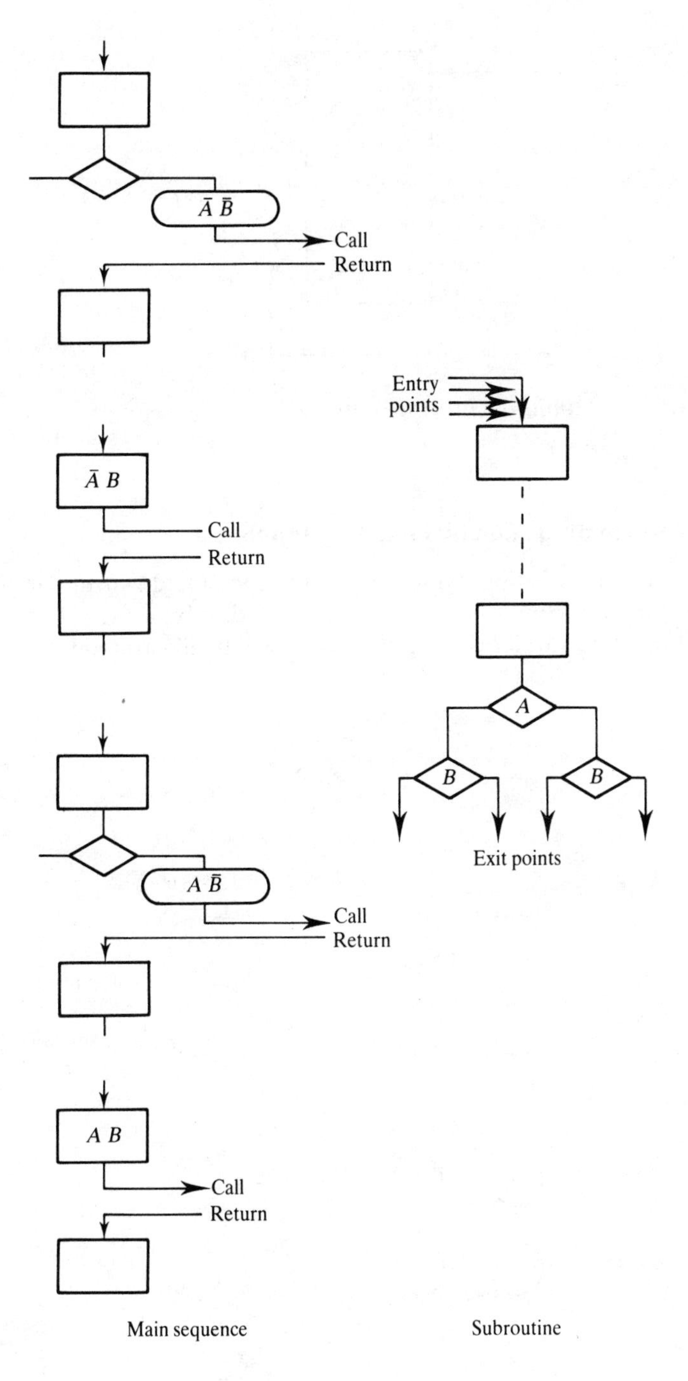


**Figure 7.12** (cont.) (b) Subroutine linkage with flag register.

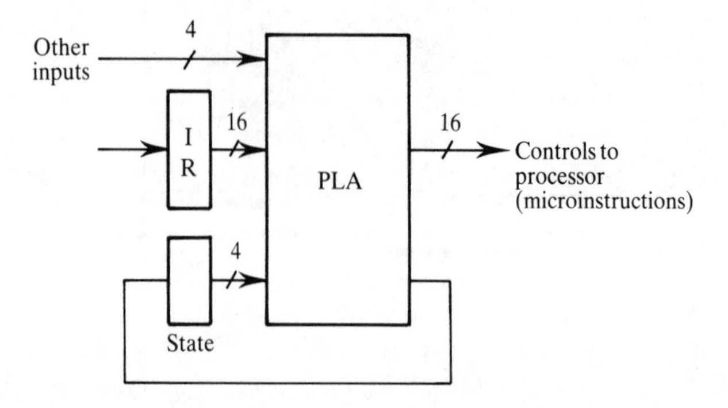


**Figure 7.13** Computer control sequencer.

### 7.4.2 Augmenting state by including inputs

Another method of simplifying documentation cuts down the amount of input testing and conditional output specification by using selected input variables as state variables. This technique will be illustrated by example.

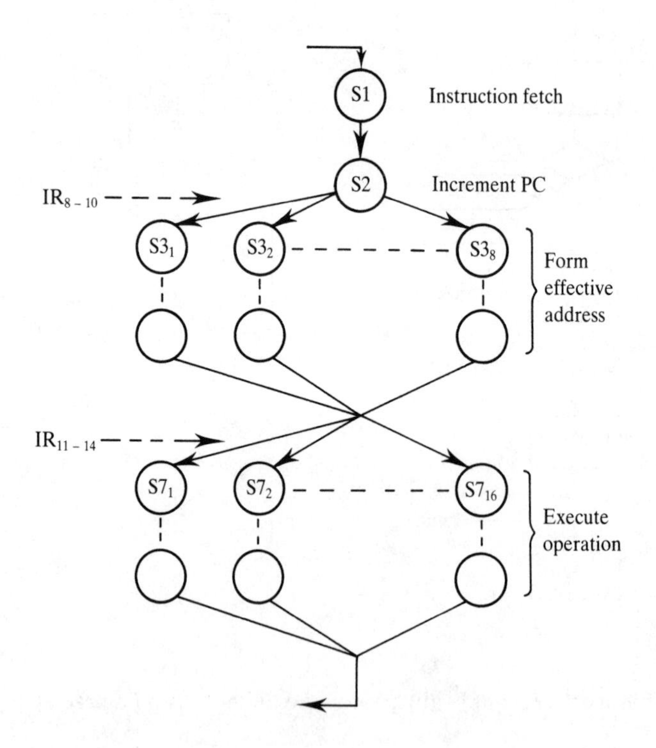


**Figure 7.14** State augmentation through use of inputs.

Figure 7.13 shows the PLA-based control sequencer of a simple computer. The inputs to the PLA are the four bits of the state register, the 16 bits of the instruction register IR, and four bits of miscellaneous inputs. There are four next state outputs and 16 control outputs to the processor (microinstructions). The function of the sequencer is to initiate the fetching of instructions and then to control fetching of data and execution of the required operation. The memory addressing mode and operation are defined in fields of the instruction word held in IR.

The state diagram is shown in outline in Figure 7.14. 16 basic states are defined by the four bits of the state register, but these are augmented by use of the parts of IR to define substates. For example, state S3 has substates $S3_1$ to $S3_8$ by taking IR bits 8 to 10 to be part of the state. The branch taken from S2 is determined by the contents of this field of IR. Each of the eight sequences generates the control sequence for the formation of an effective address. These sequences do not have to be of the same length. In a similar manner 16 sequences are defined for state S7 onwards. Here 1 of 16 possible operations is evoked. This type of state machine could be specified in the conventional way, with just 16 states, but the diagram would have been much more complex and difficult to understand.

## 7.5 State assignment methods

The choice of state encoding strongly affects the complexity of the combinational logic of a state machine, as it influences both the number of state variables and the number of product terms. There are two related minimization problems:

(1) Of those assignments which minimize the number of product terms required, find that which has the smallest number of state variables.

(2) Of those assignments of given code length, find that which requires the fewest product terms.

In general it is not possible to satisfy both criteria simultaneously. Therefore, which of these is to be solved depends on the resources of the PLD available. Of course, if a simple and arbitrary state assignment does not violate any constraints on number of products, registers or pins, then optimization is unnecessary, indeed undesirable, since the simple correspondence between state table and PLA personality could be broken down. This makes modification a more tedious and error-prone process when done manually.

It is possible to calculate bounds on the number of state variables and product terms needed. The minimum number of state variables required is of course given by $\lceil \log_2 N_s \rceil$, where $N_s$ is the number of states, and the maximum is equal to $N_s$, the case in which one state variable is

**Table 7.3** State table.

| Present state | Input state $I_1$ | $I_2$ | $I_3$ | $I_4$ | $I_5$ |
|---|---|---|---|---|---|
| s1 | s3 | s2 | s2 | s7 | s3 |
| s2 | s5 | s2 | s1 | s7 | s3 |
| s3 | s5 | s4 | s3 | s6 | s4 |
| s4 | s6 | s5 | s4 | s2 | s4 |
| s5 | s7 | s5 | s4 | s1 | s6 |
| s6 | s1 | s6 | s4 | s1 | s6 |
| s7 | s1 | s2 | s3 | s3 | s6 |

assigned to every state. A crude estimate of the maximum number of product terms is $N_s \times N_I$, where $N_I$ is the number of state machine input combinations. This estimate assumes that all possible transitions occur from every state, and that no terms can be combined. The minimum number of products required, a much more useful number, can also be calculated. The procedure for doing this will be outlined using the machine described by the state table of Table 7.3.

The upper bound on number of products is $7 \times 5 = 35$, the number of states multiplied by the number of input combinations. However, it is likely that this is an overestimate since each state does not need five link paths if the input coding is chosen appropriately. For example, if the inputs are encoded thus:

$I_1$, 10000; $I_2$, 01000; $I_3$, 00100; $I_4$, 00010; $I_5$, 00001

the products required for transitions from s1 are:

s1 · *000*     s1 · 0**00     s1 · 00010

This is possible in every state, so the total number of products is thus $3+5+4+4+5+3+4=28$. Even lower bounds than this can be found if the table is examined column by column. In the $I_1$ column, for example, there are five **destination sets**, (s1) → s3, (s2, s3) → s5, (s4) → s6, (s5) → s7, (s6, s7) → s1. Therefore, if the states are coded in a manner which allows each of these sets to be identified by a single product, then only five products are required for this column. The total number of destination sets, and thus products required, is $5+4+4+5+3=21$. If there are identical destination sets in different columns, then these can share the same product if a suitable input coding can be found. There are none in the example.

Choosing the best state assignment for a state machine with more than a few states is a difficult problem. It can be shown that the number of distinct assignments for a machine with $N_s$ states and which uses $q$ state variables is

$$\frac{(2^q - 1)!}{(2^q - N_s)!\,q!}$$

(distinct assignments are those which cannot be obtained from another by complementation or permutation of variables). This number becomes enormous for even quite small state machines. For example, with $N_s = 12$ and $q = 4$ it is over 2 billion.

A number of automatic state assignment procedures have been devised, but most are difficult to apply to typical PLD-implemented state machines. In addition, many of the published methods have computation times which rapidly explode as numbers of inputs and states increase. Some of the methods can be applied manually to the state table description, but even simple controllers typically have many input variables (five upwards), which makes these methods unworkable since a state table requires a column for every input combination. In addition, as seen in the previous chapter, there are likely to be constraints on a state assignment – for example,

- asynchronous inputs,
- asynchronous outputs,
- use of state variables as outputs, and
- externally set initial state

all reduce the freedom to select an assignment which minimizes logic complexity. Finally, most recent work on automation of state assignment has been oriented towards PLAs for VLSI, where *J–K* and *R–S* flip–flops are not normally used. The designer, therefore, must hope that finding a near-optimal state assignment is not necessary but, where some optimization is needed, intelligent use of an automated procedure may sometimes help.

## 7.6 Partitioning state machines

The partitioning of a state machine into two or more linked machines may sometimes enable PLD resource limitations to be overcome. Two techniques will be described here, one for use with a single device, and the other for splitting a state machine between PLDs.

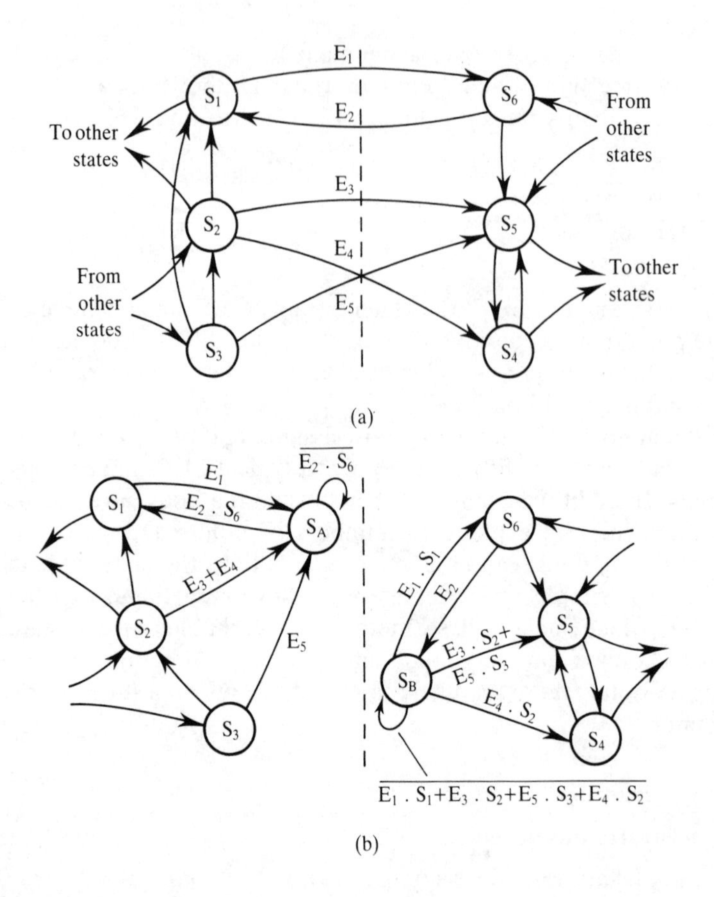


**Figure 7.15** Partitioning a state machine by introducing idle states: (a) section of machine to be partitioned; (b) the partition.

The first method is useful for PAL-type PLDs where products have a fixed allocation to registers. A large state machine implemented in such a device may have excessive product term demands for one or more state variables. These may be reduced in some cases by partitioning the design into two separate machines, only one of which is active at any time. The state machine is split by partitioning the state vector and introducing 'idle' states into each partition. Figure 7.15(a) shows a part of the state machine which is to be split at the dotted line. Figure 7.15(b) shows the result, with the introduced idle states $S_A$ and $S_B$. Transitions between the two machines now operate in two parts. A transition from machine A to machine B becomes two concurrent transitions – one from a state of machine A into idle state $S_A$, and one from idle state $S_B$ into a state of machine B. Subsequent transitions within machine B cause machine A to

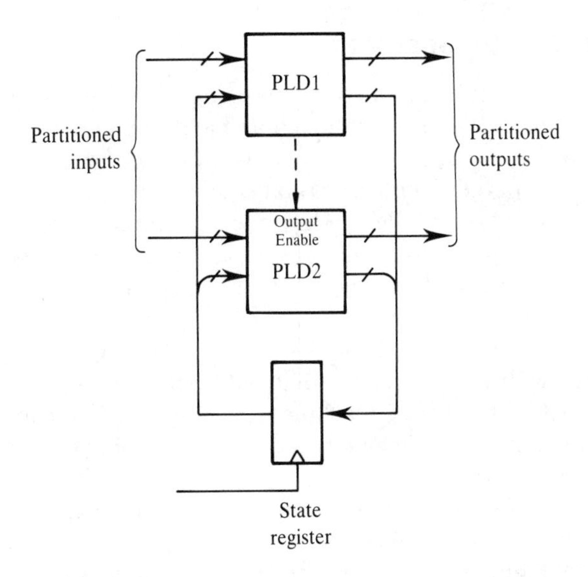


**Figure 7.16** State machine split between two PLDs.

remain in idle state $S_A$. Transitions from B to A work in the same manner through idle states $S_B$ and $S_A$. The product terms required are marked on the links of Figure 7.15(b). This method works because, in a PAL-implemented state machine, the number of product terms ORed into each state register input depends on the number of transitions in the machine. Therefore for a smaller machine, with fewer transitions, there will be fewer terms per state register bit. In a PLA-implemented machine, such a partitioning would not have any benefit.

A single state machine can also be split among two or more PLDs if no PLD can be found with enough resources for the design. One way of doing this is shown in Figure 7.16. Here the state machine is split into two parts, each of which requires a different subset of the input variables, and generates a different subset of the outputs. Each PLD has access to the state and can set any value of next state. States are allocated sequentially to the PLDs. The next state outputs must be wire ORed, since these signals are driven by both PLDs. It may be possible to reduce the number of PLD inputs required by not feeding all present state variables to all PLDs. In this case, 'output enable' signals must be generated for those PLDs which could produce conflicting next state outputs when the states in another PLD are active.

Other forms of state machine decomposition are possible, but many are of more theoretical than practical interest. Also, the combinational function decompositions of Section 5.6 are sometimes useful in state machine design.

## 7.7 Linked state machines

It is sometimes the case that a controller is best specified as two or more cooperating state machines; each machine handles a certain aspect of the control task but at certain points they must interlock or synchronize their operation. These **parallel controllers** control data paths or external devices which themselves have parallel, independently operating parts. The state machines may all operate from the same clock or have independent clocks, and may be all in the same PLD or in more than one. Here we shall only consider the single-clock case.

The subroutines of Section 7.4.1 are an example of linked state machines, but with the restriction that only one is active at any instant. These are **serially linked** state machines. Here we shall be concerned with **parallel linked** machines in which two or more component state machines can be operating at the same time.

Let us look first at the case of a single controller controlling two data processors operating in parallel, as shown in Figure 7.17. Each processor has its own data inputs and outputs, and each requires its own sequence of commands from the controller. Let us also assume that the calculations performed by the processors take an amount of time which is dependent on the data values input (many binary arithmetic algorithms have this property), and that the outputs must be made available to the succeeding processing unit at the same instant. The controller sends a signal READY to indicate the availability of new data at the outputs of the data processors. If we assume that each processor is sequenced by a separate subcontroller, one of these must enter a waiting loop until the other has completed its actions. At this point, the signal READY can be generated and the next pair of computations can proceed.

The manner in which the two state machines link is shown in Figure 7.18. When, for example, machine 1 completes its sequence, it will reach state SYNC1 where input $B$ is tested. If machine 2 has not yet completed

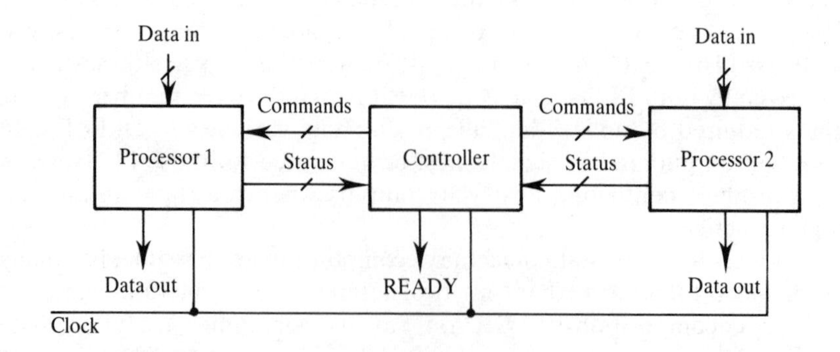


**Figure 7.17** Parallel control of two processors.

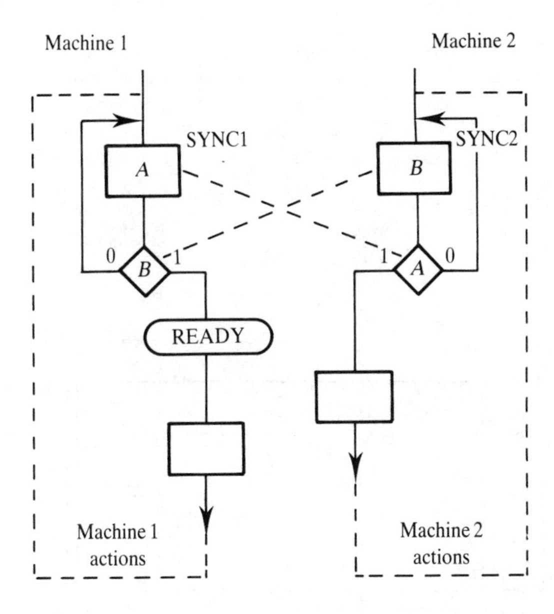


**Figure 7.18** Parallel state machines with synchronization.

its sequence, it will not have reached state SYNC2 and output $B$ will not be asserted. Machine 1 will thus remain in state SYNC1 until machine 2 reaches state SYNC2. At this point, both $A$ and $B$ will be asserted, and both machines proceed again. One of the machines will need to generate the output READY – it does not matter which. Of course, if machine 2 completes first, the same actions occur, except that the waiting will be at state SYNC2.

Figure 7.19 shows how the two finite machines communicate. Each

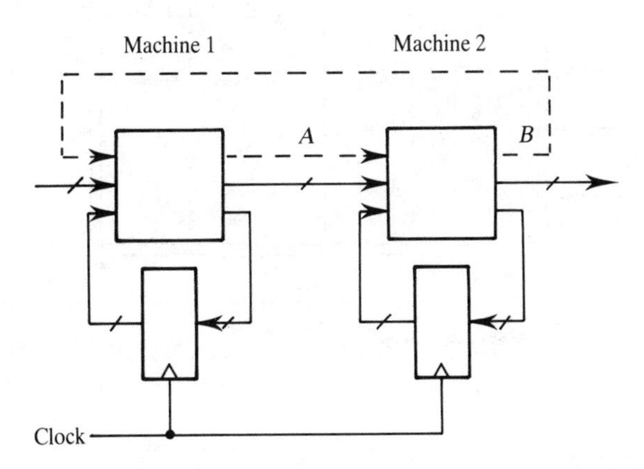


**Figure 7.19** Connections between parallel state machines.

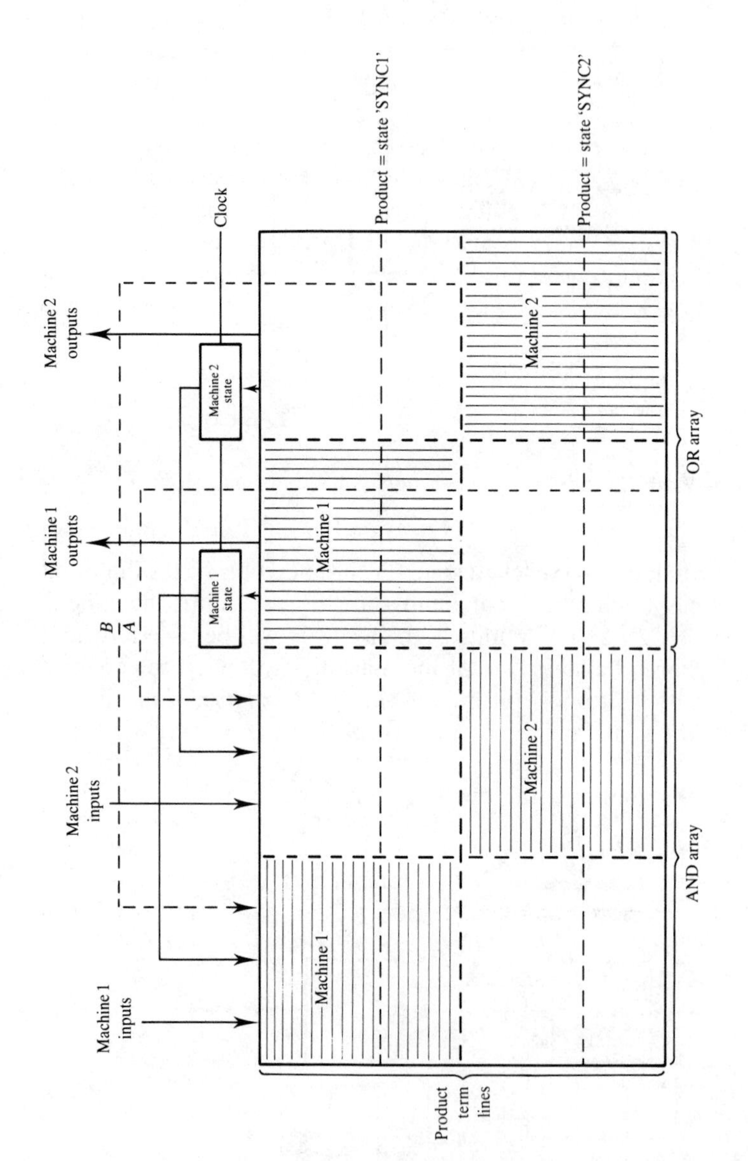


**Figure 7.20** Communicating state machines in PLA.

machine has its own state register and combinational logic block. Signals *A* and *B* are the only physical links (apart from the clock). This diagram shows a closed loop through the combinational logic blocks created by signal wires *A* and *B*. In general, if both machines are Mealy machines, and if output *B* depends on input *A* and vice versa, the closed loop could cause incorrect behaviour such as oscillation or locking into an undefined state. However, this cannot occur here as both outputs depend only on the state. Figure 7.20 is the same diagram, but drawn as a single PLA. Here are shown the product terms which generate the link signals *A* and *B*. The blank areas in the AND and OR arrays represent unused parts of the PLA. This is the price to pay for placing loosely coupled machines in the same matrix. (Some of the recent large PLDs are segmented so as to reduce this inefficiency, as almost all large designs are composed of loosely coupled parts. A discussion of these arrays is beyond the scope of this book.)

Another form of linking parallel state machines is through 'flag' or 'semaphore' bits. These are bits of the state register dedicated to holding information written by one state machine and readable and resettable by another. Figure 7.21 shows how such a semaphore is linked to two state machines. The semaphore is best thought of as a state machine in its own right, with the flowchart of Figure 7.22. This could be implemented most economically as a single *S*–*R* of *J*–*K* flip–flop. Use of state machines linked with semaphores is particularly useful in interface protocol conversion, where data has to be passed from one bus standard to another; one state machine controls each interface, with the semaphore indicating when a data item is ready for transfer between the buses.

Designing with semaphores must be approached very carefully to avoid such problems as two state machines writing to the bit at the same time, and two machines each waiting for the other to set the bit. These are in fact the problems of parallel process synchronization well known to computer scientists.

A method which addresses the problems of both efficient state assignment and process synchronization has recently been developed. It is based on a Petri net description of the parallel controller. There is no space

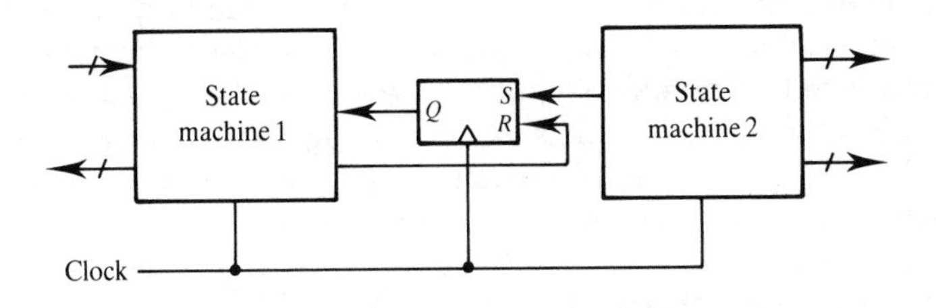


**Figure 7.21** State machines communicating through semaphore.

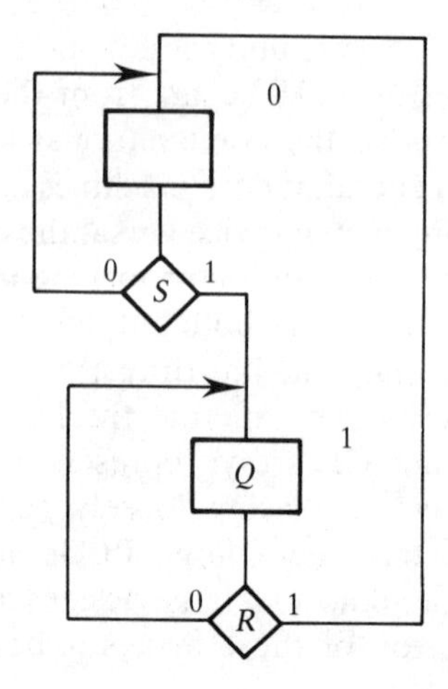


**Figure 7.22** Semaphore flowchart.

to discuss the details of this method, but further details are available in the reference given in the bibliographical notes.

---

## SUMMARY

In theory every state machine design can be transformed into one with the minimum number of states. However, methods of doing this are difficult to apply, but usually simple hand optimizations are adequate for practical purposes. Sequencers with 2-bit input decoders enable state machines to be implemented with fewer product terms, but these devices are not generally available. PAL devices can be used for state machines, but the design process is more cumbersome. The method of map-entered variables is useful here for hand minimization. Documentation can be simplified by describing repeatedly used sequences and subroutines. There are two methods of performing this, one by partitioning the state vector, the other by introducing flag bits. Documentation can be simplified in state machines with large numbers of inputs by using inputs to augment the state vector. Any practical state machine has a huge number of possible state assignments. Finding the best one is usually impossible, but some manual juggling can often produce the small reduction generally sought. Where a PAL-implemented state machine has too many products, a partitioning into two or more devices can be performed by the introduction of idle states. Concurrently operating linked state machines are often required in interfacing applications. These can be designed either by cross-connecting certain inputs and outputs or by using semaphore bits.

---

## BIBLIOGRAPHICAL NOTES

State reductions techniques are well covered in Lewin (1985), and, more formally, in Friedman (1986) and McCluskey (1986). 2-bit input decoded sequencer application is discussed in Logue *et al.* (1975). There are many PAL state machine design examples in the various Monolithic Memories and Advanced Micro Devices Application handbooks. A method like that presented here is in Chang (1985). Most of the methods in Clare (1973) are applicable to PALs rather than PLAs. The method of map-entered variables was first described in Schultz (1967), and formalized in Clare (1973). The computer controller example where inputs are used as states is from Gorman (1973). The method of estimating the minimum number of states is from Unger (1969) and the state table of Figure 7.3 is from Papachristou and Sarma (1983). The expression for the number of state assignments possible is derived in McCluskey and Unger (1959). Recent work on state assignment for PLAs is represented by De Micheli *et al.* (1985), Acha and Calvo (1985), Coppola (1986), De Micheli (1986), Saucier *et al.* (1987), Varma and Trachtenberg (1988) and Huertas and Quintana (1988, 1989). Some practical advice on state assignment is given in Sharp and Barbehenn (1988). The partitioning example of Figure 7.15 is from McCarthy (1987). A method for performing the decomposition of Figure 7.16 based on a modified state machine flowchart is described in Johnson (1976). Linked state machines are discussed in Clare (1973). The Petri net method of parallel controller design is described in Amroun and Bolton (1989).

## EXERCISES

**7.1** A very basic washing machine controller is to be designed to the following specification:

- INPUTS
  - Hot hot water required
  - Start when true start washing, when false stop, even in mid-cycle
  - Full drum is filled with water
  - Empty drum is empty
  - Time time has reached zero
- OUTPUTS
  Hot select hot water input
  - Pump turn on pump
  - Fill when true water is pumped in, out when false
  - Wash start washing and reset timer
  - Spin start spinning and reset timer

When the controller receives the start signal, the washing machine is filled with the correct temperature water and washes until the timer reaches zero. It empties the soapy water and fills the machine with cold rinsing water and washes again until the timer reaches zero. Finally, after emptying the rinsing water, it spins the clothes dry, completing the cycle.

Design a flowchart which meets this specification, using as few states as possible. (Make maximum use of conditional outputs.)

**7.2** Design a state machine for a serial adder, with inputs $a$, $b$ and output $s$. The carry is represented by the value of the state. First draw a flowchart for implementation in a PLA with 1-bit input decoding, and then for one with 2-bit decoding. How many link paths are there in each case? (Note that two-variable decision boxes are testing four combinations of the variables.)

**7.3** Design a flowchart which evaluates the parity function of four variables in a PLA with 2-bit input decoding. How many link paths are required?

**7.4** Design a 4-bit BCD counter for implementation in a registered PAL device. First produce the PLA table, and from this the minimized equation for each flip–flop input. Ensure that there is an escape from the illegal states.

Modify the design for a PAL with complemented outputs. How is the product term demand affected?

**7.5** The counter of the previous question is to be adapted in the following way – at count 0, inputs $X$ and $Y$ are tested. The value of $XY$ (that is 0, 1, 2 or 3) defines the next count value. At count 9, if the input HOLD is true, then the counter remains in this count until HOLD becomes false.

Design the logic for a PAL implementation of this counter, using variable-entered maps.

**7.6** The counter is to be further modified to allow parallel loading of a 4-bit number, in any state, under the control of an extra input bit. Why is the map-entered variable method unsuitable for such a design? (More suitable techniques will be discussed in the next chapter.)

**7.7** A binary counter is required which can count in the following sequences:

0: 0000 0001 0010 ... 1111 0000 etc.
1: 0000 0010 0100 ... 1110 0000 etc.
2: 0000 0011 0110 1001 1100 1111 0000 etc.
3: 0000 0100 1000 1100 0000 etc.

In state 0000, two inputs $A$ and $B$ are tested. The value of $AB$ determines which sequence is to be entered. (Assume that $A$ and $B$ are only valid in state 0000.)

Design the logic for a 6-bit registered PAL implementation.

**7.8** Two 4-bit counters, counter $\alpha$ and counter $\beta$, are to be implemented in a single PLD, driven by the same clock. Counter $\alpha$ is a standard binary counter. Whenever counter $\alpha$ reaches states 3, 5, 7 and 9, counter $\beta$ goes through the sequence 3, 4, 5, 6, ... 14, 15, 1, 2. After this counter $\alpha$ resumes its counting.

Design a flowchart for this design, using a subroutine. What PLD resources are required?

**7.9** A continuously operating 8-bit successive-approximation analogue–digital converter is to be designed, using the configuration of Figure 7.23. The components are an 8-bit digital–analogue converter, a

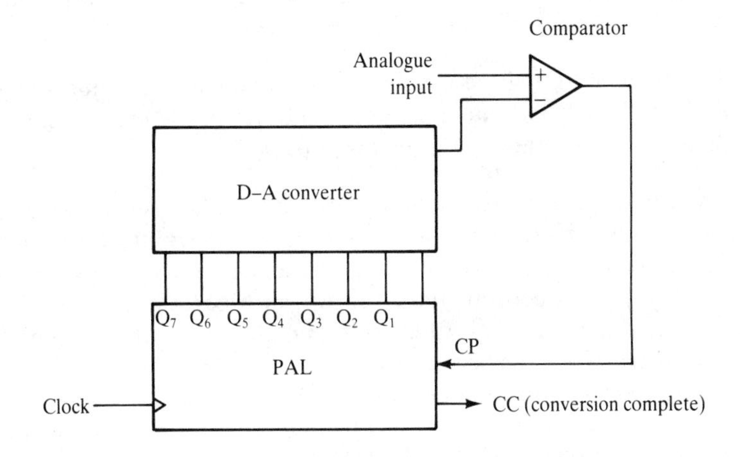


**Figure 7.23**

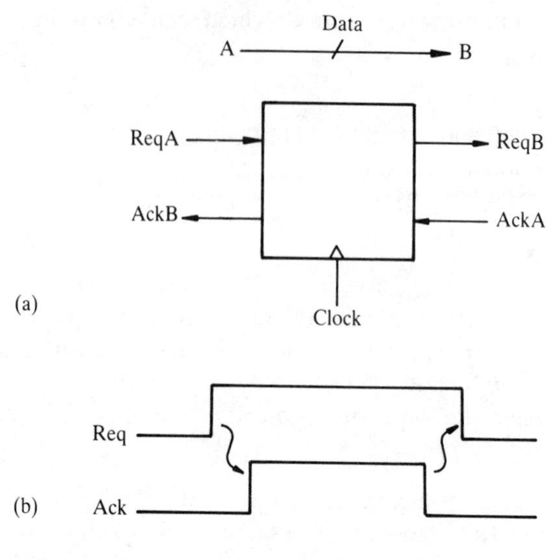


**Figure 7.24**

comparator, and a registered PAL device. The mode of operation is as follows:

The PAL first outputs the code $Q_7$–$Q_0$ = 10000000. If the analogue input is greater than this (CP = 1), then $Q_7$ remains 1 and the code 11000000 is output and further comparison is done. If the input is smaller, then the next code output is 01000000 and the next comparison is done. This process continues until the last comparison is performed on $Q_0$. $Q_7$–$Q_0$ now represents the digital equivalent of the analogue input. At this stage, the signal CC is asserted to indicate that conversion is complete.

Specify the PAL logic as a state machine in the most economical way you can find. Do a state assignment and derive the logic. (The state vector must be shared with the outputs $Q_7$–$Q_0$.)

**7.10** An interface is required between two pairs of handshake signals, as shown in Figure 7.24(a), for the purpose of controlling a transfer of data between systems *A* and *B*. Each pair of 'request' and 'acknowledge' signals is coordinated as shown in Figure 7.24(b). The data transfer sequence is initiated by signal Req*A* becoming true, and terminates when this becomes false again.

Design two state machines, each with three states and linked by a flag bit, which implement this interface. Derive the equations for a PAL implementation, using D flip–flops.

CHAPTER 8

# Data Path Functions, Counters and Arithmetic

**OBJECTIVES**

When you have completed studying this chapter you should be able

- to determine which types of data path element are candidates for PLD implementation;
- to set up the Boolean equations defining data storage and routing blocks;
- to calculate the performance limits of PLD-implemented data paths;
- to construct all types of synchronous counters using both XOR and conventional PAL devices;
- to use XOR PAL devices with 2-bit decoders for arithmetic functions;
- to decide when ROMs would be the most suitable option in a numerical application;
- to combine data and control blocks into a single PLD, taking account of their temporal interaction.

## 8.1 Introduction

In the two previous chapters we have studied techniques suitable for designing the control parts of digital systems. However, programmable logic devices also have their part to play in the data processing parts. As discussed in Chapter 1, identification of the control and data sections of a digital system is part of the initial planning, or 'top level' design. In this chapter it is assumed that the architecture of the data paths has been determined, and that the problem therefore is to convert these efficiently into a logic design. The following will be looked at: where programmable devices can be used, which types of PLD are most useful, and some design techniques suitable for application to data path functions.

First the general properties of data paths will be surveyed, and some examples will be given of some simple but frequently used functions. One common requirement is for counters of various types. Design techniques for this type of block will be given, concentrating on those PLDs which contain exclusive OR gates as part of their logical structure. After looking at further applications of these devices, the problems of implementing arithmetic operators will be discussed. Finally, systems which combine both control and data sections, and the interaction between them, will be examined.

## 8.2 Data path elements

### 8.2.1 Characteristics of data paths

Data paths store, route and transform digital signals which represent the data variables (and constants) in an algorithm. In order to perform these functions, two things are required: firstly an architecture, or network of storage, interconnection and operator blocks, and secondly a schedule defining the sequencing of data signals through this network. It is the purpose of the controller (or controllers) to provide this sequence.

Figure 8.1 is an example of a controller and data processor which together perform the algorithm of multiplying two numbers using the sequential 'shift and add' method. The operands are stored in a memory and the result is written back to this memory. In the diagram are shown the different types of signal which pass information between the controller and the data processor. Those passing from left to right are the outputs from the controller, the **instructions** or **commands**. Those passing from right to left are the inputs to the controller – the data path status signals. In this example commands are required which address the memory, select the mode of the ALU, shift register, counter and memory, set the number of shift/add cycles, and enable the three-state buffer. Two status signals are required: the least-significant bit of the shift register (which is the bit of the

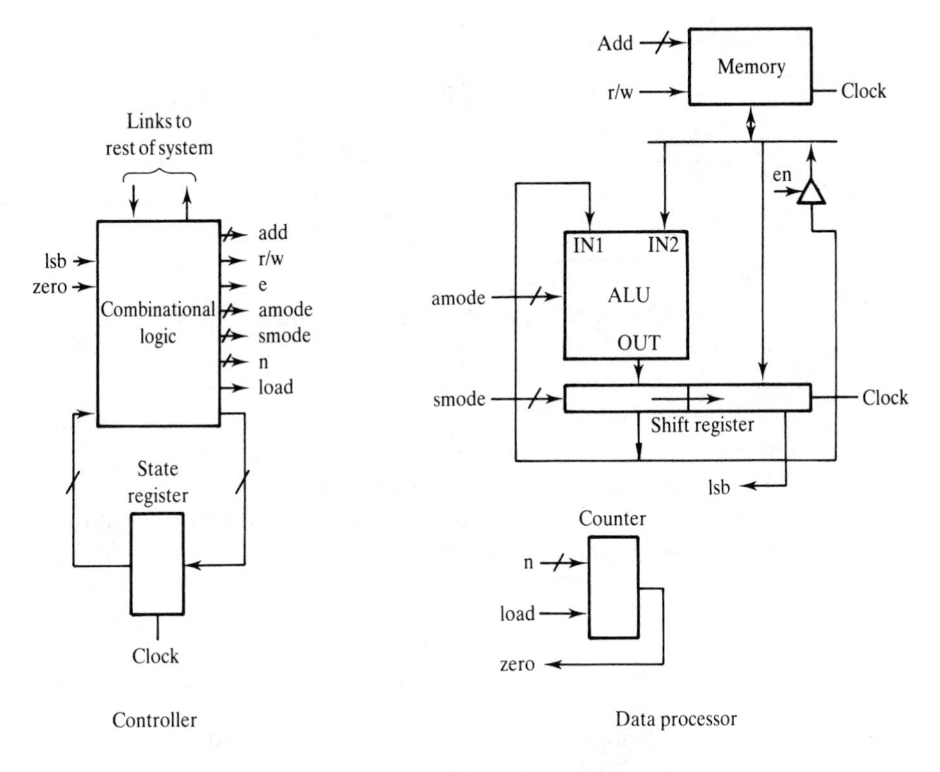


**Figure 8.1** Controller and data processor.

| | | |
|---|---|---|
| Commands | add | data memory address |
| | r/w | memory read/write control |
| | en | three-state buffer control |
| | amode | ALU mode |
| | smode | shift register mode |
| | n | counter limit |
| | load | load counter |
| Status | lsb | least-significant bit of shift register |
| | zero | counter = zero |

multiplier currently being examined) and a signal which is true when the counter content is zero. In this system there are two other types of signal, the data signals themselves, and the internal states of the controller. All of these signals will have to be encoded before logic design can be done.

A different method of encoding is used for the four kinds of signals. The data signal encoding will have been chosen at an early stage and there

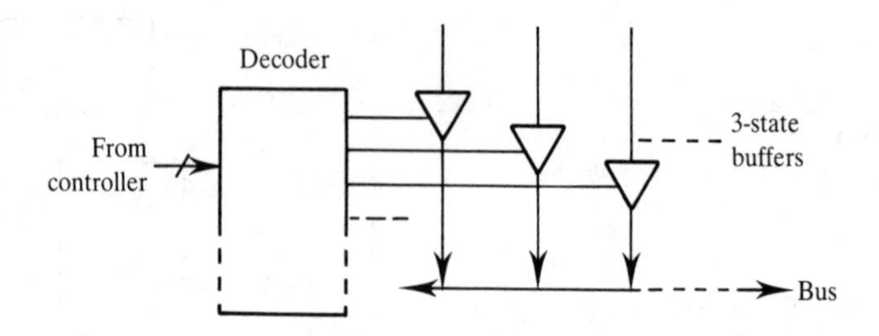


**Figure 8.2** Decoding a control signal.

will be a rule (or rules) consistently applied throughout the system for this (for example, binary two's complement, IEEE standard floating point). The encoding of the controller internal states will be chosen to optimize the controller logic using methods discussed in previous chapters. The control and status signals will generally have their encoding fixed by the requirements of the data path elements themselves. However, if these are built with PLDs there will a certain freedom in choosing the encoding of, for example, mode control signals. Sometimes the number of interconnections and the size of the controller can be reduced by further encoding of a group of signals. Figure 8.2 shows an example of this. Here a bus is driven by a number of blocks through three-state buffers, only one of which can be active at any instant. The binary enabling signals are thus mutually exclusive and can be encoded into a signal requiring $\log_2 n$ bits, where $n$ is the number of wires.

The data processor of Figure 8.1 is highly **sequential**. Few data path elements are used, but a complex control sequence is required. On the other hand, a highly **parallel** data path demands a more complex network of data processing blocks, but in general a much simpler control. Highly parallel data paths are usually **pipelined**. Part of a pipeline for the multiplication algorithm which is implemented sequentially in the architecture of Figure 8.1 is shown in Figure 8.3. In this step one new partial product is calculated by adding (or not adding) the multiplicand. For maximum efficiency, each stage of a pipeline is always busy on its step of the computation. Each stage contains some combinational logic feeding into a register, unless it is a delay stage when it will contain only the register.

A fundamental choice for the encoding of the data signals representing numbers is the **digit width**, where a digit is the basic unit of information processed by the arithmetic elements. A digit width equal to the length of the binary-encoded numbers defines **parallel arithmetic**, while a digit width of one corresponds to **serial arithmetic**. These are not the only possibilities: for example, 32-bit numbers may be processed in units of 8 bits. It is not always immediately obvious which is best choice of digit size. While it is usually true that the fastest systems can be built using parallel arithmetic,

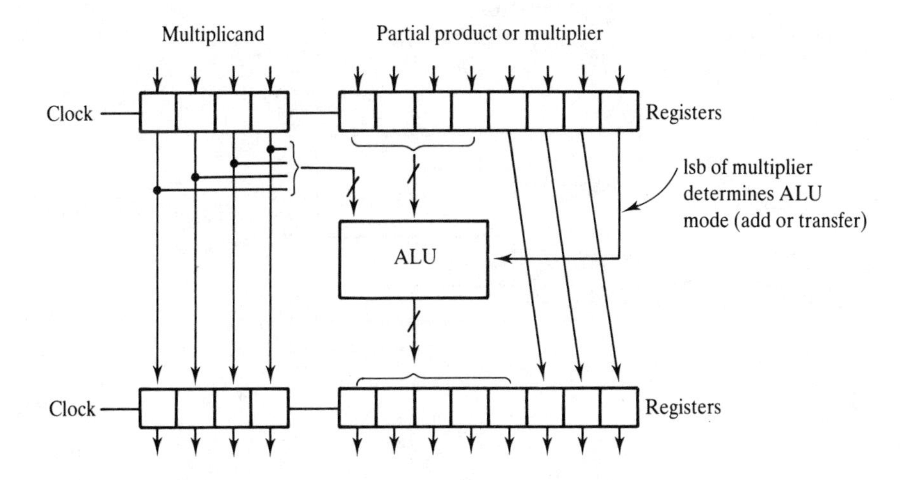


**Figure 8.3** Part of a multiplier pipeline (4-bit example).

the most efficient solution may sometimes be obtained with a smaller digit. Bit serial arithmetic units are very simple to specify as state machines, since they generally only require one or two flip–flops and thus have few states (see for example the serial adder of Figure 2.19). On the other hand, it would be a mistake to try to describe a parallel arithmetic unit as a state machine; the number of states would be very large and the state transition diagram or flowchart would have little meaning. Most data path elements are best described in terms of the logical operations performed on the arrays of bits representing the numbers. All the designs studied in this chapter will be treated in this way.

As mentioned in Section 6.1, sequential machine blocks fall into two broad classes: those in which the combinational logic has no obvious structure, and those in which the logic is a bitwise array of similar sections (Figure 6.1). Most parallel data path blocks can be placed in the latter class, thus making PAL-structured devices the usual choice for programmable logic implementations. The product term sharing of PLAs is not an advantage, as each output of the array is formed from the sum of unique products. The multiplexer of Figure 3.24 is an example of this. In this chapter, therefore, the emphasis will be on design techniques for PAL-structured PLDs.

### 8.2.2 Examples of data path elements

The general form of a parallel data path element is shown in Figure 8.4. The processing function is performed by the logic array, and the results are stored in the data register, which is usually, but not necessarily, in the same

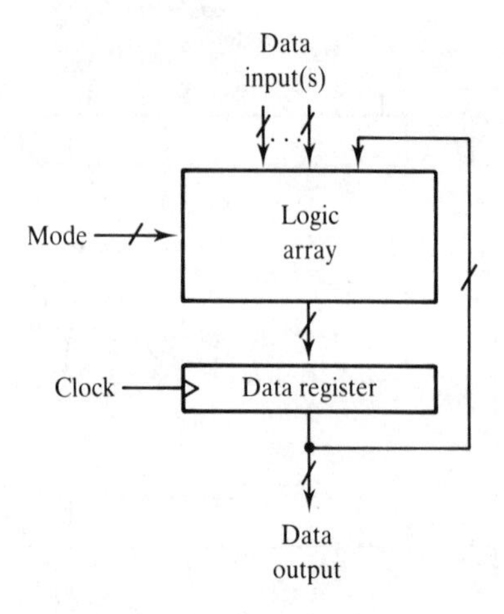


**Figure 8.4** Structure of a data path element.

PLD as the logic array. Feedback from this register is required for sequential (non-pipelined) operations. A mode control input determines which processing function is to be performed.

Many data path elements have a data routing function (or functions) in their set of operational modes. These are very easy to describe as array operations. Referring again to Figure 3.24, the function of the multiplexer can be described as

$$O_i = A_i\,\overline{\mathrm{sel}} + B_i\,\mathrm{sel} \qquad (i = 0, 1, 2, 3)$$

In this case the mode control signal is a binary one. Another frequently needed function is that of shifting. Figure 8.5 shows how a register should be connected to perform either a right shift of one bit or no shift (hold) in each cycle. This may be expressed as

$$O_i.d = O_i\,\overline{\mathrm{shift}} + O_{i+1}\,\mathrm{shift} \qquad (i = 0, 1, 2, 3)$$

where $O_4$ is data in, and $O_i.d$ is the $D$ input to the $O_i$ flip–flop

This procedure can be easily extended to handle left shifts, multiple bit shifts, and rotations (or cyclic shifts). Bidirectional shifting can make use of the controllable three-state outputs available in many PAL devices. Since left and right shifts never occur at the same time serial data input and output pins can be shared. The principle is illustrated in Figure 8.6. The three-state buffer is enabled for left shifts and disabled for right shifts, allowing the 'right in/left out' pin to be used as an input. There must be a control term, as shown in Figure 3.25, which can be programmed to control this buffer.

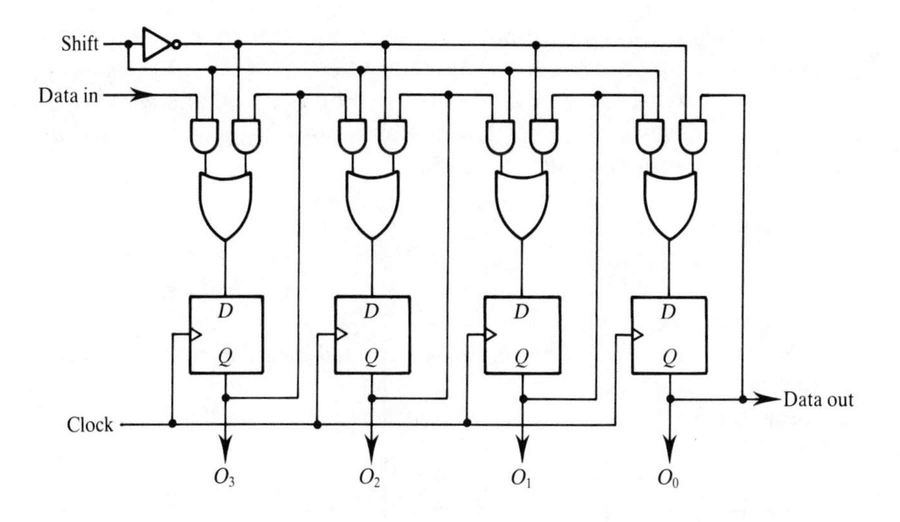


**Figure 8.5** Shift register.

Because of the small number of registers available in PLDs, it is not practical to use them for memory functions, except where the unit of information to be stored is small. For example, a PAL device can be used for a 1-bit addressable memory. The function may be described as follows:

$$O_i.d = A_i\text{data} + (1 - A_i)O_i \qquad (i = 0, 1, \ldots)$$

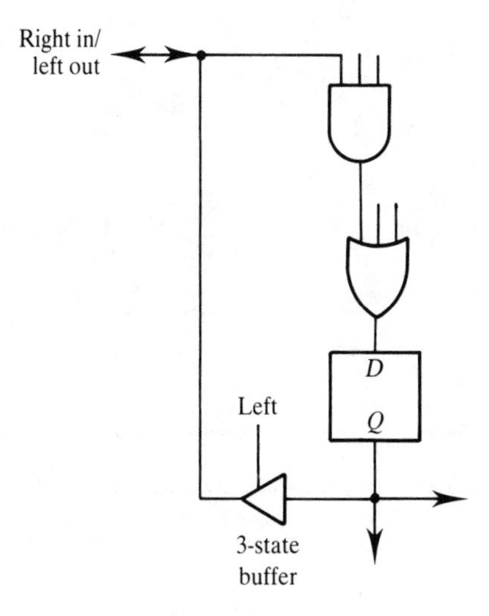


**Figure 8.6** Left-hand end of bidirectional shift register.

where 'data' is the 1-bit data input and $A_i$ is the multivalued address of bit $i$. When a bit is not addressed, its value must be held; $(1 - A_i)$ is the set of address values which does not include $A_i$. For the example of a 16-bit memory, the addresses are encoded as 4-bit strings $(a_3, a_2, a_1, a_0)$, and the equation for location 6 would be

$$
\begin{aligned}
O_6.\mathrm{d} &= a_3\bar{a}_2a_1\bar{a}_0\,\mathrm{data} + \overline{(a_3\bar{a}_2a_1\bar{a}_0)}\,O_6 \\
&= a_3\bar{a}_2a_1\bar{a}_0\,\mathrm{data} + (\bar{a}_3 + a_2 + \bar{a}_1 + a_0)\,O_6
\end{aligned}
$$

which requires five products per output.

Some arithmetic operators can be created easily in PAL-structured devices. For example, a single full adder can be constructed using the two equations for the sum and carry out (extracted from the K map of Figure 2.24):

$$\mathrm{sum} = a\bar{b}\bar{c}_{\mathrm{in}} + ab\,c_{\mathrm{in}} + \bar{a}b\bar{c}_{\mathrm{in}} + \bar{a}\bar{b}\,c_{\mathrm{in}} \quad \mathbf{(8.1)}$$

$$c_{\mathrm{out}} = a\,c_{\mathrm{in}} + ab + b\,c_{\mathrm{in}} \quad \mathbf{(8.2)}$$

It is not efficient to build two-input operand parallel adders using an array of these elements (slow carry propagation), or to extend the equations to define them directly in sum-of-products form (too many products). However, one use for simple full adders is in a 'carry save' network for summing multiple operands. Registered PAL devices programmed with multiple copies of Equations 8.1 and 8.2 allow a pipelined carry save adder to be created. The carry save principle is illustrated in Figure 8.7, a network

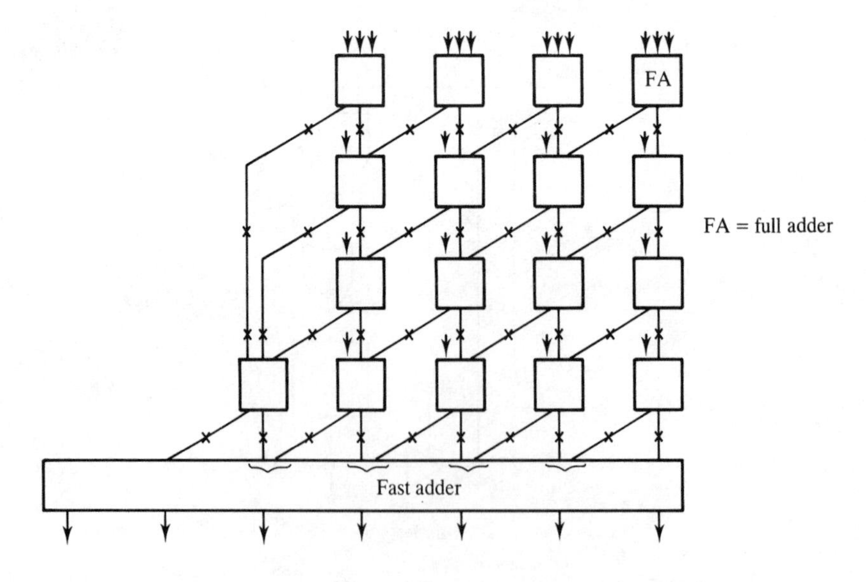


**Figure 8.7** Carry save adder network (FA, full adder).

designed to sum six 4-bit unsigned operands. The longest carry propagation path through this network is diagonal and has four adder propagation delays, the same length of path as that in a 4-bit ripple carry adder. The final stage is a conventional fast adder of the carry lookahead or bypass type; if the carry save network was continued, in effect this final stage could be performed with a ripple carry adder. The pipelining is enabled by inserting registers at the points marked '×'. The inputs to the lower rows would also have to be delayed one, two and three cycles to preserve timing. Four full adders with output registers can be fitted into a 24-pin registered PAL device. Such fast multiple-operand adders are frequently used in fast multipliers, but most applications can be handled with off-the-shelf parts.

### 8.2.3 Performance calculation

Timing calculations in PAL-based data processing networks are generally very straightforward. The principles are the same as those which were covered in Section 6.3. Here three cases will be considered:

(a) stage with feedback within device;
(b) stage with external feedback;
(c) stage with no feedback.

For each variation the maximum frequency, $f_{MAX}$, will be calculated. For all three cases $f_{MAX}$ is given by

$$f_{MAX} = 1/(t_{REG} + t_{LOGIC} + t_{SU}) \tag{8.3}$$

where $t_{REG}$ is the maximum register propagation delay, $t_{LOGIC}$ is the maximum array propagation delay, and $t_{SU}$ is the register set-up time.

The three cases are shown in Figure 8.8. In case (a) all delays are internal. $t_{REG}$ is the delay from clock edge to an internal logic array input, $t_{CF}$. The sum of $t_{LOGIC}$ and $t_{SU}$, $t_{SU(PAL)}$ is usually given in the data sheet; this is the register set-up time translated to the array inputs. This parameter is used because the register inputs are inaccessible, making the conventional set-up time unusable. The maximum operating frequency is thus given by

$$f_{MAX} = 1/(t_{CF} + t_{SU(PAL)}) \tag{8.4}$$

This is the figure generally given in data sheets. For case (b) the register delay is the delay from clock edge to output pin, $t_{CLK}$. Thus the maximum clock rate is given by

$$f_{MAX} = 1/(t_{CLK} + t_{SU(PAL)}) \tag{8.5}$$

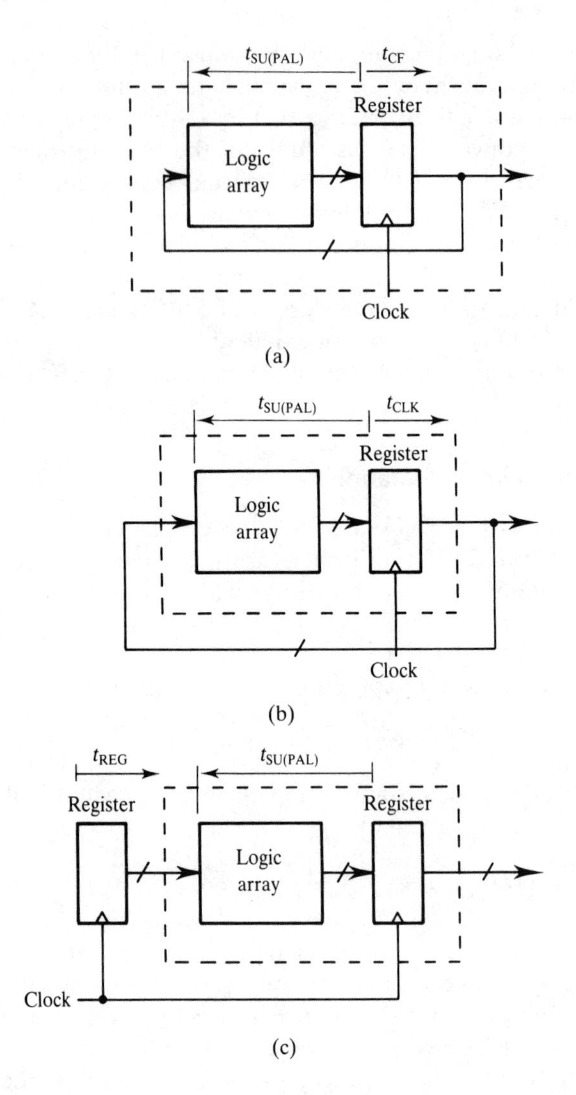


**Figure 8.8** PAL device timing: (a) internal feedback; (b) external feedback; (c) no feedback.

In case (c) the input to the device is fed from an external register with propagation delay from clock edge of $t_{REG}$. The expression is now

$$f_{MAX} = 1/(t_{REG} + t_{SU(PAL)}) \tag{8.6}$$

In a system design, the clock rate would be given by the worst of these figures, derated to take account of the worst-case clock skew (skew adds directly to the minimum clock period).

## 8.3 Counters

### 8.3.1 Building counters

Counters are often required in data paths. A simple example is the loop counter in Figure 8.1. Counters can of course be specified as state machines and standard techniques used for the derivation of the logic equations – indeed a PLA example was given in Section 6.9. However, it is worth looking at counters separately, since there are some useful design techniques which can be applied. In this section the use of conventional PAL devices will be discussed, while in the next the use of types of PAL devices specially useful for counter design will be covered.

The basic counter is the binary up-counter, whose PLA table is given in Table 8.1. From this table the K maps of Figure 8.9 can be drawn. The four PAL equations are as follows:

$$O_0.d = \overline{O}_0 \quad \textbf{(8.7)}$$

$$O_1.d = O_0 \oplus O_1 \quad \textbf{(8.8)}$$

$$O_2.d = (O_0O_1) \oplus O_2 \quad \textbf{(8.9)}$$

$$O_3.d = (O_0O_1O_2) \oplus O_3 \quad \textbf{(8.10)}$$

**Table 8.1**

| *Present state* | | | | *Next state* | | | |
|---|---|---|---|---|---|---|---|
| $O_3$ | $O_2$ | $O_1$ | $O_0$ | $O_3.d$ | $O_2.d$ | $O_1.d$ | $O_0.d$ |
| 0 | 0 | 0 | 0 | 0 | 0 | 0 | 1 |
| 0 | 0 | 0 | 1 | 0 | 0 | 1 | 0 |
| 0 | 0 | 1 | 0 | 0 | 0 | 1 | 1 |
| 0 | 0 | 1 | 1 | 0 | 1 | 0 | 0 |
| 0 | 1 | 0 | 0 | 0 | 1 | 0 | 1 |
| 0 | 1 | 0 | 1 | 0 | 1 | 1 | 0 |
| 0 | 1 | 1 | 0 | 0 | 1 | 1 | 1 |
| 0 | 1 | 1 | 1 | 1 | 0 | 0 | 0 |
| 1 | 0 | 0 | 0 | 1 | 0 | 0 | 1 |
| 1 | 0 | 0 | 1 | 1 | 0 | 1 | 0 |
| 1 | 0 | 1 | 0 | 1 | 0 | 1 | 1 |
| 1 | 0 | 1 | 1 | 1 | 1 | 0 | 0 |
| 1 | 1 | 0 | 0 | 1 | 1 | 0 | 1 |
| 1 | 1 | 0 | 1 | 1 | 1 | 1 | 0 |
| 1 | 1 | 1 | 0 | 1 | 1 | 1 | 1 |
| 1 | 1 | 1 | 1 | 0 | 0 | 0 | 0 |

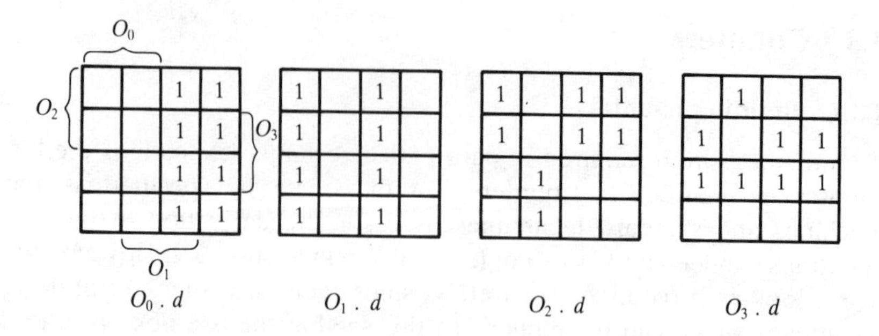


**Figure 8.9** K maps for 4-bit binary counter.

These equations require one, two, three and four products when expanded. In the general case, for an $(n+1)$-bit counter, the final equation is

$$O_n.d = (O_0O_1 \ldots O_{n-2}O_{n-1}) \oplus O_n \tag{8.11}$$

which requires $n+1$ products. A conclusion is that PAL devices with $D$ flip–flops could run out of products with long counters. A binary down-counter can be similarly derived. For this the equivalent to Equation 8.11 is

$$O_n.d = (\overline{O}_0\overline{O}_1 \ldots \overline{O}_{n-2}\overline{O}_{n-1}) \oplus O_n \tag{8.12}$$

Counters can be combined with the data routing functions of Section 8.2.1. For example, bit $i$ of a counter with modes 'load', 'count_up', 'count_down' and 'hold' can be described thus:

$$\begin{aligned} O_i.d = {} & \text{load}\, I_i \\ & + \text{count\_up}\,\{(O_0O_1 \ldots O_{i-2}O_{i-1}) \oplus O_i\} \\ & + \text{count\_down}\,\{(\overline{O}_0\overline{O}_1 \ldots \overline{O}_{i-2}\overline{O}_{i-1}) \oplus O_i\} \\ & + \text{hold}\, O_i \end{aligned} \tag{8.13}$$

where $I_i$ is the $i$th input. The mode variables would be encoded as a 2-bit binary string. This equation when expanded has $2i+1$ products, making it impractical for conventional PAL device implementation.

Modulo counters, or $n$-bit counters with a cycle length less than $2^n$, need modified logic to enable the register to be reset when the maximum count is reached. Some PAL devices have a control term which provides a synchronous reset or preset of all the register flip–flops. This term can be programmed to detect the end of the count sequence, thus allowing the counter to be designed conventionally. Counters such as these which do not use all the register states must be designed so that, if an unused state is entered, the counter will make a transition to a defined state.

### 8.3.2 Use of XOR PALs

All the equations in the last section contained the exclusive OR operator. Because of this the expanded equations require many products, often more than can be accommodated in a PAL device, especially for the higher order bits. For this reason, PAL devices have been designed which allow the exclusive OR operator to be implemented directly. These devices are listed in Tables A.6 and A.7. Figure 8.10 shows a registered PAL device with the additional exclusive OR gates, referred to here as an 'XOR PAL'. In such a PLD, equations 8.7–8.10 each require two products. An $n$-bit counter will thus require only $2n$ products.

Equation 8.13 can also take advantage of the exclusive OR structure. It may be rewritten as

$$\begin{aligned} O_i.d = {} & \{\text{load}\, I_i + (\text{hold} + \text{count\_up} + \text{count\_down})\, O_i\} \\ & \oplus \{\text{count\_up}(O_0 O_1 \ldots O_{i-2} O_{i-1}) \\ & + \text{count\_down}(\overline{O}_0 \overline{O}_1 \ldots \overline{O}_{i-2} \overline{O}_{i-1})\} \end{aligned} \quad \textbf{(8.14)}$$

With a suitable encoding of the mode variable, this equation requires only four products.

It is also possible to use XOR PALs for the synthesis of counters which count up or down in steps other than 1. The design technique is based on the construction of a parallel adder with a constant for one of the operands. The adder equations are derived using the lookahead principle outlined in Section 2.6. The equations are built up as follows: for the least-significant bit,

$$s_0 = a_0 \oplus b_0 \oplus c_0 \quad \textbf{(8.15)}$$

where $s_0$ is the sum bit, $a_0$ and $b_0$ are the inputs, and $c_0$ is the carry input to this stage. For the next bit,

$$\begin{aligned} s_1 &= a_1 \oplus b_1 \oplus c_1 \\ &= a_1 \oplus b_1 \oplus (G_0 + P_0 c_0) \end{aligned} \quad \textbf{(8.16)}$$

where $G_0 = a_0 b_0$, the stage 0 'carry generate', and $P_0 = a_0 + b_0$ or $a_0 \oplus b_0$, the stage 0 'carry propagate'; and for bit $i$,

$$s_i = a_i \oplus b_i \oplus (G_{i-1} + P_{i-1}(G_{i-2} + \ldots + P_0 c_0) \ldots)) \quad \textbf{(8.17)}$$

If we assume that one of the operands, $a$ say, is a constant, then these equations can be simplified. If $a_i = 0$, then $G_i = 0$, $P_i = b_i$, while if $a_i = 1$, then $G_i = b_i$ and $P_i = 1$ or $\overline{b}_i$. Let us first verify the equations for a 1-bit-increment up-counter. Here $a_0 = 1$, and $a_i = 0$, $i \neq 0$. From Equation 8.15, with $c_0 = 0$,

$$s_0 = \overline{b}_0 \quad \textbf{(8.18)}$$

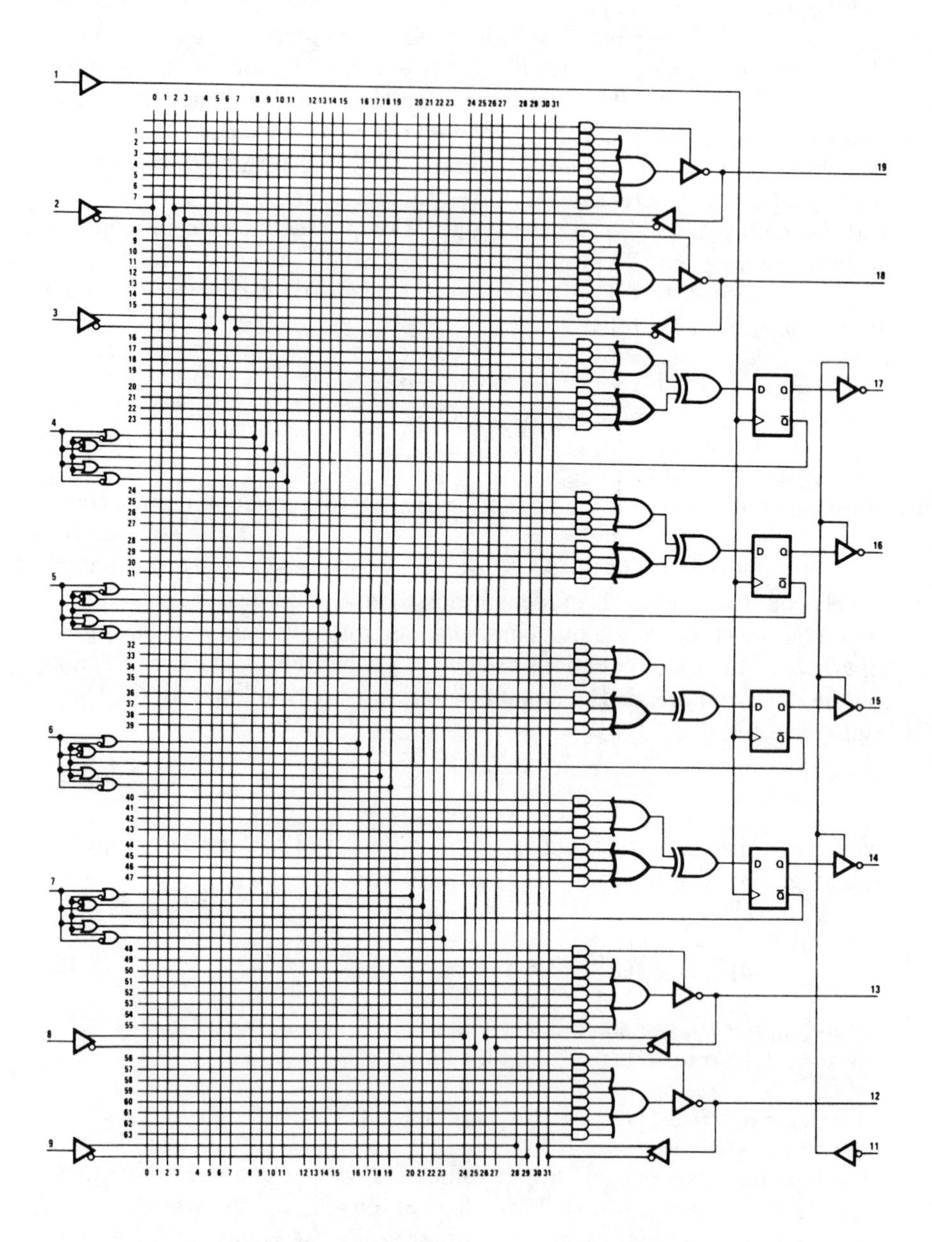


**Figure 8.10** XOR PAL.

from Equation 8.16,

$$s_1 = 0 \oplus b_1 \oplus (b_0 + 0) = b_1 \oplus b_0 \quad \textbf{(8.19)}$$

and from Equation 8.17, for $i \neq 0$,

$$\begin{aligned} s_i &= 0 \oplus b_i \oplus (0 + b_{i-1}(0 + b_{i-2}(0 + \ldots + b_1(b_0 + 0))\ldots)) \\ &= b_i \oplus b_{i-1}b_{i-2}\ldots b_1 b_0 \end{aligned} \quad \textbf{(8.20)}$$

which is the same as Equation 8.12, as expected.

Now let us derive the equations for a more interesting counter, one which counts up in fives. Here $a_2 = a_0 = 1$, and $a_i = 0$, $i \neq 0, 2$. From Equation 8.15,

$$s_0 = \overline{b}_0 \quad \textbf{(8.21)}$$

from Equation 8.16,

$$s_1 = b_1 \oplus b_0 \quad \textbf{(8.22)}$$

and from Equation 8.17, for $i \neq 0, 2$,

$$\begin{aligned} s_i &= 0 \oplus b_i \oplus (0 + b_{i-1}(0 + b_{i-2} + \ldots \\ &\quad + b_3(b_2 + 1(0 + b_1(b_0 + 0)))\ldots)) \\ &= b_i \oplus (b_{i-1}b_{i-2}\ldots b_3 b_2 + b_{i-1}b_{i-2}\ldots b_3 b_1 b_0) \end{aligned} \quad \textbf{(8.23)}$$

This equation requires at most three products per bit position in a PAL device with the exclusive OR structure. Other constant-increment up and down counters can be designed in a similar manner.

## 8.4 Arithmetic elements

### 8.4.1 Use of PALs

Rejecting ripple-carry adders as being too slow, in this section the use of PALs for building some arithmetic functions will be looked at. It will be seen that simple sum-of-products devices are inadequate in this application.

The equation for a sum bit in a carry lookahead adder was given in Equation 8.17. Expanding these equations into sum-of-products form results in 4 products for $s_0$, 12 for $s_1$, 28 for $s_2$, and so on. Building an adder in a standard PAL device is plainly impractical.

The XOR PALs of the type of Figure 8.10 can offer some saving in products. Looking again at Equation 8.17, it can be seen that the equation

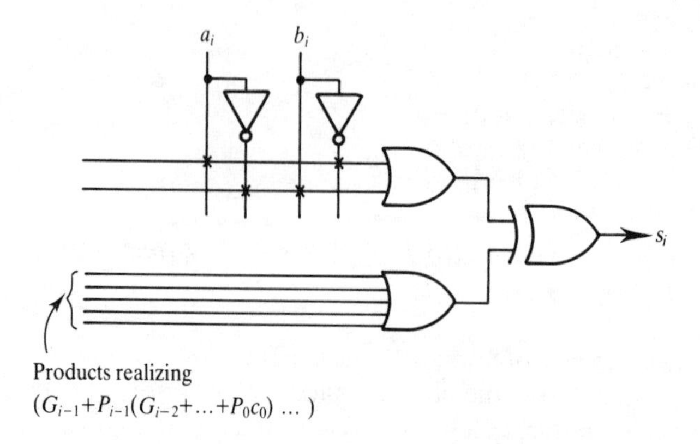


**Figure 8.11** Use of XOR PAL structure for carry lookahead adder.

can be split into two parts which can be exclusively ORed with each other:

$$a_i \oplus b_i \quad \text{and} \quad (G_{i-1} + P_{i-1}(G_{i-2} + \ldots + P_0c_0)\ldots)$$

The array realization is shown in Figure 8.11. The first part requires two products in all cases $(a_i\bar{b}_i + \bar{a}_ib_i)$. The second varies with sum bit position; $s_0$ requires 1 term, $s_1$ 3, $s_2$ 7, $s_3$ 15, $s_4$ 31, and so on. Even though this is an improvement on the simple PAL case, building an adder still requires too many products for any available PLD. However, a further modification can be made to the XOR structure which enables adders to be built with a reasonable number of products.

The 'arithmetic' PALs combine the XOR structure of Figure 8.10 with the 2-bit decoders which were discussed in Section 7.3.1. The structure is shown in Figure 8.12. The 2-bit decoders allow the $P_i$ $(= a_i + b_i$ or $a_i \oplus b_i)$ functions to be used directly as terms in a product. Thus $s_0$ (Equation 8.15) requires $1 + 1 = 2$ terms $(a_0 \oplus b_0)$ and $c_0$. $s_1$ (Equation 8.16) requires $1 + 2 = 3$ terms $(a_1 \oplus b_1$ and $G_0 + P_0c_0)$. Similarly, $s_2$ requires $1 + 3 = 4$ terms and $s_3$ requires $1 + 4 = 5$ terms. These products are shown in Figure 8.13.

Other functions (for example, 'load', 'hold', 'shift') can be combined with an adder by using more products feeding the upper OR gates in each pair of Figure 8.13. When the function is not 'add', all products feeding the bottom ORs must be set to '0'. For both addition and subtraction, either one of the inputs must be two's complemented, or a second set of products activated to perform the lookahead subtraction. The subtract equations do not have any products in common with the add equations.

The arithmetic PALs are also very useful for the construction of comparators. The comparison of two numbers, $A$ and $B$, can generate the outputs: $A = B$, $A > B$, $A \geqslant B$, $A < B$, $A \leqslant B$. The equation for the first of

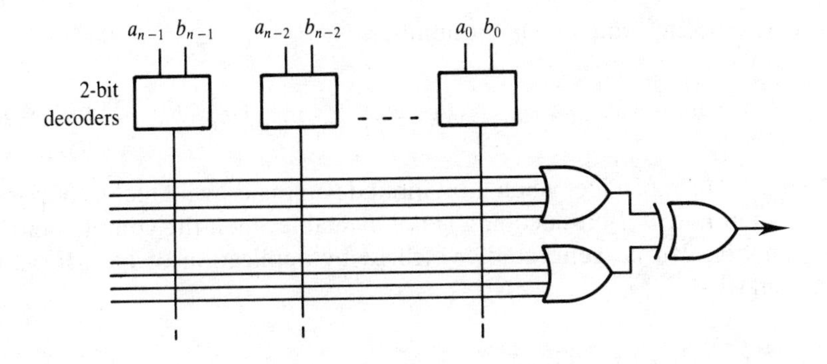


**Figure 8.12** Structure of arithmetic PAL.

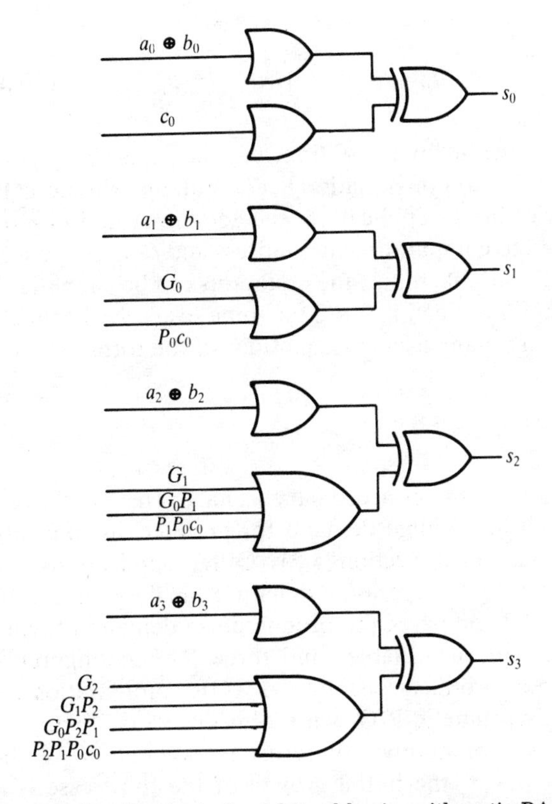


**Figure 8.13** Products for 4-bit adder in arithmetic PAL.

these when comparing two $n$-bit numbers is

$$(A = B) = (a_{n-1} \oplus b_{n-1})(a_{n-2} \oplus b_{n-2}) \ldots (a_0 \oplus b_0) \qquad \textbf{(8.24)}$$

which is a single product when 2-bit input decoding is available, as opposed to $2^n$ when not. If 2-bit decoding is not available, then the complement of the function can be generated, which is, by application of De Morgan's theorem,

$$(A \neq B) = (a_{n-1} = b_{n-1}) + (a_{n-2} = b_{n-2}) + \ldots + (a_0 = b_0)$$

This requires $2n$ products. An 8-bit comparison can be performed in those PAL devices with 16 products on at least one output.

The equation for $A > B$ is more complex:

$$\begin{aligned}(A > B) = {} & (a_{n-1}\overline{b}_{n-1}) \\ & + (a_{n-1} = b_{n-1})(a_{n-2}\overline{b}_{n-2}) \\ & + (a_{n-1} = b_{n-1})(a_{n-2} = b_{n-2})(a_{n-3}\overline{b}_{n-3}) \\ & \ldots \\ & + (a_{n-1} = b_{n-1})(a_{n-2} = b_{n-2}) \ldots (a_0\overline{b}_0) \qquad \textbf{(8.25)}\end{aligned}$$

This result is obvious by inspection, but the same result could have been derived by applicaton of Equation 8.17. With an arithmetic PAL, the only practical device in this application, the equation requires $n$ products.

Related to comparators are address and range decoders. Since these have only one variable input, the equations can be simplified on a case-by-case basis. Refer to Section 5.4.2 for some examples of this.

There are many uses for equations of the form

$$f = a \oplus b \oplus c \oplus d \oplus e \ldots \qquad \textbf{(8.26)}$$

where $a$, $b$, $c$ and so on are binary signals. This is of course the parity function which has a huge demand for products in conventional sum-of-products devices (see Section 5.5). Other applications are in pseudo-random sequence generation, signature analysis and error-correcting codes. Table 8.2 compares the product term demand of equation 8.26 for different numbers of variables and three PAL configurations. First the standard sum of products, second the XOR configuration of Figure 8.10, and third the arithmetic PAL with 2-bit decoders (Figure 8.12). In each case the growth of number of terms is exponential in the number of variables. However, the initial growth of the third case is much slower, making the arithmetic PALs again the only suitable devices for this task.

**Table 8.2** Number of products required for realization of functions of the form $f = x_1 \oplus x_2 \oplus \ldots \oplus x_n$ for three configurations.

| *Number of variables (n)* | *Configuration 1* | *Configuration 2* | *Configuration 3* |
|---|---|---|---|
| 2 | 2 | 1 + 1 = 2 | 1 |
| 3 | 4 | 2 + 1 = 3 | 1 + 1 = 2 |
| 4 | 8 | 2 + 2 = 4 | 1 + 1 = 2 |
| 5 | 16 | 4 + 2 = 6 | 2 + 1 = 3 |
| 6 | 32 | 4 + 4 = 8 | 2 + 1 = 3 |
| 7 | 64 | 8 + 4 = 12 | 2 + 2 = 4 |
| 8 | 128 | 8 + 8 = 16 | 2 + 2 = 4 |
| 9 | 256 | 16 + 8 = 24 | 4 + 2 = 6 |
| 10 | 512 | 16 + 16 = 32 | 4 + 2 = 6 |
| 11 | 1024 | 32 + 16 = 48 | 4 + 4 = 8 |
| 12 | 2048 | 32 + 32 = 64 | 4 + 4 = 8 |

### 8.4.2 Table lookup methods

As stated in Section 5.2, memories are often the only practical way of realizing some functions. Many arithmetic applications come into this category. Conversely, some arithmetic techniques have been conceived from the outset for memory implementation; two examples will be briefly mentioned at the end of this section.

Function generation is an obvious application for memory. The address inputs are fed with a signal representing the independent variable, and the outputs represent the function value. Economies are sometimes possible for functions possessing a symmetry. It is not necessary, for example, to store a complete cycle of a sine or cosine waveform; only the first quarter-cycle needs to be stored with adjustment of the memory inputs and outputs changing the waveform according to the quadrant. Figure 8.14 shows how this arrangement works. Another method of reducing memory size is by storing differences rather than function values. This is only suitable for inputs which change step by step, and requires an accumulator at the output to hold the current function value. Functions which can be approximated by a Taylor series can sometimes be economically generated term by term with memories. Since successive terms represent smaller and smaller numbers, the full dynamic range is not required for their representation, thus reducing the memory sizes required.

Memories can sometimes be useful for standard functions such as multiplication and division when one of the operands is a constant. The

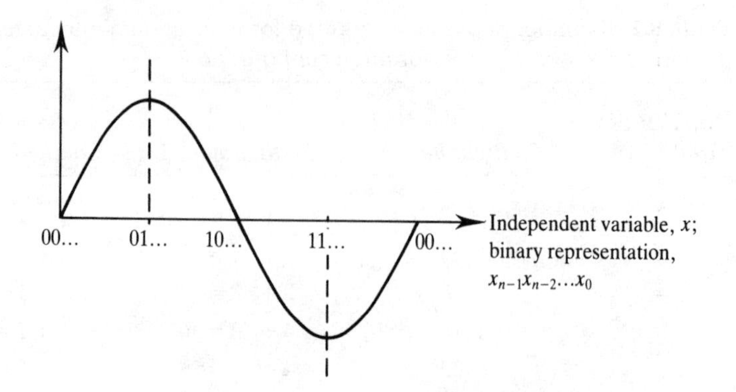


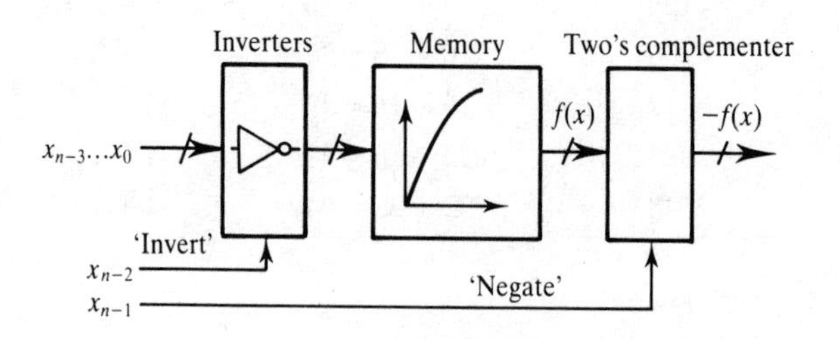


**Figure 8.14** Generation of a sine function.

memory implementation can be more economical than the general arithmetic circuit, and certainly requires fewer pins. Another application for table lookup arithmetic is **residue** arithmetic.

Residue arithmetic, based on the residue number system (RNS), avoids the problem of carry propagation of conventional arithmetic. Residue numbers are coded as a string of the remainders obtained when dividing by a specially chosen set of relatively prime moduli. For example with a set of moduli $P = \{3, 4, 5\}$ the number 12 is represented by

$$(12 \bmod 3,\ 12 \bmod 4,\ 12 \bmod 5) = (0, 0, 2)$$

The operations of addition, subtraction and multiplication can be performed on the RNS digits independently. So, for example,

$$3\ (0, 3, 3) \times 13\ (1, 1, 3)$$

is

$$((0 \times 1) \bmod 3,\ (3 \times 1) \bmod 4,\ (3 \times 3) \bmod 5) = (0, 3, 4)$$

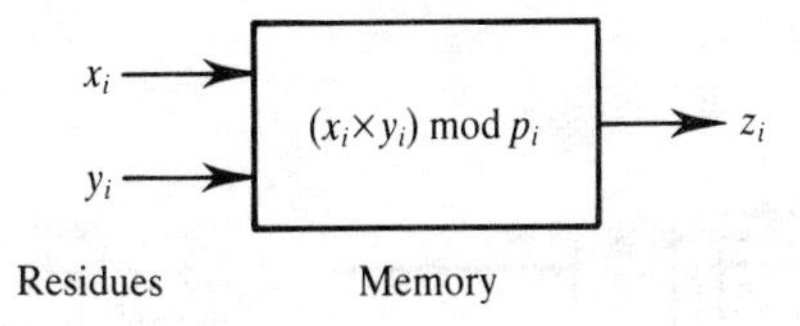


**Figure 8.15** Use of memory in residue arithmetic.

Each of the operations on the residues can be performed with a memory as shown in Figure 8.15. When using residue arithmetic, there is the overhead of code conversion at input and output to be considered.

Yet another method of computation based on table lookup is **distributed arithmetic**. This is a method of computing sums of products of integers of the form:

$$y = \sum_{i=1}^{m} a_i x_i \tag{8.27}$$

where the $a_i$ are a set of coefficients. This type of calculation is very common in digital signal processing. It is also the basic operation in matrix multiplication. Figure 8.16 shows a block of $m$ words, each of $n$ bits, which is to be subjected to the transformation of Equation 8.27. In a conventional implementation, using multipliers and accumulators, the words are used

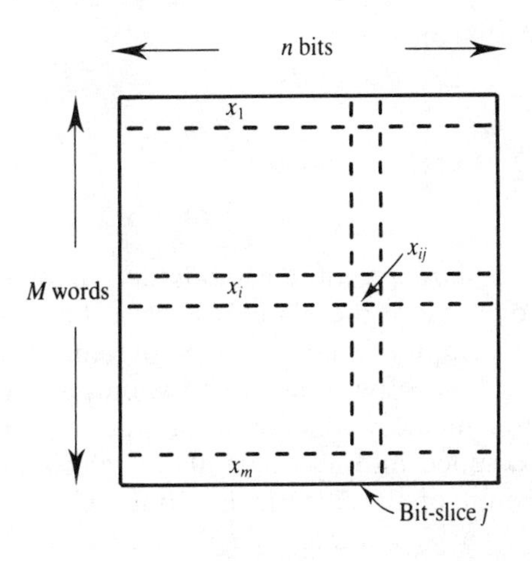


**Figure 8.16** Data block for calculation of

$$y = \sum_{i=1}^{m} a_i x_i$$

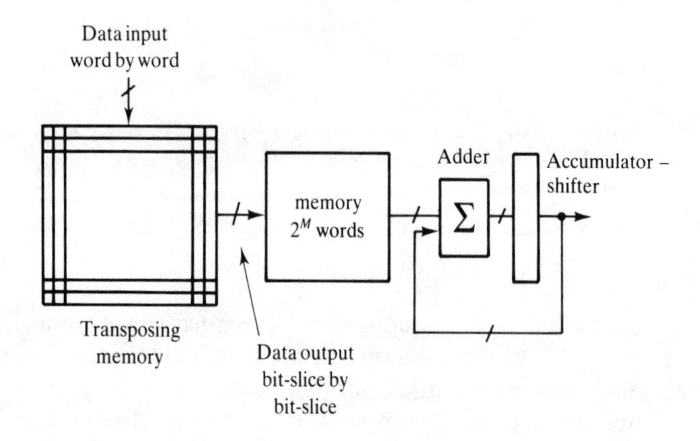


**Figure 8.17** Distributed arithmetic – basic architecture.

row by row. However, the computation can be expressed in an alternative form in which the data is used column by column. Equation 8.27 can be expressed as a double summation by expressing the $x_i$s as weighted sums of their bits:

$$y = \sum_{i=1}^{M} a_i \left( \sum_{j=0}^{n-1} x_{ij} 2^j \right) \tag{8.28}$$

which can be rewritten as:

$$y = \sum_{j=0}^{n-1} 2^j \left( \sum_{i=1}^{M} a_i x_{ij} \right) \tag{8.29}$$

The second summation represents a combination of the coefficients, as the $x_{ij}$ have values 0 or 1. Since there are $M$ words, there will be $2^M$ of these combinations. The computation can now be organized as shown in Figure 8.17. The block of data to be transformed is output bit-slice by bit-slice. Each slice is fed to a memory which looks up the required combination of the $a_i$s. These are added into an accumulator which shifts the sum each cycle to take account of the $2^j$ term in Equation 8.29. The amount of memory required can be reduced by splitting the second summation of Equation 8.29 into two, giving the arrangement of Figure 8.18 (for $M$ an even number). This can be a considerable economy, and can be split even further if necessary, at the expense of more adders. This partitioning cannot be done with the multipliers of the conventional solution.

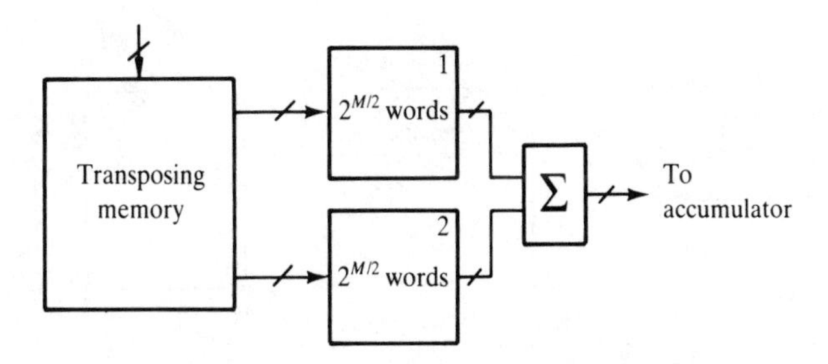


**Figure 8.18** Distributed arithmetic with partitioned memories: memory 1 has combinations of $a_1$ to $a_{m/2}$; memory 2 has combinations of $a_{m/2+1}$ to $a_m$.

## 8.5 Control + data

### 8.5.1 General

So far the design of the control and data subsystems have been considered as separate problems. In this section how these interact with each other, and then how they may be combined in a single array, will be examined. The section will end with an example of a complete design which unites control and data parts.

### 8.5.2 Timing considerations and pipelining

In Section 7.7 it was shown how two state machines could be linked. Here this will be extended to linked control and data state machines and their array implementation.

Figure 8.19 shows the general case, in which a controller and data processor, both Mealy machines, communicate. (This is a simplified version of Figure 8.1.) The command outputs from the controller feed directly into the logic of the data state machine, while two possibilities are shown for the status signals. These can be either Mealy outputs, coming directly from the logic, or Moore outputs, coming from the data (state) register. If the former are present, then the problem previously mentioned in Section 7.7 can arise. If, in a particular controller state, a conditional command output affects one of the Mealy status outputs, which in turn affects the command output, an instability or incorrect action can occur. To avoid this, only the Moore outputs from the data path can be used. However, this scheme has another disadvantage. In one clock cycle the following times have to be accommodated: the maximum propagation delay of the controller state register, the maximum propagation delay of the controller logic,

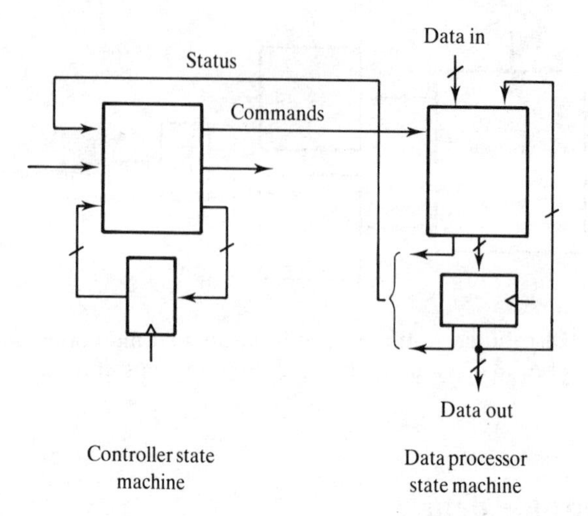


**Figure 8.19** Linked control and data state machines.

the maximum propagation delay of the data processor logic, the set-up time of the data register, and some allowance for clock skew. The clock rate is thus limited by the fact that two logic propagation delays have to be included in one cycle. For maximum clock rate, these delays must be split. This can be achieved by interposing a **pipeline register**, as shown in Figure 8.20.

The minimum clock cycle must now include the longer of the following: the register maximum propagation delays, the maximum logic delays, the register set-up times (plus an allowance for clock skew). It is assumed that the Moore status outputs are used to avoid the second long path containing both logic blocks. Thus, the conclusion is that: to avoid having to fit two logic delays in a cycle, both control and data machines must be of

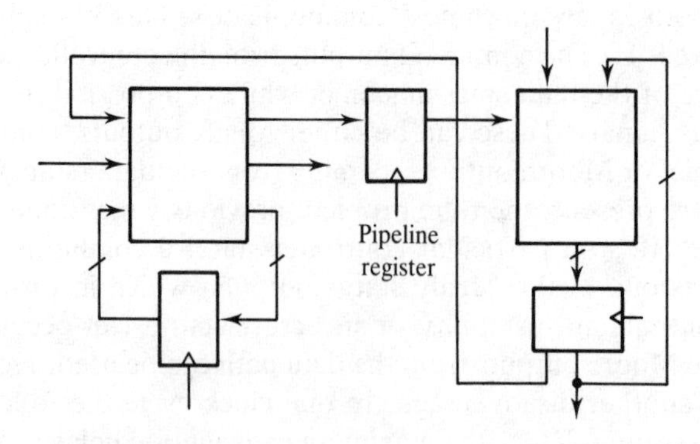


**Figure 8.20** Modification of Figure 8.19 to include pipeline register.

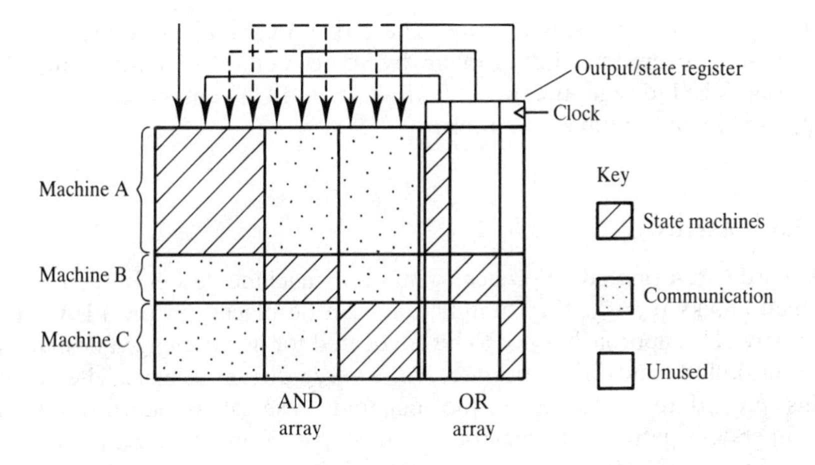


**Figure 8.21** Three Moore machines in an array.

the Moore type. The case of a single controller and data path can be generalized to any number of controllers and data processors; they must all be Moore machines. It is now possible to look at how these can be accommodated in a single array.

In Figure 8.21 are shown three Moore machines in a PLA together with their links. Three areas can be identified in the array:

(1) The areas in the AND and OR arrays which correspond to the state machines. In the AND array are the areas where external inputs and present state variables meet the product lines, and in the OR array the links between these lines and the next state and output registers.

(2) The area in the AND array where inputs from other machines meet the products – the communication area. This will be sparsely occupied for loosely coupled machines.

(3) The unused areas in the OR array where the product lines never contribute to a register input because it belongs to another machine.

Product term sharing between partitions would break down this simple division into areas. The same diagram could be drawn for the PAL structure; in this case the AND array would be the same, but the OR array would not be present. Of course, no product term sharing is possible in this case.

This illustration demonstrates that there is no benefit in attempting to merge the separate state machine descriptions into a single larger description. This is done automatically when placing them in the array. It also illustrates the inefficiency which usually results when placing more than one machine in an array. There is thus a limit to the useful size of a

PLD consisting of a single array. The larger PLDs all in different ways attempt to overcome this problem by some method of partitioning. In custom VLSI design the wasted areas of a PLA can be removed by applying layout optimization tools.

### 8.5.3 Macros

A 'hardware-oriented' approach to multiple machine design is possible, in which blocks representing subfunctions can be placed on the PLA table directly. This approach is not to be advocated for inexperienced designers, but in skilled hands it can produce some very efficient designs. The key to this procedure is to make the maximun use of standard position-independent patterns, or macros. An example of one of these patterns is the counter of Section 6.9 (Table 8.3).

Such a pattern can be placed wherever it is needed (this will be in one of the hatched areas of Figure 8.21). Note that the macro does not include the full horizontal extent of the array. A data macro for loading a register in reverse bit order when a control input (which may be from another block, perhaps a state machine controller) has the value '01' has the form shown in Table 8.4.

**Table 8.3**

| *Term number* | *Present state* | *Next state* |
|---|---|---|
| $i$ | ---------L | ---------H |
| $i+1$ | --------LH | --------HL |
| $i+2$ | -------LHH | -------HLL |
| $i+3$ | ------LHHH | ------HLLL |
| | etc. | |

**Table 8.4**

| *Term number* | *Present state* | *Next state* |
|---|---|---|
| $j$ | 01-1------ | ---------L |
| $j+1$ | 01--1----- | --------L- |
| $j+2$ | 01---1---- | -------L-- |
| | etc. | |

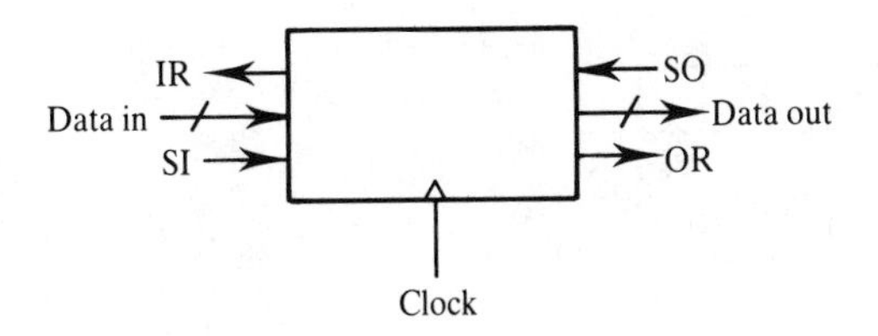


**Figure 8.22** Synchronous FIFO.

### 8.5.4 Design example – FIFO

The purpose of this example is to show how the equations can be derived for an application containing multiple control and data blocks. The task is to synthesize a synchronous first-in first-out memory (FIFO) using a single PLD. The inputs and outputs are shown in Figure 8.22. There are two parallel data ports, one for input and one for output. There are four single-bit control and status signals:

- SI (shift in): indicates that a new data word is ready for input;
- IR (input ready): indicates that there is space for a new data word;
- SO (shift out): indicates that a data word is to be shifted out;
- OR (output ready): indicates that there is a data word ready to be shifted out.

The mode of operation is illustrated in Figure 8.23, which shows the contents of the data cells. The contents of the data registers are shown in the post-clocking condition. (1) shows the FIFO with no data stored. In (2) a data word 'a' is loaded into the last register. A further word is loaded in (3). A data word is then shifted out and word 'b' moves up one place – both of these actions occur simultaneously. In (5) two actions occur: data word 'b' is shifted out and a new word 'c' is loaded. (6) shows the FIFO in its full condition, and (7) the state after a simultaneous input and output.

Figure 8.24 is the block diagram of the FIFO. At each word position there is a register and controller. The registers have three modes:

hold: $O_i.d = O_i$ **(8.30)**

load: $O_i.d = D$ **(8.31)**

shift: $O_i.d = O_{i+1}$ **(8.32)**

Each controller requires two states, 'full' and 'empty', indicating the status of the corresponding data register. The algorithm for each controller

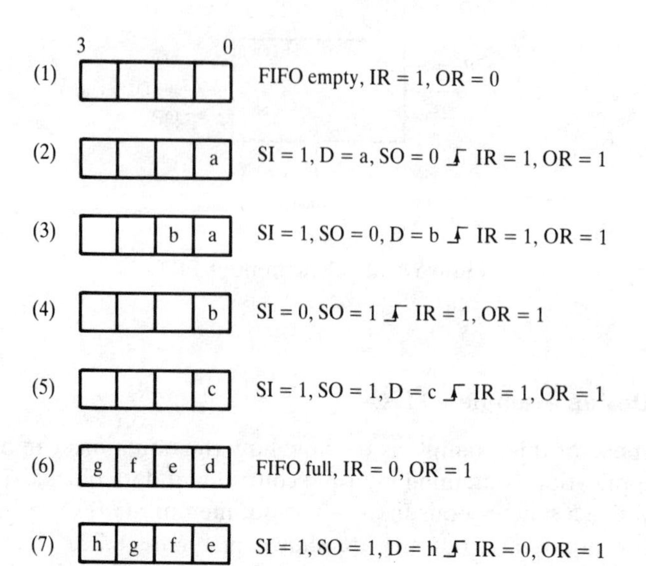


**Figure 8.23** FIFO mode of operation.

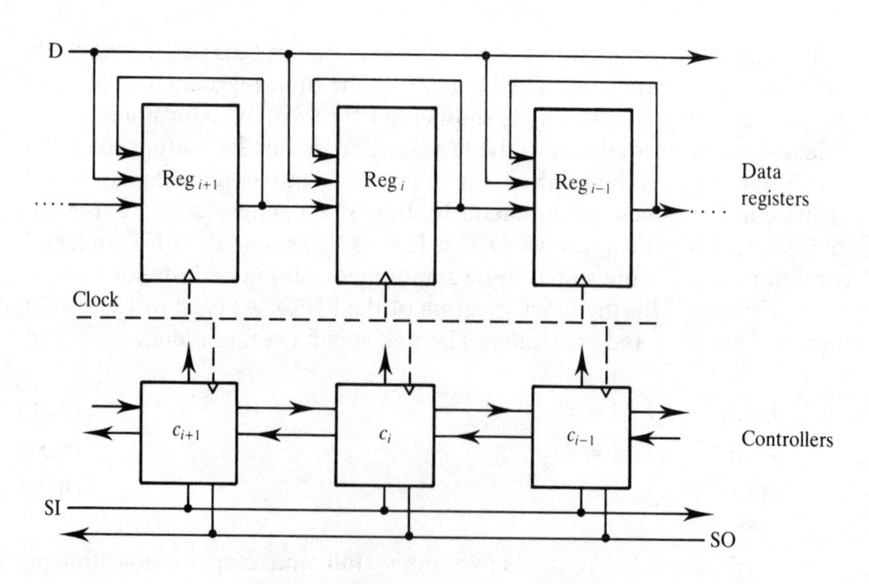


**Figure 8.24** FIFO block diagram.

(except for the first and the last) $F_i$ is as follows:

empty: if SI = 1 and SO = 0 and $F_{i-1}$ = full
  then mode = load; go to full
  else go to empty;
full: if SI = 1 and SO = 1 and $F_{i+1}$ = empty
  then mode = load; go to full;
 if SO = 1 and $F_{i+1}$ = 1
  then mode = shift; go to full;
 if SO = 0
  then mode = hold; go to full;
 go to empty;

The state machine flowchart for this is given in Figure 8.25. Notice that the outputs specifying the register mode are not always defined; this is because the register contents are not of interest when 'empty'. The PLA table is given in Table 8.5. The state assignment is as follows: 'empty' → $F_i = 0$, 'full' → $F_i = 1$.

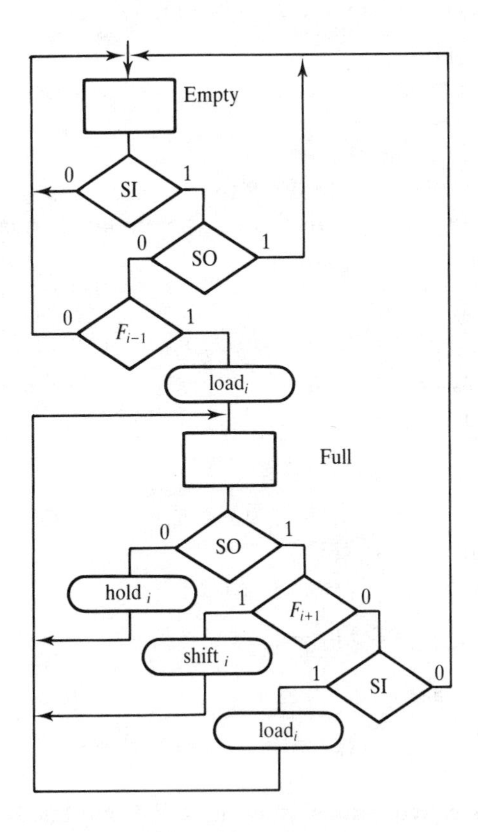


**Figure 8.25** Controller$_i$ flowchart.

**Table 8.5**

| $F_i$ | SI | SO | $F_{i-1}$ | $F_{i+1}$ | $NF_i$ | $hold_i$ | $shift_i$ | $load_i$ |
|---|---|---|---|---|---|---|---|---|
| 0 | 0 | * | * | * | 0 | – | – | – |
| 0 | 1 | 0 | 0 | * | 0 | – | – | – |
| 0 | 1 | 0 | 1 | * | 1 | 0 | 0 | 1 |
| 0 | 1 | 1 | * | * | 0 | – | – | – |
| 1 | * | 0 | * | * | 1 | 1 | 0 | 0 |
| 1 | * | 1 | * | 1 | 1 | 0 | 1 | 0 |
| 1 | 1 | 1 | * | 0 | 1 | 0 | 0 | 1 |
| 1 | 0 | 1 | * | 0 | 0 | – | – | – |

The K maps for $NF_i$ (the 'next state' variable), $hold_i$, $shift_i$ and $load_i$ are given in Figure 8.26. The equations obtained are as follows:

$$NF_i = F_i SI + F_i\overline{SO} + F_iF_{i+1} + SI\,\overline{SO}\,F_{i-1} \quad (8.33)$$
$$hold_i = F_i\overline{SO} \quad (8.34)$$
$$shift_i = SO\,F_{i+1} \quad (8.35)$$
$$load_i = SO\,\overline{F}_{i+1} + \overline{F}_i \quad (8.36)$$

For the first stage, $F_{i+1}$ is always 0' that is there is never a 'shift' output, and for the last stage $F_{i-1}$ is always 1'. The modified equations are

- first stage:

$$NF_{n-1} = F_{n-1}SI + F_{n-1}\overline{SO} + SI\,\overline{SO}\,F_{n-2} \quad (8.33a)$$
$$hold_{n-1} = F_{n-1}\overline{SO} \quad (8.34a)$$
$$load_{n-1} = \overline{F}_{n-1} \quad (8.36b)$$

- last stage:

$$NF_0 = F_0 SI + F_0\overline{SO} + F_0F_1 + SI\,\overline{SO} \quad (8.33b)$$
$$hold_0 = F_0\overline{SO} \quad (8.34b)$$
$$shift_0 = SO\,F_1 \quad (8.35b)$$
$$load_0 = SO\,\overline{F}_1 + \overline{F}_0 \quad (8.36b)$$

The FIFO outputs are

$$IR = \overline{F}_{n-1} \quad \text{and} \quad OR = F_0 \quad (8.37)$$

The register equations may now be modified to include the expanded mode signals; these are of course internal to the PLD. Now that

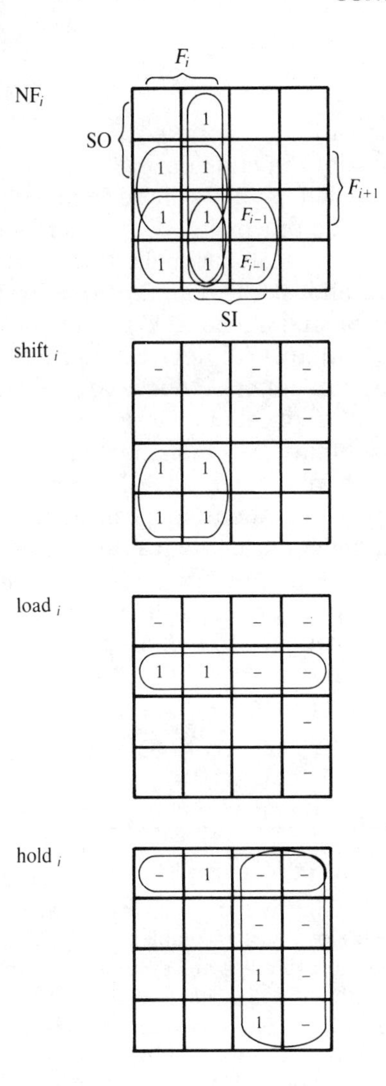


**Figure 8.26** Controller$_i$ K maps.

all of the equations have been derived, the resources required can be determined. If the data width is $m$ bits, the total number of flip–flops needed is $(m+1)n$. Only $(m+2)$ of these need access to pins, so the number of buried flip–flops is $(m+1)n - (m+2)$. If a PAL-structured device is used, then the maximum number of products per $D$ flip–flop is four. The number of signal pins is $2m+4$. With clock, output enable and power, the total is $2m+8$. Thus for any given values of $m$ and $n$, a suitable PLD, if it exists, may be selected from Appendix A. The equations may be readily transcribed into one of the PLD Boolean design languages.

## SUMMARY

Data paths are responsible for storing, routing and transforming data signals. Their complexity depends on the form of control selected. In general the simpler the data path, the more complex is the controller and the more sequential is the processing. Controllers and data paths interact through command and status signals. PAL devices are particularly suitable for data applications. The defining equations are usually simple to set up, being vector operations. PALs with registers are useful in pipelined systems. Standard PAL devices are not suitable for building long counters, as they run out of products. XOR PAL devices, however, are very useful in this application. These devices can implement all types of synchronous counter in conjunction with, if required, the standard data storage and routing tasks. XOR PALs with 2-bit decoders can perform some arithmetic operations not possible with other PLDs. ROMs are suitable for arithmetic and numerical tasks based on table lookup. There exist methods of computation only practical with ROMs. For maximum speed, linked control and data path state machines should both be of the Moore type. These linked machines can be placed in a single PLD if resources permit.

## BIBLIOGRAPHICAL NOTES

Data path structures and design methods are covered well in Ercegovac and Lang (1985). Examples of the use of PALs in complex data paths are given in Kitson and Rosen (1983). Many design examples are available in Advanced Micro Devices (1988). The standard arithmetic algorithms are described in Waser and Flynn (1982). Counter design techniques are covered in Lewin (1985). Jay (1987) discusses the use of XOR PALs in simple counter design. A compiler for complex counters in XOR PALs is described in Terry (1987). The structure of a PLA optimized for arithmetic is given in Jones (1975a); the arithmetic PALs are derived from this. Weinberger (1979) describes compact adders using these PLAs. He shows that an 8-bit adder with carry-out requires 25 products. An arithmetic PAL (if one were available this large) would require 65. Several memory applications in arithmetic are given in Monolithic Memories (1984). For more detail consult for example Hemel (1970, 1972) (table lookup methods in arithmetic), Schmid and Busch (1970) (function generation), Spicer (1973) and Benedek (1975) (BCD–binary code conversion). An explanation of residue arithmetic is available in Taylor (1984), and of distributed arithmetic in Buttner and Schussler (1976). PLA table design using macros was developed at IBM in the early days of array logic; see Jones (1975a). A multiple-PLA design specified in this way is described in Logue *et al.* (1975) and Jones (1975b, 1975c, 1975d). More recent examples of this approach are Britt (1986) and Cavlan and Britt (1986).

## EXERCISES

**8.1** Draw the flowchart for a multiplication routine for the architecture of Figure 8.1.

**8.2** Produce the complete set of equations for the 16 location addressable memory given in Section 8.2.2.

Add a read/write control input and show how the design can be augmented to allow data to be read through a single bit output.

**8.3** A multifunction shift register (most-significant end of a set) is required with the inputs and outputs, and function table as specified in Figure 8.27 (see page 266). The outputs are $Q_3$–$Q_0$, the inputs $D_3$–$D_0$. RO/LI ('right output/left input') is for cascading with other shift registers. The function control inputs are $F_2$–$F_0$. Right shifts are of the arithmetic type (that is, msb repeated) when AR = 1, otherwise they are logic shifts, when the value of LI is entered at the most-significant end. If, on an arithmetic right shift, OVR = 1, the repeated sign bit is inverted.

Design the logic for a PAL implementation of this function.

**8.4** The function table for an 8-bit barrel shifter with inputs D7–D0, outputs $Q_7$–$Q_0$ and function control bits $F_2$–$F_0$ is given below:

| $F_2$ | $F_1$ | $F_0$ | $Q_7$ | $Q_6$ | $Q_5$ | $Q_4$ | $Q_3$ | $Q_2$ | $Q_1$ | $Q_0$ |
|---|---|---|---|---|---|---|---|---|---|---|
| 0 | 0 | 0 | D7 | D6 | D5 | D4 | D3 | D2 | D1 | D0 |
| 0 | 0 | 1 | D6 | D5 | D4 | D3 | D2 | D1 | D0 | D7 |
| 0 | 1 | 0 | D5 | D4 | D3 | D2 | D1 | D0 | D7 | D6 |
| 0 | 1 | 1 | D4 | D3 | D2 | D1 | D0 | D7 | D6 | D5 |
| 1 | 0 | 0 | D3 | D2 | D1 | D0 | D7 | D6 | D5 | D4 |
| 1 | 0 | 1 | D2 | D1 | D0 | D7 | D6 | D5 | D4 | D3 |
| 1 | 1 | 0 | D1 | D0 | D7 | D6 | D5 | D4 | D3 | D2 |
| 1 | 1 | 1 | D0 | D7 | D6 | D5 | D4 | D3 | D2 | D1 |

What PAL resources are needed for implementing this specification?

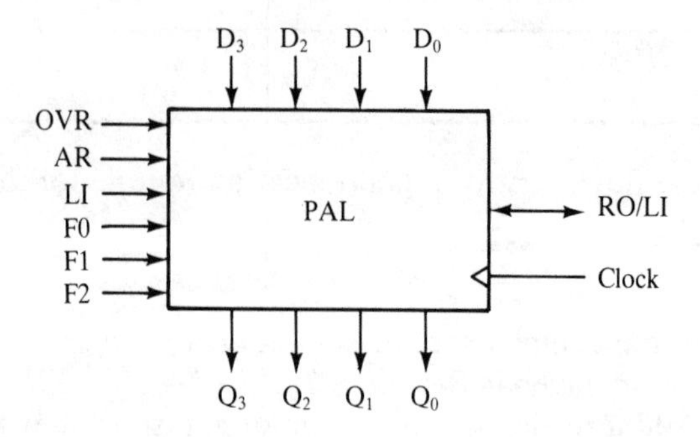


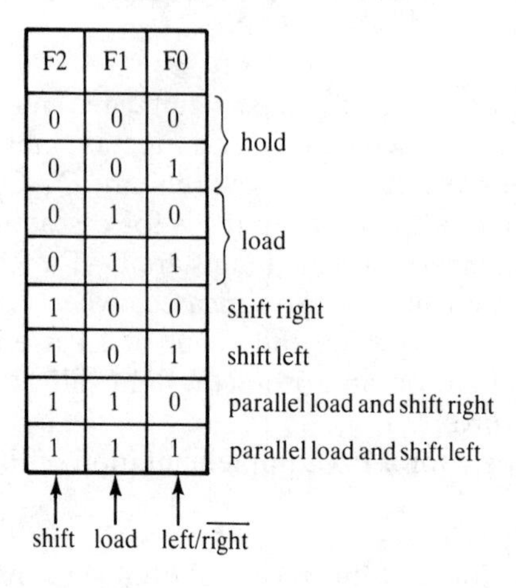

| F2 | F1 | F0 | |
|---|---|---|---|
| 0 | 0 | 0 | hold |
| 0 | 0 | 1 | hold |
| 0 | 1 | 0 | load |
| 0 | 1 | 1 | load |
| 1 | 0 | 0 | shift right |
| 1 | 0 | 1 | shift left |
| 1 | 1 | 0 | parallel load and shift right |
| 1 | 1 | 1 | parallel load and shift left |

shift load left/$\overline{\text{right}}$

**Figure 8.27**

**8.5** A PAL device has the following worst-case timing parameters:

$$t_{PD} = 25 \text{ ns}$$
$$t_{CLK} = 15 \text{ ns}$$
$$t_{CF} = 13 \text{ ns}$$
$$t_{SU(PAL)} = 15 \text{ ns}$$

and is to be used in a synchronous system together with registers having an 8 ns clock-to-output delay. What will be the maximum clock frequency in the worst-case configuration?

**8.6** Design a counter which counts up or down in threes depending on the state of a control input. What are the product term demands in:

(a) a conventional PAL
(b) an XOR PAL
(c) an arithmetic PAL?

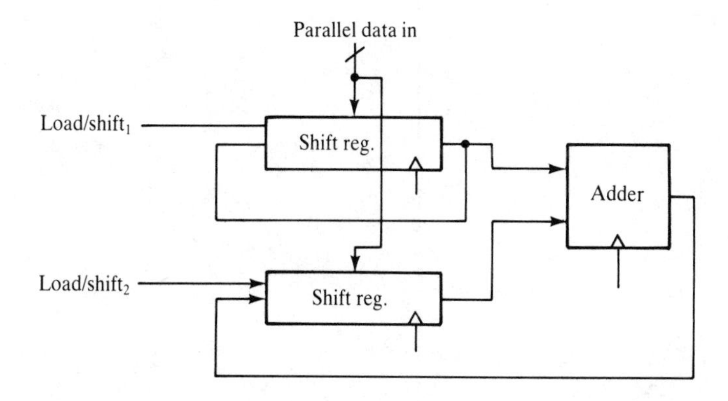


**Figure 8.28**

**8.7** Some PLDs have flip–flops which can be programmably configured into $D$, $J$–$K$ or $T$ types. Is there an occasion when more than one type would be required in a single PLD design? Why would each be chosen?

**8.8** Look at the problems of building parallel comparators in PLDs. Take as an example a comparator with two 4-bit inputs $A$ and $B$, and which produces outputs $A > B$, $A = B$ and $A < B$. What would be the ideal PLD.

**8.9** The serial-data computation system of Figure 8.28 is to be constructed in a PLA. The two 4-bit shift registers can be loaded in parallel. When data is shifted out, the two streams are added in a serial adder.

Design PLA macros for each of the three elements. Then show how they can be combined in a single PLA.

What does this demonstrate about large PLAs?

**8.10** What are the largest FIFOs, built according to the design of Section 8.5.4, which can be made from the PAL structured PLDs listed in the Appendix?

CHAPTER 9
# Asynchronous Design

---

**OBJECTIVES**

When you have completed studying this chapter you should be able

- to understand the Huffman model of asynchronous sequential circuits, and how these are related to synchronous circuits;
- to design simple asynchronous circuits starting from a flow table and which are free of race and hazard faults;
- to build custom latches and flip–flops into PLDs;
- to use flowcharts to design reliable asynchronous state machines using combinational PAL devices;
- to apply memories to asynchronous design;
- to design self-clocked asynchronous circuits using PLDs with dual-triggered flip–flops;
- to estimate the reliability of synchronizers.

---

## 9.1 Introduction

Conventional wisdom (and some company design manuals) state that asynchronous sequential circuits should never be used. Why, therefore, is this chapter here? There are two reasons: firstly, there are and always will be applications for this type of circuit, and secondly, a knowledge of asynchronous circuit behaviour is necessary for the proper understanding of synchronous circuits in all their modes of operation.

Asynchronous circuits have the advantage that they respond immediately to an input change; they can thus operate faster than a synchronous circuit and have a variable state time. Some high speed bus and data communication protocol implementations rely on asynchronous state machines. Synchronous circuits are tied to a rigid clocking scheme. When interfacing components with complex and differing clocking requirements, building an asynchronous circuit is often the neatest solution. However, there are problems. Asynchronous design is more laborious and many more potential operational errors have to be checked for. In addition, there are restrictions on the manner in which inputs can change relative to each other. Finally, it may be necessary to collect additional timing data on the PLD to be used to ensure that certain new types of hazard cannot cause incorrect sequential operation. Provided that these conditions can be met, a satisfactory and reliable design is usually possible.

The fundamental unit of synchronous systems, the clocked flip–flop, is itself an asynchronous circuit, and as such can also be upset by some combinations of input changes. Over the years, this behaviour has been studied in depth, and should be mentioned in any modern digital design textbook. The final section of this chapter is devoted to this topic.

The heart of the chapter is a flowchart-based systematic method for designing asynchronous state machines in PLDs. This is followed by a description of less restrictive methods which can be used in arrays for which additional information on their dynamic behaviour is available (unfortunately not always the case).

## 9.2 Sequential machines revisited

A combinational logic circuit has outputs which only depend on the current values of the inputs (disregarding propagation delays), whereas the output of a sequential circuit depends not only on the current inputs, but on past inputs as well. It has memory. So far we have assumed that this memory was a set of clocked flip–flops and that the sequential circuit was synchronous. In this section the underlying principles of digital memory will be looked at, with the aims of both giving a deeper understanding of synchronous circuits and introducing some design techniques for asynchronous circuits.

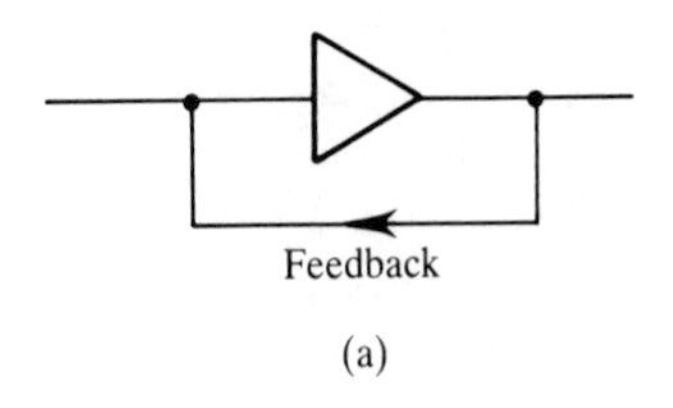


(a)

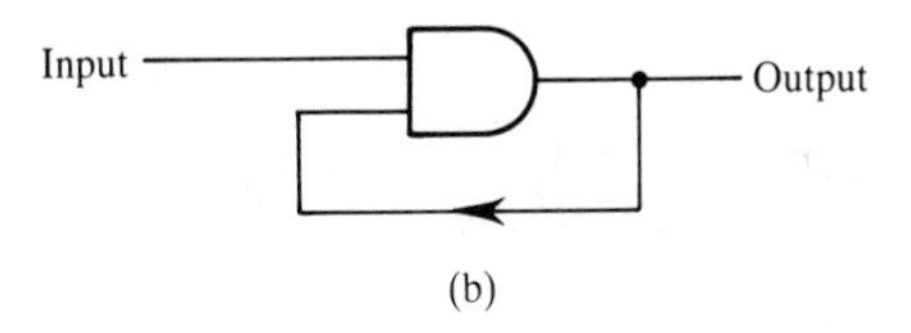


(b)

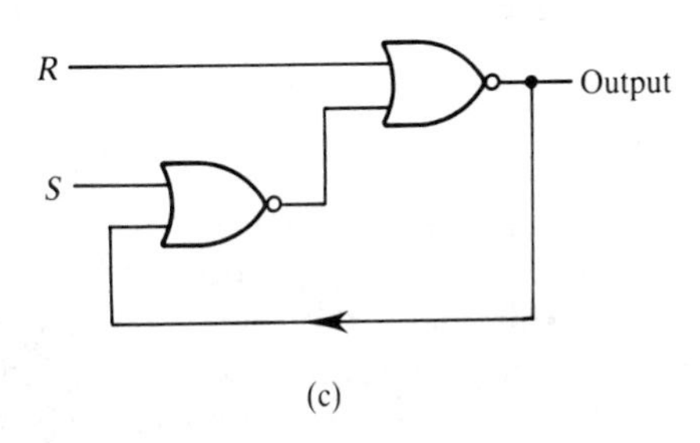


(c)

**Figure 9.1** (a) A circuit with two stable states. (b) A circuit which can be partially controlled. (c) A fully controllable two-state circuit.

For a variable signal to be maintained indefinitely, feedback is required to permit regeneration. Figure 9.1(a) shows the simplest possible memory circuit built in this way. This circuit can have two stable states: if the output is 1, the input is equal to 1 and thus the output is kept constant; the same applies for the 0 state. However, once determined, the state of this circuit cannot be altered, except by forcing the output into the opposite state. Figure 9.1(b) shows how a two-input gate can be made into a circuit with two stable states. Assume first that the output is in state 0. The feedback of this value will ensure that the input can have no effect on the stored state. However, if both inputs have the value 1, then the output will remain at this value until the input becomes 0. Neither of these circuits is useful when built at the logic gate level. The simplest useful sequential circuit is shown in Figure 9.1(c). With both inputs at 0, the output can have values 0 or 1, as the circuit in this condition is equivalent to that of Figure 9.1(a); a two-input NOR gate with one input set to 0 acts as an inverter,

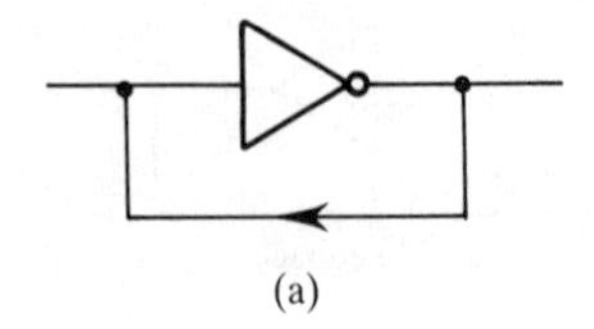

(a)

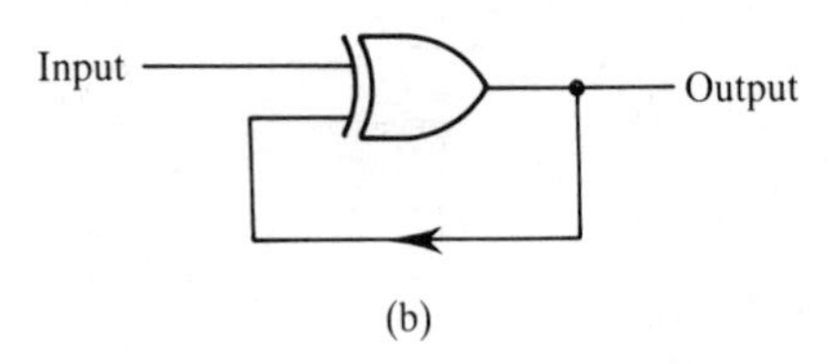


(b)

**Figure 9.2** (a) A circuit which has no stable state. (b) A circuit with both stable and unstable states.

and two inverters in series cancel. When input $R$ is set to 1, the output becomes 0 and the value fed back to the second input of the upper NOR gate is 1 – a value which will maintain the output at its new value. $S$ has the opposite effect; it causes the output to attain and hold the value 1. If both $S$ and $R$ have the value 1, then the output will become 0. Which state it takes next depends on which of the inputs returns to 0 first. This circuit is the ***S–R* latch**, a useful 1-bit memory element. Note the single regeneration path.

In none of the circuits of Figure 9.1 is a propagation delay essential to the explanations given; they would work as described with ideal delay-free circuit elements and interconnections. This is not always the case, however, and in fact delays are essential for the production of unstable states. Figure 9.2(a) shows the simplest circuit with such states. With a zero propagation delay this circuit would have an undefined behaviour owing to contradiction implied by the feedback, that is $0 = 1$. If, however, there is a propagation delay, the circuit can exist in a state where the input and output have opposite values. This is, of course, the transient or switching state of the inverter. The circuit therefore is in a permanently unstable condition oscillating between its two states with a period of about twice the inverter propagation delay. Figure 9.2(b) illustrates a circuit which can exist in either a stable state or a condition of oscillation. An input of 0 allows the circuit to settle in a stable state, while an input of 1 causes instability.

In the examples studied so far, there has only been one feedback connection. These circuits have two states. Circuits with more than a single

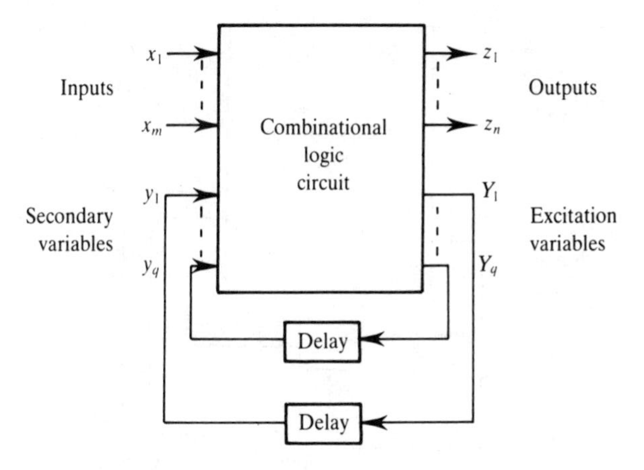


**Figure 9.3** Model of an asynchronous sequential circuit.

feedback link can potentially settle into more than two stable states. This leads to the classical model of the sequential circuit, or **Huffman circuit**, of Figure 9.3. Here the delays, which always exist in real circuits, are lumped and shown in the feedback paths. In the steady state, the 'next state' or excitation, variables will be equal to the 'present state', or secondary, variables (so called because in Huffman's electromagnetic relay technology circuits, the inputs controlled 'primary' relays and the excitations controlled 'secondary' relays), the inputs are constant, and the outputs, being functions of the input and secondary variables, will likewise be steady. If an input variable changes, one or more of the excitation variables could change. The circuit will now temporarily be in a state where the excitation variables are not equal to the secondary variables, an unstable state. After one feedback delay, these become equal and the combinational logic circuit generates a new output. This may or may not represent a stable state. If it does, the circuit now settles, but if it does not, the circuit will continue to step through states until equilibrium is reached (or not in the case of an oscillating circuit). Here, then, is a finite state machine, as it possesses internal states, a next state function and an output function.

The internal states of the circuit may be made explicit by defining separate state variable storage elements, for example, the latch of Figure 9.1(c). Figure 9.4 is a sequential circuit built along these lines. Note that twice as many excitations as before are required since each latch has $S$ and $R$ inputs. Each latch stores a state variable.

The sequential circuits above are asynchronous; changes of state can happen at any time in response to input changes. The circuit of Figure 9.4 can be made synchronous by modifying the latches to have a clock input which will only allow a change of state when it has the value 1. If a further modification is made by allowing only a single input ($D$), the circuit of

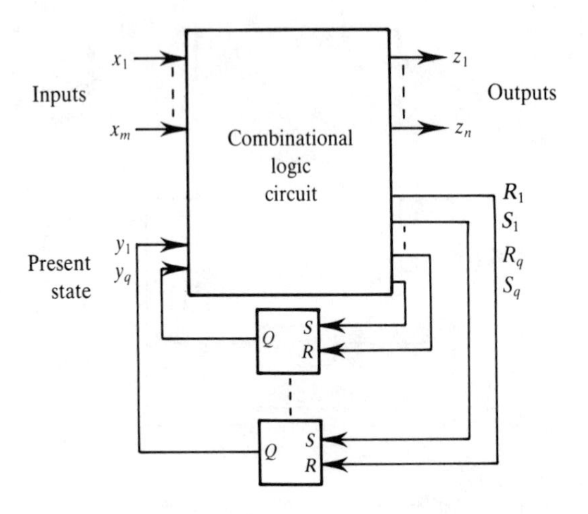


**Figure 9.4** Asynchronous sequential circuit with latches.

Figure 9.5(a) results – the ***D* latch**. (Note the *S–R* latch drawn in its more familiar form.) When the clock is 1 the output takes the value of the input, and when the clock is low it holds this value. Figure 9.5(b) shows the complete synchronous circuit.

The advantage of this type of circuit is that there are far fewer restrictions on the way the inputs can change. There is a period, during which the clock is 0, when any input change is possible without upsetting the operation of the circuit. There is one major drawback with this type of circuit, however. When the clock is 1 the circuit behaves as a simple asynchronous circuit like that of Figure 9.3. Consider the following chain of events: the clock is 0 and the circuit is in a stable state, the inputs change to a value which will cause a state transition when the clock becomes 1, the clock changes from 0 to 1, the new values of each state variable are stored in the latches and fed into the combinational logic, and the transition function defines new excitations which start to appear at the latch inputs, some of these are stored before the clock has returned to 0 – in consequence the circuit settles into the wrong state. To avoid this type of race, a constraint has to be applied: the time for which the clock is 1 must be less than the sum of the minimum propagation delays of a latch and the combinational logic. This is a very difficult constraint since minimum propagation delays are not generally known and it is not easy to maintain the width of narrow pulses in a system. The closed loop which exists when the clock is 1 must be removed if the circuit is to be free of this constraint.

This can be achieved by defining a two-phase clock, as shown in Figure 9.6. State variables are stored in a pair of cascaded latches each fed

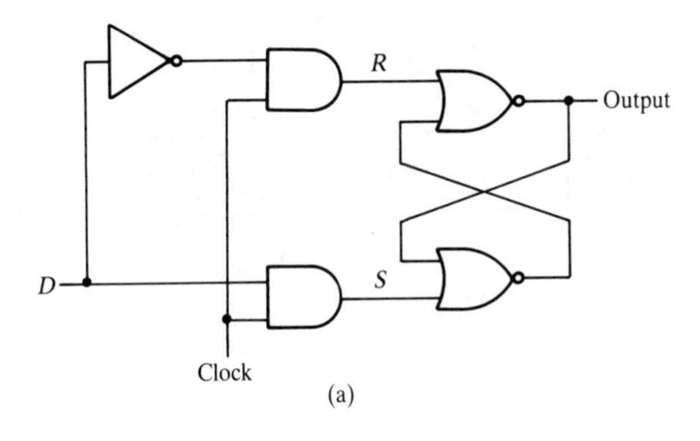


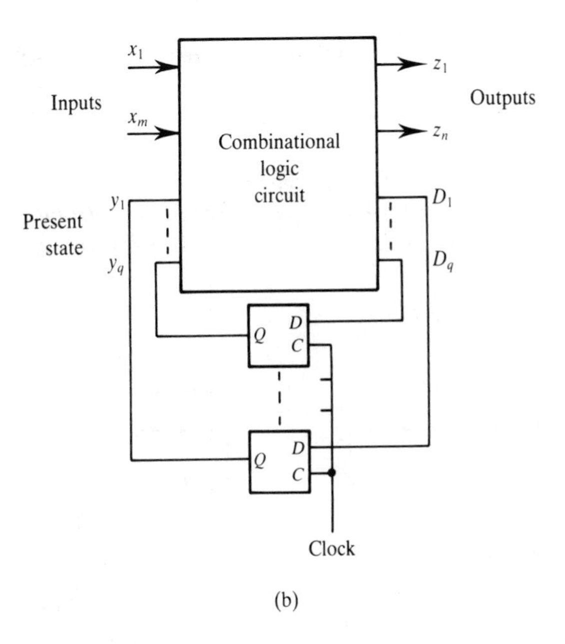


**Figure 9.5** (a) A $D$ latch. (b) A synchronous sequential circuit.

with a separate clock. If the clocks do not overlap, there is never a time when a closed path exists between $D_i$ and $Y_i$. A transition race like that described in the previous paragraph cannot occur. In one cycle of operation, the excitations are first latched in the $\phi_1$, or master, latches, and then transferred to the $\phi_2$, or slave, latches. This second action allows a new excitation to be evaluated, which, however, cannot affect the logic

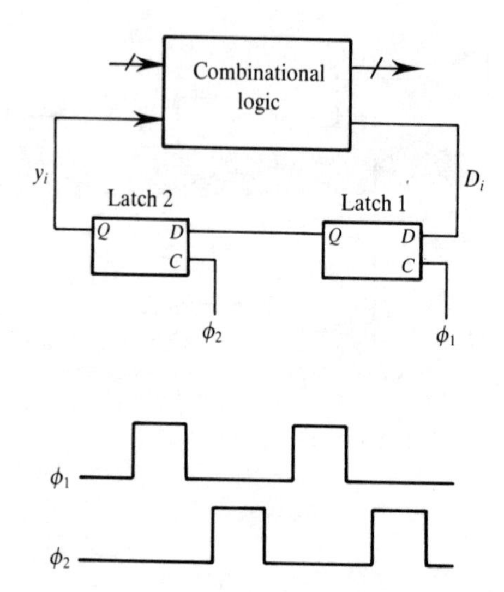


**Figure 9.6** Synchronous circuit using latches and two-phase clock.

inputs until the next cycle. When designing with standard logic components, this two-phase operation is hidden. In an edge-triggered flip–flop, the active edge causes $\phi_1$ and $\phi_2$ to be generated internally, as shown in Figure 9.7.

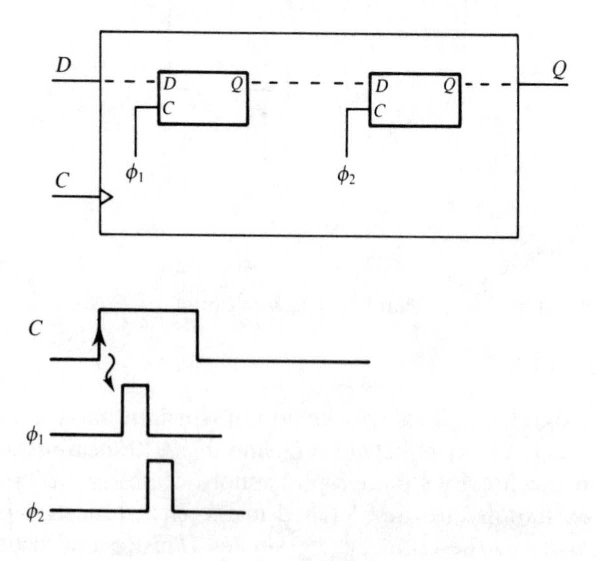


**Figure 9.7** Edge-triggered flip–flop.

## 9.3 Asynchronous machine basics

In this section the standard design techniques for asynchronous sequential circuits based on the Huffman model of Figure 9.3 will be reviewed. As will be seen, all of this can be applied directly to PLA and PAL designs.

The primary form of specification for an asynchronous sequential circuit is the **flow table**. The flow table has the same form as the state tables used in Chapter 2 for synchronous machines. As before, entries in a flow table are next states and outputs, but we must now distinguish **stable states** and **unstable states**. A synchronous machine can be stable in every defined state, at least for the duration of a clock cycle. An asynchronous machine can only be stable in those states in which the next state evaluated by the transition function is equal to the present state, because of the unbroken feedback loop (Figure 9.3). The flow table will be introduced through a simple example, a *D* latch.

Figure 9.8(a) shows the input and output signals of the latch, and Figure 9.8(b) the flow table constructed from knowledge of the behaviour of the latch. This flow table has one stable state per row, and is known as a **primitive** flow table. It is constructed as follows. First let us assume that both inputs are 0 and that the output is also 0. This is a stable condition and corresponds to the upper left box in the table. Each box of the flow table defines a **total state** of the machine, given by the values of the internal state and of the inputs. An input change causes the total state to change by moving it to another box in the same row – the internal state cannot change instantaneously, and thus neither can the row. The restriction will be made that only one input bit can change at a time, and that another change must not occur until the machine is in a stable state again. This is the so-called **fundamental mode**. If this restriction was not enforced, it would never be possible to be sure of the effective order of 'simultaneous' input changes. Returning to the latch flow table, it is assumed now that the *D* input changes to 1. This takes us to the second box, which must direct us to another stable total state, this time with input 01 and output 0 again. This new stable state is placed in the second row. If the *D* input returns to 0, stable state 1 is returned to again. Note that in the first row the content of the box corresponding to input 11 is undefined. This is because it can only be entered in response to a transition from stable state 1 with both inputs changing from 0 to 1, violating the fundamental mode restriction. By following similar reasoning the remainder of the table can be filled in. Notice that in each row there is one box with undefined contents, corresponding to the two-input-bit-change transition from the single stable state.

Examination of this primitive flow table reveals that certain rows appear very similar. For example, given that the undefined boxes can contain anything that is wanted (they can never be entered), the first three rows can be merged into one. States 1, 2 and 3 are thus equivalent. Likewise, the last three rows can be merged, making states 4, 5 and 6

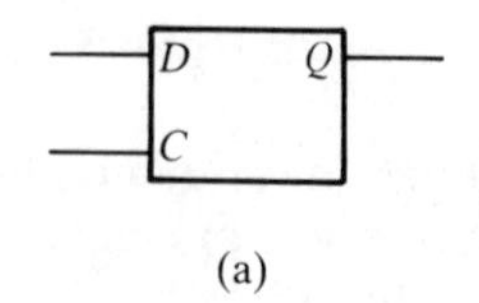


(a)

| Internal state | Inputs, $C, D$ 00 | 01 | 11 | 10 |
|---|---|---|---|---|
| 1 | (1), 0 | 2, 0 | – | 3, 0 |
| 2 | 1, 0 | (2), 0 | 4, 0 | – |
| 3 | 1, 0 | – | 4, 0 | (3), 0 |
| 4 | – | 5, 1 | (4), 1 | 3, 1 |
| 5 | 6, 1 | (5), 1 | 4, 1 | – |
| 6 | (6), 1 | 5, 1 | – | 3, 1 |

(b)

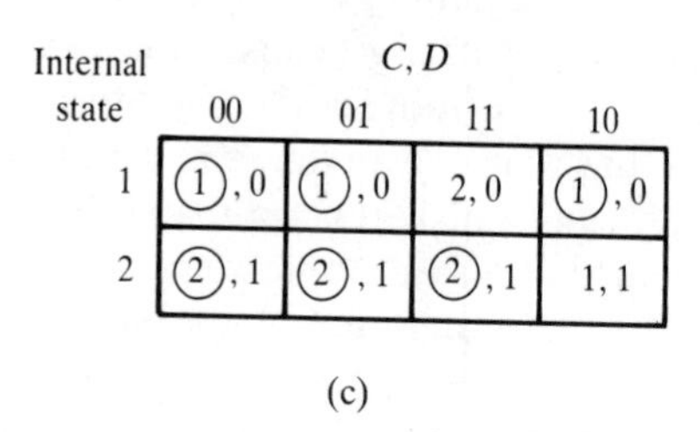

| Internal state | $C, D$ 00 | 01 | 11 | 10 |
|---|---|---|---|---|
| 1 | (1), 0 | (1), 0 | 2, 0 | (1), 0 |
| 2 | (2), 1 | (2), 1 | (2), 1 | 1, 1 |

(c)

**Figure 9.8** *D* latch design: (a) block diagram; (b) primitive flow table; (c) merged flow table.

equivalent. The **merged** flow table is shown in Figure 9.8(c). This machine requires two internal states. The merging was made possible by choosing appropriate values for the output in the unstable states; since these are transient, our specification can be met equally well by for example $0 \rightarrow 0 \rightarrow 1$ or $0 \rightarrow 1 \rightarrow 1$ output sequences for a $0 \rightarrow 1$ change between stable states (of course $0 \rightarrow 1 \rightarrow 0$ and $1 \rightarrow 0 \rightarrow 1$ are unacceptable). This merging of rows is analogous to the state reduction for synchronous machines considered in Section 7.2. A tabular procedure can be applied for more complex examples. This is described in the classical switching theory texts.

It is now possible to perform the logic design for the *D* latch. Figure 9.8(d) shows the circuit form. A single state variable is required to

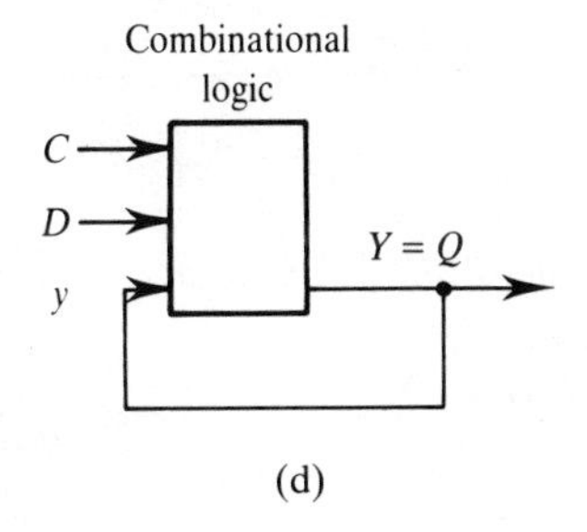


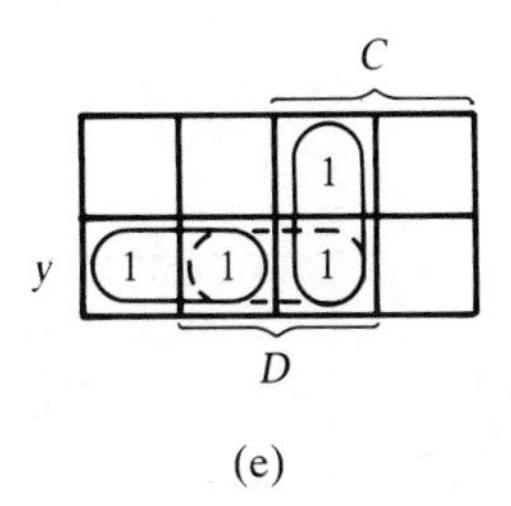


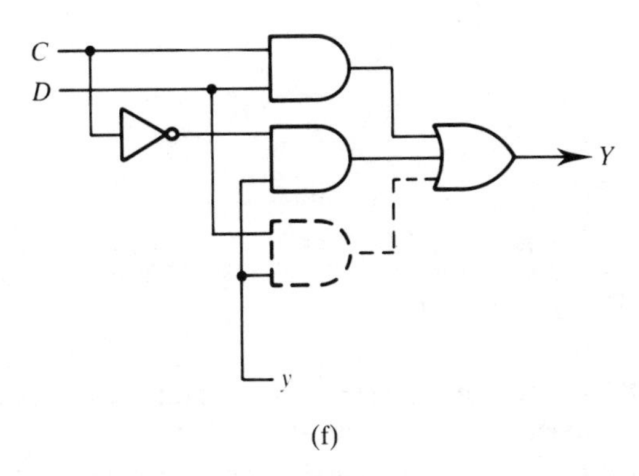


**Figure 9.8** (cont.) *D* latch design: (d) the asynchronous circuit; (e) K map for y; (f) combination logic.

distinguish the two states. If this is chosen to have the value 1 in state 2, the output can be derived directly from the state variable. The K map for the excitation $Y$ is shown in Figure 9.8(e), leading to the sum-of-products form in Figure 9.8(f). There is a static 1-hazard in this function. Can this be a problem? Let us examine its effects. $Y$ could become momentarily 0 if $y = 1$ and $C, D$ makes a $01 \rightarrow 11$ or $11 \rightarrow 01$ transition. In the first case, the movement is between the 01 and 11 columns of the flow table. After the input change, if $Y$ becomes 0, then the total state moves into the first row,

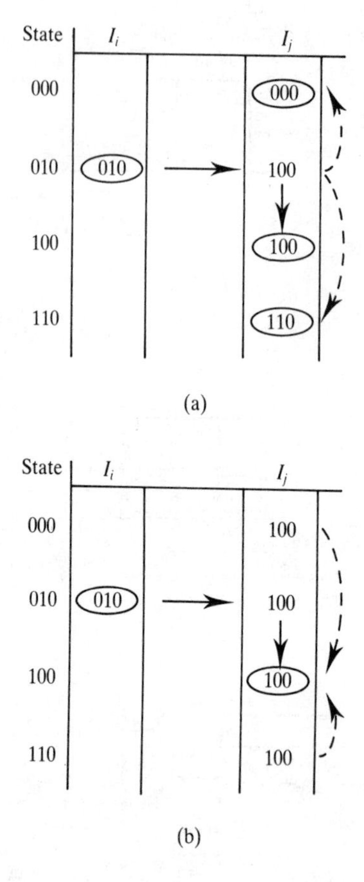


**Figure 9.9** Race between state variables: (a) critical race; (b) non-critical race.

but since the 11 box contains a transition to state 2, the required destination, no error can occur. However, in the 11→01 transition, the upper box in the 01 column contains a stable state which could be entered instead of the one below, the expected destination. The hazard must therefore be covered. The cover is shown in Figures 9.8(e) and 9.8(f). The logic could be programmed directly into a PLD, with the feedback being either internal or external.

In the above example there was only one state variable, so races could not be a problem. However, in general, these must be considered. Look at the partial flow table shown in Figure 9.9(a), on which the state codes are shown directly. If the machine is stable in state 010 and the input changes from $I_i$ to $I_j$ (with a single-bit change), the new state should be 100. For this transition two state variables must change. These cannot, of course, be guaranteed to be simultaneous. If the first variable changes first, then the internal state would be momentarily 110, a stable state in column

$I_j$. If the second bit changes first, then the transition could be to 000, another stable state in this column. This is a **critical race** between state variables (critical races are the same as the function hazards of Section 5.7.2). In Figure 9.9(b) is shown a modified table in which all the three unstable states which could be entered lead to the desired destination. The race is now **non-critical.**

The major design task in asynchronous design is to find a state assignment which is free of critical races. The simplest way is to allow only one state bit to change at every transition. To do this, all possible transitions between pairs of states must be examined. This can be illustrated on an **adjacency graph**. An arc joining a pair of states indicates that these states must be given adjacent codes. If there are cycles containing an odd number of arcs, then a race-free assignment cannot be found (see Exercise 2.2). For example, the machine whose adjacency graph is shown in Figure 9.10 cannot be given such an assignment. There are two types of solution to this problem, one which entails assigning a set of codes to each state instead of a single code, and one which relies on races being non-critical.

The first method, the method of **connected row set assignments**, allows transitions between non-adjacent states to occur as a sequence of single-bit changes. States are assigned sets of adjacent codes, one of which is adjacent to one of the codes of each destination state. A very simple example of this idea is given in Figure 9.11(a). Here the adjacency graph and encoding for a three-state machine is shown. State 'a' is given codes 00 and 01. 00 is adjacent to 10 (state 'b'), and 01 is adjacent to 11 (state 'c'). If the machine is in state 'a' it could be stable in states 00 or 01. A transition from state 'a' could take two steps, as can be seen in the partial flow table of Figure 9.11(b). The two-step transitions are shown dotted. These transitions require two passes round the feedback loop, and thus take twice as long as single-step transitions. Connected row set assignments therefore reduce the maximum operating speed of an asynchronous machine. Such an assignmernt can always be found, but may require more than the minimum number of state variables. For an $n$-state machine it can be shown that no more than $2S_0 - 1$ state variables are required, where $S_0 = \lceil \log_2 n \rceil$. For the machine of Figure 9.10, the following assignment will work:

| a: *100 | b: 000* | c: 0011 | d: 0111 | e: 0110 |
|---|---|---|---|---|
| f: *010 | g: 1000 | | | |

Here again the maximum transition time is two delays because the largest row set contains two codes.

The second state assignment method does not require a sequence of single-bit state variable changes, thus allowing maximum speed of operation. Codes are assigned to rows in such a way that transitions are direct, and the multiple state variable changes do not have any critical races. The

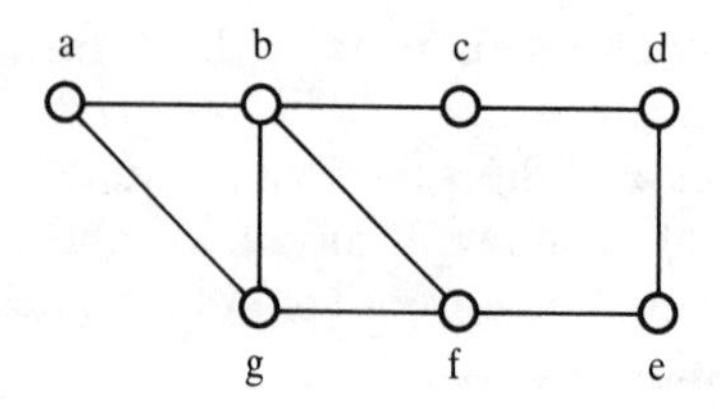


**Figure 9.10** Adjacency graph.

procedures for finding such an assignment (single transition time or STT assignments) are too lengthy to be described here and can be found in the standard texts.

One further cause of failure in asynchronous machines needs to be mentioned – the **essential hazard**. This can be demonstrated by the toggle circuit whose block diagram, timing diagram and flow table are shown in Figure 9.12(a). Figure 9.12(b) shows the state assignment and implementation, and in Figure 9.12(c) are shown the K maps for the two excitations. These show implicants $D$ and $E$ covering the two static 1-hazards. Are these necessary? $D$ covers the transition from state c to state d, with a $0 \rightarrow 1$ change of CK. $Y_1$ should remain 1, while $Y_2$ has a $1 \rightarrow 0$ change. The

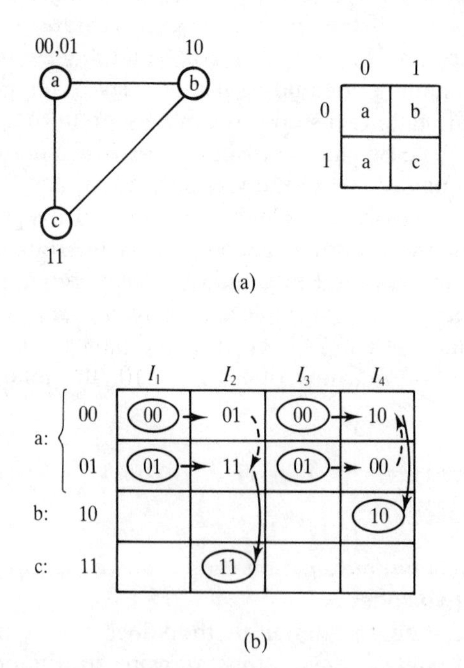


**Figure 9.11** Connected row set assignment for three-state machine: (a) adjacency graph and encoding; (b) partial flow table.

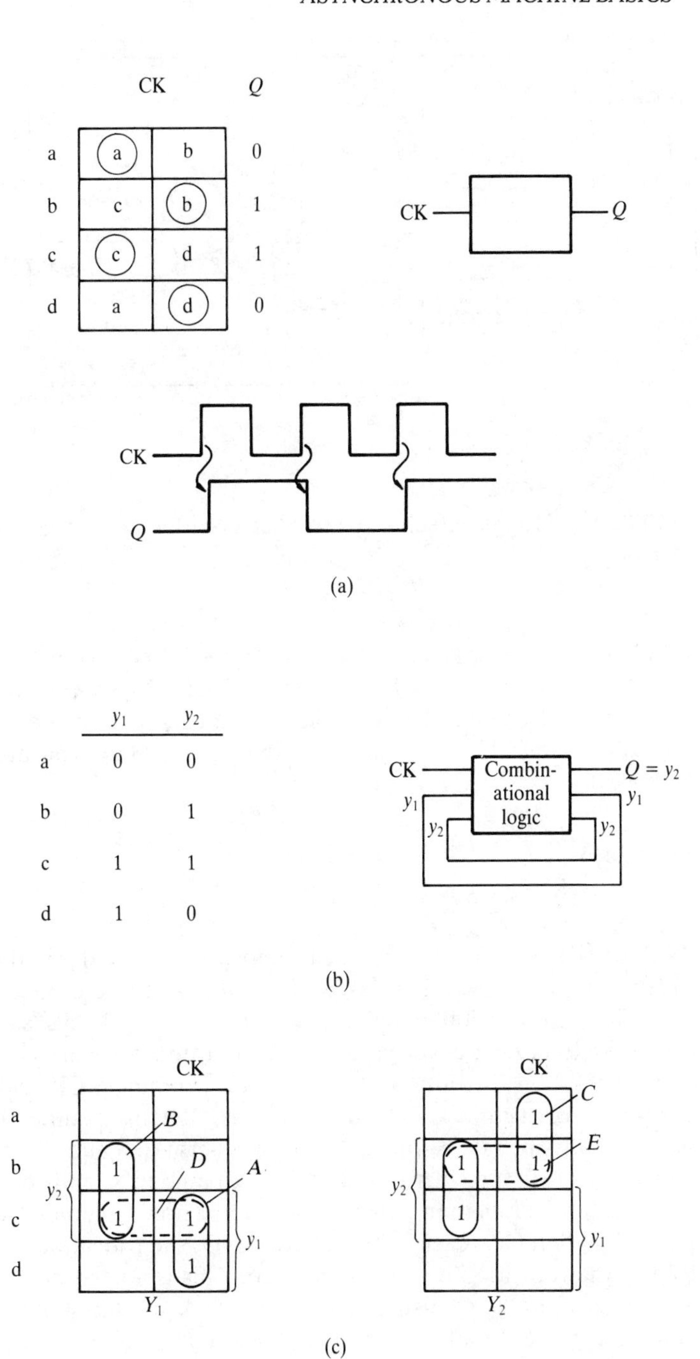


**Figure 9.12** Toggle circuit with essential hazard: (a) specification; (b) state assignment; (c) transition functions (continued overleaf).

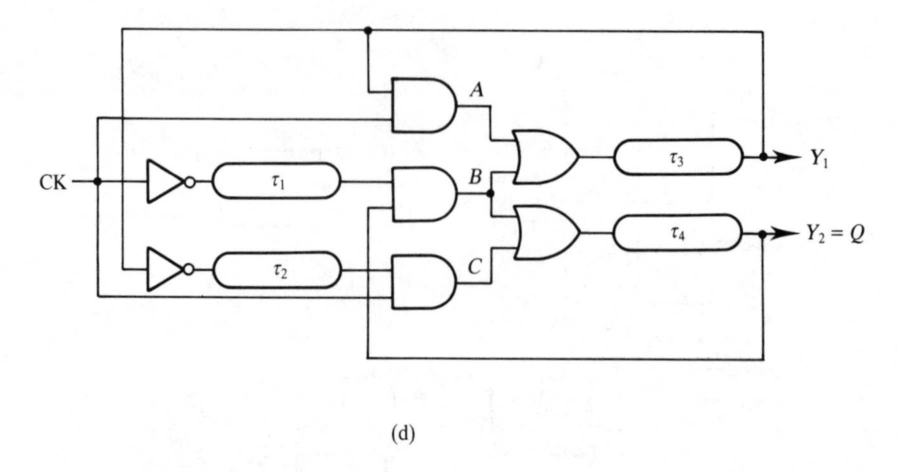


**Figure 9.12** (cont.) Toggle circuit with essential hazard: (d) combinational logic showing delays.

hazard could cause an incorrect transition to state a. *E* covers the transition from state b to state c, with a $1 \to 0$ change of CK. $Y_2$ should remain 1, while $Y_1$ has a $0 \to 1$ change. There could be an incorrect transition to state a. The covers are therefore necessary and the equations are (hazard cover in parentheses):

$$Y_1 = y_1 . \mathrm{CK} + y_2 . \overline{\mathrm{CK}} \ (+ y_1 \cdot y_2)$$
$$Y_2 = y_2 . \overline{\mathrm{CK}} + \bar{y}_1 . \mathrm{CK} \ (+ \bar{y}_1 \cdot y_2)$$

With this flow table there exists another potential malfunction, independent of logic hazards. This is illustrated with reference to the circuit for the combinational logic, drawn to include delays as Figure 9.12(d) (the logic hazard covering terms are omitted for clarity). Delays are shown lumped on the output of the inverter producing $\overline{\mathrm{CK}}$ and at the outputs of the two sum-of-products structures. Let us assume that the machine is initially in state a with CK = 0 (products *A*, *B* and *C* are all 0). CK now changes to 1 (product *C* and thus $Y_2$ change to 1, and the state is now b). If delay $\tau_4$ is less than delay $\tau_1$, product *B* now becomes 1 and the next state is c. When $\overline{\mathrm{CK}}$ reaches the middle AND, the transition is to state d, instead of the transition $\mathrm{a} \to \mathrm{b}$, as required. This is an essential hazard, which can occur if the delay distribution allows it. Again the standard texts show how the presence of an essential hazard in a flow table can be detected.

Although this hazard may be possible, how realistic is the assumption of the relative magnitudes of the delays? It was assumed that the feedback reached the sum-of-products array before the other phase of an input. This cannot occur in any realistic PLD. Essential hazards are therefore not of interest in PLD design. However, for a production design, it should be ascertained by device characterization that essential hazards are truly impossible with the device chosen.

All the standard design methods for asynchronous sequential circuits apply directly to PLD implementations. It has been shown that one of the standard hazards does not apply to PLDs, and indeed later in this chapter it will be shown that other classical rules can also be relaxed when using PLDs.

## 9.4 Building latches and flip–flops in PLDs

Even when there is no need to build custom asynchronous machines, it is sometimes useful to use small ones in the form of latches in synchronous designs. Latches are useful for capturing asynchronous events at interfaces, and single latches are often required in digital systems design. They can easily be built into a larger design which is based on conventional synchronous principles.

It is important to choose the correct circuit form, so as not to waste PLD resources. For example it is possible to build a $D$ latch using the common form of Figure 9.5(a). This would require two PLD outputs, and thus could waste a pin. Choosing the form of Figure 9.8(f), on the other hand, requires only one output, although it requires an extra product term to cover the hazard, which is unlikely to be a problem. The same applies to the $S$–$R$ latch. Figure 9.13 shows a design which requires two products and a single PLD output instead of two in the more usual form consisting of cross-coupled gates. The equations for latches such as those above can often be merged with those of the other parts of the design using the same PLD, thus compacting the specification.

Although less likely to be useful, master–slave flip–flops can also be constructed in PLD arrays. These will require at least two outputs and are not an efficient use of PLD resources; using PLDs with programmable output cells is now a more economical way of obtaining flip–flops even if only one or two are needed.

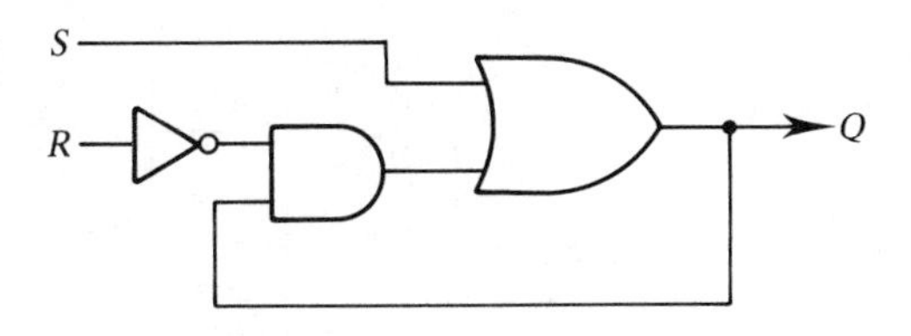


**Figure 9.13** $S$–$R$ latch.

## 9.5 A flowchart-based design method

It was shown in Chapter 6 how to use state machine flowcharts for the specification of synchronous machines. They can also be used for asynchronous machines, as would be expected. Here, too, they are most suitable for problems either where there are a few inputs or where the transitions from a state depend only on a small subset of the inputs. Fortunately many problems fall into this category. Once a flowchart has been drawn, and a suitable state assignment found, there is a direct translation into the next state and output equations. After this stage we need to check for the presence of any logic hazards which may cause incorrect transitions. Although this method works reliably, it is more difficult to produce a minimal design than with the flow table based procedure. However, since we are concerned with PLD implementations, absolute minimality is often unnecessary.

In Figure 9.14 is shown the flowchart specification for the behaviour of the latch of Figure 9.8. By tracing through all the link paths, it can be seen that it is equivalent to the merged flow table of Figure 9.8(c). To draw a flowchart corresponding to the primitive flow table (Figure 9.8(a)) would be possible but unnatural, as in this form of specification only one input combination per state defining a link back to the same state is allowed. In an asynchronous state machine flowchart, the sequencing mechanism is different from that in the synchronous case. Instead of a link path's becoming effective at a state transition time defined by the clock, in an

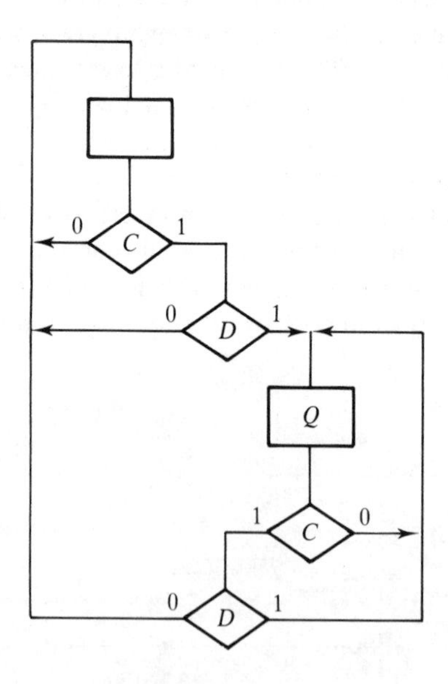


**Figure 9.14** Flowchart for *D* latch.

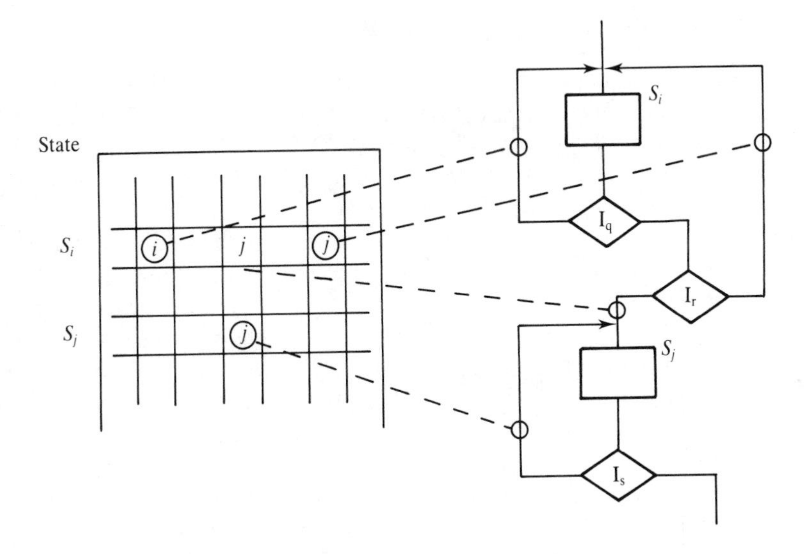


**Figure 9.15** Relation of merged flow table to flowchart.

asynchronous flowchart there is always an active link. For the machine to be in a stable state with a constant input, the active path must be one which loops back to the state box from which it originated. An input change (single variable of course for fundamental mode) causes an alternative link path to become continually active. If this link is to another state, a transition occurs, and then another path defining a loop around the new state becomes active. The transition link path, which is only active for one loop delay, corresponds to an unstable state in the flow table. Figure 9.15 illustrates the relationship between flow tables and flowcharts.

The equations for the transition and output functions can be derived from the flowchart in exactly the same way as studied previously. After a critical race-free state assignment has been chosen, each link path is followed and a product created. For the flowchart of Figure 9.14, the equation for the single excitation, $Y$, is

$$Y = \bar{y}.C.D + y.\overline{C} + y.C.D$$

This is the same cover as before, which can now be minimized and checked for logic hazards.

For more complex flowcharts intended for PAL implementation, the method of map-entered variables can be used to simplify minimization. Hazard detection is also possible with this method, whose operation will be introduced through an example.

The block diagram and flowchart for the asynchronous machine to be realized are shown in Figures 9.16(a) and 9.16(b). There are five inputs,

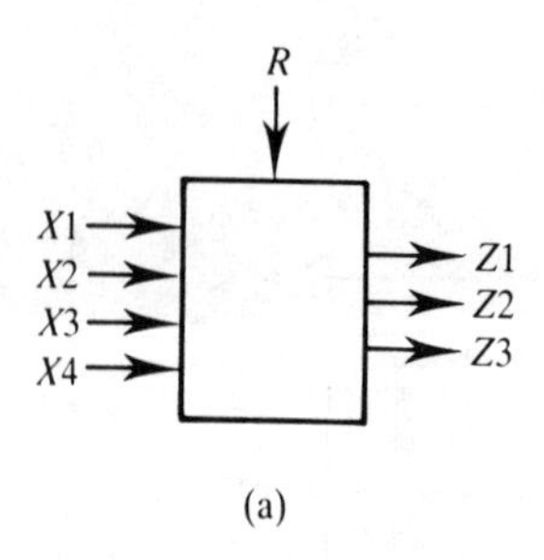


(a)

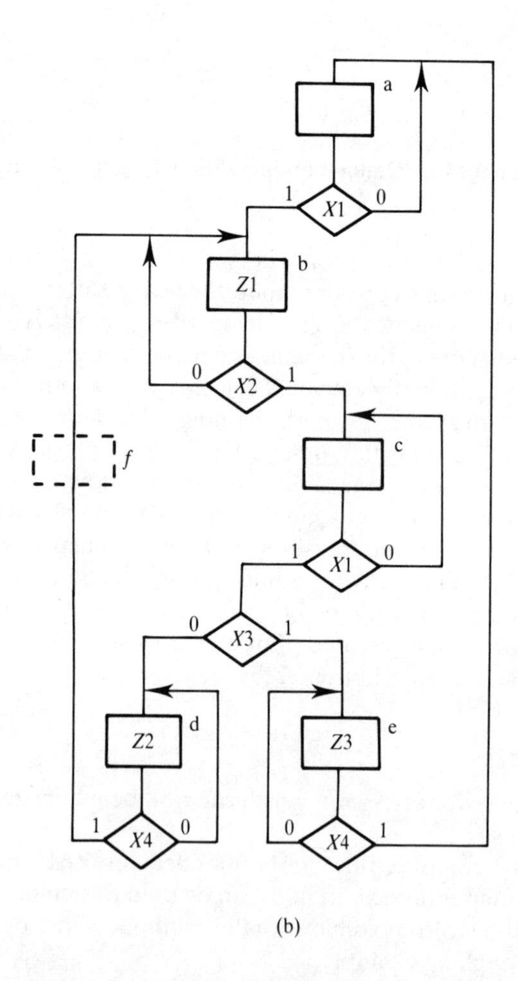


(b)

**Figure 9.16** Asynchronous machine design example: (a) block diagram; (b) flowchart.

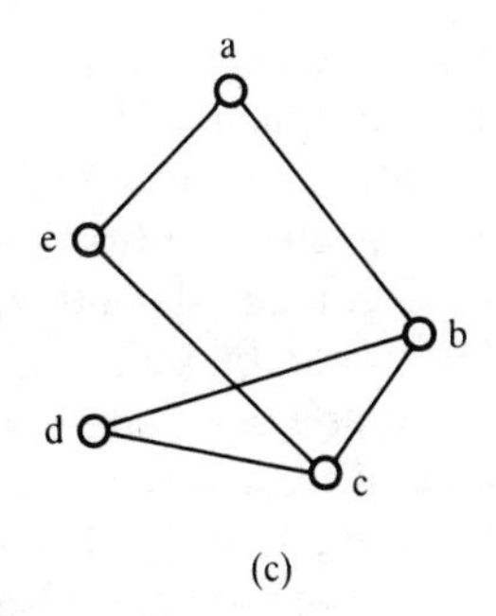


(c)

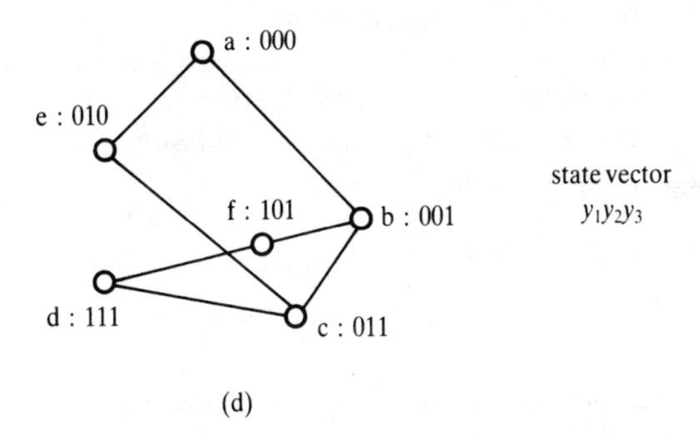


(d)

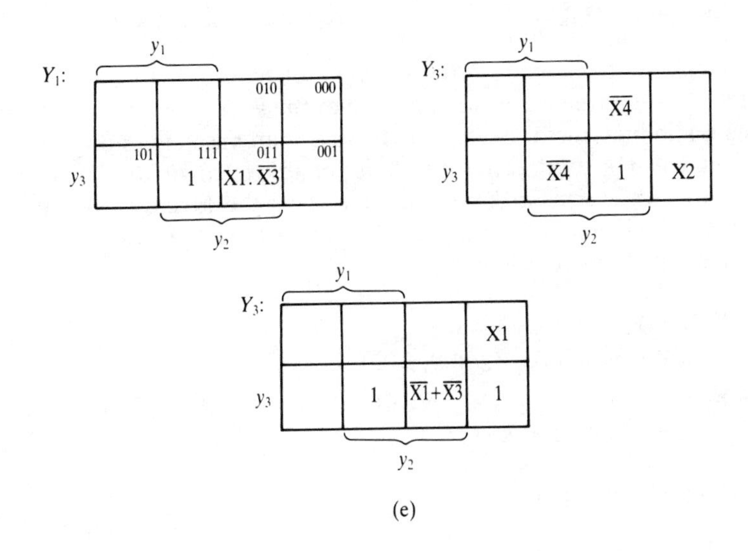


(e)

**Figure 9.16** (cont.) Asynchronous machine design example: (c) adjacency graph; (d) adjacency graph of modified machine with state assignment; (e) maps for excitations.

$X1$, $X2$, $X3$, $X4$ and $R$, and three outputs, $Z1$, $Z2$ and $Z3$. Input $R$ is a reset input – when it is true, the machine returns to its initial state. The flowchart defines five stable states, a, b, c, d and e. Note that every one of these states has a loop back to itself. The first step in the realization is to find a critical race-free state assignment. To aid this, the adjacency graph is drawn in Figure 9.16(c). Here it can be seen that states b, c and d form a cycle of length 3, which means that a one-code-per-state assignment cannot be found. A simple solution in this case is to add an extra, unstable, state f. A coding can now be found, and is shown in Figure 9.16(d). This additional state is shown dotted on the flowchart. Because it is an unstable state, there is no loop around the state box. The excitation function variable-entered maps can now be created directly from the link paths of the flowchart; these are shown in Figure 9.16(e).

These functions must now be examined for logic 1-hazards (remember this is the only type possible in a PLA structure). This is a little more complex with variable-entered maps, but the following four rules, adapted from the standard map rule, can be used:

(1) the standard case: adjacent groupings of 1s (Figure 9.17(a));
(2) adjacent groupings of map-entered variables (Figure 9.17(b): cover required is $x_2x_3\bar{x}_4V$);
(3) adjacent groupings of 1s and map-entered variables (Figure 9.17(c): cover required is $\bar{x}_1x_2x_4V$);
(4) grouping of a map-entered variable and its complement that cover the same 1 (Figure 9.17(d): cover required is $x_1x_2\bar{x}_3x_4$).

Applying these now to the example of Figure 9.16, it can be seen that each of the three maps has a hazard of the third type, not all of which may cause an incorrect transition. (The fuse-map-based method of Section 5.7.2 could also be used.) However, it is possible to cover all of these at the cost of two extra terms in $Y_3$ by first encircling the 1s and then extending the cover of all map-entered variables to include the adjacent 1. The excitation equations thus become:

$$Y_1 = y_1y_2y_3 + y_2y_3\,\mathrm{X1}\,\overline{\mathrm{X3}}$$
$$Y_2 = \bar{y}_1y_2y_3 + \bar{y}_1y_3\,\mathrm{X2} + \bar{y}_1y_2\,\overline{\mathrm{X4}} + y_2y_3\,\overline{\mathrm{X4}}$$
$$Y_3 = \bar{y}_1\bar{y}_2y_3 + \underline{y_1y_2y_3} + \bar{y}_1\bar{y}_2\,\mathrm{X1} + \bar{y}_1y_3(\overline{\mathrm{X1}} + \overline{\mathrm{X3}}) + y_2y_3(\overline{\mathrm{X1}} + \overline{\mathrm{X3}})$$

Finally, the output equations are:

$$\mathrm{Z1} = \bar{y}_1\bar{y}_2y_3$$
$$\mathrm{Z2} = y_1y_2y_3$$
$$\mathrm{Z3} = \bar{y}_1y_2\bar{y}_3$$

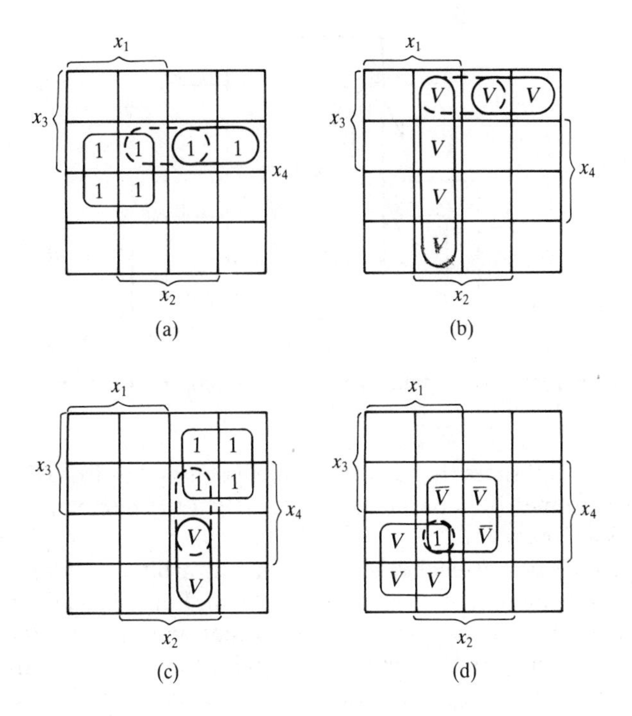


**Figure 9.17** Hazard covers in variable-entered maps.

The reset input must now be included. Since this returns the machine to state 000, it is enough to AND $\overline{R}$ with all terms in the excitation equations. The resources required for this design are thus five inputs, six outputs (three with internal feedback), and a maximum of seven products per output.

## 9.6 Use of ROMs

All the asynchronous design techniques considered so far have assumed a **pure delay** model for circuit delays. A pure delay element will pass through it any signal unaltered; the output will only be delayed by an amount equal to the value of the pure delay. However, real circuits do not behave like this. Pulses shorter than a certain minimum value will not pass through the circuit. **Inertial delay** elements have this property and are a more accurate model of real circuit behaviour. An inertial delay $d$ will delay a signal by $d$ and will not respond to a signal of duration less than $d$. The model for the delay of a memory device contains both pure and inertial delay components. Recognizing this enables most of the design rules elaborated above for asynchronous circuits to be relaxed.

Figure 9.18 shows an asynchronous circuit realized by a memory device. The conditions which the memory has to meet for this circuit not to

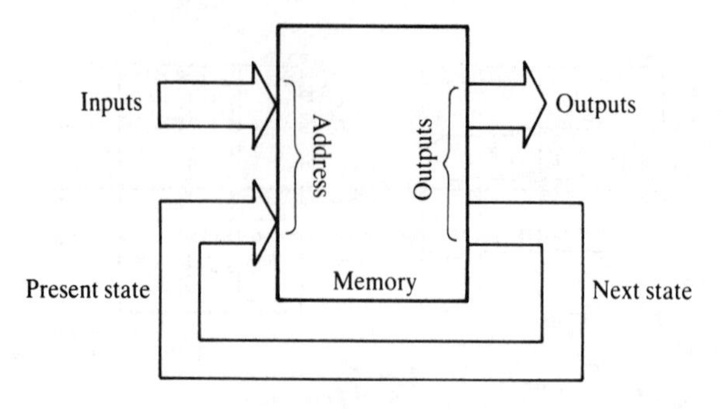


**Figure 9.18** Memory used as asynchronous circuit.

suffer from critical races, logic hazards and essential hazards will be looked at. If these are met by a particular device, then the circuit will work with any state assignment.

First consider critical races. Assume an arbitrary state assignment which has not been designed with races in mind. Following an input change causing a transition, two or more of the excitation outputs will change. In the worst case, the first to change will be after the minimum memory propagation delay, $t_{pd(min)}$, and the last to change will be after the maximum memory propagation delay $t_{pd(max)}$. Let the difference between these two delays be $\Delta t_{pd}$. Therefore, during the state transition, the memory present state input will have a potentially incorrect value for a time equal to $\Delta t_{pd}$. Now if this is less than the inertial component of the memory delay $d$, that is

$$\Delta t_{pd} < d$$

then there will be no critical race. The problem in applying this test is that values for the minimum propagation delay and the inertial delay are not given in data sheets. They therefore have to be determined by measurement. If $d = kt_{pd(min)}$, then

$$t_{pd(max)} < (1 + k)t_{pd(min)}$$

Measurements on small memories have shown $k$ to vary between 0.3 and 1.

If the above conditions hold, then logic hazards will not cause incorrect transitions, as the maximum glitch duration is also equal to $\Delta t_{pd}$. An essential hazard cannot cause a fault if the sum of the delays from an input to an excitation plus the delay from present state to another excitation is greater than a delay from a second input to excitation. That is, in the worst case

$$t_{pd(min)} + t_{pd(min)} = 2t_{pd(min)} > t_{pd(max)}$$

When using these inequalities, knowledge of the decoder arrangement of the memory is helpful. Taking feedback signals to inputs which are wired to the same decoder will reduce delay spread and thus make the constraints easier to meet.

These arguments do not in fact apply to memories alone, but to any PLD. If a PLA or PAL device is found to meet these constraints, it too can be used in this type of asynchronous circuit. However, it is usually considered safer to design the circuit in the conventional way owing to the unavailability of precise timing data.

## 9.7 A self-clocked design technique

A **self-clocked** asynchronous circuit is one which uses standard flip–flops for storing the state, and whose clock signals are derived internally instead of from an external signal. The clock or clocks are activated in response to input transitions. The general model is shown in Figure 9.19. The potential advantage of this arrangement is that races and hazards do not have to be considered if the internal clock signals can be generated appropriately. A number of design methods have been developed for self-clocked circuits over the past 30 years, some of which are suitable for PLD application. Here, one particularly easily applied method will be described. Like the method of the previous section it depends on the PLD's conforming to certain constraints on timing parameters.

A number of PLDs have flip–flops with clock inputs which can be generated internally. These are listed in Table A.8. One particular type is very useful for realizing asynchronous circuits specified in the standard way

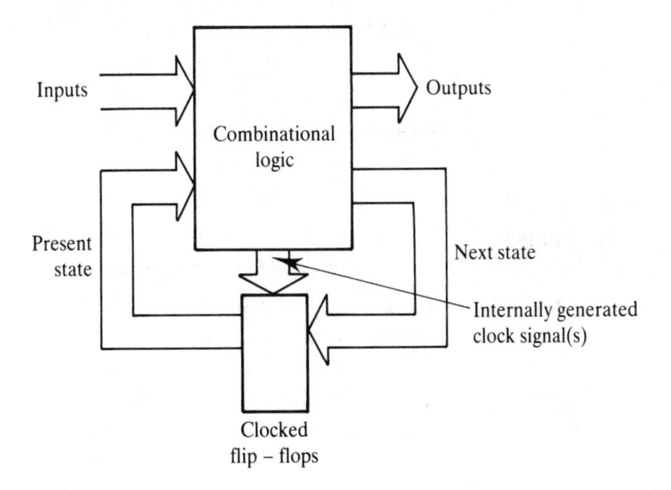


**Figure 9.19** General form of a self-clocked asynchronous sequential circuit.

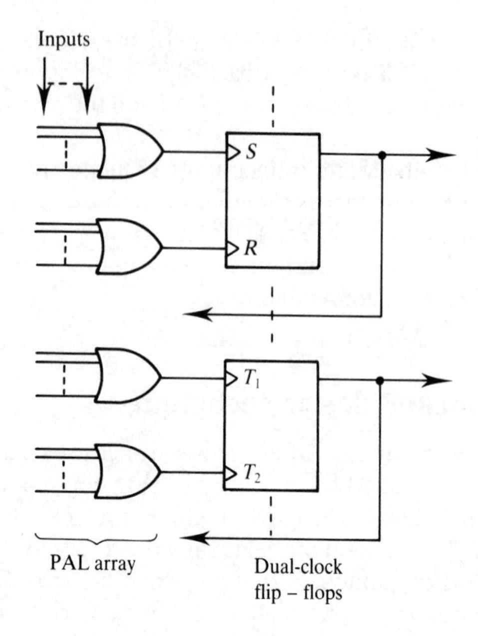


**Figure 9.20** PAL-structured device with dual-clock flip–flops.

**Table 9.1**

| *Present state* | | *Next state* | *Inputs* *S* | *R* |
|---|---|---|---|---|
| 0 | → | 0 | – | – |
| 0 | → | 1 | ↑ | – |
| 1 | → | 0 | – | ↑ |
| 1 | → | 1 | – | – |

**Table 9.2**

| *Present state* | | *Next state* | *Inputs* $T_1$ | $T_2$ | | | |
|---|---|---|---|---|---|---|---|
| 0 | → | 0 | – | – | or | ↑ | ↑ |
| 0 | → | 1 | ↑ | – | or | – | ↑ |
| 1 | → | 0 | ↑ | – | or | – | ↑ |
| 1 | → | 1 | – | – | or | ↑ | ↑ |

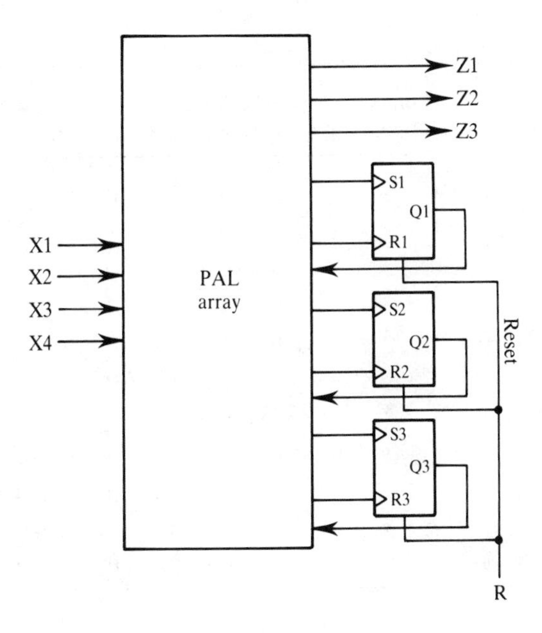


**Figure 9.21** Self-clocked realization of example of Figure 9.16.

(that is, with flow tables or flowcharts). The structure of this device is shown in Figure 9.20. It consists of a normal PAL array from which pairs of outputs drive the two clock inputs of edge-activated *S–R* or dual-toggle flip–flops. The excitation tables for the two types of flip–flop are shown in Tables 9.1 and 9.2. In these tables the symbol '–' indicates all states other than a rising edge (that is 0, 1, falling edge). The use of edge-activated *S–R* flip–flops in self-clocked design will be considered.

Whenever a transition is to occur, rising edges must be generated at the appropriate *S* and *R* inputs to change flip–flop states. When there is no transition in response to an input change, no clocks need to be generated. Let us now see how the machine of Figure 9.16 could be implemented as a self-clocked circuit. The five states require three flip–flops, giving the structure of Figure 9.21. Note that the reset input *R* can be taken directly to the flip–flop asynchronous reset inputs. The following arbitrary state assignment is chosen:

a, 000; b, 001; c, 010; d, 011; e, 100

The mode of operation of this circuit is as follows. When the machine is in a stable state, all *S* and *R* inputs must be 0. During a transition, when the machine enters an unstable state, selected *S* and *R* inputs become 1, thus defining a rising edge. When the machine enters the new stable state, all *S* and *R* inputs fall again to 0 (the falling edges do not

**Table 9.3**

| | *Present state* | | | *Inputs* | | | | *Next state* | | | *Excitations* | | | | | |
|---|---|---|---|---|---|---|---|---|---|---|---|---|---|---|---|---|
| | *Q1* | *Q2* | *Q3* | *X1* | *X2* | *X3* | *X4* | *Q1* | *Q2* | *Q3* | *S1* | *R1* | *S2* | *R2* | *S3* | *R3* |
| | 0 | 0 | 0 | 0 | * | * | * | 0 | 0 | 0 | 0 | 0 | 0 | 0 | 0 | 0 |
| * | 0 | 0 | 0 | 1 | * | * | * | 0 | 0 | 1 | 0 | – | 0 | – | 1 | 0 |
| | 0 | 0 | 1 | * | 0 | * | * | 0 | 0 | 1 | 0 | 0 | 0 | 0 | 0 | 0 |
| * | 0 | 0 | 1 | * | 1 | * | * | 0 | 1 | 0 | 0 | – | 1 | 0 | 0 | 1 |
| | 0 | 1 | 0 | 0 | * | * | * | 0 | 1 | 0 | 0 | 0 | 0 | 0 | 0 | 0 |
| * | 0 | 1 | 0 | 1 | * | 0 | * | 0 | 1 | 1 | 0 | – | – | 0 | 1 | 0 |
| * | 0 | 1 | 0 | 1 | * | 1 | * | 1 | 0 | 0 | 1 | 0 | 0 | 1 | 0 | – |
| | 0 | 1 | 1 | * | * | * | 0 | 0 | 1 | 1 | 0 | 0 | 0 | 0 | 0 | 0 |
| * | 0 | 1 | 1 | * | * | * | 1 | 0 | 0 | 1 | 0 | – | 0 | 1 | – | 0 |
| | 1 | 0 | 0 | * | * | * | 0 | 1 | 0 | 0 | 0 | 0 | 0 | 0 | 0 | 0 |
| * | 1 | 0 | 0 | * | * | * | 1 | 0 | 0 | 0 | 0 | 1 | 0 | – | 0 | – |

affect the flip–flops). The logic design problem is thus to generate appropriate 1s at the unstable states. The PLA table for the machine is shown in Table 9.3. Unstable states are indicated by an asterisk. The outputs are not included, as these are simple functions of the state.

The variable-entered maps can be constructed directly from this table. These are shown in Figure 9.22. The excitation equations derived from them are as follows:

$$S1 = \overline{Q1}\,Q2\,\overline{Q3}\,X1\,X3$$
$$S2 = \overline{Q1}\,\overline{Q2}\,Q3\,X2$$
$$S3 = \overline{Q1}\,\overline{Q2}\,\overline{Q3}\,X1 + \overline{Q1}\,Q2\,\overline{Q3}\,X1\,\overline{X3}$$
$$R1 = Q1\,\overline{Q2}\,\overline{Q3}\,X4$$
$$R2 = \overline{Q1}\,Q2\,Q3\,X4 + \overline{Q1}\,Q2\,\overline{Q3}\,X1\,X3$$
$$R3 = \overline{Q1}\,\overline{Q2}\,Q3\,X2$$

This completes the design. However, what about races and hazards? The excitations have no logic hazards, as there are no $1 \rightarrow 1$ transitions. Critical races are a potential problem as the state assignment was arbitrary. Because of differing flip–flop delays, unwanted excitation pulses may occur. However, with the real device these are not a problem. The PAL22IP6 device is fully specified for this mode of operation. The maximum difference between flip–flop outputs' changing is 8 ns, but the minimum pulse width required for triggering a flip–flop is 17 ns. Thus glitches caused on clock inputs due to races cannot cause incorrect transitions.

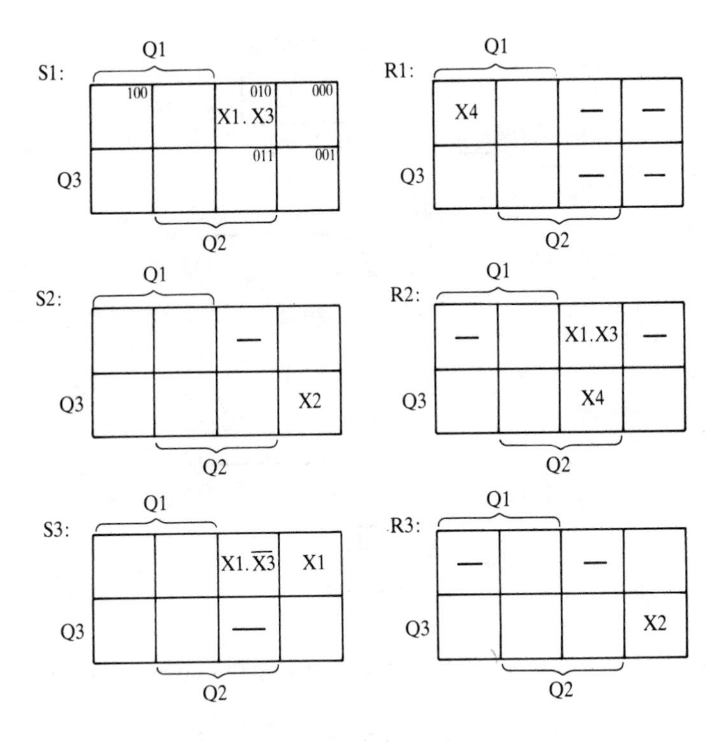


**Figure 9.22** Maps for excitations.

## 9.8 Metastability

In Chapter 6, when asynchronous inputs to synchronous machines were considered, we postponed treatment of one serious problem. Even if we design our state machine to be safe from transition races due to asynchronous inputs, or if we synchronize all asynchronous inputs, there is still a failure mode. This is due to a fundamental property of all bistable storage devices, their inability to resolve instantly inputs which change close to the active clock edge. This is illustrated for a *D* flip–flop in Figure 9.23. Flip–flop data sheets specify that the *D* input must be stable by the set-up time, $t_s$, and remain stable until the hold time, $t_h$. It is not stated what will happen if this constraint is violated. We can gain some understanding by recognizing that an edge-triggered flip–flop has two internal *D* latches, as shown in Figure 9.7. Each one of these latches functions like that of Figure 9.5(a). If we study the *S* or *R* signals in the master latch when the *D* input changes in the ambiguity region, we see that these can be very short pulses. These pulses may not be long enough to change the state of the latch correctly. Responses such as those in Figure 9.24 might occur. If the set pulse is too short, not enough energy can be given to the latch to move it completely over to the other state. It may fall back into the reset

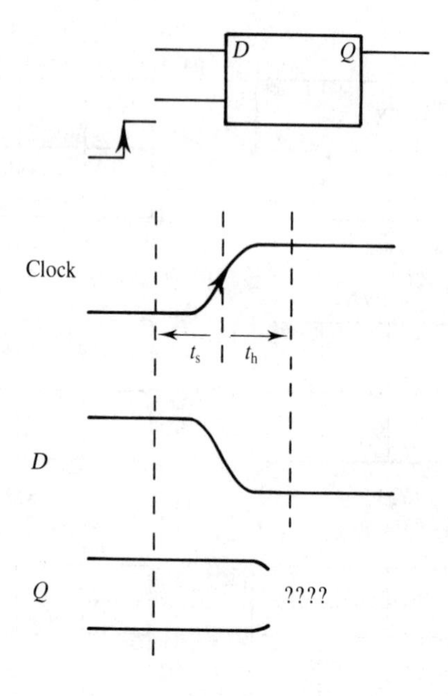


**Figure 9.23** Synchronizer with input changing during ambiguity region.

state, or it may linger in the **metastable state** for an indeterminate period before either returning to the reset state or eventually moving to the set state. Every bistable device has a metastable state, a state between the set and reset states and in which it can remain (in theory) indefinitely; it is a

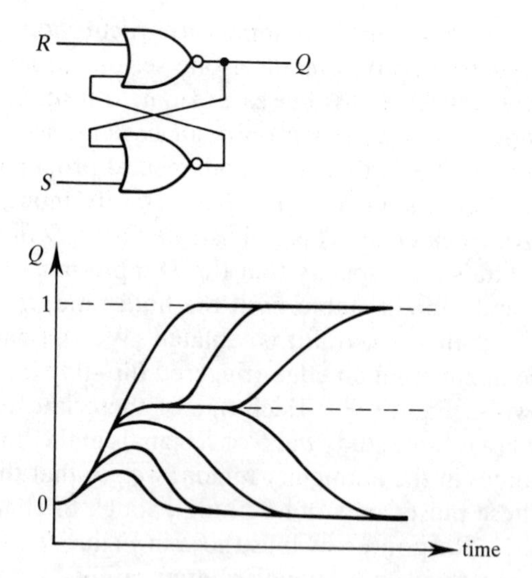


**Figure 9.24** Responses of a latch to short $S$ pulses.

state of unstable equilibrium. The slave latch of the flip–flop sees as input the output from the first latch, but sampled at a later instant. If the master latch has not yet resolved, the slave latch can also exhibit a response like one of those in Figure 9.24. The net effect is that, when a $D$ input changes during the ambiguity region, the flip–flop will take a longer time than the normal propagation delay to settle. This time can only be determined statistically.

Numerous experimental and theoretical studies have confirmed that the following equation is an accurate model of the metastable response.

$$\text{MTBM} = (1/f_c f_d W)\exp(t_R/\tau)$$

where MTBM is the mean time between metastable responses lasting longer than $t_R$, $t_R$ is the resolving time allowed, $f_c$ is the clock frequency, $f_d$ is the average data frequency, $W$ is a constant roughly equal to the interval during which data changes can cause metastability and $\tau$ is a constant dependent on flip–flop circuit parameters.

The exponential dependence on $t_R$ indicates that modest extensions to this time can greatly reduce the failure rate. Given that this is usually the only controllable parameter, most methods of increasing reliability operate by delaying the sampling of the flip–flop output.

Unfortunately the above model is not usable directly with embedded PLD flip–flops, and very little data is generally given in data sheets. However, it is easy to assess the reliability of a PLD used as a synchronizer, and to ensure that a given design has a low enough failure rate, certainly lower than that due to component failure.

The measurement circuit is given in Figure 9.25. The output of the PLD flip–flop under test is used as the input to a synchronous state

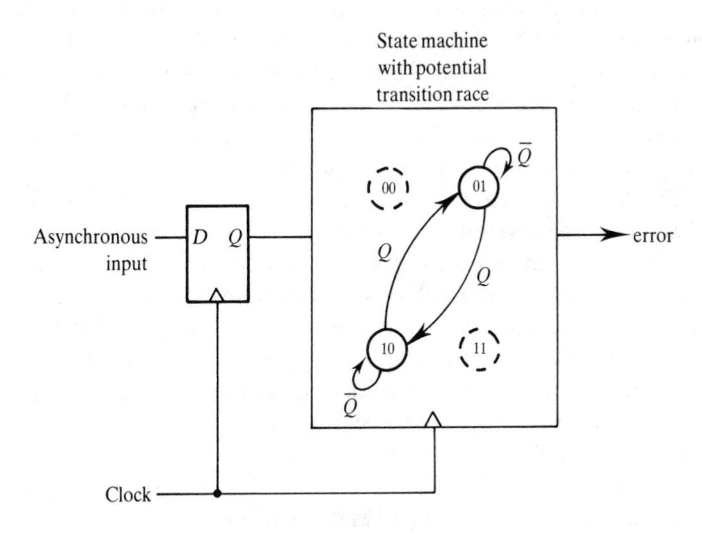


**Figure 9.25** Reliability measurement circuit.

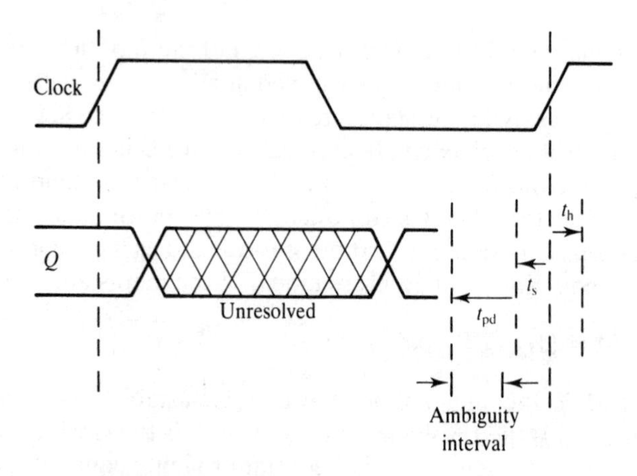


**Figure 9.26** Timing diagram for Figure 9.25.

machine whose state transitions are controlled by this input. When $Q = 1$ a transition between states 01 and 10 is enabled (states 00 and 11 could also be chosen). Because both state variables change during this transition, a race is possible if the input changes to 1 too late in the clock cycle. This could occur if the propagation delay of the synchronizer is extended as a result of metastability. The possible behaviour of $Q$ is shown in the timing diagram of Figure 9.26. Here $t_{pd}$ is the propagation delay of the state machine's combinational logic, $t_s$ is the set-up time of the state machine flip–flops, and $t_h$ is their hold time. The ambiguity window of the state machine is brought forward by an amount equal to $t_{pd}$. An error can thus occur whenever the synchronizer resolves during this interval. If it is assumed that the metastable state of the synchronizer output is consistently interpreted as 0 or 1 by the state machine input, then half of the potential error-inducing events will be missed. Also, the location of the metastability window is not known exactly. The reliability measurements will thus be of the synchronizer–state machine system, rather than of the flip–flop alone. This, however, is what is required in practice.

The test is set up as in Figure 9.25, where the PLD under test is programmed to behave as a synchronizer and state machine. Any of the device's flip–flops can be chosen as the synchronizer, but results will vary between flip–flops. Additional logic is programmed into the PLD to generate an error signal whenever states 00 or 11 are entered, and to reset the machine into a defined state after one cycle. The clock and data input terminals are connected to two totally independent signal generators, and the error outout is connected to a counter. The timing for the PLD version is shown in Figure 9.27. $t_{CLK}$ is the propagation delay of the flip–flops and $t_{su}$ their set-up time, which now includes the propagation delay of the array. $t_1$ and $t_2$ define the start and end of the ambiguity interval, which has duration $\Delta$. $t_{ext}$ is the extent to which the period $T$ exceeds the minimum

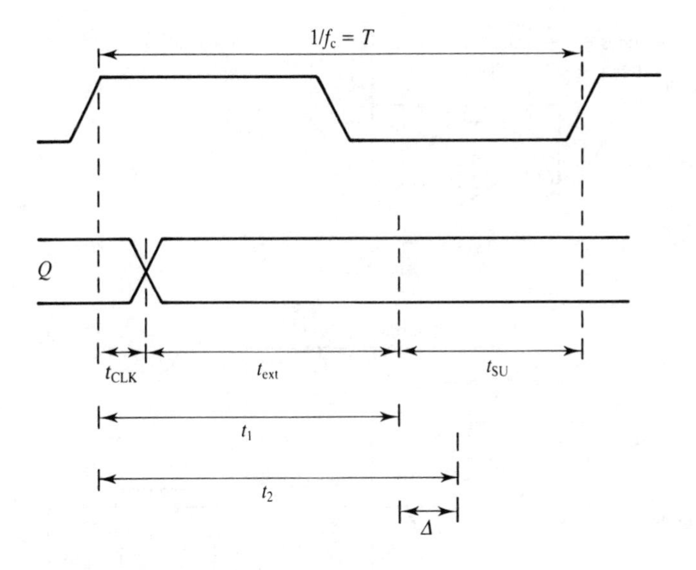


**Figure 9.27** Timing diagram for PLD test circuit.

possible period. The probability of the synchronizer's resolving in the window is given by:

$$P(t_1 < t < t_2) = P(t > t_1) - P(t > t_2)$$

The probabilities on the right-hand side are inversely related to the MTBM, hence

$$\begin{aligned} P(t_1 < t < t_2) &= \text{const}_1[\exp(-t_1/\tau) - \exp(-t_2/\tau)] \\ &= \text{const}_1 \exp[(-t_1/\tau)(1 - \exp(-\Delta/\tau))] \\ &= \text{const}_2 \exp[(-t_1/\tau)] \end{aligned}$$

assuming that $\Delta$ is constant.

The failure rate for the system is thus

$$\text{MTBF(system)} = k/f_c f_d \exp(t_1/\tau)$$

where $k$ is a constant for the system. Now

$$t_1 = 1/f_c - t_{su}$$

hence

$$\text{MTBF(system)} = k'/f_c f_d \exp(1/f_c \tau)$$

where $k'$ is another constant.

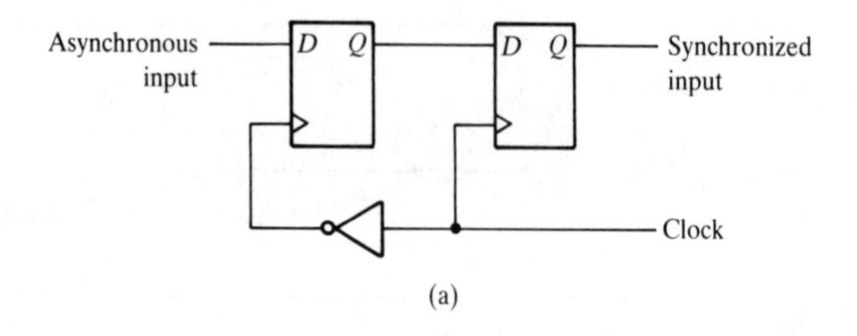


(a)

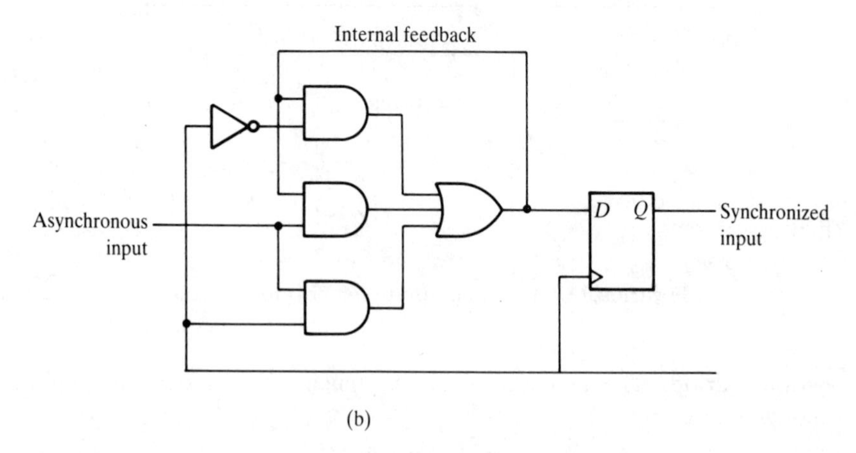


(b)

**Figure 9.28** (a) Increasing synchronizer reliability by cascading flip–flops. (b) PLD realization.

It is now possible to fit experimental data to this relationship to estimate values of $k'$ and $\tau$. Notice that this equation is more complex than the original equation, since $f_c$ appears twice; it affects both the synchronization event rate and the allowed resolving time. In a system application, $f_c$ and $f_d$ are usually both determined by external constraints. Thus, if the MTBF is found to be too low, some means must be found to increase it. Either a more suitable PLD must be found, or more time must be allowed for resolution. One means of achieving the latter is to cascade two flip–flops as shown in Figure 9.28(a). In some PLDs this can be done internally by constructing a latch using the method of Figure 9.8. This is shown in Figure 9.28(b). The reliability should also be experimentally determined in this configuration. No data sheet parameters can help in estimating this.

## SUMMARY

Asynchronous sequential circuits are often needed in interfacing applications. The simplest synchronous circuits are constructed by directly feeding back the outputs of a combinational circuit. This is the Huffman model, which is directly applicable to combinational PLDs. Traditionally, asynchronous circuits are specified by the flow table. The flow table can be manipulated to minimize the number of states required and used to find a critical race-free state assignment. The resulting logic must be free of logic hazards which could cause incorrect transitions, and have a delay distribution which prevents essential hazards. Simple asynchronous circuits in the form of latches and flip–flops can be built into a larger PLD design. The state machine flowcharts of Chapters 6 and 7 are also applicable to asynchronous design, and a similar design procedure can be followed, except that races and hazards must be detected and eliminated. The large inertial delays of some ROMs enable the normal asynchronous design rules to be relaxed, no consideration of races and hazards being necessary. These methods can also be applied to self-clocked design with dual-triggered flip–flops. Again the flowchart method can be readily applied. All flip–flops and latches can suffer from metastability when operated in non-fundamental mode. This affects the reliability of synchronizers. A simple test procedure can be used to estimate this reliability at the system level in PLDs.

## BIBLIOGRAPHICAL NOTES

The classical methods of asynchronous sequential circuit design are all covered in Unger (1969). Of the current generation of logic design textbooks, Friedman's (1986) gives a good concise treatment. Construction of an oscillator using part of a PLD is described in Signetics (1985a). Leininger (1970), Thurber and Berg (1971), Bennett (1974), Signetics (1985c), Bennett (1983), Monolithic Memories (1983) and Haas (1988) all show how to build latches and flip–flops in arrays. State assignment methods for PLA-based asynchronous circuits are described in Lemberskii *et al.* (1976), Lemberskii (1979), Lange (1979), Yakubaitis *et al.* (1980) and Lemberskii (1983). The flowchart design method is adapted from Clare (1973) and Fletcher (1980). Fletcher's method is applied to PAL design in Corbett (1981). A recent complex PLD design example, in which hazards are ignored, is given in Kopec (1988). Sholl and Yang (1975) extend classical procedures to memory-implemented asynchronous machines. Constraints for race- and hazard-free memory application are given in Ditzinger and Lipp (1979) and Thomas and Chandrasekharan (1981). Other examples of this approach are Nichols (1967), Kvamme (1970), Fletcher and Despain (1971) and Ettinger and Tillier (1985). The self-clocked design technique given was inspired by McIntosh and Weinberg (1969). The PLD metastability measurement method was formalized in Bolton (1987b). Jigour (1988) shows how an internal latch can be constructed to improve reliability.

## EXERCISES

**9.1** Following the procedure of Figure 9.8, design an $S$–$R$ latch in sum-of-products form. (The latch sets when $S = 1$, and resets when $R = 1$.) Is there a hazard? Two designs are possible, which behave differently when $S = R = 1$. To which one does the design of Figure 9.13 correspond?

**9.2** Show how the $S$–$R$ latch of the previous question can be extended to have multiple $S$ and $R$ inputs in a PLD implementation.

**9.3** In the conversion of a conventional logic diagram for part of a process control system into a PLD realization, the input latches of Figure 9.29 were encountered. Inputs $A$ and $B$ are external, while output $Z$ is fed into further internal logic.

Design the sum-of-products logic for this latch. How many PLD pins are required?

**9.4** Why cannot a 3-bit state assignment be found for the machine of Figure 9.10?

**9.5** Why, in the self-clocked design procedure described in Section 9.7, are unstable states not allowed?

**9.6** Convert the toggle circuit flow table of Figure 9.12(a) into a flowchart. How many states are required? Transform this into a self-clocked design using edge-activated $S$–$R$ flip–flops. Why can't this design be realized with a single flip–flop?

**9.7** It was been argued that state assignment is unimportant in the self-clocked design procedure described in this chapter. However, some assignments may be better than others. Why?

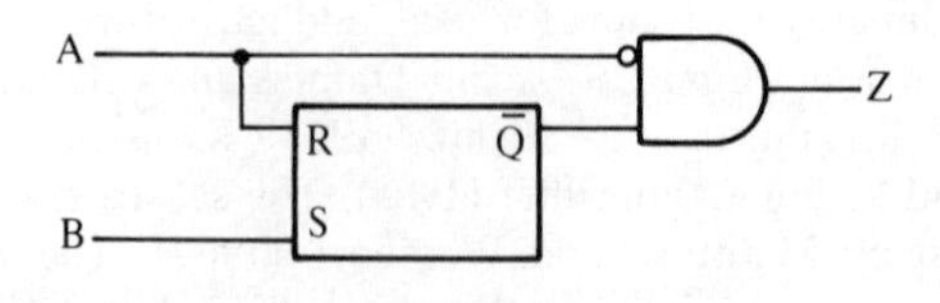


**Figure 9.29**

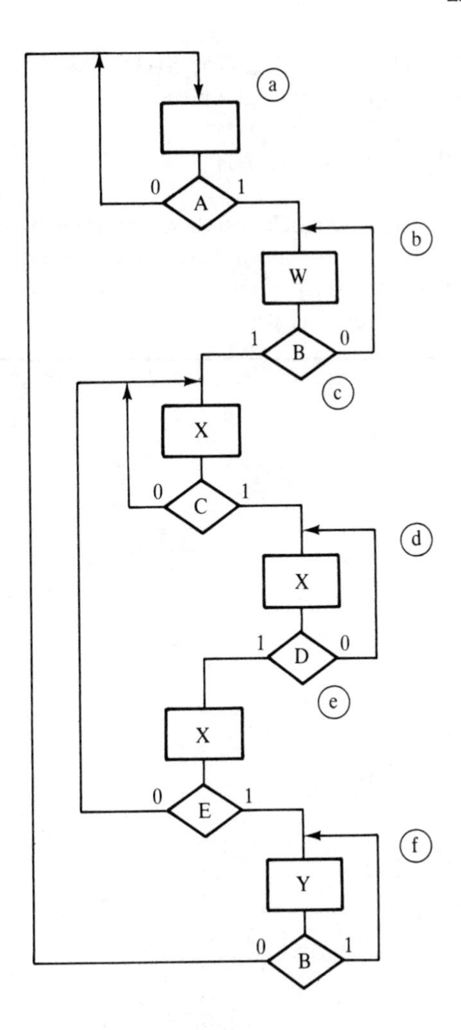


**Figure 9.30**

**9.8** Design a self-clocked circuit which behaves according to the flowchart of Figure 9.30. Ensure that the outputs do not suffer from glitches.

Why would a state assignment be difficult if this was to be implemented in the Huffman form?

**9.9** How could the self-clocked design method be adapted for use with dual toggle flip–flops?

**9.10** How is metastability in latches and flip–flops related to the fundamental mode restriction in asynchronous circuits?

**9.11** The PAL16R4D device ($f_{max} = 55$ MHz) has a mean time between failures due to metastability given by:

$$\text{MTBF} = k/f_c f_d \exp(1/f_c))$$

where $f_c$ and $f_d$ are the clock and data frequencies, $k$ has a worst-case value of 0.27 $\mu s^{-1}$, and $\tau$ has a worst-case value of 1.0 ns.

What is the MTBF if the clock frequency is 40 MHz and the average data frequency is 10, 20, 30 and 40 MHz?

---

CHAPTER 10

# Specification Languages, Simulation and Testing

**OBJECTIVES**

When you have completed studying this chapter you should be able

- to list the requirements of a modern PLD design system;
- to understand the difference between structural and behavioural forms of specification;
- to learn quickly how to use one of the commonly used PLD specification languages;
- to understand the role of simulation and device testing.

## 10.1 Introduction

In this chapter, the principles of programmable logic specification languages will be looked at, with illustrations from some of the more important or interesting examples. There is not space (and also it would be very boring) to describe all the languages available, but fortunately they are quite closely related. The languages can be divided into two major categories – those provided by semiconductor manufacturers and supporting only that manufacturer's parts, and those produced by independent companies and designed to support as many PLDs as possible. In general, the latter lag in their support of new devices and in the degree of logic optimization possible. No standard language has as yet emerged but, as programmable logic CAD becomes more integrated into general-purpose electronic CAD systems, these languages will probably move more into the mainstream of hardware description languages.

Each language is part of a PLD CAD system, some very limited, such as PALASM, and some comprising a set of many interacting programs. Here only the languages will be described and compared. As the same requirements apply to any PLD CAD system, whatever the specification language, the features of the different systems will not be covered (although it must be said that some facilities are constrained by the limitations of the language). However, before going on to details of the languages, it is necessary to consider what an ideal programmable logic CAD system should do.

After a design has been specified and compiled into a PLD program, it needs to be verified. At present, this task is performed by simulation. The PLD can then be programmed, after which the device should be tested again, to ensure that there are no circuit faults. To enable this testing, the design should not have parts which are untestable or difficult to test. The final section of the chapter will offer some brief guidance on designing for testability.

## 10.2 Requirements of a PLD design system

The type of design system that would be desirable is best explained by examining how a designer would ideally go about designing a digital system which includes PLDs. It is assumed that the PLD design tools can be integrated into a 'host' CAD system which permits designs to be entered and simulated hierarchically, but could also be used alone if required. The hypothetical design sequence would proceed as follows.

After the initial conceptual studies and analysis, the designer would create the architecture of the system by defining the highest level functional blocks and their interconnection, as described in Chapter 1, possibly using a graphical schematic capture tool. These blocks may or may not be directly realizable; a block called 'microprocessor' would, while a block called 'custom FIFO', for example, would not. At this stage a high level, or symbolic, simulation is possible by writing models in whatever behavioural modelling language is provided in the host system. Hierarchical decomposition of the structure would be continued to a point where the functional blocks defined are either standard components or assemblies of components, or candidates for a PLD implementation.

Where blocks have been identified which look suitable candidates for PLDs, the PLD CAD comes into play. The functions of these blocks must first be defined in the abstract – no particular PLD should be assumed. These blocks could therefore be too small to use any PLD economically or too large to fit into one. To allow for different design styles, alternative methods of functional specification must be allowed for. These should include truth tables, waveforms, text, or schematics constructed from a library of logic primitives. (The latter form has not been considered in this book as it is but a 'bridge' from older design practices.) These functional descriptions must now be transformed into a standard form (a 'virtual array') to allow a uniform treatment at the next stage.

A suitable standard for this virtual array is the two-level sum-of-products form since all Boolean functions can be expressed in this way and most PLDs are based on this structure. In addition, logic blocks described in this way can be readily split, merged and minimized. The CAD system should also allow the designer to select a particular PLD at this early stage and to specify its personality directly by defining the product and sum terms. The textual language should also therefore serve this requirement.

Assuming that there now exist two-level blocks selected for PLD implementation, the tools must at this stage aid the designer in selecting the most suitable device or network of devices. To enable this process, a two-level block must have appended to it a list of resources required. These will include number of inputs, number of outputs, total number of products, number of products per output, number and type of registers and clocking arrangements, three-state outputs, etc.

Various CAD programs which operate on these two-level arrays may now be executed. The most important are minimization, simulation, device fitting and splitting/merging. Device fitting is a crucial part of this system. With the explosion in the number of PLDs available and the increasing complexity of these parts it is becoming more difficult to select the most appropriate one for an application. The task of a 'fitter' program is to match the resource requirements of a virtual array with a database of PLD resources. Its output is a report listing the PLD types which could realize the design and the percentage utilization in each case. Such a fitter program would ideally have a rule-based structure, in which additional information such as propagation delay, power consumption and cost could easily be incorporated. Constraints on these factors could be introduced before the fitting process. Not only must the raw resource requirements be matched, but the interactions between resources would have to be considered. For example, it may not be possible to use the maximum number of inputs and outputs of a PLD at the same time.

Two possibilities for backtracking now exist. In the first case, the block specified is too large for any PLD. The user will now have to specify a division into two blocks with the aid of a splitter program and try the fitting process again. If, on the other hand, the resources of the PLDs chosen were poorly utilized, two or more blocks may have to be merged. With the larger PLDs, merging will be essential as it is unlikely that a single functional block could be neatly specified to fill the whole device. After both operations the minimizer could again be applied.

A 'fuse' file can now be generated. This is a straightforward process, relying on files containing device-specific data. The final stages of simulation can now be performed, with the characteristics of the chosen PLDs used in models compatible with the host CAD system's simulator. Also at this stage, test patterns must be generated for each PLD to allow post-programming verification.

The specification language for the PLD functional blocks must be designed in such a way that all the above processes are easy to perform. In designing a hardware specification–description language it is essential to distinguish between **structural** and **behavioural** (or functional) descriptions. The language must be able to handle both of these.

A structural description specifies the interconnection of the primitive logical elements of a block. These elements operate on and are connected by Boolean signals, and the description has a 1:1 correspondence with the programmed PLD – in effect it is a PLD internal 'wirelist'. Examples of structural elements are multiple-input AND gates (for products), exclusive OR gates and flip–flops. Structural descriptions may be made more compact by defining signal vectors and constructs for selection ('CASE' and 'IF ... THEN') and repetition ('FOR'). State machines can also be described in a structural language if a state assignment is made, because of the direct correspondence of transitions to products.

A behavioural description specifies the behaviour of a block in terms of its inputs, outputs and internal signal variables. The simplest form of functional description is a truth table. For eventual PLD realization, a functional description must be converted into a structural description. Often, however, the two descriptions are the same. For example, a truth table can be directly stored in a ROM, and a set of products describing a state machine can map directly into a sum-of-products based PLD with $D$ flip–flops. Behavioural descriptions which cannot be mapped directly are state machines with symbolic states, data operations with high level data and mode selection signals, and arithmetic operators. These descriptions cannot be translated into structural descriptions without some knowledge of the type of PLD to be used. For example, ROMs and PLAs with different flip–flop types all have to be treated differently. Also, exclusive OR gates, when present, must be accommodated.

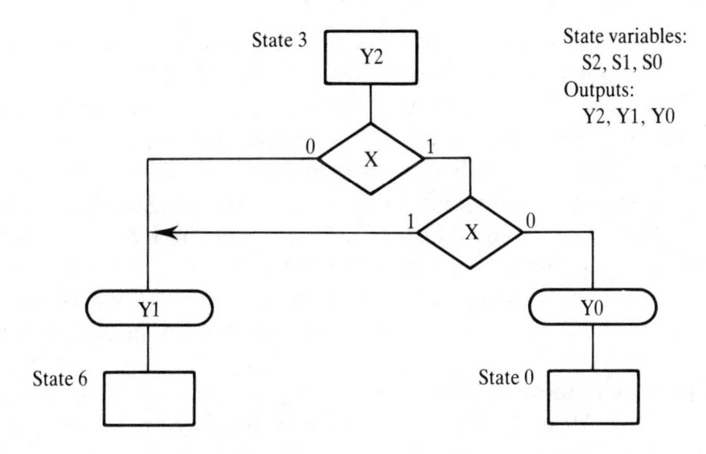


**Figure 10.1** Flowchart fragment.

It is necessary to bear in mind these general principles when examining and comparing the different languages. When comparing state machine notations, the ASM fragment of Figure 10.1 will be used.

## 10.3 Specification languages

### 10.3.1 PALASM and its relations

PALASM was first introduced by Monolithic Memories in 1977 as the supporting software for the first PALs. The source code of the PALASM program, written in FORTRAN, has always been made available to customers. Other PAL device manufacturers have based their assemblers on PALASM, and indeed it has been the basis of much of the thinking behind PLD specification language development. PALASM has also been built into PAL programmers to allow 'instant assembly'.

The following is a simple example of a PALASM specification file:

```
PAL20X8                                PAL DESIGN SPECIFICATION
PART1234                                  A.DESIGNER 7/9/89
2-DIGIT BCD COUNTER
MMI
CLK /CE1 D1A D1B D1C D1D D2A D2B D2C D2D /LD  GND
/OC  /CO  Q2D Q2C Q2B Q2A Q1D Q1C Q1B Q1A CE2 VCC
/Q1A :=  /LD * /Q1A          ;HOLD FIRST BIT OF 1 DECIMAL
      +  LD * /D1A           ;LOAD D1A
     :+: /LD * CE1 * CE2     ;COUNT

...
IF (VCC) CO = Q1A*Q1D*Q2A*Q2D      ;CARRY OUT
```

The first four lines must always be present, but only the PAL type is checked. The pin list has to start on line 5. It is a list of the symbolic names given to pin variables. CLK, VCC, GND and NC (no connection) are reserved names. The defining equations follow. Each equation is an assignment to an output pin variable, = for combinational, and := for registered. Where an output is complemented, the / symbol must appear either in front of the variable's entry in the pin list, or at the left-hand side of its defining equation. This information is used in defining the output polarity of PALs where this is programmable. Where it is not, a negation must be present if the PAL has inverting outputs; PALASM does not perform De Morgan's theorem.

The operations available are AND (*), OR (+), XOR (:+:), and XNOR (:*:). XOR and XNOR are designed to be used with PALs possessing these types of gate; an expansion into ANDs and ORs is not done. All equations must refer to pin variables, and thus intermediate variables and expression substitution are not possible. The IF( ) construct is used to define output enabling control terms. Its use in the example above indicates that CO will always be enabled, since VCC is always true.

PALASM is thus a direct description of every product term required in a PAL design. Specifications can be long and very opaque, especially where the equations are the result of hand manipulation in, for example, state machine designs. The handling of complemented PAL outputs in designs where no output complementation is required is also very prone to error.

Other PAL manufacturers have adopted PALASM as the basis of their support software. These include AMPALASM from Advanced Micro Devices, PLAN from National Semiconductor, HELP from Harris Semiconductor and EPLASM from Panatech/Ricoh. Improvements with respect to the original PALASM include better error messages and expression macros for substitution into equations (PLAN and HELP). EPLASM is for the 'EPL' devices which have programmable output cells. The usage of product terms and XOR operators determines the programming of these cells, provided that the configuration required is possible. PLAN additionally supports ECL PALs which do not have a high impedance output state. Here the enabling term specified by IF( ) is combined by the program with the relevant product terms of an equation to allow wired OR to be used instead.

PLEASM is cousin to PALASM, being a FORTRAN program adapted from PALASM for the purpose of specifying the function on PROMs used as logic elements. The specification format is basically that of PALASM, with some small differences. The pin list is specified in two parts, one starting with the keyword .ADD lists the address (input) pin names, and one starting with .DAT lists the data (output) pin names, both least-significant bit first. The equations are listed in a similar manner, except that IF( ) is not used because, in PROMs, outputs are enabled externally by means of enable pins.

The major difference with PALASM is that arithmetic operators are allowed in PLEASM equations, since these can be easily expanded into PROM truth tables, where there is no product term limitation. The new operators are .+. and .*., indicating addition and multiplication respectively. Together with these there is the ability to define vectors of pin variables which are interpreted as binary numbers. Here are some examples of PLEASM equations:

```
EQ = A3:*:B3 * A2:*:B2 * A1:*:B1 * A0:*:B0        ;like PALASM
S7,S6,S5,S4,S3,S2,S1,S0 = X3,X2,X1,X0
                          .*. Y3,Y2,Y1,Y0          ;S=X*Y
C,C3,C2,C1,C0 = /A3,/A2,/A1,/A0
                .+. B3,B2,B1,B0.+.CIN              ;B–A+1+CIN
P3,P2,P1,P0 = A1,A0.+.B1,B0.+.C1,C0
              .+.D1,D0.+.E1,E0                     ;P=A+B+C+D+E
```

The arithmetic operators are defined for unsigned operands and numbers are specified most-significant bit first. PLEASM does not support the mixing of logical and arithmetic operations in the same equation, as would be required for defining an ALU, for example.

### 10.3.2 State machine languages

The structure of the PLA makes design directly onto a programming table very simple for many applications; in fact these are still supplied by some manufacturers. A reduced truth table for a multiple-output function may be entered directly, as illustrated in Chapter 3. State machines described as flowcharts may also be converted into PLA tables, as was shown in Chapter 6 – each link path maps directly into a product term, assuming that no minimization has been performed. Much early PLA CAD was based on tables.

Signetics produced a CAD program in about 1980 written in BASIC for the Intel Intellec Microcomputer Development System (MDS) ('the IBM PC of the 1970s'), for assembling FPLA and FPLS design specifications. The program ran interactively, prompting the user for a header block, a pin block and an equation block. In the pin block, in addition to symbols, pin functions are specified as input, output or bidirectional. Internal flip–flops are given reserved 'pin numbers' such as ⟨P0⟩.

The equation format is very similar to PALASM's. The inputs to *S–R* flip–flops, for example, are handled as

```
/Y: S = /TEST * /A * /B
    R = /TEST * /A * /B + TEST * A * B
```

A *D* flip–flop may be defined by using a *J–K* thus:

```
X: J  = A * B
   K = /J
```

(The FPLS devices supported only have *J–K* or *R–S* flip–flops.) Notice how the colon is used to represent the presence of the clock.

Predefined symbols are used for control inputs (for example, preset), control terms and the complement array sum term. The latter is defined as an additional combinational equation. The IF construct is used to define the action of control inputs and terms in a similar manner to PALASM. For example,

```
IF(D0 = /A) Y = /(B * C)
```

defines the control term D0 and the output Y. D0 is a predefined symbol for one of the control terms.

This form of description is thus purely structural and device specific. A design has first to be conceived with close reference to the FPLA/FPLS circuit diagram and then converted into equational form.

Out of this program grew the AMAZE program, written in Pascal and released in 1983. AMAZE has a more elaborate user interface, with many menus and IC package pictures for pin symbol assignment. The equation syntax is simplified by dividing the specification into blocks such as 'logic equation'. 'I/O direction' and 'flip–flop control'. A major improvement to AMAZE was added in 1985 (the tenth anniversary of the FPLA), a state machine form of design entry. State machines are described in a separate file from the device file, the latter containing pin symbol and non-state-machine information. The state machine file defines transitions between Boolean state vectors. One state machine file may refer to more than one device and more than one state machine may be defined in a single file.

The state machine specification consists of two parts: vector definitions and state transitions. State, input and output vectors are defined separately. Two methods are available for vector definition, Boolean or coded sets. Examples of the former are as follows:

```
   IN_VECT  = /I1 * I15;
STATE_VECT  = /REG_1 * /REG_2 * /REG_3;
  OUT_VECT  = OUT2, /OUT1, /OUT7, OUT8;
  OUT_VECT' = OUT2', /OUT1', /OUT7', OUT8';
```

Notice first the different ways of specifying input and output vectors and the use of ′ to denote registered outputs. Examples of the coded set method for state vector definition are

```
[ Q0,Q4,Q1,Q7 ]
STATE_00 = 0 H;      (hexadecimal)
STATE_02 = 2 H;
STATE_09 = 9 H;
STATE_14 = E H;

[ Q3,Q5 ]
ST_0 = 00 B;         (binary)
ST_1 = 01 B;
ST_3 = 11 B;
```

and for a set of output vectors

```
[ REG1,REG2 ]
OUTA'  1  -  B;
OUTB'  0  1  B;
OUTC'  0  0  B;
```

The state machine syntax is easily understood by looking at the coding of the example of Figure 10.1

```
WHILE [state_3] : [Y2]
IF [ X * /Y ] THEN [state_0] WITH [Y0]
ELSE [state_6] WITH [Y1]
```

There is thus a direct translation from the flowchart. Vectors state_3 etc. will have been defined previously. The combinations of the inputs X and Y could also have been represented by values of a vector. Each IF represents one link path and thus one product term in the FPLS. Note the use of the ELSE line. This is taken to mean that the complement array is to be used in this state – it is not therefore translated into products. Registered outputs are denoted by ′, as in the vector definitions, for example [Y0′]. Multiple IFs may be replaced with the CASE...ENDCASE construct, in which an ELSE may be included if required.

The major restrictions of the AMAZE state machine syntax are as follows:

(1) one flip–flop type (*J–K* or *R–S*, depending on target device) is assumed in the translation to tables,

(2) the 'ELSE' clause only applies to the use of the complement array, and

(3) state machine description cannot be used with FPLAs.

### 10.3.3 Improved manufacturer-specific languages

PALASM 2 is the replacement for PALASM. It was introduced in 1985 to support the newer Monolithic Memories PAL products in addition to a ROM-based sequencer and some FPLS devices. The differences in the specification language are the minimum necessary to enable the new devices, with their programmable output cells, to be programmed.

The design specification file contains two sections: declarations and a functional description. In addition to the usual designer, PLD type and pin variable information, up to 20 strings can be defined. These are expressions which can be substituted into equations to allow more compact specifications. The substitution is purely a textual replacement. Additional declarations are required for certain devices: these include names given to internal global set and reset signals, and buried registers.

The functional description section, introduced by the keyword EQUATIONS, contains equations assigning values to outputs or to internal registers or signals which have been declared. The syntax for these is the same as PALASM's. Exclusive ORs are now expanded where the target device does not have these gates. Extensions are used to indicate flip–flop inputs which can be defined by logical terms. For example, flip–flop OUT may require the following four equations:

```
OUT       := ...
OUT.SETF  = ...
OUT.RSTF  = ...
OUT.CLKF  = ...
```

The first equation defines the D input, according to the PALASM convention. The IF( ) construction is no longer used for enable terms. For consistency, the syntax

```
OUT.TRST = ...
```

is used. A device specification in PALASM 2 is thus a complete structural description of a PAL circuit, and may be related directly to a fuse plot.

PALASM 2 also has a state machine syntax. A state machine specification is in two parts, one (STATE) which contains the state assignment and machine description, and one (CONDITIONS) which gives names to input conditions. (The reason for the latter is that the MMI programmable sequencer (PROSE) contains a PAL device for the encoding of input conditions.) The example of Figure 10.1 would be encoded as

```
STATE
MEALY_MACHINE
  STATE_3 = /S1 * S2 * S3      ;STATE ASSIGNMENT
  ...
```

```
    STATE_3          := COND_1 -> STATE_6
                      + COND_2 -> STATE_0
    STATE_3.OUTF =  COND_1 -> Y1 * Y2
                      + COND_2 -> Y0 * Y2
    ...
CONDITIONS
    COND_1 = /X
    COND_2 = X * /Y
```

An 'ELSE' is possible by using the 'local default' construct +-> INIT without a condition name. If the keyword MOORE_MACHINE is used, then the output line needs no conditions. Because outputs of the PROSE device are registered, all designs can be described as Moore machines. Additional facilities are DEFAULT_BRANCH, which is the state which is entered if no condition is true in any state, and OUTPUT_HOLD or DEFAULT_OUTPUT, which can shorten the output specification lines. A simple sequential automatic state assignment is possible.

PLPL was AMD's 'second generation' design software developed to support their own PALs, but with the capability for having other device descriptions added to its database. It was announced in 1983 and became available in the middle of 1984. It is worth looking at in a little more detail since it contains many ideas from modern computer languages, illustrating the trend towards more formalism in hardware description languages.

A PLPL device description contains at least a heading, a pinlist and an equation section. The example below illustrates the main features.

```
DEVICE SHFT8BIT (AMPAL22V10)
        "This is an example of an eight-bit shift register"
PIN     CLOCK     = 1        RESET = 13    SELECT[1:0] = 2,11
        RILO      = 23       "Right Shift input, Left Shift output"
        LIRO      = 14       "Left Shift input, Right Shift output"
        DATA[7:0] = 3:10
        Q[7:0]    = 22:15;
DEFINE  LOAD  = 0;      'constants'
        SHFTR = 1;
        SHFTL = 2;
        HOLD  = 3;
BEGIN
        IF (RESET) THEN ARESET ();
        IF (SHFTL) THEN ENABLE (RILO);
        RILO = Q[7];
        IF (SHFTR) THEN ENABLE (LIRO);
        LIRO = Q[0];
```

```
        CASE (SELECT[1:0])
        BEGIN
          LOAD)  Q[7:0] := DATA[7:0];
          SHFTR) Q[7:0] := RILO,Q[7:1];
          SHFTL) Q[7:0] := Q[6:0],LIRO
          HOLD)  Q[7:0] := Q[7:0];
        END;
END.
```

The heading consists of the keyword DEVICE followed by the design name and device type to be used. The pinlist can assign names to pins in any order. Notice that pin vectors can be defined. The next, optional, section defines 'macros'. These are numerical constants or expressions, or Boolean constants or expressions, which can be substituted later. In the example, numerical constants are defined in order to clarify the meaning of the CASE in the equation section. This construct specifies the input conditions for all eight registers, generating $8 \times 4 = 32$ product terms. Note the standard use of := to indicate register. Here the CASE allowed the specification of the shift register in a form which can be read functionally, but which is in fact a direct statement of the logic. The equations generated are

```
Q[7] :=   DATA[7] * /SELECT[1] * /SELECT[0]
        + RILO    * /SELECT[1] *  SELECT[0]
        + Q[6]    *  SELECT[1] * /SELECT[0]
        + Q[7]    *  SELECT[1] *  SELECT[0];
etc.
```

The equations could be written directly in this form. Equations in this section are assignments to pin variables. = indicates a combinational output, according to the normal convention. In PLPL a multiple assignment to a pin variable causes all the right-hand sides to be ORed; this can be seen in the CASE example, and indeed PLPL relies on this for the expansion of its higher level constructs.

PLPL also provides a FOR construct for generating equations. For example, the shift register equations could be expresed as

```
FOR (PIN_NUM = 1 TO 8) DO
  Q[PIN_NUM] := LOAD  * DATA[PIN_NUM] +
                SHFTR * Q[PIN_NUM PLUS 1] +
                SHFTL * Q[PIN_NUM MINUS 1] +
                HOLD  * Q[PIN_NUM];
```

where LOAD etc. have been defined as Boolean expresions, RILO as Q[9] and LIRO as Q[0]. Also, PIN_NUM would have to be declared in a VAR section. To use this construct the registers have to be renumbered from 1 to 8 as Q[-1] is not allowed. Arithmetic '+' and '−' are PLUS and MINUS in PLPL. It is important to note that these operators cannot be used to define device functions, for example

```
Q[0:7] := Q[0:7] PLUS 1;
```

is definitely not allowed. In other words, 'program variables' must not be confused with 'device variables'. The same qualifications apply to the use of the relational operators <, > etc. However, Boolean results of a relational operation can be included in equations, and the result of an arithmetic operation can be assigned to a Boolean vector.

Address decoding can be handled with the CASE construct. The following example should be self-explanatory (#B starts a binary constant):

```
CASE (A[15:11])
BEGIN
  #B00000, #B00001) MEM[1] = MEMOP;
  #B00010, #B00011) MEM[2] = MEMOP;
           #B00100) MEM[3] = MEMOP;
END;
```

The other equations use the IF...THEN construct and invoke the predefined functions ARESET and ENABLE which define the asynchronous reset and output/enable actions of the 22V10 device. User-defined functions were to be a future addition.

The CASE and IF...THEN...ELSE constructs make state machine description in PLPL quite straightforward. The ASM example could be coded as follows:

```
DEFINE state0 = 0;      "state assignments"
       state1 = 1;
       ...
BEGIN
       CASE (S[2:0])
       BEGIN
         state0) ...
         state1) ...
         ...
         state3) BEGIN Y[2] = 1; "state output"
                       IF X * /Y THEN BEGIN
                                      Y[0]   = 1; "cond. o/p"
                                      S[2:0] := state0; "trans."
                                      END;
                                    ELSE BEGIN
                                      Y[1]   = 1;
                                      S[2:0] := state6;
                                    END;
                 END;
         ...
         DEFAULT)
END.
```

Here the CASE is used to enumerate all the states and the IFs are used to define link paths. The default selector in the CASE is useful for defining a transition to a safe state in case of error. In the example, ELSE was used to define two link paths. Two product terms would be generated, though. Of course IFs could be used again, or even a CASE if the input combinations were enumerated. A global reset could be defined by enclosing the entire state machine description within an IF reset THEN ... ELSE ... construct. This avoids having to place a test in every state. The outputs Y[2:0] could be registered – the only difference would be the use of := since *D* registers are assumed.

The equations generated by this language will have redundancies in them which can be eliminated by a simple checker. For example, a state variable being set to 0 will generate a product including a 0.

All constructs in PLPL can be nested, as in Pascal, a language to which PLPL has obvious similarities. However, it must always be remembered that PLPL is only an 'equation generator' and not all design specifications can be read directly as functional descriptions.

One of the most highly developed of manufacturer-specific design systems is A+PLUS from Altera. Recognizing that many applications are described as schematics, the language enables PLD function to be specified either as a netlist of primitive components or as Boolean equations. A conversion program is thus necessary to convert the netlist into a set of equations in sum-of-products form. A state machine form of description is also allowed.

### 10.3.4 Universal languages

The increase in the number of manufacturers and PLD architectures in the early 1980s created a market for universal PLD CAD systems. The two first were CUPL, from Assisted Technology in 1982, and ABEL from DATA I/O in 1983. Both of these systems have languages with a syntax closely related to those described above, so they will not be described here. However, there are some interesting language design issues in universal languages, so two other, rather different, universal languages, Perfect and LOG/iC, will be discussed below.

Perfect, conceived by one of the designers of CUPL, was introduced in 1986. The method of description goes some way towards resolving the problem of describing PLDs with complex multimode macrocells. The first-generation languages were designed before PLDs had such flexible cells and it has proved difficult to adapt them; in fact, these languages are unable to describe all macrocell modes in some PLDs. Perfect addresses this problem by defining firstly **Boolean statements**, which describe the logical operations in the array, and secondly **netlist statements**, which describe networks of wires and logical elements. Wire variables can be pins, or internal nodes.

Two types of Boolean statement are possible, those which assign the value of an expression to a variable which will be used later, for example

```
y = a & b # c & d
```

or those which bind the value of an expression to a node or output pin, for example

```
clock state2 = a & !b
```

which binds an array output to the clock input of the macrocell flip–flop associated with wire state2. (& is ‘AND’, # is ‘OR’, ! is negation). A truth table and state machine syntax are also provided to allow alternative forms of relationship between variables to be described.

LOG/iC has evolved from the LOGE CAD system developed at the University of Karlsruhe. It was originally a state machine design system, but has been extended to include more general logic specification capabilities. Whereas all the languages described so far have been modelled on programming languages (with PLPL being the best example), LOG/iC allows the designer to operate almost exclusively at the function table and state machine levels. Here for example is the specification for an address decoder:

```
*DECLARATIONS
  x-variables = 16
  y-variables = 6
*X-NAMES
  a[15..0]           ;address bus
*Y-NAMES
  ramsel,            !select system RAM
  romsel,            !select system ROM
  csver,             !select version ROM
  bse[1..3]          ;select block address in version ROM
*FUNCTION TABLE
  $ (a[15..0])     : ((ramsel,romsel,csver)), (bsel[3..1]);
8000H..0FFFFH :    0      1      1   ,    – ; select RAM
0400H..00480H :    1      1      1   ,   0D; select range 1
0481H..0057FH :    1      1      0   ,   1D; select range 2
0580H..005FFH :    1      1      0   ,   2D; select range 3
3E80H..03F00H :    1      1      0   ,   3D; select range 4
3F18H..03FBFH :    1      1      0   ,   5D; select range 5
3FC0H..03FFFH :    1      1      0   ,   6D; select range 6
3F01H..03F17H :    1      1      0   ,   7D; select range 7
REST          :    1      0      1   ,    – ; select ROM
*PAL
  type = PAL20L8
*PINS
  a[0..15] = [1..11,13,14,20,21,23],
  ramsel = 15, romsel = 16, csver = 22, bsel[1..3] = [17..19];
```

Notice that this specification first specifies a block of logic in terms of named X and Y variables and later binds these to a device and pin numbers. A LOG/iC design file can specify several functional blocks and more than one PLD. The compiler generates and minimizes the equations derived from the function table. The LOG/iC method of state machine description is illustrated by the following example of a 93-state counter:

```
*DECLARATIONS
  x-variables = 3
  y-variables = 1
  z-variables = 7
*X-NAMES
  reset = 1, count = 2, down = 3;
*Y-NAMES
  carry = 1;
*Z-NAMES
  QQ[6..0] = [7..1];
*Z-VALUES
  S[1..93] = [0..92]
*FLOW-TABLE
  S[1..93], X1--, Y0, F1;            reset condition
  S[1..93], X00-, Y0, F[1..93];      hold
  S[1..92], X010, Y0, F[2..93];      count up
  S93     , X010, Y1, F1;            carry
  S[2..93], X011, Y0, F[1..92];      count down
  S1      , X011, Y1, F93;           carry
*STATE ASSIGNMENT
  z-values
*PAL
  type = PAL32VX10
*PINS
  reset = 3, count = 4, down = 5,
  carry = 22, QQ[0..6] = [15..21];
*FLI
  t-flipflop
```

This is a very compact form of state machine description. (The use of the term 'flow table' here is unconventional.) S indicates present state, and F indicates next state. Again, the function is described independently of the device. The state assignment and flip–flop type instructions are necessary for the compiler to generate the equations.

LOG/iC also allows structural descriptions in a manner similar to PALSAM 2. This should only be necessary if special features of the device are to be used. This is in fact a problem of all device-independent descriptions; the devices are often designed with such flexibility that a compiler for each device type would be necessary in order to make maximum use of all possible features. This argument is in fact used by manufacturers of CAD tools which are tailored to their own architectures.

## 10.4 Simulation of PLD designs

Once the function of a PLD has been specified using one of the available languages, and it has been compiled into a fuse map, it is necessary to ensure that the programmed device will behave as expected. In the absence of formal mathematically based methods, we must rely on **simulation**. All PLD development tools include a simulator. A simulator enables the responses of a programmed PLD to a given input sequence, the input **vectors**, to be calculated and displayed. For combinational designs it is often possible to perform an exhaustive test; every possible input is applied and the response checked. This can become impractical with large numbers of inputs, however. Likewise, except with trivial cases it is impractical to apply every possible input sequence to a sequential design – there are simply too many of them. Intelligently applied simulation can thus only increase confidence that a design is correct.

Some thought should be applied during the design stage about how the design can be made easily verifiable. This is especially important with sequential designs, where the circuit has to be initialized into different states for the various tests. PLDs with register preload considerably simplify this task. Asynchronous sequential circuits cause particular problems, since simulators generally have only a simple and fixed delay model. The result of a simulation could be that correctly designed circuits will not be simulated correctly (outputs may oscillate, for example) or that designs suffering from races and hazards will appear to be correct on simulation.

Some design systems have some quite powerful simulation aids. For example, PALASM 2 has a simulation vector generation language, an tool which both cuts down on the amount of typing for entry of vectors and makes the input files more readable and easily relatable to device function. A statement is defined for setting inputs to given values, for example

```
SETF READ /START A B C
```

sets READ, A, B and C to 1 and START to 0, and there is a similar statement for preloading registers (PRLDF) (when the device allows this). A clock pulse can be generated on one of the clock pins using the command

```
CLOCKF CLK1
```

Sequences of vectors can be generated using looping constructs, for example

```
WHILE (/OUT1 * READ) DO
  BEGIN
    SETF A C
    CLOCKF CLK2
  END
```

or

```
FOR I := 1 TO 4 DO
  BEGIN
    SETF B
    CLOCKF CLK
  END
```

An IF...THEN...ELSE construct allows conditional vector generation and the statement CHECK allows expected outputs to be compared with simulation results. After a simulation has been run, a set of inputs and outputs can be displayed as waveforms.

Where a complete digital design system is being developed on a CAD system, it is necessary to incorporate the PLDs into the simulation. Many general-purpose simulators now permit this to be done, by interpreting PLD program files and translating them into the simulator's modelling language. A PLD would thus be simulated and debugged first using a PLD design package, and then simulated again in the context of the system in which it is embedded.

## 10.5 Device testing

When the PLD has been programmed, there is the problem of verifying there are no faults due to circuit failures. In general, the simulation vectors applied to the chip are inadequate for this task, since they cannot be guaranteed to detect all possible faults. A set of **test vectors** is required for this task.

Erasable PLDs present the fewest testing problems, since the chips can be fully tested using standard test patterns and then erased before final programming. Even so, many users will require a final test of the programmed device. This is essential with fuse-programmed PLDs since the chips cannot be fully tested during manufacture; the final stage of manufacturing test must be performed by the user. Generation of the required test vectors must be done, except in trivial designs, by a test vector generation program.

A number of test generation programs are available for PLAs in general, and for PLDs. These programs operate by first assuming a **fault model** for the device. The fault model lists the assumed modes of failure, for example a product 'stuck' at 0 or 1, or a fuse not blown when it should be and vice versa. The fuse faults are known as **cross-point faults**. The test vectors should be able to detect as many of these postulated faults as possible by comparison of output responses with a fault-free response. Ideally, all faults should be detectable, but in practice this is difficult to achieve. The **fault coverage** is a number which specifies the percentage of faults detectable with a given set of test vectors. A low fault coverage may be improved by modifications to the design, by for example using spare input and output pins to increase the controllability and observability of internal parts of the circuit.

---

## SUMMARY

A PLD CAD system should allow PLD designs to be developed before PLD selection is done since a single design may have to be spread over more than one PLD or it may not occupy a whole device. A PLD design can be described either functionally or structurally. Functional specifications are more easily understood. A number of PLD specification languages have been defined. The first of these were closely tied to a small set of device architectures and permitted logical products to be defined one by one. The more recent languages are able to handle a wider range of device types, and a greater degree of functional specification. There is no universal language which can be used for the functional specification of all PLDs. Designs are verified by simulation, which cannot always guarantee correctness. Testing of programmed devices is necessary for the detection of faults due to circuit defects. The needs of simulation and testing should be taken into account at the design stage.

---

## BIBLIOGRAPHICAL NOTES

The introductory parts of this chapter are from Bolton (1986). A design methodology based on the manipulation of two-level arrays is described in Maissel and Phoenix (1983). An early PLD design system which used a virtual array was HELP (Harris Semiconductor, 1985), and one which had a simple fitter was PLAN (National Semiconductor, 1985). PALASM is described in Monolithic Memories (1978) and Birkner (1978). PLEASM is described in Monolithic Memories (1984). AMAZE is introduced in Signetics (1984) and its use is illustrated in Wong (1985). PALASM 2 is described in Schmitz and Greiner (1984). PLPL was introduced in Kitson and Ow-Wing (1984). CUPL was first described in Osann (1982) and ABEL in Burrier (1984). Perfect is described in Aronson and Abrams (1986). LOGE, the predecessor of LOG/iC, was introduced in Grass and Lipp (1979). A more recent reference is Ditzinger and Tatje (1987). For definitive details of language syntax and compiler capabilities refer to the latest manuals. Alford (1989) surveys a wide range of PLD development systems. Yee (1984) discusses the requirements and options for simulation and testing of programmable logic. Osann (1984) gives a useful practical survey of issues and a design example showing simulation and test vectors. Sievers (1984) describes how the manufacturer designs testability into fuse-programmable devices. Methods for PAL test generation based on the stuck fault model are given in Vafai (1983), Bengali and Coli (1983), Gruebel (1983) and Wang (1984). Guidelines for testable PLD design may be found in Advanced Micro Devices (1988).

Appendix

# Programmable Logic Device Architecture Tables

In this appendix, all known PLDs are listed. Their architectures are characterized by dividing the devices into categories and including within each the minimum information necessary to describe the essential features of the device.

This information has been extracted from data books, data sheets and descriptions in technical articles. Some of the devices are now obsolete, and some may never have entered production. However, their details have been included to illustrate the evolution of programmable device architectures. For definitive data on any device, reference should be made to the latest manufacturers' literature.

## A.1 PLAs

PLAs are combinational PLDs which have complete AND and OR arrays. The structure of PLAs is shown in Figure 3.23, and a specific example is shown in Figure 5.2. PLA architectures are listed in Table A.1. Sequencers have the structure shown in Figure 6.2, with an example shown in Figure 6.3. The sequencer architectures are listed in Table A.2.

## A.2 PAL-structured devices

### A.2.1 General

PAL devices are PLAs with no OR array, but a set of OR gates which sum sets of products. The structure of combinational PAL devices is shown in Figure 3.25 (see Figure 5.4 for a specific example). The 20-pin combinational devices are listed in Table A.3, and the 24-pin devices are listed in Table A.4.

Address Decoders, or Field Programmable Gate Arrays (FPGAs) are PAL-like combinational PLDs which generally have no OR array; products are taken directly to outputs. They are particularly useful for address decoding. The architectures are listed in Table A.5.

Registered PALs have output registers fed from the logic array like that of the device shown in Figure 7.7. Tables A.6 and A.7 list the architectures. All these devices have an external common clock and are thus appropriate for synchronous designs.

### A.2.2 Programmable output cells and generic architectures

To serve as many applications as possible, a large number of PAL architectures would be required. To overcome this problem, PALs with generic architecture have been devised. These are devices with output cells, or macrocells, of variable configuration. The structure of a generic PAL is shown in Figure A.1. The set of output cell configurations which have been used is shown in Figure A.5. Each generic device is able to emulate a number of fixed-architecture devices in addition to being adaptable into unique architectures. The first generic PAL was the 22V10.

Being able to generate register clock signals internally increases the flexibility of a registered PAL device, allowing use in multiclock systems, and for the construction of self-clocked circuits. PALs with such flexible clocking are listed in Table A.8.

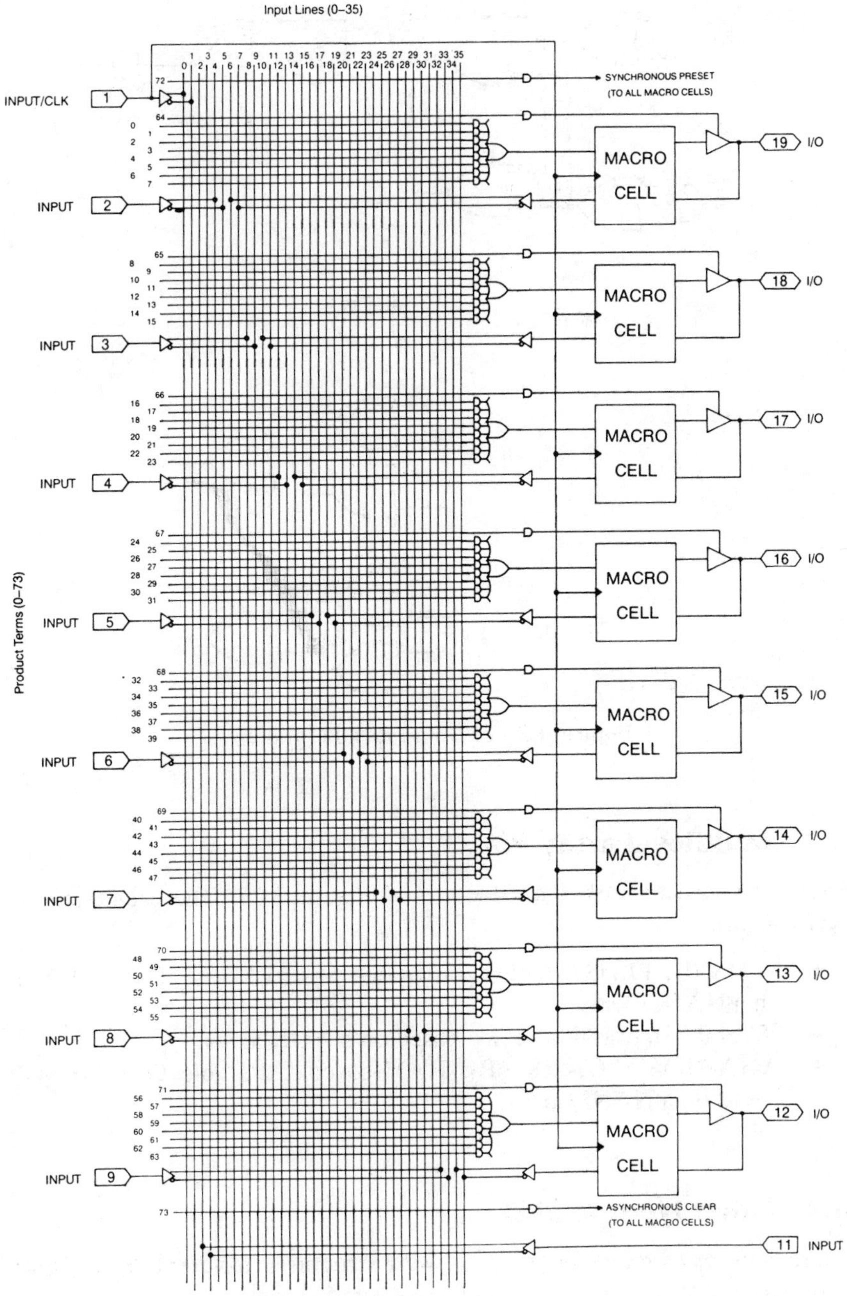

Input Lines (0–35)

0 1 2 3 4 5 6 7 8 9 10 11 12 13 14 15 16 17 18 19 20 21 22 23 24 25 26 27 28 29 30 31 32 33 34 35

Product Terms (0–73)

INPUT/CLK 1

72 SYNCHRONOUS PRESET (TO ALL MACRO CELLS)

64 0 1 2 3 4 5 6 7 MACRO CELL 19 I/O

INPUT 2

65 8 9 10 11 12 13 14 15 MACRO CELL 18 I/O

INPUT 3

66 16 17 18 19 20 21 22 23 MACRO CELL 17 I/O

INPUT 4

67 24 25 26 27 28 29 30 31 MACRO CELL 16 I/O

INPUT 5

68 32 33 34 35 36 37 38 39 MACRO CELL 15 I/O

INPUT 6

69 40 41 42 43 44 45 46 47 MACRO CELL 14 I/O

INPUT 7

70 48 49 50 51 52 53 54 55 MACRO CELL 13 I/O

INPUT 8

71 56 57 58 59 60 61 62 63 MACRO CELL 12 I/O

INPUT 9

73 ASYNCHRONOUS CLEAR (TO ALL MACRO CELLS)

11 INPUT

**Figure A.1** Generic PAL.

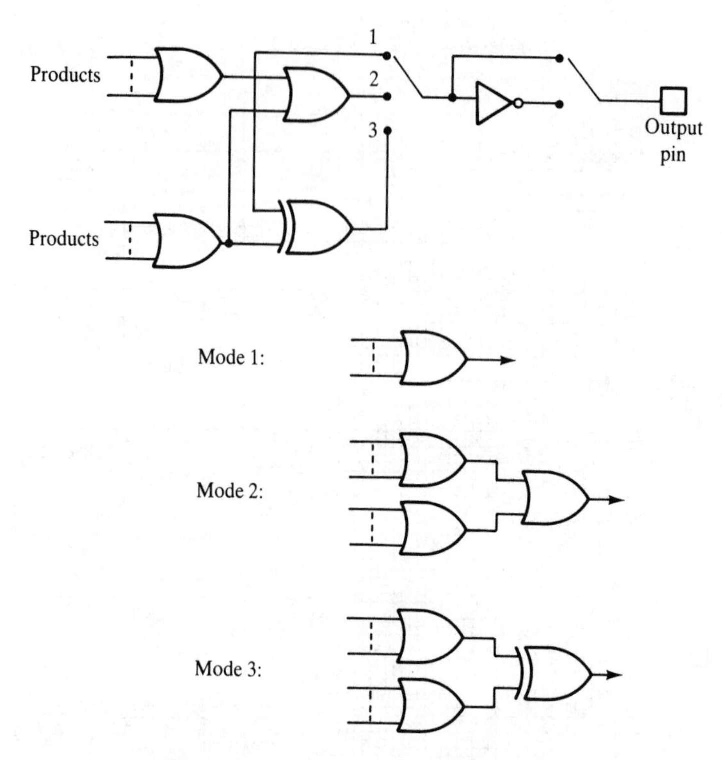


**Figure A.2** EPL output cell (Type 1).

## A.3 Multilevel array PLDs

These are devices with the structure of Figure 3.27. The architectures available are:

- PLHS501, PLHS502: 'Programmable Macro Logic' devices based on a NAND array,
- 78C800: An erasable device based on a NOR array,
- AGA-1K16, AGA-1K16P4: RAM-based 'Alterable Gate Arrays' based on a NAND array.

## A.4 Other types of PLD

There now exist many large PLDs with structures different from those considered in this book. The families are listed below.

- Microprogrammed PLDs:
  - 29CPL141, 29CPL142, 29CPL144, 29CPL151, 29CPL152, 29CPL154

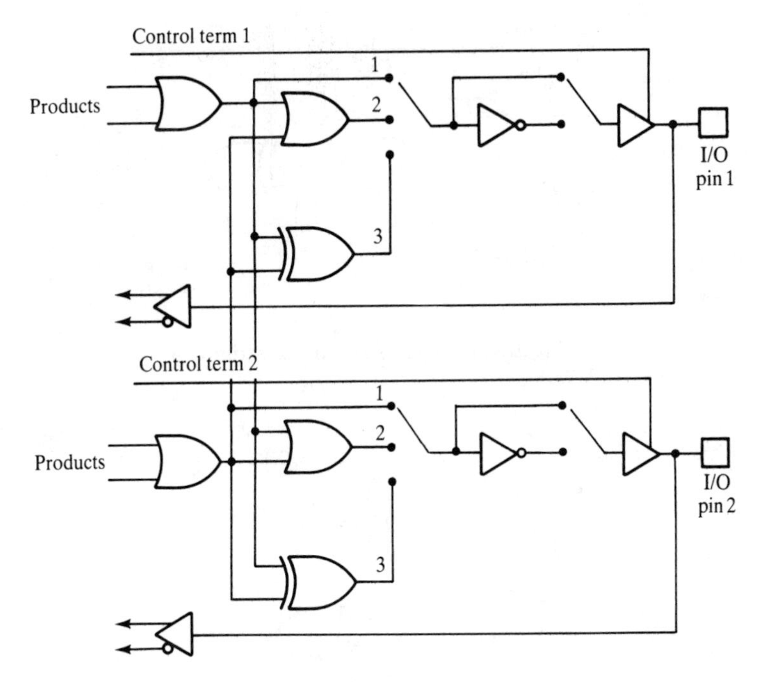


**Figure A.3** EPL output cell (Type 2).

- 14R21 'PROSE'
- EPS444, EPS448 'SAM'

- Bus Interface PLDs:
  - 5CBIC, 85C960
  - EPB1400 'Buster'
  - PLX448, PLX464
  - MCA1200, EPB2001, EPB2002 (for Micro Channel)
  - VME3000 (for VME bus)

- PLD for parallel controllers:
  - 7C361

- PLDs with Matrix or Partitioned Arrays:
  - XC2064, XC2018, XC3020, XC3030, XC3042, XC3064, XC3090 (Logic Cell Arrays)
  - ACT1 (gate array structured with universal combinational cells)
  - ERA60100 (gate array structured with 2-input NAND cells)
  - EPM5016, EPM5024, EPM5032, EPM5064, EPM5127, EPM5128 ('MAX')
  - PA7024, PA7028, PA7040, PA7068 ('PEEL Arrays')
  - CAL1024 (Algatronix configurable array)

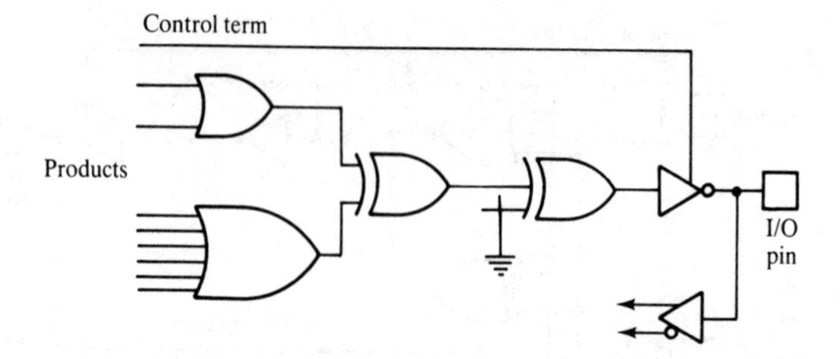


**Figure A.4** 22XP10 output structure.

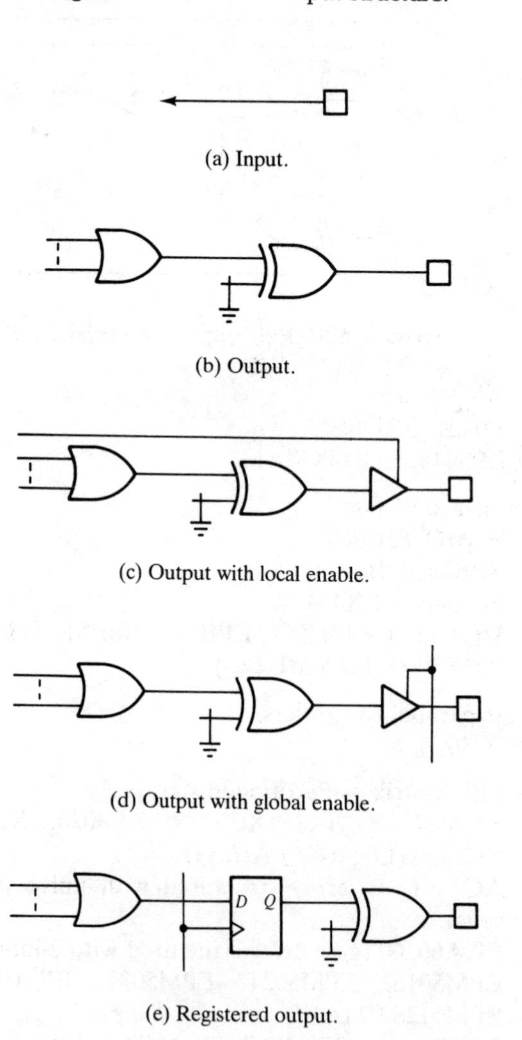


(a) Input.

(b) Output.

(c) Output with local enable.

(d) Output with global enable.

(e) Registered output.

**Figure A.5** Generic PAL output cell modes.

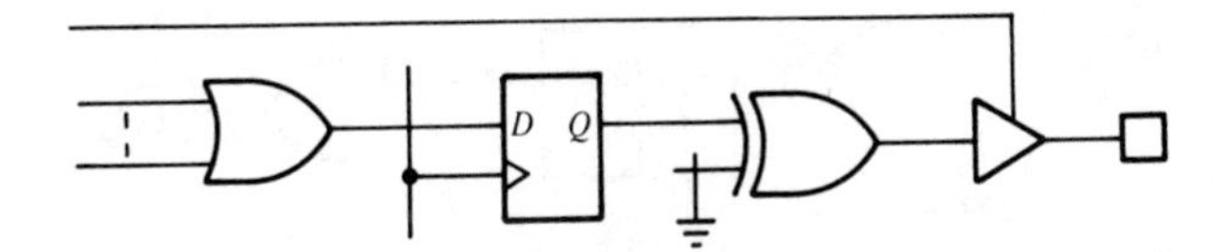


(f) Registered output with local enable.

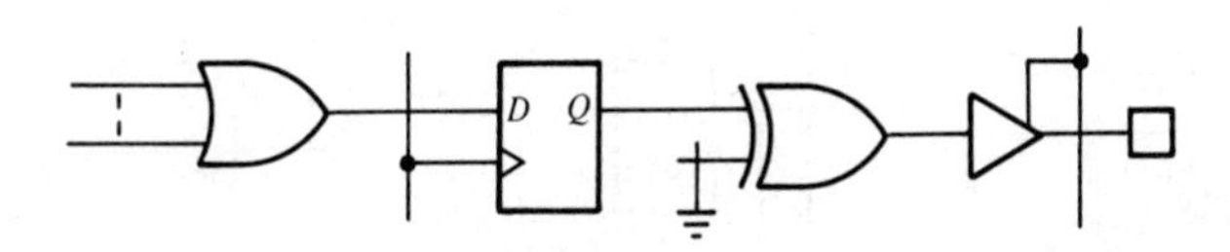


(g) Registered output with global enable.

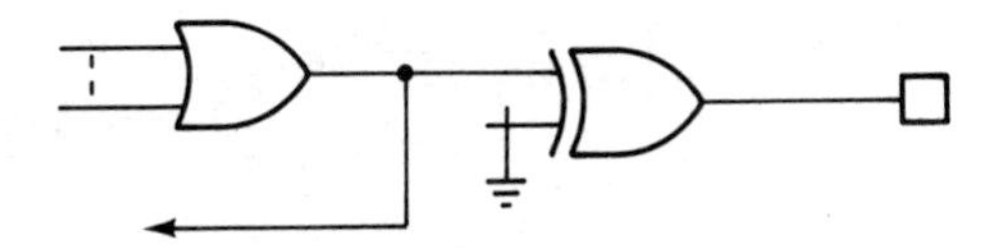

(h) Combinational output and feedback.

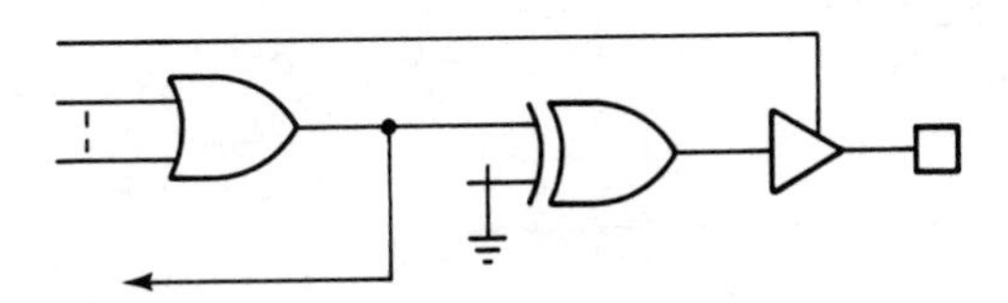

(i) Combinational output and feedback with local enable.

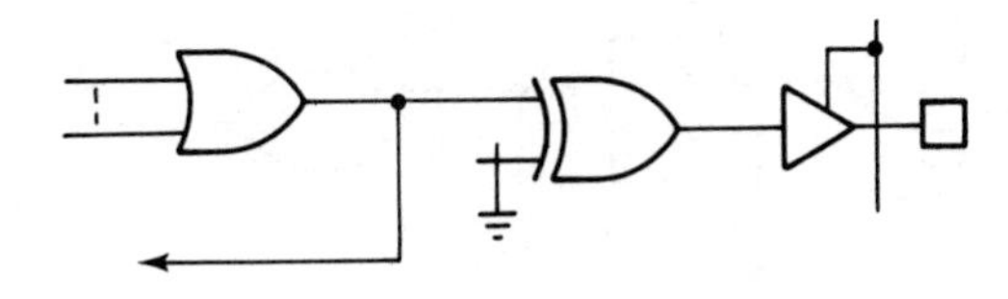

(j) Combinational output and feedback with global enable.

**Figure A.5** (cont.) Generic PAL output cell modes.

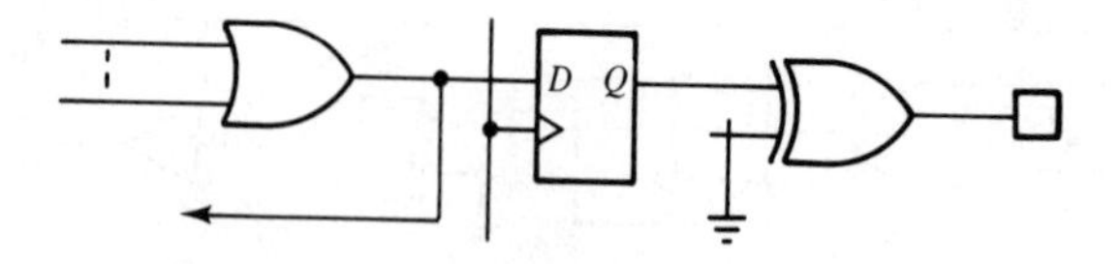


(k) Registered output, combinational feedback.

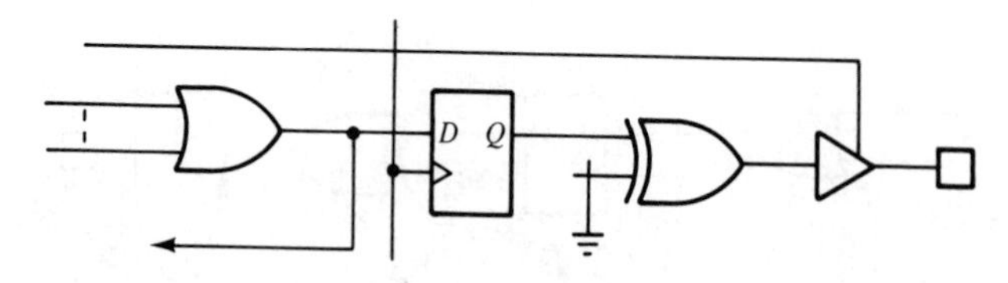


(l) Registered output, combinational feedback, local enable.

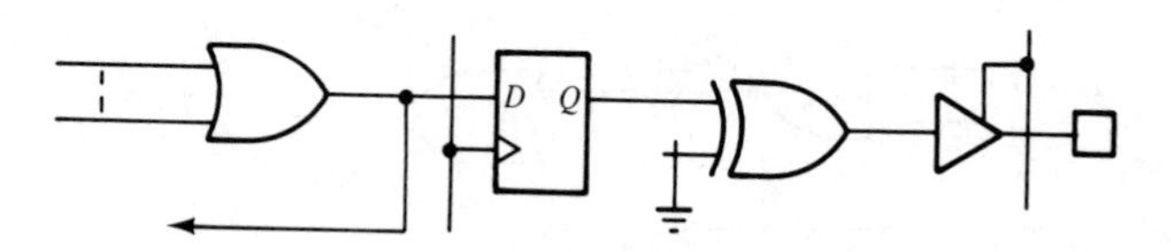


(m) Registered output, combinational feedback, global enable.

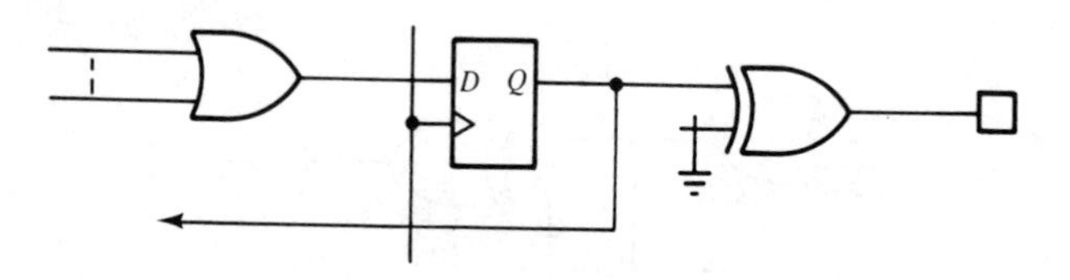


(n) Registered output and feedback.

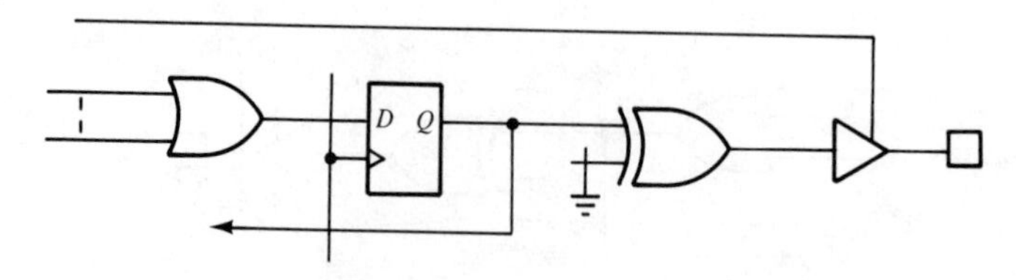


(o) Registered output and feedback, local enable.

**Figure A.5** (cont.) Generic PAL output cell modes.

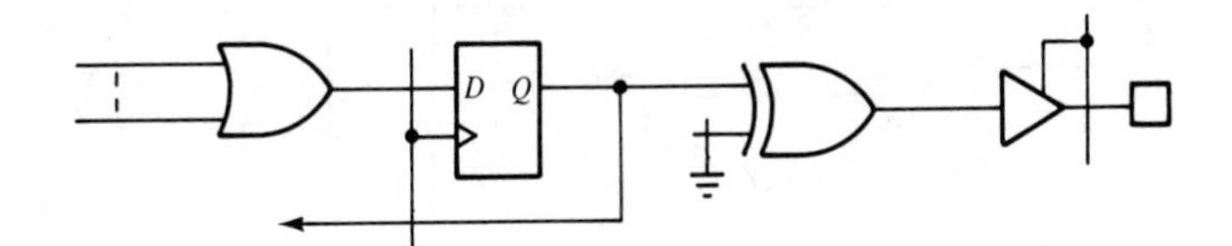


(p) Registered output and feedback, global enable.

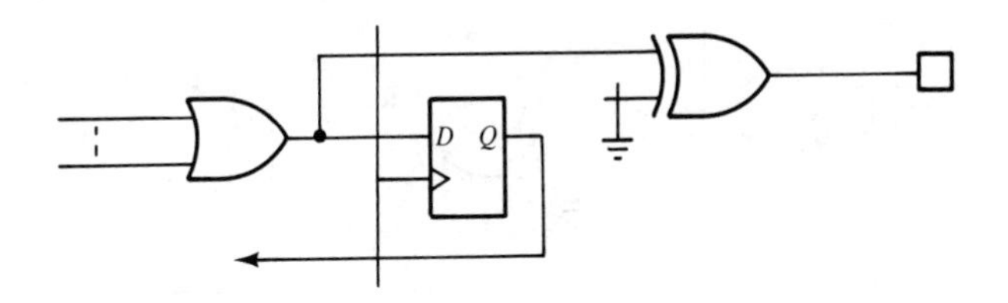


(q) Combinational output, registered feedback.

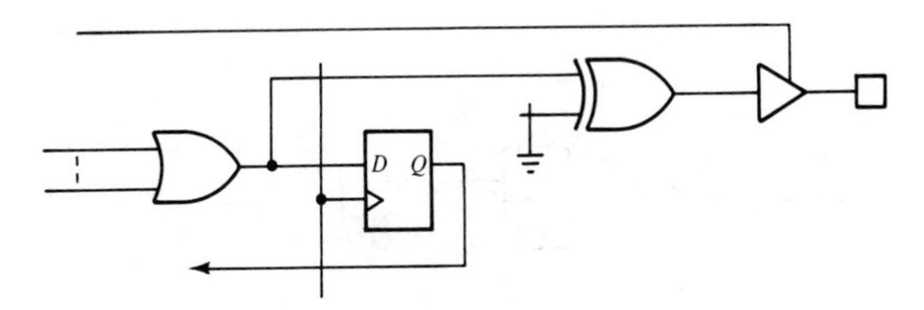


(r) Combinational output, registered feedback, local enable.

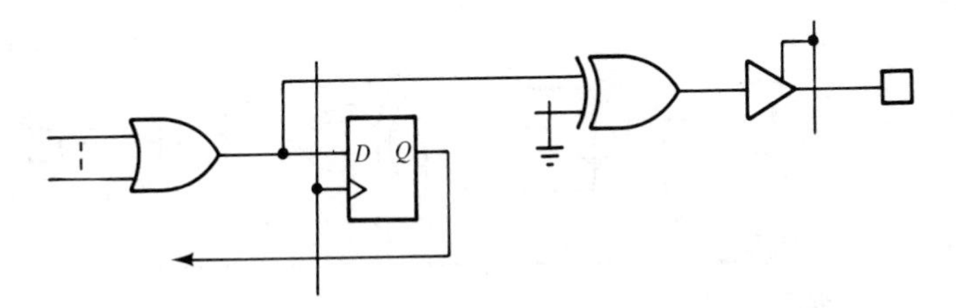


(s) Combinational output, registered feedback, global enable.

**Figure A.5** (cont.) Generic PAL output cell modes.

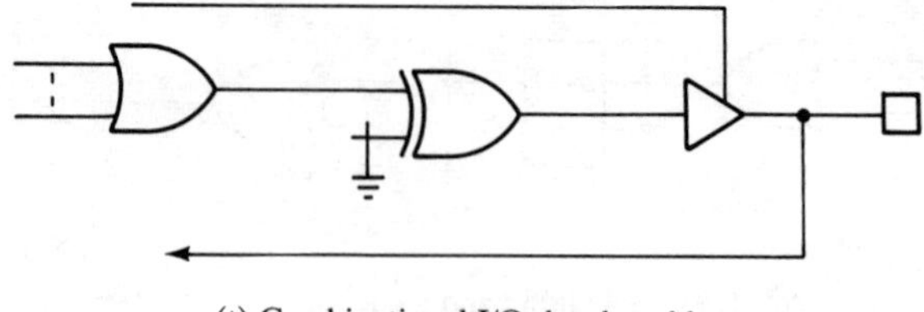

(t) Combinational I/O, local enable.

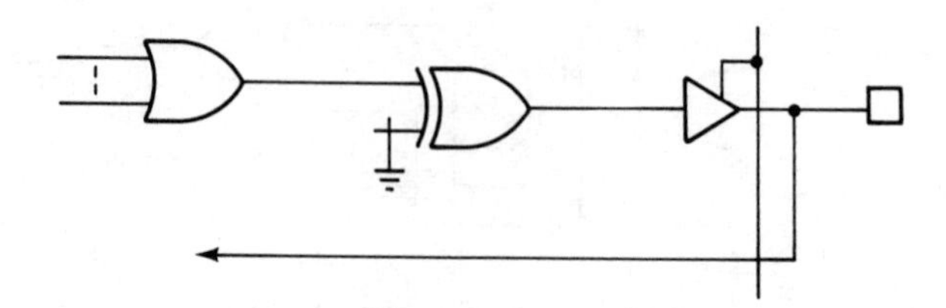

(u) Combinational I/O, global enable.

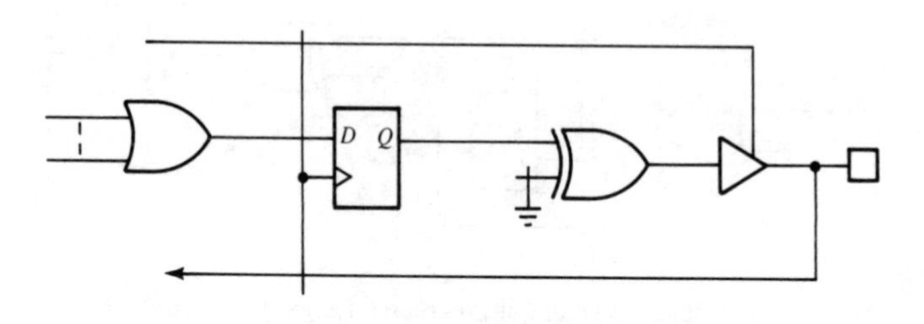


(v) Registered I/O, local enable.

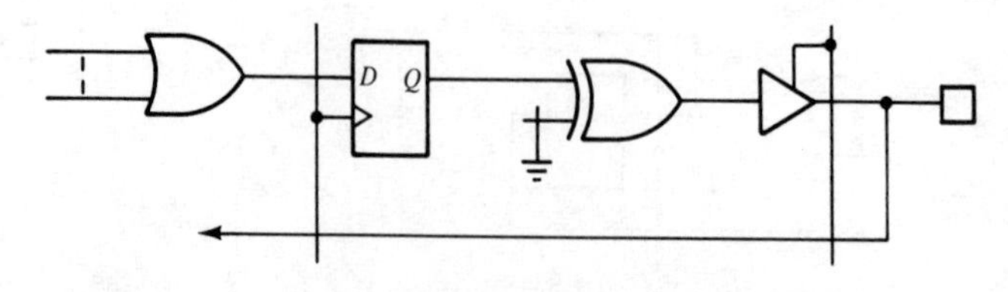


(w) Registered I/O, global enable.

**Figure A.5** (cont.) Generic PAL output cell modes.

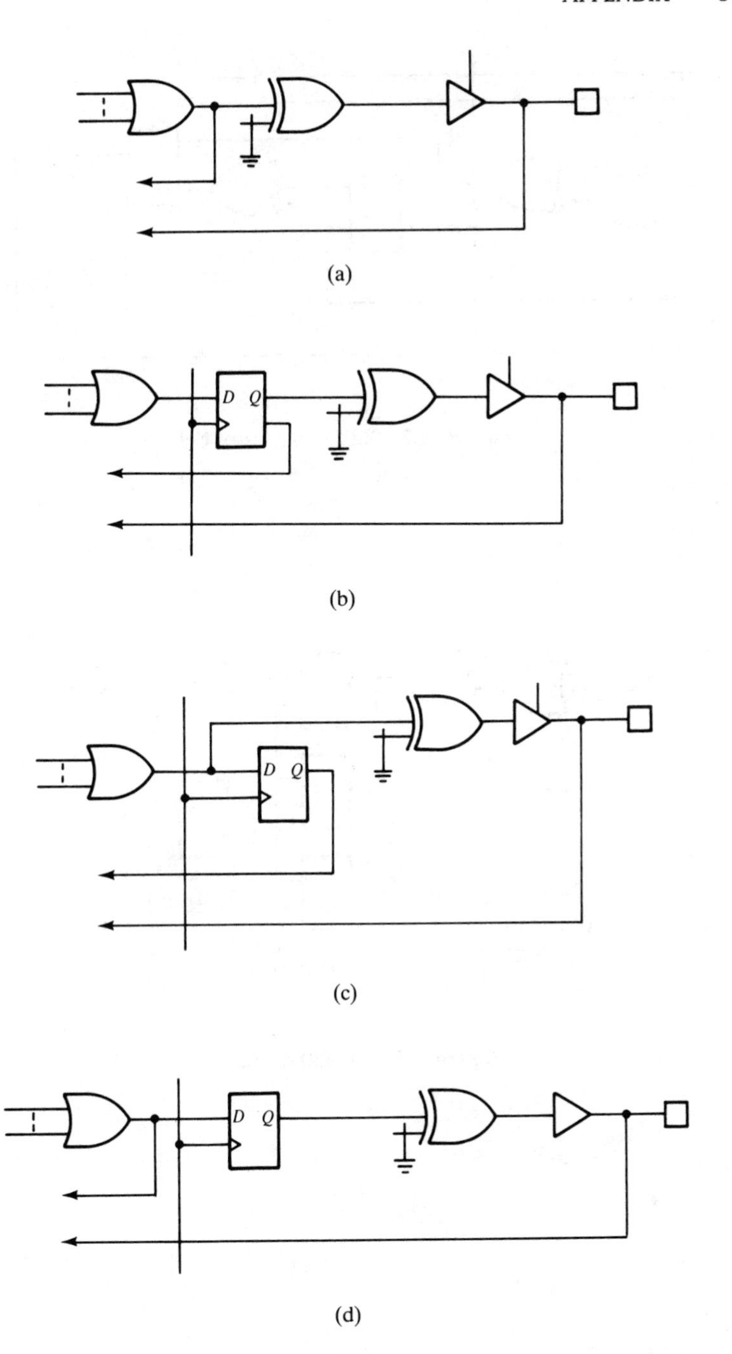


**Figure A.6** (a) Combinational output and feedback *or* combinational feedback and input. (b) Registered output and feedback *or* registered feedback and input. (c) Combinational I/O and registered feedback. (d) Combinational feedback and registered I/O.

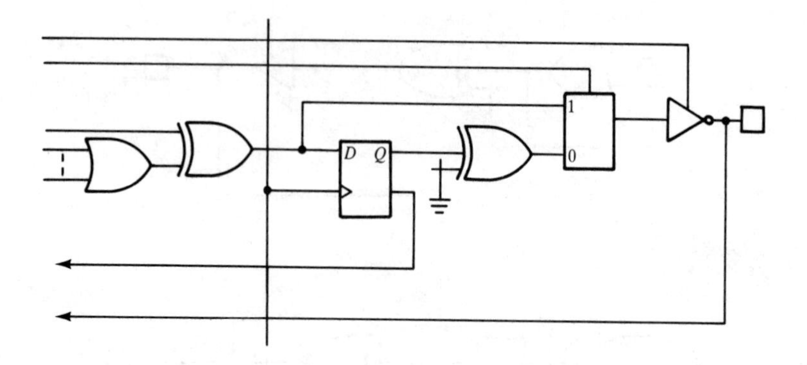


**Figure A.7** 32VX10 output cell.

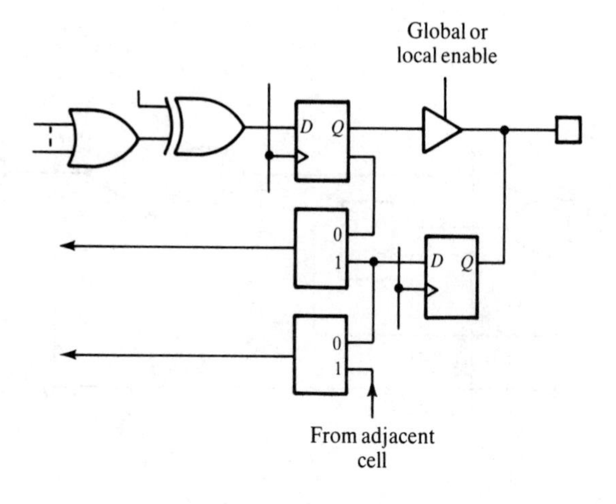


**Figure A.8** 7C330 output cell.

**Table A.1** PLA architectures.

| Name | No. of inputs | No. of outputs[1] | No. of I/Os | Max. no. of inputs | No. of products | No. of control terms | No. of pins | Year of disclosure | Notes |
|---|---|---|---|---|---|---|---|---|---|
| 8575/6 | 14 | 8 | – | 14 | 96 | – | 24 | 1973 | 2,3 |
| IM5200 | 14 | 8 | – | 14 | 48 | – | 24 | 1975 | |
| PLS100/1 | 16 | 8 | – | 16 | 48 | – | 28 | 1975 | 2,4 |
| 74S330/1 | 12 | 6 | – | 12 | 50 | – | 20 | 1976 | 2,5,6 |
| 82S106/7 | 16 | 8 | – | 16 | 48 | – | 28 | 1977 | 2,6,7 |
| PLS152/3 | 8 | – | 10 | 17 | 32 | 10 AND | 20 | 1980 | 8 |
| TIFPLA839/40 | 14 | 6 | – | 14 | 32 | – | 24 | 1981 | 2,9 |
| 100459 | 16 | $8+\overline{8}$ | – | 16 | 24 | – | 64 | 1983 | 10 |
| PLS161 | 12 | 8 | – | 12 | 48 | – | 24 | 1983 | 4 |
| PLS173 | 12 | – | 10 | 21 | 32 | 10 AND | 24 | 1985 | 8 |
| PLHS473 | 11 | 2 | 9 | 20 | 24 | 11 OR | 24 | 1985 | 8 |
| PEEL253 | 8 | – | 10 | 17 | 42 | 10 OR | 20 | 1987 | 8 |
| PEEL273 | 12 | – | 10 | 21 | 42 | 10 OR | 24 | 1987 | 8 |

**Table A.2(a)** Sequencer architectures.

| Name | No. of inputs | No. of unregistered | | No. of registers | | | No. of products | Complement array | Control terms | No. of pins | Year of disclosure | Notes |
|---|---|---|---|---|---|---|---|---|---|---|---|---|
| | | Outputs | I/Os[1] | Buried | State+ output[1] | Output | | | | | | |
| TMS2000 | 17 | 18 | – | 8J–K | – | – | 60 | No | – | 40 | 1970 | 2 |
| TMS2200 | 13 | 10 | – | 5J–K | – | – | 72 | No | – | 28 | 1970 | 2 |
| HPLA-0174 | 19 | 16 | – | 12D | – | – | 70 | No | – | 28 | 1975 | 2 |
| PLS104/5 | 16 | – | – | 6S–R | – | 8S–R | 48 | Yes | – | 28 | 1977 | 3,4 |
| PLS154/5 | 4 | – | 8(P) | – | 4J–K/D(P) | – | 32 | Yes | 11 | 20 | 1980 | 4,5,6,7 |
| PLS156/7 | 4 | – | 6(P) | – | 6J–K/D(P) | – | 32 | Yes | 11 | 20 | 1980 | 4,5,6,7 |
| PLS158/9 | 4 | – | 4(P) | – | 8J–K/D(P) | – | 32 | Yes | 11 | 20 | 1980 | 4,5,6,7 |
| 74PL333/5 | 12 | – | – | 4J–K | – | 6D | 32 | No | – | 24 | 1981 | 4,5,8,9 |
| PLS167 | 14 | – | – | 6S–R | 2S–R | 4S–R | 48 | Yes | – | 24 | 1983 | 3 |
| PLS168 | 12 | – | – | 6S–R | 4S–R | 4S–R | 48 | Yes | – | 24 | 1984 | 3 |
| PLS179 | 8 | – | 4(P) | – | 8J–K/D(L) | – | 32 | Yes | 11 | 24 | 1986 | 4,5,6,7 |
| PSG507 | 13 | See Note 11 | – | 8S–R | – | 8S–R | 80 | No | 6 | 24 | 1986 | 10,11,12,13 |
| 21F10 | 11 | – | See Note 11 | – | 10D(P) | – | 32 | No | 12 | 24 | 1985 | 5,11,14,15,16,17 |
| GAL6001 | 11 | – | 10 | 8D–E | 10D–E(L) | – | 64 | No | 11 | 24 | 1986 | 18,19,20,21,22 |
| PLUS405 | 16 | – | – | 8S–R/ J–K | – | 8S–R/ J–K | 64 | 2 | – | 28 | 1986 | 23,24 |
| PLS506 | 13 | See Note 11 | – | 16S–R | – | 8S–R | 97 | Yes | – | 24 | 1987 | 11,12 |

**Table A.2(b)** Sequencers with 2-bit decoders.

| Name | No. of inputs | No. of unregistered | | No. of registers | | | No. of products | Comple-ment array | Control terms | No. of pins | Year of disclosure | Notes |
|---|---|---|---|---|---|---|---|---|---|---|---|---|
| | | Outputs | I/Os[1] | Buried | State+ output[1] | Output | | | | | | |
| IBM PLA | 18 | – | – | 13J–K | – | 16D | 70 | No | – | 48 | 1974 | 2 |
| μPB450 | 24 | – | – | 16J–K | – | 16D | 72 | No | – | 48 | 1985 | 25 |

**Table A.3(a)** 20-pin combinational PAL devices.

| Name | No. of inputs | No. of outputs | No. of I/Os | Max. no. of inputs | Product term distribution | No. of control products | Output polarity | Year of disclosure | Notes |
|---|---|---|---|---|---|---|---|---|---|
| 10H8 | 10 | 8 | – | 10 | 8(2) | – | H | 1977 | 1 |
| 10L8 | 10 | 8 | – | 10 | 8(2) | – | L | 1977 | 1 |
| 10P8 | 10 | 8 | – | 10 | 8(2) | – | P | 1983 | 1,7 |
| 12H6 | 12 | 6 | – | 12 | 4,4(2),4 | – | H | 1977 | 1 |
| 12L6 | 12 | 6 | – | 12 | 4,4(2),4 | – | L | 1977 | 1 |
| 12P6 | 12 | 6 | – | 12 | 4,4(2),4 | – | P | 1983 | 1,7 |
| 14H4 | 14 | 4 | – | 14 | 4(4) | – | H | 1977 | 1 |
| 14L4 | 14 | 4 | – | 14 | 4(4) | – | L | 1977 | 1 |
| 14P4 | 14 | 4 | – | 14 | 4(4) | – | P | 1983 | 1,7 |
| 16H2 | 16 | 2 | – | 16 | 2(8) | – | H | 1977 | 1 |
| 16L2 | 16 | 2 | – | 16 | 2(8) | – | L | 1977 | 1 |
| 16P2 | 16 | 2 | – | 16 | 2(8) | – | P | 1983 | 1,7 |
| 16C1 | 16 | $1+\bar{1}$ | – | 16 | 16 | – | H and L | 1977 | 1,2 |
| 16H8 | 10 | 2 | 6 | 16 | 8(7) | 8 | H | 1982 | |
| 16HD8 | 10 | 8 | – | 16 | 8(8) | – | H | 1982 | 1,3 |
| 16HE8 | 10 | 2 | 6 | 16 | 8(8) | – | H/P | 1983 | 4 |
| 16L8 | 10 | 2 | 6 | 16 | 8(7) | 8 | L | 1977 | 5,6 |
| 16LD8 | 10 | 8 | – | 16 | 8(8) | – | L | 1982 | 1,3 |
| 16LE8 | 10 | 2 | 6 | 16 | 8(8) | – | L/P | 1983 | 4 |
| 16P8 | 10 | 2 | 6 | 16 | 8(7) | 8 | P | 1983 | |
| 16SP8 | 10 | 2 | 6 | 16 | 7,3(7\|7),7 | 8 | P | 1986 | |
| 18P8 | 10 | – | 8 | 18 | 8(8) | 8 | P | 1984 | |
| EPL10P8 | 10 | 8 | – | 10 | 8(2\|2) | – | P | 1984 | 7,8 |
| EPL12P6 | 12 | 6 | – | 12 | 4\|4,4(2\|2),4\|4 | – | P | 1984 | 7,8 |
| EPL14P4 | 14 | 4 | – | 14 | 4(4\|4) | – | P | 1984 | 7,8 |
| EPL16P2 | 16 | 2 | – | 16 | 2(8\|8) | – | P | 1984 | 7,8 |
| EPL16P8 | 10 | 2 | 6 | 16 | 4(7\|7) | 8 | P | 1984 | 7,9 |

**Table A.3(b)** Programmable multiplexers.

| Name | No. of inputs | No. of outputs | No. of I/Os | Max. no. of inputs | Product term distribution | No. of control products | Output polarity | Year of disclosure | Notes |
|---|---|---|---|---|---|---|---|---|---|
| R29693 | 10 | 4 | – | 10 | N/A | – | L | 1978 | 10 |

**Table A.4(a)** 24-pin combinational PAL devices.

| Name | No. of inputs | No. of outputs | No. of I/Os | Max. no. of inputs | Product term distribution[1] | No. of control products | Output polarity[2] | Year of disclosure | Notes |
|---|---|---|---|---|---|---|---|---|---|
| 12H10 | 12 | 10 | – | 12 | 10(2) | – | H | 1984 | 1 |
| 12L10 | 12 | 10 | – | 12 | 10(2) | – | L | 1981 | 1 |
| 12P10 | 12 | 10 | – | 12 | 10(2) | – | P | 1983 | 1 |
| 14H8 | 14 | 8 | – | 14 | 4,6(2),2 | – | H | 1984 | 1 |
| 14L8 | 14 | 8 | – | 14 | 4,6(2),4 | – | L | 1981 | 1 |
| 14P8 | 14 | 8 | – | 14 | 4,6(2),4 | – | P | 1985 | 1 |
| 16H6 | 16 | 6 | – | 16 | 2(4),2(2),2(4) | – | H | 1984 | 1 |
| 16L6 | 16 | 6 | – | 16 | 2(4),2(2),2(4) | – | L | 1981 | 1 |
| 16P6 | 16 | 6 | – | 16 | 2(4),2(2),2(4) | – | P | 1985 | 1 |
| 18H4 | 18 | 4 | – | 18 | 6,2(4),6 | – | H | 1984 | 1 |
| 18L4 | 18 | 4 | – | 18 | 6,2(4),6 | – | L | 1981 | 1 |
| 18P4 | 18 | 4 | – | 18 | 6,2(4),6 | – | P | 1985 | 1 |
| 20H2 | 20 | 2 | – | 20 | 2(8) | – | H | 1984 | 1 |
| 20L2 | 20 | 2 | – | 20 | 2(8) | – | L | 1981 | 1 |
| 20P2 | 20 | 2 | – | 20 | 2(8) | – | P | 1985 | 1 |
| 20C1 | 20 | $1+\bar{1}$ | – | 20 | 16 | – | H and L | 1981 | 1,2 |
| 20L8 | 14 | 2 | 6 | 20 | 8(7) | 8 | L | 1982 | 7 |
| 20P8 | 14 | 2 | 6 | 20 | 8(7) | 8 | P | 1985 | |
| 20L10 | 12 | 2 | 8 | 20 | 10(3) | 10 | L | 1981 | |
| 20S10 | 12 | 2 | 8 | 20 | $7,4(7 \mid 7),7$ | 10 | P | 1983 | |
| 22P10 | 12 | – | 10 | 22 | 10(8) | 10 | P | 1986 | |
| 22XP10 | 12 | – | 10 | 22 | $10(2 \mid 6)$ | 10 | P | 1986 | 3 |

**Table A.4(b)** ECL devices.

| Name | No. of inputs | No. of outputs | No. of I/Os | Max. no. of inputs | Product term distribution[1] | No. of control products | Output polarity[2] | Year of disclosure | Notes |
|---|---|---|---|---|---|---|---|---|---|
| 20P8 | 12 | – | 8 | 20 | 4(4\|4) | 8 | P | 1983 | 4 |
| 16P8 | 12 | 4 | 4 | 16 | 8(8) | 4 | P | 1985 | 4,5 |
| 16P4 | 16 | 4 | – | 16 | 4(8) | – | P | 1987 | 4,5 |
| 12C4 | 12 | $4+\overline{4}$ | – | 12 | 4(8) | – | H,L | 1988 | 4,5 |
| 16C4 | 16 | $4+\overline{4}$ | – | 16 | 4(8) | – | H,L | 1989 | 4,5,6 |

**Table A.5** Address decoder/FPGA architectures.

| Name | No. of inputs | No. of outputs | No. of I/Os | Max. no. of inputs | No. of products/ output | No. of control products | Output polarity | No. of pins | Year of disclosure | Notes |
|---|---|---|---|---|---|---|---|---|---|---|
| PLS102/3 | 16 | 9 | – | 16 | 1 | – | P | 28 | 1977 | 1 |
| PLS150/1 | 6 | – | 12 | 17 | 1 | 3 | P | 20 | 1980 | 2 |
| HPL-77061 | 12 | 4 | 6 | 18 | 2 | – | P | 24 | 1983 | 3 |
| PLS162 | 16 | 5 | – | 16 | 1 | – | P | 24 | 1984 | 1 |
| PLS163 | 12 | 9 | – | 12 | 1 | – | P | 24 | 1984 | 1 |
| HPL-82C339 | 11 | 8 | – | 11 | 1 | – | L | 24 | 1984 | 4,5,6,7 |
| HPL-82C338 | 8 | 8 | – | 8 | 1 | – | L | 20 | 1985 | 4,7,8 |
| HPL-82C138 | 7 | 4 | – | 7 | 1 | – | L | 16 | 1985 | 4,6,7,9 |
| HPL-82C139 | 7 | 4 | – | 7 | 1 | – | L | 16 | 1985 | 4,6,7,10 |
| PAL6L16 | 6 | 16 | – | 6 | 1 | – | L | 24 | 1985 | 4 |
| PAL8L14 | 8 | 14 | – | 8 | 1 | – | L | 24 | 1985 | 4 |
| TIFPGA529 | 8 | 8 | – | 8 | 1 | – | L | 20 | 1985 | 11 |
| TIBPAD16N8 | 10 | 2 | 6 | 16 | 1 | 8 | L | 20 | 1987 | 12 |
| TIBPAD18N8 | 10 | – | 8 | 18 | 1 | – | L | 20 | 1987 | 13 |
| 85C508 | 16 | 8 | – | 16 | 1 | – | L | 28 | 1988 | 14,15 |

**Table A.6(a)** 20-pin synchronous registered PAL devices.

<table>
<tr><th>Name</th><th>No. of inputs</th><th>No. of registers with feedback</th><th>No. of I/Os</th><th>Max. no. of inputs</th><th>Product term distribution</th><th>No. of control products</th><th>Output polarity</th><th>Year of disclosure</th><th>Notes</th></tr>
<tr><td>16R8</td><td>8</td><td>8</td><td>–</td><td>16</td><td>8(8)</td><td>–</td><td>L</td><td>1977</td><td>1</td></tr>
<tr><td>16RP8</td><td>8</td><td>8</td><td>–</td><td>16</td><td>8(8)</td><td>–</td><td>P</td><td>1983</td><td>1</td></tr>
<tr><td>16R6</td><td>8</td><td>6</td><td>2</td><td>16</td><td>7,6(8),7</td><td>2</td><td>L</td><td>1977</td><td>1</td></tr>
<tr><td>16RP6</td><td>8</td><td>6</td><td>2</td><td>16</td><td>7,6(8),7</td><td>2</td><td>P</td><td>1983</td><td>1</td></tr>
<tr><td>16R4</td><td>8</td><td>4</td><td>4</td><td>16</td><td>2(7),4(8),2(7)</td><td>4</td><td>L</td><td>1977</td><td>1</td></tr>
<tr><td>16RP4</td><td>8</td><td>4</td><td>4</td><td>16</td><td>2(7),4(8),2(7)</td><td>4</td><td>P</td><td>1983</td><td>1</td></tr>
<tr><td>16X4</td><td>8</td><td>4</td><td>4</td><td>16</td><td>See Note 3</td><td>4</td><td>L</td><td>1978</td><td>1,2,3</td></tr>
<tr><td>16A4</td><td>8</td><td>4</td><td>4</td><td>16</td><td>See Note 4</td><td>4</td><td>L</td><td>1978</td><td>1,2,4</td></tr>
<tr><td>HPL-77000</td><td>10</td><td>8</td><td>–</td><td>18</td><td>8(4)</td><td>16</td><td>P</td><td>1982</td><td>5,6,7</td></tr>
<tr><td>EPL16RP8</td><td>8</td><td>8</td><td>–</td><td>16</td><td>4(8|8)</td><td>–</td><td>L</td><td>1985</td><td>1,8,9</td></tr>
<tr><td>EPL16RP6</td><td>8</td><td>6</td><td>2</td><td>16</td><td>(7|8),2(8|8),(8|7)</td><td>2</td><td>L</td><td>1985</td><td>1,8,9</td></tr>
<tr><td>EPL16RP4</td><td>8</td><td>4</td><td>4</td><td>16</td><td>(7|7),2(8|8),(7|7)</td><td>4</td><td>L</td><td>1985</td><td>1,8,9</td></tr>
</table>

**Table A.6(b)** 20-pin synchronous generic PALs.

| Name | No. of inputs | No. of output cells | Output cell modes[10] | Max. no. of inputs | Product distribution | Year of disclosure | Notes |
|---|---|---|---|---|---|---|---|
| EP300* | 10 | 8 | i,l,o,r,t,v | 18 | 8(8) | 1984 | 9,11,12 |
| 16V8 | 10 | 8 | p,t *or* (c),t *or* a,b | 16 | 8(8) | 1984 | 9,11,13,14 |
| 16F8 | 10 | 8 | o,p,t,u,v,w | 18 | 4(8\|8 *or* 6\|10 *or* 3\|13 *or* 1\|15) | 1986 | 11,13,14,15 |
| 23S8 | 9 | 4 (See Note 16) | o,r,t,v | 17 | 2(6),6(8),4(10),2(12) | 1986 | 12,17,18 |
| 18CV10 | 8 | 10 | o,t | 18 | 2(8),2(10),2(12),2(14),2(16) | 1986 | 11,12 |
| 18V8 | 10 | 8 | a,b,p,t | 18 | 8(8) | 1987 | 9,11,13 |
| 18U8 | 10 | 8 | o,p,t,u | 18 | 8(8) | 1987 | 9,11,12,13 |

* Also known as 5C030 and 18CV8

**Table A.7(a)** 24-pin synchronous registered PAL devices.

| Name | No. of inputs | No. of registers with feedback | No. of I/Os | Max. no. of inputs | Product term distribution | No. of control products | Output polarity | Year of disclosure | Notes |
|---|---|---|---|---|---|---|---|---|---|
| 20R4 | 12 | 4 | 4 | 16 | 2(7),4(8),2(7) | 4 | L | 1982 | 1,2 |
| 20RS4 | 10 | 4 | 6 | 16 | 7,(7\|7),2(8\|8),(7\|7),7 | 6 | P | 1983 | 1 |
| 20RP4 | 10 | 4 | 6 | 16 | 10(8) | 6 | P | 1986 | 1 |
| 20X4 | 10 | 4 | 6 | 16 | 3(3),4(2,2),3(3) | 6 | L | 1981 | 1,3 |
| 20XRP4 | 10 | 4 | 6 | 16 | 3(8),4(2,6),3(8) | 6 | P | 1986 | 1,4 |
| R19R4 | 11 | 4 | 4 | 15 | 2(7),4(8),2(7) | 4 | L | 1982 | 1,5,6 |
| T19R4 | 11 | 4 | 4 | 15 | 2(7),4(8),2(7) | 4 | L | 1982 | 1,5,7 |
| 20R6 | 12 | 6 | 2 | 14 | 7,6(8),7 | 2 | L | 1982 | 1,2 |
| 20RP6 | 10 | 6 | 4 | 14 | 10(8) | 4 | P | 1986 | 1 |
| 20XRP6 | 10 | 6 | 4 | 14 | 2(8),6(2,6),2(8) | 4 | P | 1986 | 1,4 |
| R19R6 | 11 | 6 | 2 | 13 | 7,6(8),7 | 2 | L | 1982 | 1,5,6 |
| T19R6 | 11 | 6 | 2 | 13 | 7,6(8),7 | 2 | L | 1982 | 1,5,7 |
| 20R8 | 12 | 8 | – | 12 | 8(8) | – | L | 1982 | 1,2 |
| 20RS8 | 10 | 8 | 2 | 12 | 7,4(8\|8),7 | 2 | P | 1983 | 1 |
| 20RP8 | 10 | 8 | 2 | 12 | 10(8) | 2 | P | 1986 | 1 |
| 20X8 | 10 | 8 | 2 | 12 | 3,8(2,2),3 | 2 | L | 1981 | 1,3 |
| 20XRP8 | 10 | 8 | 2 | 12 | 8,8(2,6),8 | 2 | P | 1986 | 1,4 |
| R19R8 | 11 | 8 | – | 11 | 8(8) | – | L | 1982 | 1,5,6 |
| T19R8 | 11 | 8 | – | 11 | 8(8) | – | L | 1982 | 1,5,7 |
| 20RS10 | 10 | 10 | – | 10 | 8,4(8\|8),8 | – | P | 1983 | 1 |
| 20RP10 | 10 | 10 | – | 10 | 10(8) | – | P | 1986 | 1 |
| 20X10 | 10 | 10 | – | 10 | 10(2,2) | – | L | 1981 | 1,3 |
| 20XRP10 | 10 | 10 | – | 10 | 10(2,6) | – | P | 1986 | 1,4 |
| R19L8 | 13 | 2 | 6 | 19 | 8(7) | 8 | L | 1982 | 5,6,8 |
| T19L8 | 13 | 2 | 6 | 19 | 8(7) | 8 | L | 1982 | 5,7,8 |

**Table A.7(b)** ECL devices.

| Name | No. of inputs | No. of registers with feedback | No. of I/Os | Max. no. of inputs | Product term distribution | No. of control products | Output polarity | Year of disclosure | Notes |
|---|---|---|---|---|---|---|---|---|---|
| 16RC8 | 8 | 8 | – | 8 | 8(8) | – | P | 1986 | 1,9,10,11 |
| 16LC8 | 8 | 8 | – | 8 | 8(8) | – | P | 1986 | 1,9,10,11,13 |
| 16RD8 | 8 | 8 | – | 8 | 8(8) | – | P | 1986 | 1,10,11,12 |
| 16LD8 | 8 | 8 | – | 8 | 8(8) | – | P | 1986 | 1,10,11,12,13 |
| 16RC4 | 8 | 4 | 4 | 12 | 8(8) | – | P | 1986 | 1,9,10,11 |
| 16LC4 | 8 | 4 | 4 | 12 | 8(8) | – | P | 1986 | 1,9,10,11,13 |
| 16RD4 | 8 | 4 | 4 | 12 | 8(8) | – | P | 1986 | 1,10,11,12 |
| 16LD4 | 8 | 4 | 4 | 12 | 8(8) | – | P | 1986 | 1,10,11,12,13 |
| 16RM4 | 12 | – | 4 | 16 | 4(8) | – | P | 1987 | 10,11,12,14,15,16 |
| 16LM4 | 12 | – | 4 | 16 | 4(8) | – | P | 1987 | 10,11,12,13,14,15,16 |

**Table A.7(c)** 24-pin synchronous generic PALs.

| Name | No. of inputs | No. of output cells | Output cell modes[17] | Max. no. of inputs | Product distribution | Year of disclosure | Notes |
|---|---|---|---|---|---|---|---|
| 22V10 | 12 | 10 | o,t | 22 | 2(8),2(10),2(12),2(14),2(16) | 1982 | 2,18,19 |
| 20V8 | 12 | 8 | p,t *or* c,t *or* a,b | 20 | 8(8) | 1984 | 18,20,21,22 |
| 22RX10 | 12 | 10 | c,d,i,j,l,m,o,t, m,u,w | 22 | 10(4,4) | 1985 | 18,19,20,21,23 |
| 32V10 | 12 | 10 | See Figure A.6 | 22 | 2(8),2(10),2(12),2(14),2(16) | 1985 | 18,19,21 |
| 22VP10 | 12 | 10 | o,t,v | 22 | 2(8),2(10),2(12),2(14),2(16) | 1985 | 18,19 |
| 22RX8 | 14 | 8 | o,t | 22 | 8(1,8) | 1985 | 18,24,25 |
| 32VX10 | 12 | 10 | See Figure A.7 | 22 | 2(1,8),2(1,10),2(1,12),2(1,14),2(1,16) | 1985 | 18,19 |
| 20G10 | 12 | 10 | o,p,t,u | 22 | 10(8) | 1985 | 18,19,20,21 |
| 16Z8 | 10 | 8 | p,t *or* c,t *or* a,b | 16 | 8(8) | 1986 | 18,21,22,26 |
| PLC20V8 | 12 | 8 | a,b,p,t | 20 | 8(9) | 1987 | 18,20,21 |
| 29M16 | 5 | { 8 single feedback<br>8 dual feedback | o,p,r,s,t,u,v,w<br>See Figure A.6 | 21 | 8(8),4(12),4(16) | 1987 | 18,20,21,25,27,28,29 |

**Table A.7(d)** ECL devices.

| Name | No. of inputs | No. of output cells | Output cell modes[17] | Max. no. of inputs | Product distribution | Year of disclosure | Notes |
|---|---|---|---|---|---|---|---|
| 20EV8 | 12 | 8 | o,r,t,v | 20 | 4(8),4(12) | 1985 | 10,11,18,19 |
| 20EG8 | 12 | 8 | o,r,t,v | 20 | 4(8),4(12) | 1985 | 10,11,13,18,19 |
| 20G8 | 12 | 8 | I/O and registered I/O | 20 | 4(4\|4) | 1986 | 10,12,30 |

**Table A.7(e)** Larger synchronous generic PALs.

| Name | No. of inputs | No. of output cells | Output cell modes[17] | Max. no. of inputs | Product distribution | No. of pins | Year of disclosure | Notes |
|---|---|---|---|---|---|---|---|---|
| 7C330 | 11 | 12 (See Note 32) | See Figure A.8 | 23 | 2(1,8),3(1,10),3(1,12),3(1,14),3(1,16),3(1,18) | 28 | 1986 | 18,20,21,31,32,33 |
| 7C332 | 13 | 12 | See Note 35 | 25 | 2(1,8),2(1,10),2(1,12),2(1,14),2(1,16),2(1,18) | 28 | 1986 | 7,8,20,21,27,28,30,34,35 |
| 26V12 | 14 | 12 | o,r,t,v | 26 | 4(8),2(10),2(12),2(14),2(16) | 28 | 1988 | 19,20,28,30 |
| 24V10 | 16 | 10 | p,t *or* (c),t *or* a,b | 24 | 10(8) | 28 | 1989 | 18,20,21,22 |
| 32R16 | 16 | 16 | I/O and registered I/O | 32 | 8(8\|8) | 40 | 1983 | 36 |
| 64R32 | 32 | 32 | I/O and registered I/O | 64 | 16(8\|8) | 84 | 1983 | 37 |
| EP1200 | 12 | 24 (See Note 32) | c,o,t,v | 36 | 6(4),4(6),12(8),4(10),2(12) | 40 | 1984 | 7,20,30,32,38,39,40 |

**Table A.8** PAL-structured PLDs with programmable clocks.

| Product name | Clock |
|---|---|
| 16RA8, 20RA10 | 20- and 24-pin PALs with bypassable D flip–flops. One product drives each clock. |
| EP610, EP910, EP1810 | 24-, 40- and 68-pin EPLDs with flip–flops configurable as D, J–K, R–S or T types. One product per clock, or global clock. |
| 7C331 | 28-pin EPLD with output cell similar to 7C330, but with one product driving clock. |
| 29MA16 | 24-pin EPLD similar to 29M16 but with optional local clocking from one product. |
| V750, V850, V2500 | 24-, 28- and 40-pin EPLDs with two D flip–flops per output cell, each driven by one term. |
| 5AC312 (EP512), 5AC324 | 24- and 40-pin EPLDs with global or local clocking of flip–flops configurable as D or T types. Two products per clock. |
| 22IP6 | 24-pin PAL with structure as shown in Figure 9.20. Nine products allocatable between pairs of S, R or $T_1$, $T_2$ inputs. |

**Notes applying to all tables**

(1) Where different part numbers exist for the same architecture, the generic or best known one is given. Prefixes have been omitted whenever this would not cause confusion.

(2) All devices have 3-state outputs unless otherwise indicated.

(3) All devices are 'one-time' programmable unless otherwise indicated.

(4) Product term distribution refers to numbers of logical products fed to each OR gate. $m(n)$ means $m$ OR gates each with $n$ inputs. $m(n|n)$ means $m$ pairs of gates each fed by $2n$ products. This is applicable to devices with product steering or certain special types of output cell. (See Figure 5.5.)

(5) 'P' denotes programmable output polarity.
'H' denotes high output polarity.
'L' denotes low output polarity.

**Notes for Table A.1**

(1) All devices have programmable output polarities unless otherwise indicated.

(2) Open-collector version available.

(3) Mask programmed device.

(4) One output enable pin provided.

(5) One input convertible to output enable.

(6) Output disabled if no product active.

(7) Output pin provided indicating that a product is active.

(8) Erasable version available.

(9) Two ANDed output enables provided.

(10) An ECL device.

**Notes for Table A.2(a) and Table A.2(b)**

(1) Polarity indicated where not H. (P = programmable.)

(2) Mask programmed device.

(3) Preset/output enable pin.

(4) Open-collector version available.

(5) Output enable pin.

(6) Flip–flops in two groups for P,R, output enable and load control.

(7) Flip–flops loadable from pins.

(8) State register clock and reset from OR array.

(9) Outputs are latched.

(10) Contains a 6-bit counter controllable by sequencer.

(11) Output registers programmably bypassable.

(12) Output enable pin shared with an input.

(13) Clock polarity programmable.

(14) Programmably bypassable input registers.

(15) Input register clock pin, 2 state/output register clock pins.

(16) Clocks shared with inputs.

(17) Synchronous and asynchronous initialize terms.

(18) Programmably bypassable input registers/latches.

(19) Ouputs and state registers programmably bypassable.

(20) Flip–flops clocked individually or from common clock.

(21) Input clock shared with input.

(22) An erasable device.

(23) Programmable preset/resets shared with output enable pin.

(24) Two clocks, one shared with an input.

(25) State flip–flops connected in scan path for testing purposes.

**Notes for Table A.3(a) and Table A.3(b)**

(1) Totem pole outputs.

(2) The two outputs are complementary.

(3) Six outputs have internal feedback to the AND array. The ‘D’ signifies ‘dedicated outputs’, that is none can be disabled and used as external inputs.

(4) Outputs have programmable polarity, I/O 3-state buffers fuse programmable.

(5) Once the most popular 20-pin combinational PAL device.

(6) Available in an erasable version.

(7) ‘EPL’ (Electronically Programmable Logic) devices are erasable.

(8) The output cell is shown in Figure A.2. In the first mode, the EPL is equivalent to the PAL device of the same name.

(9) The output cell is shown in Figure A.3. In the first mode, the EPL is equivalent to the PAL device of the same name.

(10) Structure is shown in Figure 3.33.

**Notes for Table A.4(a) and Table A.4(b)**

(1) Totem pole outputs.

(2) The two outputs are complementary.

(3) The output structure is shown in Figure A.4.

(4) ECL 10KH compatible.

(5) ECL 100K compatible.

(6) A 28-pin device.

(7) Erasable version available.

**Notes for Table A.5**

(1) One output enable pin.

(2) Each control term able to programmably control a bank of 4 I/Os.

(3) One input convertible to output enable. Each output can be either permanently enabled, disabled or under the control of the aformentioned pin.

(4) Totem pole outputs.

(5) Address inputs divided: 7 ms bits|2 ls bits|high bank bit|low bank bit. Outputs in 2 4-bit banks, each of which is decode of ls address bits, and selected if ms bits match programmed address.

(6) 'Match' output true if ms bits equal to programmed address.

(7) Inputs latched by 'ALE' input. Outputs conditional on 'select' input.

(8) Address inputs divided: 5 ms bits|3 ls bits. One of 8 outputs asserted according to ls bits, and if ms bits match programmed address.

(9) Address inputs divided: 5 ms bits|2 ls bits. One of 4 outputs asserted according to ls bits, and if ms bits match programmed address.

(10) Address inputs divided: 4 ms bits|1 ls bit|high bank bit|low bank bit. Outputs in 2 2-bit banks, each of which is decode of ls address bits, and selected if ms bits match programmed address.

(11) Outputs split into two banks of four, each one controllable by an enable pin.

(12) Has same I/O configuration as 16L8 PAL. This is the fastest device in the table.

(13) High speed feedback path from each output.

(14) Erasable device.

(15) Outputs latched by ALE input.

**Notes for Table A.6(a) and Table A.6(b)**

(1) One output enable pin.

(2) 2-bit input decoders for each of four input/feedback pairs.

(3) Device illustrated in Figure 8.10.

(4) Device as shown in Figure 8.10, but with additional preprogrammed products.

(5) Inputs and feedbacks decoded in pairs.

(6) Outputs are latched.

(7) Latch enables and output polarities controlled by products.

(8) Product distribution as shown in Figure A.3.

(9) An erasable device.

(10) Output cell modes given in Figure A.5.

(11) Clock pin shared with input.

(12) Global synchronous preset and asynchronous reset products.

(13) Output enable pin shared with input.

(14) One less product per output available if local enable used.

(15) Split clocking; second clock pin shared with output enable.

(16) In addition to output cells, has four registered I/Os and six buried registers.

(17) Output enable terms have programmable polarity.

(18) Product term for enabling external observation of buried register state.

**Notes for Tables A.7(a)–(e)**

(1) One output enable pin.

(2) Erasable version available.

(3) Structure shown in Figure 3.26.

(4) Product term configuration as shown in Figure A.4.

(5) One input clock/latch enable pin.

(6) Inputs bypassably registered.

(7) Inputs bypassably latched.

(8) The 2 outputs are unregistered.

(9) 2 clock/latch enable pins, signals ORed together.

(10) Available in 10KH version.

(11) Available in 100K version.

(12) Split register, 2 clock/latch enable pins.

(13) Outputs latched.

(14) Additional common clock/latch enable.

(15) One reset pin.

(16) I/Os are registered.

(17) Unless otherwise specified, cell modes given in Figure A.5.

(18) One clock shared with input pin.

(19) Global synchronous preset and asynchronous reset products.

(20) An erasable device.

(21) Output enable shared with input pin.

(22) One less product per output if local enable used.

(23) Product configurable as shown in Figure A.2.

(24) Products configured as shown in Figure A.4.

(25) Global asynchronous preset and reset products.

(26) Four extra pins allow in-system reconfiguration.

(27) Registers can be programmed to be latches.

(28) Two clocks routable to any register/latch.

(29) Additional cell mode allows registered or latched input.

(30) 2 clocks shared with input pins.

(31) 3 clock pins.

(32) 4 buried registers.

(33) Set and reset products for all output flip–flops.

(34) Clocks have polarity control.

(35) Output cell like that of 7C330 but without output flip–flop.

(36) Registers in 2 banks. 2 clock, 2 output enable, 2 preload pins.

(37) Registers in 4 banks. 4 clock, 4 output enable, 4 preload pins.

(38) Output cells have input latches.

(39) Additional products available for allocation to some outputs.

(40) Global communication of inputs and some feedbacks, other feedbacks local.

# Bibliography

Acha J.I. and Calvo J. (1985). On the implementation of sequential circuits with PLA modules. *IEE Proc., Pt. E*, **132**(5) (September), 246–50

Advanced Micro Devices (1988). *PAL Device Handbook* and *PAL Device Data Book*

Agrawal P., Agrawal V.D. and Biswas N.N. (1985). Multiple output minimization. In *Proc. 22nd ACM–IEEE Design Automation Conf.*, pp. 674–80. Silver Spring MD: Computer Society Press

Aleksander I. (1978). Structure/function considerations for digital systems that contain polyfunctional elements. *IEE J. on Computers and Digital Techniques*, **1**(4) (October), 165–70

Alford R.C. (1989). *Programmable Logic Designer's Guide*. Indianapolis, IN: Sams

Almaini A.E.A. (1986). *Electronic Logic Systems*. Englewood Cliffs NJ: Prentice-Hall International

Amroun A. and Bolton M.J.P. (1989). Synthesis of controllers from Petri net descriptions and application of ELLA. In *Preprints of IMEC–IFIP Workshop on Applied Formal Methods for Correct VLSI Design*. Amsterdam: North-Holland

Arevalo Z. and Bredeson J.G. (1978). A method to simplify a Boolean function into a near minimum sum-of-products, for programmable logic arrays. *IEEE Trans. Computers*, **27**(11) (November), 1028–39

Aronson A. and Abrams L. (1986). *PFC. The Perfect PLD Compiler for Program Logic Devices*. Valley Data Sciences

Augin M., Boeri F. and André C. (1978). An algorithm for designing multiple Boolean functions: application to PLAs. *Digital Processes*, **4**(3–4), 215–30

Bartolomeus M. and De Man H. (1985). PRESTOL-II: yet another logic minimizer for programmed logic arrays. In *Proc. ISCAS 85*, Vol. 2, pp. 447–50. New York NY: IEEE

Barton M.H. (1985). *Notes on Structured Logic Design*. Report, Department of Electrical and Electronic Engineering, University of Bristol

Bell C.G., Grason J. and Newell A. (1972). *Designing Computers and Digital Systems*. Maynard MA: Digital Press

Benedek M. (1975). Developing large binary to BCD conversion structures. In *Proc. 3rd Sym. on Computer Arithmetic*, pp. 188–96. New York NY: IEEE

Bengali I. and Coli V. (1983). Testing algorithms for LSI PALs. In *Wescon/83 and Mini Micro West Conf. Record*, pp. 13/1 1–5. Los Angeles CA: Electronic Conventions

Bennett L.A.M. (1974). Flip–flops in functional memory. *Electronics Lett.*, **10**(10) (May 16), 177, 178

Bennett S. (1983). Programmable array traps control codes. *EDN*, **28**(1) (January), 283, 284, 288

Berstis V. (1989). The V compiler: automating hardware design. *IEEE Design and Test of Computers*, **6**(2) (April), 8–17

Bibilo P.N. and Yenin S.V. (1987). *Synthesis of Combinational Networks Using the Method of Functional Decomposition*. Minsk: Nauki i Tekhnika (in Russian)

Birkner J.M. (1978). Reduce random logic complexity by using arrays of fuse-programmable circuits. *Electronic Design*, **26**(17) (August 16), 98–105

Birkner J.M. and Chua H.-T. (1977). Programmable array logic circuit. *US Patent 4,124,899*, November 7, 1978 (filed May 23, 1977)

Biswas N.N. (1984). Computer aided minimization procedure for Boolean functions. In *Proc. ACM–IEEE 21st Design Automation Conf.*, pp. 699–702. Silver Spring MD: Computer Society Press

Biswas N.N. and Gurunath B. (1986). BANGALORE: an algorithm for the optimal minimization of programmable logic arrays. *International J. Electronics*, **60**(6) (June), 691–707

Blakeslee T.R. (1979). *Digital Design with Standard MSI and LSI* 2nd edn. New York NY: Wiley

Bolton M.J.P. (1985). Designing with programmable logic. *IEE Proc.*, Pts. E and I, **132**(2) (March–April), 73–85

Bolton M.J.P. (1986). Device-independent CAD for programmable logic. In *Proc. 6th Int. Conf. on Custom and Semicustom ICs*, pp. 41.0–41.4. Saffron Walden: Prodex

Bolton M.J.P. (1987a). *Handling Asynchronous Inputs in Synchronous PLA-Based State Machines*. Report, Department of Electrical and Electronic Engineering, University of Bristol, July

Bolton M.J.P. (1987b). Measurement of metastable behaviour in programmable logic devices. In *Proc. RELCOMEX '87. 4th Int. Conf. on Reliability and Exploitation of Computer Systems*, pp. 309–16. Technical University of Wroclaw, Poland

Bonn T.H. (1955). Transistor function tables. *US Patent 2,960,681*, November 15, 1960 (filed August 25, 1955)

Bostock G. (1987). *Programmable Logic Handbook*. London: Collins

Brayton R.K., Hachtel G.D., Hemachandra L.A., Newton A.R. and Sangiovanni-Vincentelli A.L.M. (1982). A comparison of logic minimization strategies using ESPRESSO: an APL program package for partitioned logic simulation. In *Proc. 1982 Int. Sym. on Circuits and Systems*, pp. 42–8. New York NY: IEEE

Brayton R.K., Hachtel G.D., McMullen C.T. and Sangiovanni-Vincentelli A.L.M. (1984). *Logic Minimization Algorithms for VLSI Synthesis*. Boston MA: Kluwer Academic Publishers

Bricaud P. and Campbell J. (1978). Multiple output PLA minimization: EMIN. In *1978 Wescon Technical Papers*, pp. 33/3 1–9. North Hollywood CA: Western Periodicals

Britt R. (1986). Programmable-logic sequencers solve timing problems. *EDN*, **31**(4) (February 20), 209–20

Brown D.R. and Rochester N. (1949). Rectifier networks for multiposition switching. *Proc. IRE*, **37**(2) (February), 139–47

Brown D.W. (1981). A state-machine synthesizer – SMS. In *Proc. 18th ACM IEEE Design Automation Conf.*, pp. 301–5. New York NY: IEEE

Browne M.C. and Clarke E.M. (1987). SML – a high level language for the design and verification of finite state machines. In *From HDL Descriptions to Guaranteed Correct Circuit Designs*, pp. 269–92. Amsterdam: North-Holland

Bul E.S. (1980). Implementation of switching functions by a network of programmable logic arrays. *Automatic Control and Computer Sciences*, **14**(2), 11–15

Burrier D. (1984). Advanced language leads to smoother designing with programmable logic. *Electronic Design*, **32**(16) (August 9), 247–52, 254, 256, 258

Burrows D.F. (1986). SHADE: Plessey's structured hardware design environment. In *Proc. 3rd Silicon Design Conf.*, pp. 105–14. London: Silicon Design

Buttner M. and Schussler H.-W. (1976). On structures for the implementation of the distributed arithmetic. *Nachrichtentechnische Z.*, **29**(6) (June) 472–7

Carr W.N. and Mize J.P. (1972). *MOS/LSI Design and Application*. New York NY: McGraw-Hill

Caruso G. (1988). Heuristic algorithm for the minimisation of generalised Boolean functions. *IEE Proc., Pt. E*, **135**(2) (March), 108–16

Cavlan N. (1976). *Signetics' Field Programmable Logic Arrays*. Signetics, February

Cavlan N. (1977). Structure and applications of a field programmable logic sequencer. In *1977 Wescon Technical Papers*, pp. 16/2 1–12. North Hollywood CA: Western Periodicals

Cavlan N. and Britt R. (1986). A hardware oriented approach simplifies designing with Signetics' programmable logic sequencers

Cavlan N. and Cline R. (1975). Field-PLAs simplify logic designs. *Electronic Design*, **23**(18) (September 1), 84–90

Ceruzzi P.E. (1983). *Reckoners*. Westport CT: Greenwood Press

Chang D. (1985). Designing a state machine using a PAL. *Midcon/85 Conf. Record*, pp. 3/0 1–7. Los Angeles CA: Electronic Conventions Management (also in *Wescon/85*, pp. 24/2 1–3)

Chow W.T. and Henrich W.H. (1957). Storage matrix. *US Patent 3,028,659*, April 10, 1962 (filed December 27, 1957)

Chu Y. (1962a). *Digital Computer Design Fundamentals*. New York NY: McGraw-Hill

Chu Y. (1962b). Matrix logic computer. *US Patent 3,230,355*, January 18, 1966 (filed December 4, 1962)

Chu Y. (1967). Building blocks for large-scale integration of logic cirucits. In *Proc. 1966 Int. Conf. on Microelectronics*, pp. 305–18. Oldenbourg

Clare C.R. (1973). *Designing Logic Systems Using State Machines*. New York NY: McGraw-Hill

Comer D.J. (1984). *Digital Logic and State Machine Design*. New York NY: Holt, Rinehart and Winston

Cook P.W. (1974). Array logic. In *Proc. 1974 IEEE Int. Sym. on Circuits and Systems*, pp. 215–19. New York NY: IEEE

Coppola A.J. (1986). An implementation of a state assignment heuristic. In *Proc. 23rd ACM–IEEE Design Automation Conf.*, pp. 334–8. Washington DC: Computer Society Press

Corbett J.C. (1981). Applications of PALs and FPLAs to asynchronous controllers. In *Proc. 15th Asilomar Conf. on Circuits, Systems and Computers*, pp. 46–9. New York NY: IEEE

Curtis H.A. (1962). *A New Approach to the Design of Switching Circuits*. Princeton NJ: Van Nostrand

Cypress Semiconductor (1985). *PAL Application Brief*

Dagenais M.R., Agarwal V.K. and Rumin N.C. (1986). McBoole: a new procedure for exact logic minimization. *IEEE Trans. Computer-Aided Design*, **5**(1) (January), 229–38

Dagless E.L. (1983). Logic design with emphasis on the ASM method. In *Semi-Custom IC Design and VLSI* (Hicks P.J., ed.), pp. 93–107. London: Peter Peregrinus

Davio M. (1984). Algorithmic aspects of digital system design. *Philips J. Research*, **39**(4–5), 206–25

Davio M., Deschamps J.-P. and Thayse A. (1983). *Digital Systems with Algorithm Implementation*. Chichester: Wiley

De Micheli G. (1985). Symbolic minimization of logic functions. In *IEEE Int. Conf. on Computer-Aided Design ICCAD-85. Digest of Technical Papers*, pp. 293–5. Washington DC: Computer Society Press

De Micheli G. (1986). Symbolic design of combinational and sequential logic circuits implemented by two-level logic macros. *IEEE Trans. Computer-Aided Design*, **5**(4) (October), 597–616

De Micheli G., Brayton R.K. and Sangiovanni-Vincentelli A.L.M. (1986). Optimal state assignment for finite state machines. *IEEE Trans. Computer-Aided Design*, **4**(3) (July) 269–85, **5**(1) (January 1986), 239 (correction)

De Micheli G., Hofmann M., Newton A.R. and Sangiovanni-Vincentelli A.L.M. (1985). A design system for PLA-based digital circuits. In *Advances in Computer-Aided Engineering Design* Vol. 1, *Computer Aided Design of VLSI Circuits and Systems* (Sangiovanni-Vincentelli A., ed.), pp. 285–364. Greenwich CT: JAI Press

Denyer P. and Renshaw D. (1985). *VLSI Signal Processing: a Bit Serial Approach*. Wokingham: Addison-Wesley

Devadas S., Wang A.R., Newton A.R. and Sangiovanni-Vincentelli A. (1988). Boolean decomposition of programmable logic arrays. In *Proc. IEEE 1988 Custom Integrated Circuits Conf.*, pp. 2.5.1–2.5.5. New York NY: IEEE

Ditzinger A. and Lipp H.M. (1979). Use of memories and programmable logic arrays for asynchronous sequential circuits. *IEE J. Computers and Digital Techniques*, **2**(5) (October), 213–20

Ditzinger A. and Tatje J. (1987). A top down approach to PLD and gate array design. In *Wescon/87 Conf. Record*, pp. 5/2 1–6. Los Angeles CA: Electronic Conventions Management

Engeler W.E., Lowy M., Pedicone J., Bloomer J., Richotte J. and Chan D. (1988). A high speed static CMOS PLA architecture. In *Proc. 1988 Int. Conf. on Computer Design: VLSI in Computers and Processors. ICCD '88*, pp. 348–51. Washington DC: Computer Society Press

Ercegovac M.D. and Lang T. (1985). *Digital Systems and Hardware/Firmware Algorithms*. New York NY: Wiley

Ettinger G.M. and Tillier M.L. (1985). Memory-based logic sequence generation. *Microprocessors and Microsystems*, **9**(9) (November), 446–51

Fleisher H. and Maissel L.I (1975). An introduction to array logic. *IBM J. Research and Development*, **19**(2) (March), 98–109

Fleisher H., Weinberger A. and Winkler V.D. (1970). The writeable personalized chip. *Computer Design*, **9**(6) (June), 59–66

Fletcher W.I. (1980) *An Engineering Approach to Digital Design*. Englewood Cliffs NJ: Prentice-Hall

Fletcher W.I. and Despain A.M. (1971). Simplify sequential circuit designs with programmable ROMs. *Electronic Design*, **19**(14) (July 8), 70–2

Flinders M., Gardner P.L., Llewelyn R.J. and Minshull J.F. (1970). Functional memory as a general purpose systems technology. In *Proc. 1970 IEEE Int. Computer Group Conf.*, pp. 314–24. New York NY: IEEE

Friedman A.D. (1986). *Fundamentals of Logic Design and Switching Theory*. Rockville MD: Computer Science Press

Gai S., Mezzalama M. and Prinetto P. (1985). Automated synthesis of digital circuits from RT-level description. *IEE Proc., Pt. E*, **132**(5) (September), 265–77

Gardner P.L. (1971). Functional memory and its microprogramming implications. *IEEE Trans. Computers*, **20**(7) (July), 764–75

Glasser L.A. and Dobberpuhl D.W. (1985). *The Design and Analysis of VLSI Circuits*. Reading MA: Addison-Wesley

Gorman K. (1973). The programmable logic array: a new approach to micro-programming. *EDN*, **18**(22) (November 20), 68–75

Grass W. and Lipp H.M. (1979). LOGE – a highly effective system for logic design automation. *ACM SIGDA Newslett.*, **9**(2) (June), 6–13

Grass W. and Thelen B. (1981). A heuristic two-pass algorithm for minimizing multiple-output switching functions. *Digital Processes*, **7**(1), 1–19 (in German)

Green D. (1986). *Modern Logic Design*. Wokingham: Addison-Wesley

Gruebel B. (1983). Computer based functional test grading of programmable logic. In *Wescon/83 and Mini Micro West Conf. Record*, pp. 16/1 1–6. Los Angeles CA: Electronic Conventions

Gurunath B. and Biswas N.N. (1987). An algorithm for multiple output minimization. In *Proc. ICCAD–87*, pp. 74–7. Washington DC: Computer Society Press

Guzeman D. (1972). Diode switching matrices make a comeback. *Electronics*, **45**(2) (January 17), 76, 77

Haas P. (1988). SR latch design minimizes macrocells. *EDN*, **33**(19) (September 15), 240

Harris Semiconductor (1984a). *Bipolar Digital Data Book*

Harris Semiconductor (1984b). *CMOS Digital Data Book*

Harris Semiconductor (1985). *Running HELP Software: Dos and Don'ts*

Hartenstein R.W. (1973). Hierarchy of interpreters for modelling complex digital systems. In *Lecture Notes in Computer Science* Vol. 1 (GI 3. Jahrestagung), (Brauer W., ed.), pp. 261–9, 508. Berlin: Springer

Hartenstein R.W. (1977). *Fundamentals of Structured Hardware Design*. Amsterdam: North-Holland

Hartmann R.F. (1984). Estimating gate complexity of programmable logic devices. *VLSI Design*, **5**(5) (May), 100–3

Hemel A. (1970). Making small ROMs do math quickly, cheaply and easily. *Electronics*, **43**(10) (May 11), 104–11

Hemel A. (1972). Square root extraction with read-only memories. *Computer Design*, **11**(4) (April), 100–2, 104

Henle R.A., Ho I.T., Maley G.A. and Waxman R. (1969). Structured logic. In *AFIPS Conf. Proc.* Vol. 35, *1969 Fall Joint Computer Conf.*, pp. 61–7. Montvale NJ: AFIPS Press

Heutink F. (1974). Implications of busing for cellular arrays. *Computer Design*, **13**(11) (November), 95–100

Hild M. (1984). Converting PALs to CMOS gate arrays. *VLSI Design*, **5**(3) (March), 58–60, 62–4

Hong S.J., Cain R.G. and Ostapko D.L. (1974). MINI: a heuristic approach for logic minimization. *IBM J. Research and Development*, **18**(5) (September), 443–58

Huertas J.L. and Quintana J.M. (1988). A new method for the efficient state-assignment of PLA-based sequential machines. In *Proc. ICCAD–88*, pp. 156–9. Washington DC: Computer Society Press

Huertas J.L. and Quintana J.M. (1989). Efficiency of state assignment methods for PLA-based sequential circuits. *IEE Proc., Pt. E*, **136** (July), 247–53

IEEE (1984). *IEEE Standard Graphic Symbols for Logic Functions*. ANSI/IEEE Standard 91–1984. New York NY: IEEE

IEEE (1986). *IEEE Standard for Logic Circuit Diagrams*. ANSI/IEEE Standard 991–1986. New York NY: IEEE

Jay C. (1987). XOR PLDs simplify design of counters and other devices. *EDN*, **32**(11) (May 28), 205–10

Jigour R.J. (1988). PLD synchronizes asynchronous inputs. *Electronic Design International*, **1**(2) (November), 75, 76

Johnson D.W. (1976). Go from flow charts to hardware. *Electronic Design*, **24**(18) (September 1), 90–5

Jones J.W. (1975a). Array logic macros. *IBM J. Research and Development*, **19**(2) (March), 120–6

Jones J.W. (1975b). Shared macros and facilities in programmable logic arrays. *IBM Technical Disclosure Bull.*, **18**(3) (August), 823–5

Jones J.W. (1975c). Asynchronous sequential control using programmable logic arrays. *IBM Technical Disclosure Bull.*, **18**(3) (August), 826–9

Jones J.W. (1975d). Transmission-line adaptor implementation using programmable logic arrays. *IBM Technical Disclosure Bull.*, **18**(3) (August), 830–4

Kambayashi Y. (1979).Logic design of programmable logic arrays. *IEEE Trans. Computers*, **28**(9) (September), 609–17

Kamdar J.P. (1988). Commercial considerations for design with ASICs. *Microprocessors and Microsystems*, **12**(5) (June), 260–3

Kampel I. (1986). *A Practical Introduction to the New Logic Symbols* 2nd edn. London: Butterworths

Kang S. and vanCleemput W.M. (1981). Automatic PLA synthesis from a DDL-P description. *Proc. 18th ACM IEEE Design Automation Conf.*, pp. 391–7. New York NY: IEEE

Kidder T. (1981). *The Soul of a New Machine*. Boston MA: Little, Brown (London: Allen Lane, 1982, Penguin, 1982)

Kitson B. and Ow-Wing K. (1984). Logic-programming language enriches design processes. *Electronic Design*, **32**(6) (March 22), 183–92

Kitson B.S. and Rosen B.J. (1983). Logical alternatives in supermini design. *Computer Design*, **22**(13) (November), 259, 260, 262, 264–8

Kobylarz T. and Al-Najjar A. (1979). An examination of the cost function for programmable logic arrays. *IEEE Trans. Computers*, **28**(8) (August), 586–90

Kohonen T. (1980). *Content-Addressable Memories*. Berlin: Springer

Kopec S. (1989). Asynchronous state machines challenge digital designers. *EDN*, **33**(12) (June 9), 179–84, 186

Krausener J.-M. (1971). *Bipolar Read-Only-Memories SN7488*. Application Report NA 46, Texas Instruments, November

Krug H. (1986). AGAs. Eine neue Logikfamilie für Entwickler. *Elektronik Industrie*, **17**(12), 32–4

Kuo Y.-H., Wang R.-Y. and Kung L.-Y. (1988). Logic design using the PLAs with limited I/O pins and products terms. *Microprocessing and Microprogramming*, **23**(1–5) (March), 27–31

Kvamme F. (1970). Standard read-only memories simplify complex logic design. *Electronics*, **43**(1) (January 5), 88–95

Langdon Jr G.G. (1982). *Computer Design*. San Jose CA: Computeach Press

Lange E.E. (1979). Minimization of the number of states of an asynchronous finite automaton with allowance for implementation by programmable logic array. *Automatic Control and Computer Sciences*, **13**(5), 1–5

Leininger J.C. (1970).Universal logic module. *IBM Technical Disclosure Bull.*, **13**(5) (October), 1294, 1295

Lemberskii I.G. (1979). Reduction of the number of terms of the DNF in internal state assignment of asynchronous automaton implemented using a programmable logic array. *Automatic Control and Computer Sciences*, **13**(2), 51–6

Lemberskii I.G. (1983). Synthesis of asynchronous automata in the form of two-level hazard-free implementations. *Automatic Control and Computer Sciences*, **17**(5), 51–9

Lemberskii I.G., Fritsnovich G.F. and Chapenko V.P. (1976). Internal state assignment for asynchronous finite automata with a view to implementation using programmable logic arrays. *Automatic Control and Computer Sciences*, **10**(4), 10–17

Lewin D. (1985). *Design of Logic Systems*. Wokingham: Van Nostrand Reinhold

Li H.F. (1980). Programmable logic array optimization techniques. *International J. Electronics*, **49**(4) (October), 287–99

Logue J.C., Brickman N.F., Howley F., Jones J.W. and Wu W.W. (1975). Hardware implementation of a small system in programmable logic arrays. *IBM J. Research and Development*, **19**(2) (March), 110–19

McCarthy C. (1987). Partitioning adapts large state machines to PLDs. *EDN*, **32**(19) (September 17), 163–6

McCluskey E.J. (1986). *Logic Design Principles*. Englewood Cliffs NJ: Prentice-Hall

McCluskey E.J. and Unger S.H. (1959). A note on the number of internal state assignments for sequential switching circuits. *IRE Trans. Electronic Computers*, **8** (December), 439, 440

McIntosh M.D. and Weinberg B.L. (1969). On asynchronous machines with flip–flops. *IEEE Trans. Computers*, **18**(5) (May), 473

McMullen C. and Shearer J. (1986). Prime implicants, minimum covers, and the complexity of logic simplification. *IEEE Trans. Computers*, **35**(8) (August), 761, 762

Maggiore J. (1974). PLA – a universal logic element. *Electronic Products*, (April 15), 67–72, 75

Maissel L. and Phoenix R.L. (1983). IDL (interactive design language) features and philosophy. In *Proc. ICCD '83*, pp. 667–9. Silver Spring MD: Computer Society Press

Mano M.M. (1984). *Digital Design*. Englewood Cliffs NJ: Prentice-Hall

Martinez-Carballido J.F. and Powers V.M. (1983). PRONTO: quick PLA product reduction. In *Proc. 20th ACM IEEE Design Automation Conf.*, pp. 545–52. Silver Spring MD: Computer Society Press

Mathony H.-J. (1989). Universal logic design algorithm and its application to the synthesis of two-level switching circuits. *IEE Proc.*, Pt. E, **136**(3) (May), 171–7

Miles G. (1975). FPLAs offer a design alternative for the development of system logic. *EDN*, **20**(20) (November 5), 85–9

Millhollan M.S. and Sung C. (1985). A 3.6 ns ECL programmable array logic IC. In *1985 IEEE Int. Solid-State Circuits Conf.*, pp. 202, 203. Coral Gables FL: Lewis Winner

Minsky M.L. (1967). *Computation: Finite and Infinite Machines*. Englewood Cliffs NJ: Prentice-Hall

Mitarai H. and Kuo H. (1975). ROM micro-reduction techniques. In *Proc. 2nd USA–Japan Computer Conf.*, pp. 126–30. Montvale NJ: AFIPS Press

Mitchell C. (1977). *A Guide to Implementing Logic Functions Using PROMs*. Application Note, National Semiconductor, November

Monolithic Memories (1971). *ROM in Sequential and Combinatorial Logic*. Application Note 102, December

Monolithic Memories (1978). *PAL Handbook* 1st edn., July

Monolithic Memories (1983). *Programmable Array Logic Handbook* 3rd edn.

Monolithic Memories (1984). *PLE Handbook*, October

Monolithic Memories (1986). *PAL/PLE Device Programmable Logic Array Handbook* 5th edn.

Mrazek D. and Morris M. (1973). PLAs replace ROMs for logic designs. *Electronic Design*, **21**(22) (October 25), 66–70

Muroga S. (1979). *Logic Design and Switching Theory*. New York NY: Wiley

National Semiconductor (1985). *PLAN Manual*, August

Nguyen L.B., Perkowski M.A, and Goldstein N.B. (1987). PALMINI – fast Boolean minimizer for personal computers. In *Proc. 24th ACM–IEEE Design Automation Conf.*, pp. 615–21. Washington DC: Computer Society Press

Nichols J.L. (1967). A logical next step for read-only memories. *Electronics*, **40**(12) (June 12), 111–13

Novikov S.V. (1977). Synthesis of circuits using programmable logic arrays. *Automatic Control and Computer Sciences*, **11**(5), 1–4

Novikov S.V. (1980). Method of implementing a system of partial Boolean functions by means of an arrangement of programmable logic arrays. *Automatic Control and Computer Sciences*, **14**(6), 25–9

Osann R. (1982). A universal language for programmable logic. In *Wescon/82 Conf. Record*, pp. 21/3 1–8. El Segundo CA: Electronic Conventions

Osann R. (1984). Testing programmable logic: an overview. In *Midcon/84 Conf. Record*, pp. 13/1 1–7. Los Angeles CA: Electronic Conventions

Papachristou C.A. and Sarma D. (1983). An approach to sequential circuit realisation. *IEE Proc.*, Pt. E, **130**(5) (September), 159–64

Pathak J., Kurkowski H., Pugh R., Shrivastava R. and Jenne F.B. (1986). A 19-ns 250-mW CMOS erasable programmable logic device. *IEEE J. Solid-State Circuits*, **21**(5) (October), 741–9

Peatman J.B. (1980). *Digital Hardware Design*. New York NY: McGraw-Hill

Perkins S.R. and Rhyne T. (1988). An algorithm for identifying and selecting the prime implicants of a multiple-output Boolean function. *IEEE Trans. Computer-Aided Design of Integrated Circuits and Systems*, **7**(11) (November), 1215–18

Philips (1985). *Integrated Fuse Logic*. Handbook IC13N

Poretta A., Santomauro M. and Somenzi F. (1984). TAU: a fast heuristic logic minimizer. In *Proc. ICCAD–84*, pp. 206–8. New York NY: IEEE

Price J.E. (1962). Programmable circuit. *US Patent 3,191,151*, June 22, 1965 (filed November 26, 1962)

Proebsting R.J. (1969). MOS transistor integrated matrix. *US Patent 3,702,985*, November 14, 1972 (filed April 30, 1969)

Prosser F.P. and Winkel D.E. (1987). *The Art of Digital Design. An Introduction to Top-Down Design* 2nd edn. Englewood Cliffs NJ: Prentice-Hall

Ptasinki J. (1982). Glitch-free FPLA/PAL design. In *Southcon/82 Conf. Record*, pp. 12/4 1–3. El Segundo CA: Electronic Conventions

Roth C.H. (1985). *Fundamentals of Logic Design* 3rd edn. St Paul MN: West

Roth J.P. (1978). Programmed logic array optimization. *IEEE Trans. Computers*, **27**(2) (February), 174–6

Roth J.P. (1980). *Computer Logic, Testing and Verification*. Potomac MD: Computer Science Press; London: Pitman

Rudell R.L. and Sangiovanni-Vincentelli A.L.M. (1987). Multiple-valued minimization for PLA optimization. *IEEE Trans. Computer-Aided Design*, **6**(5) (September), 727–50

Saldanha A. and Katz R.H. (1988). PLA optimization using output encoding. In *IEEE Int. Conf. on Computer-Aided Design, ICCAD–88. Digest of Technical Papers*, pp. 478–81. Washington DC: Computer Society Press

Sasao T. (1981). Multiple-valued decomposition of generalized Boolean functions and the complexity of programmable logic arrays. *IEEE Trans. Computers*, **30**(9) (September), 635–43

Sasao T. (1983). *Input Variable Assignment and Output Phase Optimization of PLAs*. Report RC 1003, IBM Thomas J. Watson Research Center, June

Saucier G., Crastes de Paulet M., Poirot F. and Sicard P. (1987). ASYL: a rule-based synthesis tool. In *Proc. ICCD '87*, pp. 567–70. Washington DC: Computer Society Press

Schmid H. and Busch D. (1970). Generate functions from discrete data. *Electronic Design*, (September 27), 42–7

Schmitz N. and Greiner J. (1984). Software aids in PAL circuit design, simulation, and verification. *Electronic Design*, **32**(11) (May 31), 243–50

Schultz G.W. (1969). An algorithm for the synthesis of complex sequential networks. *Computer Design*, **8**(3) (March), 49–55

Sharp D. and Barbehenn G. (1988). Squeezing state machines into PLDs. *VLSI Systems Design*, **9**(10) (October), 70, 71, 74, 76, 78, 79, 84

Sholl H.A. and Yang S.-C. (1975). Design of asynchronous sequential networks using READ-ONLY memory. *IEEE Trans. Computers*, **24**(2) (February), 195–206

Shvartsman M.I. (1981). Output decomposition for combinational PLA-structures. *Automatic Control and Computer Sciences*, **15**(6), 9–14

Sievers W.H. (1984). How testability is designed into programmable logic. In *Midcon/84 Conf. Record*, pp. 10/2 1–10. Los Angeles CA: Electronic Conventions

Siewiorek D.P., Bell C.G. and Newell A. (1982). *Computer Structures: Principles and Examples*. New York NY: McGraw-Hill

Signetics (1984). *AMAZE, PC/MS DOS Users Manual*, August

Signetics (1985a). *Oscillator with PLS 159*. Application Note AN13, July

Signetics (1985b). *9-Bit Parity Generator/Checker with 82S153/153A*. Application Note AN21, September

Signetics (1985c). *Latches and Flip–flops with PLS153*. Application Note AN14, September

Signetics (1986). *Programmable Logic Data Manual*

Signetics (1988). *PLHS501 Application Notes*, January

Spicer D. (1973). Fast BCD to binary and binary to BCD converters. In *Semiconductor Circuit Design*, **2**, pp. 101–12. Bedford: Texas Instruments

Staff of the Harvard Computation Laboratory (1951). *Synthesis of Electronic Computing and Control Circuits. Annals of the Computation Laboratory of Harvard University*, Vol. 27. Cambridge MA: Harvard

Streicher A. (1985). *Programmable Logic Arrays (PALs)*. Application Report EB 159, Texas Instruments, March

Tang C.K. (1971). A storage cell reduction technique for ROS design. In *AFIPS Conf. Proc.* Vol. 39, *1971 Fall Joint Computer Conf.*, pp. 163–7. Montvale NJ: AFIPS Press

Taylor F.J. (1984). Residue arithmetic: a tutorial with examples. *IEEE Computer*, **17**(5) (May), 50–62

Teel W. and Wilde D. (1982). A logic minimizer for VLSI PLA design. In *Proc. 19th ACM IEEE Design Automation Conf.*, pp. 156–62. Silver Spring MD: Computer Science Press

Terry J. (1987). *A PAL Compiler for Counters*. Final Year Project Report, Department of Electrical and Electronic Engineering, University of Bristol

Texas Instruments (1988). *Programmable Logic Data Book*

Thomas B. and Chandrasekharan P.C. (1981). Economical realization of asynchronous sequential circuits using random-access memories. *IEE Proc.*, Pt. E, **128**(3) (May), 123–8

Thurber K.J. and Berg R.O. (1971). Universal logic modules implemented using LSI memory techniques. In *AFIPS Conf. Proc.* Vol. 39, *1971 Fall Joint Computer Conf.*, pp. 177–94. Montvale NJ: AFIPS Press

Uimari D.C. (1972). Diode matrices. *New Electronics*, **5**(22) (November 14), 54, 55, 63

Unger S.H. (1969). *Asynchronous Sequential Switching Circuits*. New York NY: Wiley

Unger S.H. (1989). *The Essence of Logic Circuits*. Englewood Cliffs NJ: Prentice-Hall

Vafai M. (1983). *Testing Your PAL Devices*. Application Note, Monolithic Memories

van Laarhoven P.J.M., Aarts E.H.L. and Davio M. (1985). PHIPLA – a new algorithm for logic minimization. In *Proc. 22nd ACM–IEEE Design Automation Conf.*, pp. 739–43. Silver Spring MD: Computer Society Press

Vargas P. (1987). *EPLDs, PLAs and TTL – Comparing the Hidden Costs in Production*. Application Note AP-307, Intel, January

Varma D. and Trachtenberg E.A. (1988). A fast algorithm for the optimal state assignment of large finite state machines. In *Proc. ICCAD–88*, pp. 152–5. Washington DC

Wahlstrom S.E., Fong E., Chung M.S.C., Gan J. and Chen J. (1988). An 11000 fuse electrically erasable programmable logic device (EEPLD) with an extended macrocell. *IEEE J. Solid-State Devices*, **23**(4) (August), 916–22

Wang, T (1984). *PAL Functional Testing*. Application Note 351, National Semiconductor, September

Waser S. and Flynn M.J. (1982). *Introduction to Arithmetic for Digital Systems Designers*. New York NY: Holt, Rinehart and Winston

Weinberger A. (1979). High-speed programmable logic array adders. *IBM J. Research and Development*, **23**(2) (March), 163–78

Weste N.H.E. and Eshraghian K. (1985). *Principles of CMOS VLSI Design*. Reading MA: Addison-Wesley

Wey C.-L. and Chan T.-Y. (1988). PLAYGROUND: minimization of PLAs with mixed ground true outputs. In *Proc. 25th ACM–IEEE Design Automation Conf.*, pp. 421–6. Washington DC: Computer Society Press

Wiatrowski C.A. and House C.H. (1980). *Logic Circuits and Microcomputer Systems*. New York NY: McGraw-Hill

Wilkes M.V. (1956). *Automatic Digital Computers*. London: Methuen

Wong D.K. (1985a). Designing state machines with field programmable logic sequencers. In *Southcon/85 Conf. Record*, pp. 4/4 1–18. Los Angeles CA: Electronics Conventions Management

Wong D.K. (1985b). *4-bit Binary-to-7 Segment Decoder*. Application Note AN10, Signetics, November

Wong K.-N. and Ismail M.G. (1988). New heuristics for the exact minimization of logic functions. In *Proc. 1988 IEEE Int. Sym. on Circuits and Systems*, pp. 1865–8. New York NY: IEEE

Wong S.-C., So H.-C., Hung C.-Y. and Ou J.-H. (1985). Novel circuit techniques for zero-power 25-ns CMOS erasable programmable logic devices (EPLDs). *IEEE J. Solid-State Circuits*, **21**(5) (October), 766–74

Wyland D.C. (1971). Associative read-only memory technique: a key to LSI control logic. *Computer Design*, **10**(9) (September), 61–8

Wyland D.C. (1978). Managing the flow of data is easy with programmable multiplexer. *Electronics*, **51**(10) (May 11), 132–5

Yakubaitis E.Ya., Bul E.S., Lange E.E., Lemberskii I.G., Fritsnovich G.F. and Chapenko V.P. (1980). Technique for synthesizing asynchronous automata employing programmable logic arrays. *Automatic Control and Computer Sciences*, **14**(4), 23–31

Yee J. (1984). Test methods for programmable logic. In *Southcon/84 and Mini Micro Southeast Conf. Record*, pp. 12/1 1–8. Los Angeles CA: Electronic Conventions

# Index